STUDY GUIDE

with Selected Solutions

Basic Chemistry

Karen Timberlake

Los Angeles Valley College

San Francisco Boston New York
Capetown Hong Kong London Madrid Mexico City
Montreal Munich Paris Singapore Sydney Tokyo Toronto

Cover Credit: Image of Salt Pond in Newark, California by Robert Campbell/Chamois Moon

ISBN 0-8053-3987-6

1 2 3 4 5 6 7 8 9 10 VHG 08 07 06 05 04
www.aw-bc.com

Preface

This Study Guide is intended to accompany *Basic Chemistry.* The purpose of this Study Guide is to provide students with additional learning resources to increase their understanding of the key concepts in the text. Each chapter in the Study Guide correlates with a chapter in the text. Within each chapter, there are Learning Exercises that focus on problem solving, which promote an understanding of the chemical principles of that Learning Goal. Following the Learning Exercises, a Check List of Learning Goals and a multiple-choice Practice Test provide a review of the chapter content. Finally, the Answers and Solutions to Selected Text Problems give solutions for all the odd-numbered problems in each chapter.

I hope that this Study Guide will help in the learning of chemistry. If you wish to make comments or corrections, or ask questions, you can send me an e-mail message at khemist@aol.com.

Karen C. Timberlake
Los Angeles Valley College
Valley Glen, CA

To The Student

"One must learn by doing the thing;
though you think you know it, you
have no certainty until you try."
—*Sophocles*

Here you are in a chemistry class with your textbook in front of you. Perhaps you have already been assigned some reading or some problems to do. Looking through the chapter, you may see words, terms, and pictures that are new to you. This may very well be your first experience with a science class like chemistry. At this point you may have some questions about what you can do to learn chemistry. This Study Guide is written with those considerations in mind.

Learning chemistry is similar to learning something new such as tennis or skiing or driving a car. If I asked you how you learn to play tennis or ski or drive a car, you would probably tell me that you would need to practice every day. It is the same with learning chemistry. Learning the chemical concepts and learning to work the problems depends on the time and effort you invest in it. If you practice every day, you will find that learning chemistry is an exciting experience and a way to understand the current issues of the environment, health and medicine.

Manage Your Study Time

I often recommend a study system to students in which you read one section of the text and immediately practice the questions and problems that go with it. In this way, you concentrate on a small amount of information and actively use what you learned to answer questions. This helps you to organize and review the information without being overwhelmed by the entire chapter. It is important to understand each section, because they build like steps. Information presented in each chapter proceeds from the basic to the more complex skills. Perhaps you will only study 3 or 4 sections of the chapter. As long as you also practice doing some problems at the same time, the information will stay with you.

Form a Study Group

I highly recommend that you form a study group in the first week of your chemistry class. Working with your peers will help you use the language of chemistry. Scheduling a time to meet each week helps you study and prepare to discuss problems. You will be able to teach some things to the other students in the group, and sometimes they will help you understand a topic that puzzles you. You won't always understand a concept right away. Your group will help you see your way through it. Most of all, a study group creates a strong support system whereby students can help each other complete the class successfully.

Go to Office Hours

Finally, go to your tutor's and/or professor's office hours. Your professor wants you to understand and enjoy learning this material and should have office hours. Often a tutor is assigned to a class or there are tutors available at your college. Don't be intimidated. Going to see a tutor or your professor is one of the best ways to clarify what you need to learn in chemistry.

Using This Study Guide

Now you are ready to sit down and study chemistry. Let's go over some methods that can help you learn chemistry. This Study Guide is written specifically to help you understand and practice the chemical concepts that are presented in your class and in your text. Some of the exercises teach basic skills; others encourage you to extend your scientific curiosity. The following features are part of this study guide:

1. Study Goals

The Study Goals give you an overview of what the chapter is about and what you can expect to accomplish when you complete your study and learning of a chapter.

2. Think About It

Each chapter in the Study Guide has a group of questions that encourage you to think about some of the ideas and practical applications of the chemical concepts you are going to study. You may find that you already have knowledge of chemistry in some of the areas. That will be helpful to you. Other questions give you an overview of the chemistry ideas you will be learning.

3. Key Terms

Each chapter in the Study Guide introduces Key Terms. As you complete the description of the Key Terms, you will have an overview of the topics you will be study-ing in that chapter. Because many of the Key Terms may be new to you, this is an opportunity to determine their meaning.

4. Chapter Sections

Each section of the chapter begins with the Key Concepts to illustrate the important ideas in that section. The summary of concepts is written to guide you through each of the learning activities. When you are ready to begin your study, read the matching section in the textbook and review the sample exercises in the text.

5. Learning Exercises

The Learning Exercises give you an opportunity to practice problem solving related to the chemical principles in the chapter. Each set of Exercises reviews one chemical principle. There is room for you to answer the questions or complete the exercise in this Study Guide. The answers are found immediately following each exercise. (Sometimes they will be located at the top of the next page.) Check your answers right away. If they don't match the answer in the study guide, go back to the textbook and review the material again. It is important to make corrections before you go on. In learning tennis, you hit the ball a lot from the base line before you learn to volley or serve. Chemistry, too, involves a layering of skills such that each one must be understood before the next one can be learned.

At various times, you will notice some essay questions that illustrate one of the con-cepts. I believe that writing out your ideas is a very important way of learning content. If you can put your problem-solving techniques into words, then you understand the patterns of your thinking and you will find that you have to memorize less.

6. Check List

Use the Check List to check your understanding of the Study Goals. This gives you an overview of the major topics in the section. If something does not sound familiar, go back and review. One aspect of being a strong problem-solver is the ability to check your knowledge and understanding as you go along.

7. Practice-Test

A Practice Test is found at the end of each chapter. When you have learned the material in a chapter, you can apply your understanding to the Practice Test. If the results of this test indicate that you know the material, you are ready to proceed to the next chapter. If the results indicate more study is needed, you can repeat the learning Exercises you need to work on. Answers are found at the end of the Practice Test.

Contents

Contents

1
Chemistry in Our Lives

Study Goals

- Define the term *chemistry* and identify substances as chemicals.
- Describe some physical and chemical properties of matter.
- Describe the changes in states of matter.
- Identify the activities that are part of the scientific method.
- Develop a study plan for learning chemistry.

Think About It

1. Why can we say that the salt and sugar we use on food are chemicals?

2. How can the scientific method help us make decisions?

3. Why is boiling water called a physical change?

4. What are some things you can do to help you study and learn chemistry?

Key Terms

Match each of the following key terms with the correct definition.

1. physical change **2.** chemical change **3.** scientific method
4. matter **5.** theory **6.** chemistry

a. _____ An explanation of nature validated by experiments

b. _____ The study of substances and how they interact

c. _____ A property of a substance that can change without a change in its identity

d. _____ Anything that has mass and occupies space

e. _____ The process of making observations, writing a hypothesis, and testing with experiments

f. _____ A property of a substance that converts a substance into a new substance

Answers
a. 5 **b.** 6 **c.** 1 **d.** 4 **e.** 3 **f.** 2

1.1 Chemistry and Chemicals

- A chemical is any material used in or produced by a chemical process.
- A substance is a chemical containing one type of matter that has the same composition and properties.
- In the sciences, physical quantities are described in units of the metric or International System (SI).

◆ Learning Exercise 1.1

Indicate if each of the following is a chemical:

a. ______aluminum **b.** ______ love

c. ______ sodium fluoride in toothpaste **d.** ______ ammonium nitrate in fertilizer

e. ______ time

Answers **a.** yes **b.** no **c.** yes **d.** yes **e.** no

1.2 Some Fundamental Ideas of Chemistry

- Matter is anything that has mass and occupies space.
- Physical properties are those characteristics of a substance that can change without affecting the identity of the substance.
- Chemical properties are those characteristics of a substance that change when a new substance is produced.
- The states of matter are solid, liquid, and gas.
- Melting and freezing, boiling and condensation, and sublimation are changes of state.

◆ Learning Exercise 1.2A

Classify each of the following as a physical (P) or chemical (C) property:

a. ______ Silver is shiny. **b.** ______ Water fills a glass.

c.______ Wood burns. **d.** ______ Mercury is a very dense liquid.

e. ______ Helium in a balloon is a gas. **f.** ______ Ice cubes float in water.

Answers **a.** P **b.** P **c.** C **d.** P **e.** P **f.** P

◆ Learning Exercise 1.2B

Classify each of the following as a physical (P) or chemical change (C).

a. ______ Sodium melts at 98°C. **b.** ______ Iron forms rust in air and water.

c. ______ Water condenses on a cold window. **d.** ______ Fireworks explode when ignited.

e. ______ Gasoline burns in a car engine. **f.** ______ Paper is cut to make confetti.

Answers **a.** P **b.** C **c.** P **d.** C **e.** C **f.** P

1.3 Scientific Method: Thinking Like a Scientist

- The scientific method is a process of making observations, writing a hypothesis, and testing the hypothesis with experiments.
- A theory develops when experiments that validate a hypothesis are repeated by many scientists with consistent results.

Learning Exercise 1.3

Identify each of the following as observation (O), hypothesis (H), or experiment (E).

a. ______ Sunlight is necessary for the growth of plants.

b. ______ Plants in the shade were shorter than plants in the sun.

c. ______ Plant leaves are covered with aluminum foil and their growth measured.

d. ______ Fertilizer added to plants accelerates their growth.

e. ______ Ozone slows plant growth by interfering with photosynthesis.

f._______ Ozone causes brown spots on plant leaves.

Answers **a.** H **b.** O **c.** E **d.** E **e.** H **f.** O

1.4 A Study Plan for Learning Chemistry

- Components of the text that help structure learning include Looking Ahead, Learning Goals, Questions and Problems, Key Terms, Chapter Summaries, and Answers.
- An active learner continually interacts with chemical concepts while reading the text and attending lecture.
- Working with a study group clarifies ideas and illustrates problem solving.

Learning Exercise 1.4

Which of the following activities would be included in a successful study plan for learning chemistry?

a. ______ attending lecture once in a while

b. ______ working problems with friends from class

c. ______ attending review sessions

d. ______ planning a regular study time

e. ______ not doing the assigned problems

f. ______ going to the instructor's office hours

Answers **a.** no **b.** yes **c.** eyes **d.** yes **e.** no **f.** yes

Checklist for Chapter 1

You are ready to take the self-test for Chapter 1. Be sure you have accomplished the following learning goals for this chapter. If you are not sure, review the section listed at the end of the goal. Then apply your new skills and understanding to the self-test.

After studying Chapter 1, I can successfully:

____ Describe a substance as a chemical (1.1).

____ Identify physical and chemical properties (1.2).

____ Identify physical and chemical changes (1.2).

____ Describe the volume and shape of a solid, liquid, and gas (1.2).

____ Identify the components of the scientific method (1.3).

____ Design a study plan for successful learning chemistry (1.4).

Practice Test for Chapter 1

1. Which of the following would be described as a chemical?
A. sleeping **B.** salt **C.** singing
D. listening to a concert **E.** energy

2. Which of the following is not a chemical?
A. wool **B.** sugar **C.** feeling cold
D. salt **E.** vanilla

3. Which of the following is a chemical property?
A. dynamite explodes **B.** a shiny metal **C.** a melting point of 110°C
D. rain on a cool day **E.** breaking up cement

For questions 4–6, answer with solid (S), liquid (L), or gas(G):

4. ____ Has a definite volume, but takes the shape of a container.

5. ____ Does not have a definite shape or definite volume.

6. ____ Has a definite shape and a definite volume.

7. Which of the following is a chemical property of silver?
A. density of 10.5 g/mL **B.** shiny **C.** melts at 961°C
D. good conductor of heat **E.** reacts to form tarnish

8. Which of the following is a physical property of silicon?
A. burns in chlorine **B.** has a black to grey color
C. reacts with nitric acid **D.** reacts with oxygen to form sand
E. used to form silicone

For problems 9–12, answers as physical change (P) or chemical change (C):

9. ____ butter melts in a hot pan

10. ____ iron forms rust with oxygen

11. ____ baking powder form bubbles (CO_2) during baking of a cake

12. ____ water boils

13. ____ propane burns in a camp stove

For questions 14–16, identify each statement as observation (O), hypothesis (H), or experiment (E):

14. ____ Hot water can dissolve more sugar than cold water.

15. ____ Place 20 g sugar each in a glass of cold water and a glass of hot water.

16. ____ Sugar is solid, white crystals.

For questions 17–20, answer yes or no.
To successfully learn chemistry, I can

17. ____ Work the problems in the chapter and check answers.

18. ____ Attend some lectures, but not all.

19. ____ Form a study group.

20. ____ Set up a regular study time.

Answers to the Practice Test

1. B	**2.** C	**3.** A	**4.** L	**5** G
6. S	**7.** E	**8.** B	**9.** P	**10.** C
11. C	**12.** P	**13.** C	**14.** H	**15.** E
16. O	**17.** yes	**18.** no	**19.** yes	**20.** yes

Answers and Solutions to Selected Text Problems

Section 1.1
Answers to Selected Questions and Problems

1.1 **a.** Chemistry is the science of the composition and properties of matter.
b. A chemist is a scientist who studies the composition and changes of matter.
c. A chemical is a substance that is used in or produced by a chemical process.

1.3 Many chemicals are listed on a vitamin bottle, such as vitamin A, vitamin B_3, vitamin B_{12}, vitamin C, folic acid, and so on.

1.5 Typical items found in a medicine cabinet and chemicals they contain:
Antacid tablets: calcium carbonate, cellulose, starch, stearic acid, silicon dioxide
Mouthwash: water, alcohol, glycerol, sodium benzoate, benzoic acid
Cough suppressant: menthol, beta-carotene, sucrose, glucose

1.7 No. All these ingredients are chemicals.

1.9 An advantage of a pesticide is that it protects drops from damage by various insects. Some disadvantages are that a pesticide can destroy beneficial insects, be retained in a crop that is eventually eaten by animals or humans, or pollute groundwater.

Section 1.2

1.11 **a.** Color is a physical property.
b. The ability of hydrogen to react with oxygen is a chemical property.
c. The temperature at which a substance freezes is a physical property.
d. The change in milk left in a warm room is a chemical property.

1.13 **a.** The change of water from gas to liquid is a physical change.
b. The reaction of cesium with water is a chemical change.
c. The melting of gold from solid to liquid is a physical change.
d. The change in shape is a physical change.
e. Because dissolving sugar in water only separates the sugar molecules, it is a physical change.

1.15 **a.** The reactivity of a substance is a chemical property.
b. The state of a substance is a physical property.
c. The color of a substance is a physical property.
d. The reaction with hydrogen is a chemical property.
e. The temperature at which a substance melts is a physical property.

Section 1.3

1.17 **a.** A hypothesis proposes a possible explanation for a natural phenomenon.
b. An experiment is a procedure that tests the validity of a hypothesis.
c. A theory is a hypothesis that has been validated many times by many scientists.
d. An observation is a description or measurement of a natural phenomenon.

1.19 **(1)** A change in number of sales is an observation.
(2) Changing the menu to improve sales is a hypothesis.
(3) A taste test is an experiment.
(4) The ratings of the taste test are observations.
(5) Improvement in sales is an observation.
(6) Better sales by changing the menu is a theory.

Section 1.4

1.21 There are several things a student can do to be successful in chemistry, including forming a study group, going to lecture, working sample problems and study checks, working problems and checking answers, reading the assignment ahead of class, going to the instructor's office hours, and keeping a problem notebook.

1.23 **a**. Form a study group.
c. Visit the instructor during office hours.
e. Become an active learner.

Answers to Additional Questions and Problems

1.29 **a.** Appearance is a physical property.
b. The melting point of gold is a physical property.
c. The ability of gold to conduct electricity is a physical property.
d. The ability of gold to form a new substance with sulfur is a chemical property.

1.31 **a.** Plant growth is a chemical change.
b. A change of state from liquid to solid is a physical change.
c. Chopping wood into smaller pieces is a physical change.
d. Burning wood, which forms new substances, is a chemical change.

1.33 **a.** Tablets are solid.
b. Helium in a balloon is a gas.
c. Milk is a liquid.
d. Air is a mixture of gases.
e. Charcoal is a solid.

1.35 A hypothesis, which is a possible explanation for an observation, can be tested with experiments.

1.37 **b.** Another hypothesis needs to be written when experimental results do not support the previous hypothesis.
c. More experiments are needed for a new hypothesis.

1.39 **a.** Determination of a melting point with a thermometer is an observation
b. Describing a reason for the extinction of dinosaurs is a hypothesis or theory
c. Measuring the speed of a race is an observation

1.41 Yes. Sherlock's investigation includes observations (gathering data), formulating a hypothesis, testing the hypothesis, and modifying it until one of the hypotheses is validated.

1.43 A successful study plan would include:
b. Working the sample problems throughout the chapter
c. Going to the instructor's office during office hours

2
Measurements

Study Goals

- Learn the units and abbreviations for the metric (SI) system.
- Write a standard number in scientific notation.
- Determine the number of significant figures in a measurement or problem answer.
- Use SI and metric prefixes to change base units to larger or smaller units.
- Write conversion factors using the units in an equality.
- In problem solving, convert the initial unit of a measurement to another unit.
- Calculate the density of a substance; use density to determine mass or volume.
- Calculate temperature values in degrees Celsius and kelvins.

Think About It

1. What kind of device would you use to measure each of the following: your height, your weight, and the quantity of water to make soup?

2. How do you determine the amount of money in your wallet?

3. When you do a measurement, why should you write down a number and a unit?

4. Why does oil float on water?

5. What are the different scales used for temperature measurement?

Key Terms

Match each of the following key terms with the correct definition.

1. metric (SI) system **2.** exact number **3.** significant figures
4. conversion factor **5.** density **6.** absolute zero

a. _____ All the numbers recorded in a measurement, including the estimated digit

b. _____ A fraction that gives the equal quantities of a relationship in the numerator and denominator

c. _____ The relationship of the mass of an object to its volume

d. _____ A number obtained by counting items or from a definition within the same system

e. _____ A decimal system of measurement used throughout the world

f. _____ The lowest temperature possible, which is 0 on the kelvin scale

Answers **a.** 3 **b.** 4 **c.** 5**d.** 2 **e.** 1 **f.** 6

2.1 Units of Measurement

- In the sciences, physical quantities are described in units of the metric or International System (SI).
- Length or distance is measured in meters (m), volume in liters (L), mass in grams (g), temperature in Celsius (°C) or kelvins (K), and time in seconds (s).

◆ Learning Exercise 2.1

Indicate the type of measurement in each of the following measurements:

1. length **2.** mass **3.** volume **4.** temperature **5.** time

a. _____ 45 g **b.** _____ 8.2 m **c.** _____ 215°C

d. _____ 45 L **e.** _____ 825 K **f.** _____ 8.8 s

Answers **a.** 2 **b.** 1 **c.** 4 **d.** 3 **e.** 4 **f.** 5

2.2 Scientific Notation

- A number written in scientific notation has two parts: a coefficient between 1 and 10 followed by a power of 10.
- For large numbers greater than 10, the decimal point is moved to the left to give a positive power of 10. For small numbers less than 1, the decimal point is moved to the right to give a negative power of 10.

◆ Learning Exercise 2.2A

Study Note

1. The number 2.5×10^3 means that 2.5 is multiplied by 10^3 (1 000).

$$2.5 \times 1\,000 = 2\,500$$

The number 8.2×10^{-2} means that 8.2 is multiplied by 10^{-2} (0.01).

$$8.2 \times 0.01 = 0.082$$

2. For a number greater than 10, the decimal point is moved to the left to give a number between 1 and 10 and a positive power of 10. For small numbers less than 1, the decimal point is moved to the right to give a number between 1 and 10 and a negative power of 10.

Write the following measurements in scientific notation:

a. 240 000 cm ____________ **b.** 800 m ____________

c. 230 000 kg ____________ **d.** 50 000 yr ____________

e. 0.002 m ____________ **f.** 0.000 0015 g ____________

g. 0.08 kg ____________ **h.** 0.000 1 s ____________

Answers **a.** 2.4×10^5 cm **b.** 8×10^2 m **c.** 2.3×10^5 kg **d.** 5×10^4 yr
e. 2×10^{-3} m **f.** 1.5×10^{-6} g **g.** 8×10^{-2} kg **h.** 1×10^{-4} s

◆ Learning Exercise 2.2B

Circle the larger number in each pair.

a. 2500 or 2.5×10^2 **b.** 0.04 or 4×10^{-3}

c. 65 000 or 6.5×10^5 **d.** 0.00035 or 3.5×10^{-3}

e. 300 000 or 3×10^6 **f.** 0.002 or 2×10^{-4}

Answers **a.** 2500 **b.** 0.04 **c.** 6.5×10^5
d. 3.5×10^{-3} **e.** 3×10^6 **f.** 0.002

◆ Learning Exercise 2.2C

Write each of the following in standard form:

Example: 2×10^2 m = 200 m and 3×10^{-4} g = 0.0003 g

a. 4×10^3 m _______________ **b.** 5.2×10^4 g _______________

c. 1.8×10^5 g _______________ **d.** 8×10^{-3} L _______________

e. 6×10^{-2} kg _______________ **f.** 3.1×10^{-5} g _______________

Answers **a.** 4 000 m **b.** 52 000 g **c.** 180 000 g
d. 0.008 L **e.** 0.06 kg **f.** 0.000 031 g

2.3 Measured Numbers and Significant Figures

- A measured number is obtained when you use a measuring device to determine an amount of some item.
- An exact number is obtained by counting items or from a definition that relates units in the same measuring system.
- There is uncertainty in every measured number, but not in exact numbers. Significant figures in a measured number are all reported figures, including the estimated digit.
- Zeros written in front of a nonzero number or zeros that are used as placeholders in a large number are not significant digits.

◆ Learning Exercise 2.3A

Are the numbers in each of the following statements measured (M) or exact (E)?

a. _____ There are 7 days in 1 week. **b.** _____ A concert lasts for 73 minutes.

c. _____ There are 1000 g in 1 kg. **d.** _____ The potatoes have a mass of 2.5 kg.

e. _____ A student has 26 CDs. **f.** _____ The snake is 1.2 m long.

Answers **a.** E (counted) **b.** M (use a watch) **c.** E (metric definition)
d. M (use a balance) **e.** E (counted) **f.** M (use a ruler)

◆ Learning Exercise 2.3B

Study Note
Significant figures (SFs) are all numbers reported in a measurement, including the estimated digit. Zeros are significant unless they are placeholders appearing at the beginning of a decimal number or in a large number without a decimal point.
4.255 g (four SFs)   0.0042 (two SFs)   46,500 (three SFs)

State the number of significant figures in the following measured numbers:

a. 35.24 g ____ **b.** 0.000 080 m ____

c. 55 000 m ____ **d.** 805 mL ____

e. 5.025 L ____ **f.** 0.006 kg ____

g. 268 200 mm ____ **h.** 25.0°C ____

Answers **a.** 4 **b.** 2 **c.** 2 **d.** 3 **e.** 4 **f.** 1 **g.** 4 **h.** 3

2.4 Significant Figures in Calculations

- In a calculation with measured numbers, the number of significant digits given in the answer must match the number of significant figures in the measurement with the fewest significant figures.
- When evaluating a calculator answer, it is important to count the significant figures in the measurements and round off the calculator answer properly.
- Answers in chemical calculations rarely use all the numbers that appear in the calculator. Exact numbers are not included in the determination of the number of significant figures in an answer.

◆ Learning Exercise 2.4A

Study Note
1. To round off a number less than 5, keep the digits you need and drop all digits that follow. Round 42.8254 to three significant figures → 42.8 (drop 254)
2. If the first number dropped is 5 or greater, keep the proper number of digits and increase the last retained digit by 1. Round 8.4882 to two significant figures → 8.5
2. In large numbers, maintain the value of the answer by adding nonsignificant zeros. Round 356 835 to three significant figures → 357 000

Round off each of the following to *two* significant figures:

a. 88.75 m ____________ **b.** 0.002923 g ____________

c. 50.525 g ____________ **d.** 1.6726 m ____________

e. 0.0010558 kg ____________ **f.** 82.08 L ____________

Answers **a.** 89 m **b.** 0.0029 g **c.** 51 g **d.** 1.7 m **e.** 0.0011 kg **f.** 82 L

◆ Learning Exercise 2.4B

Study Note

1. An answer from multiplying and dividing has the same number of significant figures as the initial measurement that has the smallest number of significant figures.
   1.5 × 32.546 = 48.819 → 49 *Answer rounded to two SFs*
   two SFs *five SFs*
2. An answer from adding or subtracting has the same number of decimal places as the initial number with the fewest decimal places.
   82.223 + 4.1 = 86.323 → 86.3 *Answer rounded to one decimal place*

Solve each problem and give the answer with the correct number of significant figures:

a. $1.3 \times 71.5 =$

b. $\dfrac{8.00}{4.00} =$

c. $\dfrac{0.082 \times 25.4}{0.116 \times 3.4} =$

d. $\dfrac{3.05 \times 1.86}{118.5} =$

e. $\dfrac{376}{0.0073} =$

f. $38.520 - 11.4 =$

g. $4.2 + 8.15 =$

h. $102.56 + 8.325 - 0.8825 =$

Answers
a. 93 **b.** 2.00 **c.** 5.3 **d.** 0.0479
e. 52 000 (5.2×10^4) **f.** 27.1 **g.** 12.4 **h.** 110.00

2.5 SI and Metric Prefixes

- In the metric system, larger and smaller units use prefixes to change the size of the unit by factors of 10. For example, a prefix such as *centi* or *milli* preceding the unit meter gives a smaller length than a meter. A prefix such as *kilo* added to gram gives a unit that measures a mass that is 1000 times greater than a gram.
- In the following table, some metric (SI) prefixes are shown with the most commonly used in bold type:

Prefix	Symbol	Meaning	Numerical Value	
tera	T	trillion	1 000 000 000 000	10^{12}
giga	G	billion	1 000 000 000	10^{9}
mega	M	million	1 000 000	10^{6}
kilo	k	thousand	1000	10^{3}
deci	d	one-tenth	0.1	10^{-1}
centi	c	one-hundredth	0.01	10^{-2}
milli	m	one-thousandth	0.001	10^{-3}
micro	μ	one-millionth	0.000 001	10^{-6}
nano	n	one-billionth	0.000 000 001	10^{-9}
pico	p	one-trillionth	0.000 000 000 001	10^{-12}
femto	f	one-quadrillionth	0.000 000 000 000 001	10^{-15}

- An equality contains two units that measure the *same* length, volume, or mass.
- Some common metric equalities are 1 m = 100 cm; 1 L = 1000 mL; 1 kg = 1000 g.
- Some useful metric–U.S. equalities are:

2.54 cm = 1 in. 1 kg = 2.205 lb 1L = 1.057 qt

◆ Learning Exercise 2.5A

Match the items in column **A** with those from column **B.**

A		B	
1. _____	kilo-	**a.**	millimeter
2. _____	one thousand liters	**b.**	0.1 L
3. _____	deciliter	**c.**	one-millionth of a second
4. _____	milliliter	**d.**	kiloliter
5. _____	centimeter	**e.**	0.01 m
6. _____	one-tenth centimeter	**f.**	1000 g
7. _____	microsecond	**g.**	one-thousandth of a liter
8. _____	kilogram	**h.**	one thousand times

Answers **1.** h **2.** d **3.** b **4.** g **5.** e **6.** a **7.** c **8.** f

◆ Learning Exercise 2.5B

Place the following units in order from smallest to largest.

a. kilogram milligram gram ______________________________

b. centimeter kilometer millimeter ______________________________

c. dL mL L ______________________________

d. kg mg μg ______________________________

Answers
a. milligram, gram, kilogram **b.** millimeter, centimeter, kilometer
c. mL, dL, L **d.** μg, mg, kg

◆ Learning Exercise 2.5C

Complete the following metric relationships:

a. 1 L = ________ mL **b.** 1 L = ________ dL

c. 1 m = ________ cm **d.** 1 s = ________ ms

e. 1 kg = ________ g **f.** 1 cm = ________ mm

g. 1 mg = ________ μg **h.** 1 dL = ________ L

i. 1 m = ________ mm **j.** 1 cm = ________ m

Answers
a. 1000 **b.** 10 **c.** 100 **d.** 1000 **e.** 1000
f. 10 **g.** 1000 **h.** 0.1 **i.** 1000 **j.** 0.01

2.6 Writing Conversion Factors

- Conversion factors are used in a chemical calculation to change from one unit to another. Each factor represents an equality that is expressed in the form of a fraction.
- Two forms of a conversion factor can be written for any equality. For example, the metric–U.S. equality 2.54 cm = 1 in. can be written as follows:

$$\frac{2.54\text{ cm}}{1\text{ in.}} \quad \text{and} \quad \frac{1\text{ in.}}{2.54\text{ cm}}$$

◆ Learning Exercise 2.6A

Study Note

Metric conversion factors are obtained from metric prefixes. For example, the metric equality 1 m = 100 cm gives the factors

$$\frac{1\text{ m}}{100\text{ cm}} \text{ and } \frac{100\text{ cm}}{1\text{ m}}$$

When a unit is squared or cubed, the value of the conversion factor is also squared or cubed. For example, when the metric equality 1 m = 100 cm is squared, the relationship becomes

$$(1\text{ m})^2 = (100\text{ cm})^2$$

This equality gives the factors

$$\frac{(1\text{ m})^2}{(100\text{ cm})^2} \text{ and } \frac{(100\text{ cm})^2}{(1\text{ m})^2}$$

Write two conversion factors for each of the following pairs of units:

a. millimeters and meters

b. kilogram and grams

c. kilograms and pounds

d. square inches and square centimeters

e. centimeters and meters

f. liters and quarts

g. deciliters and liters

h. millimeters cubed and centimeters cubed

Answers

a. $\frac{1000\text{ mm}}{1\text{ m}}$ and $\frac{1\text{ m}}{1000\text{ mm}}$

b. $\frac{1000\text{ g}}{1\text{ kg}}$ and $\frac{1\text{ kg}}{1000\text{ g}}$

c. $\frac{2.205\text{ lb}}{1\text{ kg}}$ and $\frac{1\text{ kg}}{2.205\text{ lb}}$

d. $\frac{(2.54\text{ cm})^2}{(1\text{ in.})^2}$ and $\frac{(1\text{ in.})^2}{(2.54\text{ cm})^2}$

e. $\frac{100\text{ cm}}{1\text{ m}}$ and $\frac{1\text{ m}}{100\text{ cm}}$

f. $\frac{1\text{ L}}{1.057\text{ qt}}$ and $\frac{1.057\text{ qt}}{1\text{ L}}$

g. $\frac{10\text{ dL}}{1\text{ L}}$ and $\frac{1\text{ L}}{10\text{ dL}}$

h. $\frac{(\text{cm})^3}{(10\text{ mm})^3}$ and $\frac{(10\text{ mm})^3}{(1\text{ cm})^3}$

◆ Learning Exercise 2.6B

Study Note

Sometimes a statement within a problem gives an equality that is only true for that problem. Then conversion factors can be written that are true only for that problem. For example, a problem states that there are 50 mg vitamin B in a tablet. The conversion factors are

$$\frac{1\text{ tablet}}{50\text{ mg vitamin B}} \quad \text{and} \quad \frac{50\text{ mg vitamin B}}{1\text{ tablet}}$$

A problem may also state a percentage that is true for that problem only. Suppose a problem states that a candy bar contains 45% by mass chocolate. This percentage equality can be written with factors using the same mass unit such as grams.

$$\frac{45\text{ g chocolate}}{100\text{ g candy bar}} \quad \text{and} \quad \frac{100\text{ g candy bar}}{45\text{ g chocolate}}$$

Write two conversion factors for each of the following statements:

a. A cracker contains 55% fat by mass.

b. In the city, a car gets 14 miles to the gallon.

c. A 125 g of steak contains 45 g protein.

d. 18-carat pink gold contains 25% copper by mass.

Answers

a. $\frac{55\text{ g fat}}{100\text{ g cracker}}$ and $\frac{100\text{ g cracker}}{55\text{ g fat}}$

b. $\frac{14\text{ mi}}{1\text{ gal}}$ and $\frac{1\text{ gal}}{14\text{ mi}}$

c. $\frac{45\text{ g protein}}{125\text{ g steak}}$ and $\frac{125\text{ g steak}}{45\text{ g protein}}$

d. $\frac{25\text{ g copper}}{100\text{ g pink gold}}$ and $\frac{100\text{ g pink gold}}{25\text{ g copper}}$

2.7 Problem Solving

- Conversion factors from metric and/or U.S. relationships and percent can be used to change a quantity expressed in one unit to a quantity expressed in another unit.

◆ Learning Exercise 2.7A

The process of solving a problem with units requires the change of the initial unit to one or more units until the final unit of the answer is obtained.

Given unit —— Conversion Factors ——→ Desired unit

Guide to Problem Solving (GPS) Using Conversion Factors
STEP 1: Identify the given unit and the final unit needed for the answer.
STEP 2: Write a plan showing the sequence of units.
STEP 3: State the appropriate equalities and their conversion factors.
STEP 4: Set up the problem by arranging the factors to cancel units and provide the final unit.

Example: How many liters is 2850 mL?

STEP 1: **Given:** 2850 mL **Need:** liters

STEP 2: **Plan:** milliliters —— **Metric factor** ——→ liters

STEP 3: **Equalities/Conversions Factors:**

1 L = 1000 mL

$\frac{1\text{ L}}{1000\text{ mL}}$ and $\frac{1000\text{ mL}}{1\text{L}}$

STEP 4: **Set Up Problem**: $2850\ \cancel{\text{mL}} \times \frac{1\text{ L}}{1000\ \cancel{\text{mL}}} = 2.85\text{ L}$

Use metric–metric conversion factors to solve the following problems:

a. 189 mL = ________ L

b. 2.7 cm = ________mm

c. 425 in.^{2} = ________ cm^2

d. 76 mg = ________g

e. How many meters tall is a person whose height is 175 cm?

f. There are 285 mL in a cup of tea. How many liters is that?

g. An 18-carat ring contains 75% gold by mass. If the total mass of the ring is 13 500 mg, how many grams of gold does the ring contain?

h. You walked 1.5 km on the treadmill at the gym. How many meters did you walk?

Answers

a. 0.189 L **b.** 27 mm **c.** 2740 cm^2 **d.** 0.076 g
e. 1.75 m **f.** 0.285 L **g.** 10.1 g **h.** 1500 m

◆ Learning Exercise 2.7B

Use metric–U.S. conversion factors to solve the following problems:

a. 18 in. = __________ cm **b.** 4.0 qt = __________ L

c. 275 mL = __________ qt **d.** 1300 mg = __________ lb

e. 150 lb = __________ kg **f.** 840 g = __________ lb

g. 15 ft = __________ cm **h.** 8.50 oz = __________ g

Answers	**a.** 46 cm	**b.** 3.8 L	**c.** 0.291 qt	**d.** 0.0029 lb
	e. 68 kg	**f.** 1.9 lb	**g.** 460 cm	**h.** 241 g

◆ Learning Exercise 2.7C

Study Note

1. For setups that require a series of conversion factors, it is helpful to write out the plan first. Work from the starting unit to the final unit. Then use a conversion factor for each change of unit.

Starting unit → unit (1) → unit (2) = final unit

3. To convert from one unit to another, select conversion factors that cancel the given unit and provide the next unit. Several factors may be needed to obtain the final unit.

$$\cancel{\text{Starting unit}} \times \frac{\cancel{\text{unit (1)}}}{\cancel{\text{Starting unit}}} \times \frac{\text{unit (2)}}{\cancel{\text{unit (1)}}} = \text{final unit}$$

Use conversion factors to solve the following problems:

a. A piece of plastic tubing measures 120 mm. What is the length of the tubing in inches?

b. A statue weighs 240 lb. What is the mass of the statue in kilograms?

c. Your friend has a height of 6 ft, 3 in. What is your friend's height in meters?

d. In a triple-bypass surgery, a patient requires 3 pt whole blood. How many milliliters of blood were given if 1 qt = 2 pt?

e. Calculate the meters squared in a rug with an area of 48 000 cm^2.

f. A mouthwash contains 22% alcohol by volume. How many milliliters of alcohol are in a 1.05-pt bottle of mouthwash if there are 2 pt in 1 qt?

g. An 18-karat gold bracelet has a mass of 2.0 oz. If 18-karat gold contains 75% pure gold, how many grams of pure gold are in the bracelet?

Answers				
	a. 4.7 in.	**b.** 110 kg	**c.** 1.9 m	**d.** 1420 mL
	e. 4.8 m^2	**f.** 110 mL	**g.** 43 g	

2.8 Density

- The density of a substance is the ratio of its mass to its volume, usually in units of grams per milliliter (g/mL) or grams per cubic centimeter (g/cm^3) (1 mL = 1 cm^3). For example, the density of sugar is 1.59 g/mL and silver is 10.5 g/mL.

$$\text{Density} = \frac{\text{mass of substance}}{\text{volume of substance}}$$

Study Note

Density can be used as a factor to convert between the mass (g) and volume (mL) of a substance. The density of silver is 10.5 g/mL. What is the mass of 6.0 mL of silver?

$$6.0 \cancel{\text{mL silver}} \times \frac{10.5 \text{ g silver}}{1 \cancel{\text{mL silver}}} = 63 \text{ g silver}$$

Density

What is the volume of 25 g olive oil (D = 0.92 g/mL)?

$$25 \cancel{\text{g olive oil}} \times \frac{1 \text{ mL olive oil}}{0.92 \cancel{\text{g olive oil}}} = 27 \text{ mL olive oil}$$

Density

◆ Learning Exercise 2.8

Calculate the density or use density as a conversion factor to solve each of the following:

a. What is the density (g/mL) of glycerol if a 200-mL sample has a mass of 252 g?

b. A small solid has a mass of 5.5 oz. When placed in a graduated cylinder with a water level of 25.2 mL, the object causes the water level to rise to 43.8 mL. What is the density of the object in grams per milliliter (g/mL)?

c. A sugar solution has a density of 1.20 g/mL. What is the mass in grams of 0.250 L of the solution?

d. A piece of pure gold weighs 0.26 lb. If gold has a density of 19.3 g/mL, what is the volume in milliliters of the piece of gold?

e. A salt solution has a density of 1.15 g/mL and a volume of 425 mL. What is the mass in grams of the solution?

f. A 50.0-g sample of a glucose solution has a density of 1.28 g/mL. What is the volume in liters of the sample?

Answers	**a.** 1.26 g/mL	**b.** 8.4 g/mL	**c.** 300 g
	d. 6.1 mL	**e.** 489 g	**f.** 0.0391 L

2.9 Temperature

- Temperature is measured in Celsius units (°C) or kelvins (K). In the United States, the Fahrenheit scale (°F) is still in use.
- The equation $T_F = 1.8T_C + 32$ is used to convert a Celsius temperature to a Fahrenheit temperature.
- When rearranged for °C, the equation is used to convert from °F to °C.

$$T_C = \frac{(T_F - 32)}{1.8}$$

- The temperature on the Celsius scale is related to the kelvin scale: K = °C + 273.

◆ Learning Exercise 2.9

Calculate the temperatures in the following problems:

a. To prepare yogurt, milk is warmed to 68°C. What Fahrenheit temperature is needed to prepare the yogurt?

b. On a cold day in Alaska, the temperature drops to −12°C. What is that temperature on a Fahrenheit thermometer?

c. A patient has a temperature of 39.5°C. What is that temperature in °F?

d. On a hot summer day, the temperature is 95°F. What is the temperature on the Celsius scale?

e. A pizza is cooked at a temperature of 425°F. What is the °C temperature?

f. A research experiment requires the use of liquid nitrogen to cool the reaction flask to −45°C. What temperature will this be on the kelvin scale?

Answers	**a.** 154°F	**b.** 10°F	**c.** 103.1°F
	d. 35°C	**e.** 218°C	**f.** 228 K

Checklist for Chapter 2

You are ready to take the self-test for Chapter 2. Be sure you have accomplished the following learning goals for this chapter. If you are not sure, review the section listed at the end of the goal. Then apply your new skills and understanding to the practice test. After studying Chapter 2, I can successfully:

_____ Write the names and abbreviations for the metric (SI) units of measurement (2.1).

_____ Write large or small numbers using scientific notation (2.2).

_____ Count the number of significant figures in measured numbers (2.3).

_____ Report an answer with the correct number of significant figures (2.4).

_____ Write a metric equality from the numerical values of metric prefixes (2.5).

_____ Write two conversion factors for an equality (2.6).

_____ Use conversion factors to change from one unit to another unit (2.7).

_____ Calculate the density of a substance, or use density to calculate the mass or volume (2.8).

_____ Given a temperature, calculate a corresponding temperature on another scale (2.9).

Practice Test for Chapter 2

Instructions: Select the letter preceding the word or phrase that best answers the question.

1. Which of the following is a metric measurement of volume?
A. kilogram **B.** kilowatt **C.** kiloliter **D.** kilometer **E.** kiloquart

2. The measurement 24 000 g written in scientific notation is
A. 24 g **B.** 24×10^3 g **C.** 2.4×10^3 g **D.** 2.4×10^{-3} g **E.** 2.4×10^4 g

3. The measurement 0.005 m written in scientific notation is
A. 5 m **B.** 5×10^{-3} m **C.** 5×10^{-2} m **D.** 0.5×10^{-4} m **E.** 5×10^3 m

4. The measured number in the following is
A. 1 book **B.** 2 cars **C.** 4 flowers **D.** 5 rings **E.** 45 g

5. The number of significant figures in 105.4 m is
A. 1 **B.** 2 **C.** 3 **D.** 4 **E.** 5

6. The number of significant figures in 0.00082 g is
A. 1 **B.** 2 **C.** 3 **D.** 4 **E.** 5

7. The calculator answer 5.78052 rounded to two significant figures is
A. 5 **B.** 5.7 **C.** 5.8 **D.** 5.78 **E.** 6.0

8. The calculator answer 3486.512 rounded to three significant figures is
A. 4000 **B.** 3500 **C.** 349 **D.** 3487 **E.** 3490

9. $16.0 \div 8.0$ is
A. 2 **B.** 2.0 **C.** 2.00 **D.** 0.2 **E.** 5.0

10. 58.5 + 9.158 is
A. 67 **B.** 67.6 **C.** 67.7 **D.** 67.66 **E.** 67.658

11. $\dfrac{2.5 \times 3.12}{4.6}$ is

A. 0.54 **B.** 7.8 **C.** 0.85 **D.** 1.7 **E.** 1.69

12. Which of these prefixes has the largest value?
A. centi **B.** deci **C.** milli **D.** kilo **E.** micro

13. What is the decimal equivalent of the prefix *centi*?
A. one-thousandth **B.** one-hundredth **C.** one-tenth
D. ten **E.** one hundred

14. Which of the following is the smallest unit of measurement?
A. gram **B.** milligram **C.** kilogram **D.** decigram **E.** centigram

15. Which volume is the largest?
A. mL **B.** dL **C.** cm^3 **D.** L **E.** kL

16. Which of the following is a conversion factor?
A. 12 in. **B.** 3 ft **C.** 20 m **D.** $\dfrac{1000\text{ g}}{1\text{ kg}}$ **E.** cm^3

17. Which is a conversion factor that relates milliliters to liters?
A. $\dfrac{1000\text{ mL}}{1\text{ L}}$ **B.** $\dfrac{100\text{ mL}}{1\text{ L}}$ **C.** $\dfrac{10\text{ mL}}{1\text{ L}}$ **D.** $\dfrac{0.01\text{ mL}}{1\text{ L}}$ **E.** $\dfrac{0.001\text{ mL}}{1\text{ L}}$

18. Which is a conversion factor for millimeters and centimeters?
A. $\dfrac{1\text{ mm}}{1\text{ cm}}$ **B.** $\dfrac{10\text{ mm}}{1\text{ cm}}$ **C.** $\dfrac{100\text{ cm}}{1\text{ mm}}$ **D.** $\dfrac{100\text{ mm}}{1\text{ cm}}$ **E.** $\dfrac{10\text{ cm}}{1\text{ mm}}$

19. 294 mm is equal to
A. 2940 m **B.** 29.4 m **C.** 2.94 m **D.** 0.294 m **E.** 0.0294 m

20. The area of the face of a tennis racket measures 115 $in.^2$. What is that area in square centimeters?
A. 742 cm^2 **B.** 17.8 cm^2 **C.** 45.3 cm^2 **D.** 292 cm^2 **E.** 115 cm^2

21. What is the volume of 65 mL in liters?
A. 650 L **B.** 65 L **C.** 6.5 L **D.** 0.65 L **E.** 0.065 L

22. What is the mass in kilograms of a 22-lb turkey?
A. 10 kg **B.** 48 kg **C.** 10 000 kg **D.** 0.048 kg **E.** 22 000 kg

23. The number of milliliters in 2 dL is
A. 20 mL **B.** 200 mL **C.** 2000 mL **D.** 20 000 mL **E.** 500 000 mL

24. A person who is 5 ft, 4 in. tall would be
A. 64 m **B.** 25 m **C.** 14 m **D.** 1.6 m **E.** 1.3 m

25. How many ounces are in 1500 g (1 lb = 16 oz)?
A. 94 oz **B.** 53 oz **C.** 24 000 oz **D.** 33 oz **E.** 3.3 oz

26. How many quarts of orange juice are in 255 mL of juice?
A. 0.255 qt **B.** 270 qt **C.** 236 qt **D.** 0.270 qt **E.** 0.400 qt

27. Your doctor places you on a 2200-Cal diet, with 18% of the Calories from fat.
How many Calories are you allowed from fat?
A. 18 Cal **B.** 2200 Cal **C.** 1800 Cal **D.** 400 Cal **E.** 3960 Cal

28. How many milliliters of a salt solution with a density of 1.8 g/mL are needed to provide 400 g of salt solution?
A. 220 mL **B.** 22 mL **C.** 720 mL **D.** 400 mL **E.** 4.5 mL

29. Three liquids have densities of 1.15 g/mL, 0.79 g/mL, and 0.95 g/mL. When the liquids, which do not mix, are poured into a graduated cylinder, the liquid at the top is the one with a density of
A. 1.15 g/mL **B.** 1.00 g/mL **C.** 0.95 g/mL **D.** 0.79 g/mL **E.** 0.16 g/mL

30. A sample of oil has a mass of 65 g and a volume of 80.0 mL. What is the density of the oil?
A. 1.5 g/mL **B.** 1.4 g/mL **C.** 1.2 g/mL **D.** 0.90 g/mL **E.** 0.81 g/mL

31. What is the mass of a 10.0-mL sample of liquid with a density of 1.04 g/mL?
A. 104 g **B.** 10.4 g **C.** 1.04 g **D.** 1.40 g **E.** 9.62 g

32. Ethyl alcohol has a density of 0.790 g/mL. What is the mass of 0.250 L of the alcohol?
A. 198 g **B.** 158 g **C.** 3.95 g **D.** 0.253 g **E.** 0.160 g

33. 105°F = ____°C
A. 73°C **B.** 41°C **C.** 58°C **D.** 90°C **E.** 189°C

34. The melting point of gold is 1064°C. The Fahrenheit temperature needed to melt gold would be
A. 129°C **B.** 623°F **C.** 1031°F **D.** 1913°F **E.** 1947°F

35. The average daytime temperature on the planet Mercury is 683 K. What is this temperature on the Celsius scale?
A. 956°C **B.** 715°C **C.** 680°C **D.** 410°C **E.** 303°C

Answers to the Practice Test

1. C	**2.** E	**3.** B	**4.** E	**5.** D
6. B	**7.** C	**8.** E	**9.** B	**10.** C
11. D	**12.** D	**13.** B	**14.** B	**15.** E
16. D	**17.** A	**18.** B	**19.** D	**20.** A
21. E	**22.** A	**23.** B	**24.** D	**25.** B
26. D	**27.** C	**28.** A	**29.** D	**30.** E
31. B	**32.** A	**33.** B	**34.** E	**35.** D

Answers and Solutions to Selected Text Problems

Section 2.1

2.1 **a.** meter; length **b.** gram; mass **c.** liter; volume
d. second; time **e.** degree Celsius; temperature

2.3 **a.** both **b.** both **c.** neither
d. both **e.** metric

2.5 **a.** gram, metric **b.** liter, metric **c.** Celsius, metric
d. meter, both **e.** second, both

Section 2.2

2.7 **a.** Move the decimal point left four decimal places to give 5.5×10^4 m.

b. Move the decimal point left two decimal places to 4.8×10^2 g.

c. Move the decimal point right six decimal places to give 5×10^{-6} cm.

d. Move the decimal point right four decimal places to give 1.4×10^{-4} s.

e. Move the decimal point right three decimal places to give 7.85×10^{-3} L.

f. Move the decimal point left six decimal places to 6.7×10^5 kg.

2.9 **a.** The value 7.2×10^3, which is also 72×10^2, is greater than 8.2×10^2.

b. The value 3.2×10^{-2}, which is also 320×10^{-4}, is greater than 4.5×10^{-4}.

c. The value 1×10^4 or 10 000 is greater than 1×10^{-4} or 0.0001.

d. The value 6.8×10^{-2} or 0.068 is greater than 0.000 52.

2.11 **a.** The standard number is 1.2 times the power of 10^4 or 10 000, which gives 12 000.

b. The standard number is 8.25 times the power of 10^{-2} or 0.01, which gives 0.0825.

c. The standard number is four times the power of 10^6 or 1 000 000, which gives 4 000 000.

d. The standard number is five times the power of 10^{-3} or 0.001, which gives 0.005.

Section 2.3

2.13 **a.** The *estimated digit* is the last digit reported in a measurement. In 8.6 m, the 6 in the first decimal (tenths) place was estimated and has some uncertainty.

b. The *estimated digit* is the 5 in the second decimal (hundredths) place.

c. The *estimated digit* would be the 0 in the first decimal (tenths) place.

2.15 Measured numbers are obtained using some kind of measuring tool. Exact numbers are numbers obtained by counting or from a definition in the metric or the U.S measuring system.

a. measured **b.** exact **c.** exact **d.** measured

2.17 Measured numbers are obtained using some kind of measuring tool. Exact numbers are numbers obtained by counting or from a definition in the metric or the U.S. measuring system.
a. The value 6 oz of meat is obtained by measurement, whereas 3 hamburgers is a counted/exact number.
b. None; both 1 table and 4 chairs are counted/exact numbers.
c. Both 0.75 lb and 350 g are obtained by measurements.
d. None; the values in a definition are exact numbers.

2.19 **a.** Zeros preceding significant digits are *not significant.*
b. Zeros between significant digits are *significant.*
c. Zeros after significant digits in a decimal number are *significant.*
d. Zeros in the coefficient of a number written in scientific notation are *significant.*
e. Zeros in a number with no decimal point are considered as placeholders only and *not significant.*

2.21 **a.** All five numbers are significant figures.
b. Only the two nonzero numbers are significant; the preceding zeros are placeholders.
c. Only the two nonzero numbers are significant; the zeros that follow are placeholders.
d. All three numbers in the coefficient of a number written in scientific notation are significant.
e. All four numbers, including the last zero in a decimal number, are significant.
f. All three numbers, including the zeros that follow a nonzero digit in a decimal number, are significant.

2.23 Both measurements in **c** have two significant figures, and both measurements in **d** have four significant figures.

2.25 **a.** 5000 is the same as 5 x 1000, which is written in scientific notation as 5×10^3.

b. 30 000 is the same as 3 x 10 000, which is written in scientific notation as 3×10^4.

c. 100 000 is the same as 1 x 100 000, which is written in scientific notation as 1×10^5.

d. 0.000 25 is the same as $2.5 \times \frac{1}{10\,000}$, which is written in scientific notation as 2.5×10^{-4}.

Section 2.4

2.27 Calculators carry out mathematical computations and display without regard to significant figures. Our task is to round the calculator's answer to the number of significant figures allowed by the number of significant figures in the original data.

2.29 To round a number, determine how many significant figures are kept and drop all remaining digits. There is no change in the retained figures if the first digit dropped is 0 to 4. However, if the first digit dropped is 5 to 9, raise the last retained digit by 1.

a. To round 1.854, drop the 4 and keep 1.85.
b. To round 184.2038, drop 2038 and keep 184.
c. To round 0.004738265, drop 8265 and increase the retained digits by 1 or 0.00474.
d. To round 8807 to three significant figures, drop 7 and increase the retained digits to 8810, keeping a zero in the one's place as a placeholder; in scientific notation, 8.81×10^3.
e. To round 1.832149, drop 2149 and keep 1.83 as the rounded value.

2.31 **a.** Drop 55 and increase the last digit by 1, which gives 56.9 m
b. Drop 25 and keep remaining digits as 0.002 28 g
c. Drop 27, keep remaining digits, and add two zeros as placeholders, 11 500 s (1.15×10^4 s).
d. Add a significant zero to give three SFs, 8.10 L.

2.33 **a.** Because the value of 0.034 has two SFs, the answer 1.6 can only have two SFs.
b. The measurement 5 has one SF, which allows one SF in the answer (0.01).
c. The measurement 1.25 has three SFs, which allows three SFs in the answer (27.6).

$$\frac{34.56}{1.25} = 27.6$$

d. The measurement 25 has two SFs, which allows two SFs in the answer (3.5).

$$\frac{(0.2465)(25)}{1.78} = 3.5$$

e. The measurement 2.8×10^4 has two SFs, which allows two SFs in the answer (0.14).

$$(2.8 \times 10^4)(5.05 \times 10^{-6}) = 0.14 \quad (1.4 \times 10^{-1})$$

f. The measurement 8×10^3 has one SF, which allows one SF in the answer (0.8).

$$\frac{(3.45 \times 10^{-2})(1.8 \times 10^5)}{(8 \times 10^3)} = 8 \times 10^{-1}\ (0.8)$$

2.35 The answer of addition and subtraction problems can have as many decimal places as the measurement with the fewest decimal places.

a.

45.48 cm	two decimal places
+ 8.057 cm	three decimal places
53.54 cm	two decimal places

b.

23.45 g	two decimal places
104.1 g	one decimal place
+0.025 g	three decimal places
127.6 g	one decimal place

c. 145.675 mL — three decimal places
$-$ 24.2 mL — one decimal place
121.5 mL — one decimal place

d. 1.08 L — two decimal places
$-$ 0.585 L — three decimal places
0.50 L — two decimal places

Section 2.5

2.37 The kilometer per hour (km/hr) markings indicate how many kilometers (how much distance) will be traversed in 1 hour's time if the speed is held constant. The miles per hour (mph) markings indicate the same distance traversed *but measured in miles* during the 1 hour of travel.

2.39 Because the prefix *kilo* means 1000 times, a *kilo*gram is equal to 1000 grams.

2.41 **a.** mg **b.** dL **c.** km **d.** kg **e.** μL **f.** ns

2.43 **a.** 0.01 **b.** 1000 **c.** 0.001 **d.** 0.1 **e.** 1 000 000 **f.** 10^{-9}

2.45 **a.** 100 cm **b.** 1000 m **c.** 0.001 m **d.** 1000 mL

2.47 **a.** A kilogram, which is 1000 g, is larger because a milligram is 0.001 g.

b. A milliliter, which is 10^{-3} L, is larger because a microliter is 10^{-6} L.

c. A kilometer, which is 10^{3} (1000) m, is larger because a centimeter is 10^{-2} (0.01) m.

d. A kiloliter, which is 10^{3} (1000) L, is larger because a deciliter is 10^{-1} (0.1) L.

Section 2.6

2.49 Because a conversion factor is unchanged when inverted $\frac{1\text{ m}}{100\text{ cm}}$ and $\frac{100\text{ cm}}{1\text{ m}}$.

2.51 The numerator and denominator are from the equality: 1 kg = 1000 g

2.53 **a.** 1 yd = 3 ft $\frac{1\text{ yd}}{3\text{ ft}}$ and $\frac{3\text{ ft}}{1\text{ yd}}$

b. 1 L = 1000 mL $\frac{1\text{ L}}{1000\text{ mL}}$ and $\frac{1000\text{ mL}}{1\text{ L}}$

c. 1 min = 60 s $\frac{1\text{ min}}{60\text{ s}}$ and $\frac{60\text{ s}}{1\text{ min}}$

d. 1 dL = 100 mL $\frac{1\text{ dL}}{100\text{ mL}}$ and $\frac{100\text{ mL}}{1\text{ dL}}$

2.55 The equalities between the metric prefixes can be written as two conversion factors.

a. 1 m = 100 cm $\frac{1\text{ m}}{100\text{ cm}}$ and $\frac{100\text{ cm}}{1\text{ m}}$

b. 1 g = 1000 mg $\frac{1\text{ g}}{1000\text{ mg}}$ and $\frac{1000\text{ mg}}{1\text{ g}}$

c. 1 L = 1000 mL $\frac{1\text{ L}}{1000\text{ mL}}$ and $\frac{1000\text{ mL}}{1\text{ L}}$

d. 1 kg = 10^6 mg $\frac{10^6\text{ mg}}{1\text{ kg}}$ and $\frac{1\text{ kg}}{10^6\text{ mg}}$

e. $(1\text{ m})^3 = (100\text{ cm})^3$ $\frac{(100\text{ cm})^3}{(1\text{ m})^3}$ and $\frac{(1\text{ m})^3}{(100\text{ cm})^3}$

2.57 An equality stated in a problem can be written as two conversion factors, which are true only for that problem.

a. 3.5 m = 1 s $\quad \frac{3.5\text{ m}}{1\text{ s}}$ and $\frac{1\text{ s}}{3.5\text{ m}}$

b. 1 mL = 0.65 g $\quad \frac{0.65\text{ g}}{1\text{ mL}}$ and $\frac{1\text{ mL}}{0.65\text{ g}}$

c. 1.0 gal = 46.0 km $\quad \frac{46.0\text{ km}}{1.0\text{ gal}}$ and $\frac{1.0\text{ gal}}{46.0\text{ km}}$

d. Percent means parts silver per 100 parts sterling silver. Using grams (g) as the mass unit
100 g sterling silver = 93 g silver $\quad \frac{93\text{ g silver}}{100\text{ g sterling}}$ and $\frac{100\text{ g sterling}}{93\text{ g silver}}$

Section 2.7

2.59 When using a conversion factor you are trying to cancel existing units and arrive at a new (desired) unit. The conversion factor must be properly oriented so unit cancellation (numerator to denominator) can be accomplished.

2.61 **a.** Plan: cm → m

$175\text{ cm} \times \frac{1\text{ m}}{100\text{ cm}} = 1.75\text{ m}$

b. Plan: mL → L

$5500\text{ mL} \times \frac{1\text{ L}}{1000\text{ mL}} = 5.5\text{ L}$

c. Plan: kg → g

$0.0055\text{ kg} \times \frac{1000\text{ g}}{1\text{ kg}} = 5.5\text{ g}$

d. Plan: $cm^3 \rightarrow m^3$

$350\text{ cm}^3 \times \frac{1\text{ m}^3}{(100)^3\text{ cm}^3} = 3.5 \times 10^{-4}\text{ m}^3$

2.63 **a.** Plan: qt → mL

$0.750\text{ qt} \times \frac{1\text{ L}}{1.057\text{ qt}} \times \frac{1000\text{ mL}}{1\text{ L}} = 710.\text{ mL}$

b. Plan: lb → kg

$11.8\text{ stones} \times \frac{14.0\text{ lb}}{1\text{ stone}} \times \frac{1\text{ kg}}{2.205\text{ lb}} = 74.9\text{ kg}$

c. Plan: in. → cm → mm

$19.5\text{ in.} \times \frac{2.54\text{ cm}}{1\text{ in.}} \times \frac{10\text{ mm}}{1\text{ cm}} = 495\text{ mm}$

d. Plan: μm → m → cm → in.

$0.50\text{ μm} \times \frac{1\text{ m}}{10^6\text{ μm}} \times \frac{100\text{ cm}}{1\text{ m}} \times \frac{1\text{ in.}}{2.54\text{ cm}} = 2.0 \times 10^{-5}\text{ in.}$

2.65 **a.** Plan: ft → in. → cm → m

$78.0\text{ ft} \times \frac{12\text{ in.}}{1\text{ ft}} \times \frac{2.54\text{ cm}}{1\text{ in.}} \times \frac{1\text{ m}}{100\text{ cm}} = 23.8\text{ m (length)}$

b. Plan: ft $\rightarrow$ in. $\rightarrow$ cm $\rightarrow$ m $\rightarrow$ m^2

$$27.0 \text{ ft} \times \frac{12 \text{ in.}}{1 \text{ ft}} \times \frac{2.54 \text{ cm}}{1 \text{ in.}} \times \frac{1 \text{ m}}{100 \text{ cm}} = 8.23 \text{ m (width)}$$

Area $= 23.8 \text{ m} \times 8.23 \text{ m} = 196 \text{ m}^2$

c. Plan: m $\rightarrow$ km $\rightarrow$ hr $\rightarrow$ min $\rightarrow$ s

$$23.8 \text{ m} \times \frac{1 \text{ km}}{1000 \text{ m}} \times \frac{1 \text{ hr}}{185 \text{ km}} \times \frac{60 \text{ min}}{1 \text{ hr}} \times \frac{60 \text{ s}}{1 \text{ min}} = 0.463 \text{ s}$$

d. Plan: $m^2 \rightarrow cm^2 \rightarrow in.^2 \rightarrow ft^2 \rightarrow$ gal $\rightarrow$ qt $\rightarrow$ L

$$196 \text{ m}^2 \times \frac{(100 \text{ cm})^2}{1 \text{ m}^2} \times \frac{(1 \text{ in.})^2}{(2.54 \text{ cm})^2} \times \frac{(1 \text{ ft})^2}{(12 \text{ in.})^2} \times \frac{1 \text{ gal}}{300 \text{ ft}^2} \times \frac{4 \text{ qt}}{1 \text{ gal}} \times \frac{1 \text{ L}}{1.057 \text{ qt}}$$

$= 53.1$ L

2.67 Each of the following requires a percent factor from the problem information.

a. Plan: g crust $\rightarrow$ g oxygen (percent equality: 100.0 g crust = 46.7 g oxygen)

$$325 \text{ g crust} \times \frac{46.7 \text{ g oxygen}}{100.0 \text{ g crust}} = 152 \text{ g oxygen}$$

b. Plan: g crust $\rightarrow$ g magnesium (percent equality: 100.0 g crust = 2.1 g magnesium)

$$1.25 \text{ g crust} \times \frac{2.1 \text{ g magnesium}}{100.0 \text{ g crust}} = 0.026 \text{ g magnesium}$$

c. Plan: oz $\rightarrow$ lb $\rightarrow$ g $\rightarrow$ g nitrogen (percent equality: 100.0 g fertilizer = 15 g nitrogen)

$$10.0 \text{ oz fertilizer} \times \frac{1 \text{ lb}}{16 \text{ oz}} \times \frac{453.6 \text{ g}}{1 \text{ lb}} \times \frac{15 \text{ g nitrogen}}{100.0 \text{ g fertilizer}} = 43 \text{ g of nitrogen}$$

d. Plan: kg pecans $\rightarrow$ kg choc. bars $\rightarrow$ lb (percent equality: 100.0 kg bars = 22.0 kg pecans)

$$5.0 \text{ kg pecans} \times \frac{100 \text{ kg choc. bars}}{22.0 \text{ kg pecans}} \times \frac{2.205 \text{ lb}}{1 \text{ kg}} = 50. \text{ lb of chocolate bars}$$

Section 2.8

2.69 Because the density of aluminum is 2.70 g/cm^3, silver is 10.5 g/cm^3, and lead is 11.3 g/cm^3, we can identify the unknown metal by calculating its density as follows:

$$\frac{217 \text{ g metal}}{19.2 \text{ cm}^3 \text{ metal}} = 11.3 \text{ g/cm}^3$$ The metal is lead.

2.71 Density is the mass of a substance divided by its volume. The densities of solids and liquids are usually stated in grams per milliliter (g/mL) or grams per cubic centimeter (g/cm^3).

$$\text{Density} = \frac{\text{mass(g)}}{\text{volume (mL)}}$$

a. $$\frac{24.0 \text{ g}}{20.0 \text{ mL}} = 1.20 \text{ g/mL}$$

b. $$\frac{0.250 \text{ lb}}{130.3 \text{ mL}} \times \frac{453.6 \text{ g}}{1 \text{ lb}} = \frac{0.870 \text{ g}}{\text{mL}}$$

c. volume of gem: 34.5 mL total $-$ 20.0 mL water = 14.5 mL

density of gem: $$\frac{45.0 \text{ g}}{14.5 \text{ mL}} = 3.10 \text{ g/mL}$$

d. $$\frac{485.6 \text{ g}}{114 \text{ mL}} = 4.26 \text{ g/mL}$$

e. $0.100\ \cancel{\text{pint}} \times \frac{1\ \cancel{\text{qt}}}{2\ \cancel{\text{pints}}} \times \frac{1\ \cancel{\text{L}}}{1.057\ \cancel{\text{qt}}} \times \frac{1000\ \text{mL}}{1\ \cancel{\text{L}}} = 47.3\ \text{mL}$

mass of syrup = 182.48 g – 115.25 g = 67.23 g

density of syrup = $\frac{67.23\ \text{g}}{47.3\ \text{mL}} = 1.42\ \text{g/mL}$

2.73 a. $1.50\ \cancel{\text{kg alcohol}} \times \frac{1000\ \cancel{\text{g}}}{1\ \cancel{\text{kg alcohol}}} \times \frac{1\ \cancel{\text{mL}}}{0.785\ \cancel{\text{g}}} \times \frac{1\ \text{L}}{1000\ \cancel{\text{mL}}} = 1.91\ \text{L}$

b. $6.5\ \cancel{\text{mL}} \times \frac{13.6\ \text{g}}{1\ \cancel{\text{mL}}} = 88\ \text{g}$

c. $225\ \cancel{\text{mL}} \times \frac{7.8\ \cancel{\text{g}}}{1\ \cancel{\text{mL}}} \times \frac{1\ \cancel{\text{lb}}}{453.6\ \cancel{\text{g}}} \times \frac{16\ \text{oz}}{1\ \cancel{\text{lb}}} = 62\ \text{oz}$

d. $74.1\ \cancel{\text{cm}^3} \times \frac{1\ \cancel{\text{mL}}}{1\ \cancel{\text{cm}^3}} \times \frac{8.92\ \text{g}}{1\ \cancel{\text{mL}}} = 661\ \text{g}$

e. $12.0\ \cancel{\text{gal}} \times \frac{4\ \cancel{\text{qt}}}{1\ \cancel{\text{gal}}} \times \frac{1000\ \cancel{\text{mL}}}{1.057\ \cancel{\text{qt}}} \times \frac{0.66\ \cancel{\text{g}}}{1\ \cancel{\text{mL}}} \times \frac{1\ \text{kg}}{1000\ \cancel{\text{g}}} = 30.\ \text{kg}$

Section 2.9

2.75 The Fahrenheit temperature scale is still used in the United States. A normal body temperature is 98.6°F on this scale. To convert temperature to the equivalent reading on the Celsius scale, the following calculation must be performed:

$$\frac{(99.8°\text{F} - 32)}{1.8} = 37.7°\text{C}$$

Because a normal body temperature is 37.0°C, the temperature of 37.7°C would be a mild fever.

2.77 In temperature calculations, the number of significant figures is determined by the measured temperature; the values of 32 and 1.8 are exact.

a. 1.8 (37.0°C) + 32 = 66.6 + 32 = 98.6°F

b. $\frac{(65.3°\text{F} - 32°)}{1.8} = \frac{33.3}{1.8} = 18.5°\text{C}$

c. –27°C + 273 = 246 K

d. 62°C + 273 = 335 K

e. $\frac{(114°\text{F} - 32)}{1.8} = \frac{82}{1.8} = 46°\text{C}$

f. $\frac{(72°\text{F} - 32)}{1.8} = \frac{40}{1.8} = 22°\text{C};\ 22°\text{C} + 273 = 295\ \text{K}$

2.79 a. $\frac{(106°\text{F} - 32)}{1.8} = \frac{74}{1.8} = 41°\text{C}$

b. $\frac{(103°\text{F} - 32)}{1.8} = \frac{71}{1.8} = 39°\text{C}$

No, there is no need to phone the doctor. The child's temperature is less than 40.0°C.

Answers to Additional Questions and Problems

2.87 **a.** Drop 8 and increase retained digits by 1 to give 0.0000126 L (1.26×10^{-5} L).

b. Drop 8 and increase retained digits by 1 to give 3.53×10^{2} kg.

c. Drop 111, keep retained digits, and add three zeros as placeholders to give 125 000 m^3 or 1.25×10^{5} m^3.

d. Drop 03 and keep retained digits, 58.7 m.

e. Add two significant zeros to give 3 SFs, 3.00×10^{-3} s.

f. Drop 26 and keep retained digits, 0.0108 g.

2.89 This problem requires several conversion factors. Let's take a look first at a possible unit plan. When you write out the unit plan, be sure you know a conversion factor you can use for each step.

Plan: ft → in. → cm → m → min

$$7500\ \cancel{\text{ft}} \times \frac{12\ \cancel{\text{in.}}}{1\ \cancel{\text{ft}}} \times \frac{2.54\ \cancel{\text{cm}}}{1\ \cancel{\text{in.}}} \times \frac{1\ \cancel{\text{m}}}{100\ \cancel{\text{cm}}} \times \frac{1\ \text{min}}{55.0\ \cancel{\text{m}}} = 42\ \text{min}$$

2.91 Plan: lb → g → onions

$$4.0\ \cancel{\text{lb onions}} \times \frac{453.6\ \cancel{\text{g}}}{1\ \cancel{\text{lb}}} \times \frac{1\ \text{onion}}{115\ \cancel{\text{g onion}}} = 16\ \text{onions}$$

Because the number of onion is a counting number, the value for onions 15.8 is rounded to a whole number 16.

2.93 **a.** Plan: oz → crackers

$$8.0\ \cancel{\text{oz}} \times \frac{6\ \text{crackers}}{0.50\ \cancel{\text{oz}}} = 96\ \text{crackers}$$

b. Plan: crackers → servings → g→ lb→ oz

$$10\ \cancel{\text{crackers}} \times \frac{1\ \cancel{\text{serving}}}{6\ \cancel{\text{crackers}}} \times \frac{4\ \cancel{\text{g}}\ \text{fat}}{1\ \cancel{\text{serving}}} \times \frac{1\ \cancel{\text{lb}}}{453.6\ \cancel{\text{g}}} \times \frac{16\ \text{oz}}{1\ \cancel{\text{lb}}} = 0.2\ \text{oz fat}$$

c. Plan: boxes → oz → servings→ mg→ g

$$50\ \cancel{\text{boxes}} \times \frac{8.0\ \cancel{\text{oz}}}{1\ \cancel{\text{box}}} \times \frac{1\ \cancel{\text{serving}}}{0.50\ \cancel{\text{oz}}} \times \frac{140\ \cancel{\text{mg}}\ \text{sodium}}{1\ \cancel{\text{serving}}} \times \frac{1\ \text{g}}{1000\ \cancel{\text{mg}}} = 110\ \text{g sodium}$$

2.95 Plan: lb → kg → pesos→ dollar→ cents

$$0.45\ \cancel{\text{lb}} \times \frac{1\ \cancel{\text{kg}}}{2.205\ \cancel{\text{lb}}} \times \frac{48\ \cancel{\text{pesos}}}{1\ \cancel{\text{kg}}} \times \frac{1\ \cancel{\text{dollar}}}{10.8\ \cancel{\text{pesos}}} \times \frac{100\ \text{cents}}{1\ \cancel{\text{dollar}}} = 91\ \text{cents}$$

Because the calculation is for a counted number of cents, the value 90.7 is rounded to 91.

2.99 This problem has two units. Convert grams to milligrams, and convert liters in the denominator to deciliters.

$$\frac{1.85\ \cancel{\text{g}}}{1\ \cancel{\text{L}}} \times \frac{1000\ \text{mg}}{1\ \cancel{\text{g}}} \times \frac{1\ \cancel{\text{L}}}{10\ \text{dL}} = 185\ \text{mg/dL}$$

2.101 The difference between the initial volume of the water and its volume with the lead object will give us the volume of the lead object.

285 mL total – 215 mL water = 70 mL lead

Using the density of lead, we can convert milliliters to the mass in grams of the lead object.

$$70.\ \text{mL lead} \times \frac{11.3\ \text{g lead}}{1\ \text{mL lead}} = 790\ \text{g lead}$$

2.103 Plan: L gas → mL gas → g gas → g oil → mL oil → cm^3 oil

$$1.00\ \text{L gas} \times \frac{1000\ \text{mL gas}}{1\ \text{L gas}} \times \frac{0.66\ \text{g gas}}{1\ \text{mL gas}} \times \frac{1\ \text{g oil}}{1\ \text{g gas}} \times \frac{1\ \text{mL oil}}{0.92\ \text{g oil}} \times \frac{1\ \text{cm}^3}{1\ \text{mL}}$$

$$= 720\ \text{cm}^3\ \text{oil}$$

2.105 **a.** Plan: kg weight → kg fat → lb (percent equality: 100.0 kg weight = 3.0 kg fat)

$$45\ \text{kg body weight} \times \frac{3.0\ \text{kg fat}}{100.0\ \text{kg body weight}} \times \frac{2.205\ \text{lb}}{1\ \text{kg}} = 3.0\ \text{lb fat}$$

b. Plan: L fat → mL → g → lb

$$3.0\ \text{L fat} \times \frac{1000\ \text{mL}}{1\ \text{L}} \times \frac{0.94\ \text{g fat}}{1\ \text{mL fat}} \times \frac{1\ \text{lb}}{453.6\ \text{g}} = 6.2\ \text{lb fat}$$

2.107 Plan: cm^3 → g → g silver → lb → oz (percent equality: 100 g sterling = 92.5 g silver)

$$27.0\ \text{cm}^3 \times \frac{10.3\ \text{g}}{1\ \text{cm}^3} \times \frac{92.5\ \text{g silver}}{100\ \text{g}} \times \frac{1\ \text{lb}}{453.6\ \text{g}} \times \frac{16\ \text{oz}}{1\ \text{lb}} = 9.07\ \text{oz pure silver}$$

2.109

$$T_C = \frac{(T_F - 32°)}{1.8} = -26°\text{C}$$

$$K = -15°\text{C} + 273 = -247\ \text{K}$$

3
Atoms and Elements

Study Goals

- Classify an example of matter as a pure substance or a mixture.
- Write the name of an element from its symbol or its period and group number.
- Classify an element as a metal or nonmetal.
- Describe the three important particles in the atom, their location, charges, and relative masses.
- Describe Rutherford's gold foil experiment and how it led to the current model of the atom.
- Use atomic number and mass number of an atom to determine the number of protons, neutrons, and electrons in the atom.
- Understand the relationship of isotopes to the atomic mass of an element on the periodic table.

Think About It

1. What is the difference between an element and a compound?

2. How are the symbols of the elements related to their names?

3. What are some elements you have seen today?

4. On a dry day, you walk across a carpet and touch a doorknob. You feel a spark. What happened?

Key Terms

Match each the following key terms with the correct definition.

a. element **b.** atom **c.** atomic number **d.** mass number **e.** isotope

1. _____ The number of protons and neutrons in the nucleus of an atom

2. _____ The smallest particle of an element

3. _____ A primary substance that cannot be broken down into simpler substances

4. _____ An atom of an element that has a different number of neutrons than another atom of the same element

5. _____ The number of protons in an atom

Answers **1.** d **2.** b **3.** a **4.** e **5.** c

3.1 Classification of Matter

- A pure substance, element or compound, has a definite composition.
- Elements are the simplest type of matter; compounds consist of a combination of two or more elements.
- Mixtures contain two or more substances that are physically, not chemically, combined.
- Mixtures are classified as homogeneous or heterogeneous.

◆ Learning Exercise 3.1A

Identify each of the following as an element (E) or compound (C):

1. _____ iron **2.** _____ carbon dioxide

3. _____ potassium iodide **4.** _____ gold

5. _____ aluminum **6.** _____ table salt (sodium chloride)

Answers **1.** E **2.** C **3.** C
4. E **5.** E **6.** C

◆ Learning Exercise 3.1B

Identify each of the following as a pure substance (P) or mixture (M):

1. _____ bananas and milk **2.** _____ sulfur

3. _____ silver **4.** _____ a bag of raisins and nuts

5. _____ water **6.** _____ sand and water

Answers **1.** M **2.** P **3.** P **4.** M **5.** P **6.** M

◆ Learning Exercise 3.1C

Identify each of the following mixtures as homogeneous (HO) or heterogeneous (HE):

1. _____ chocolate milk **2.** _____ sand and water

3. _____ lemonade **4.** _____ a bag of raisins and nuts

5. _____ air **6.** _____ vinegar

Answers **1.** HO **2.** HE **3.** HO **4.** HE **5.** HO **6.** HO

3.2 Elements and Symbols

- Chemical symbols are one- or two-letter abbreviations for the names of the elements.
- The physical properties of an element are those characteristics such as color, density, and melting and boiling point that we can observe or measure without changing the identity of the element.

◆ Learning Exercise 3.2A

Study Note

Now is the time to learn the names of the elements and their symbols. Practice saying and writing the names of the elements in the periodic table. Cover the symbols in the list of elements and practice writing the symbols for the elemental names.

Write the symbols for each of the following elements:

1. carbon ____ **2.** iron ____ **3.** sodium ____

4. phosphorus ____ **5.** oxygen ____ **6.** nitrogen ____

7. iodine ____ **8.** sulfur ____ **9.** potassium ____

10. lead ____ **11.** calcium ____ **12.** gold ____

13. copper ____ **14.** neon ____ **15.** chlorine ____

Answers

1. C	**2.** Fe	**3.** Na	**4.** P	**5.** O
6. N	**7.** I	**8.** S	**9.** K	**10.** Pb
11. Ca	**12.** Au	**13.** Cu	**14.** Ne	**15.** Cl

◆ Learning Exercise 3.1B

Write the names of the elements represented by each of the following symbols:

1. Mg ____________________ **2.** K ____________________

3. Au ____________________ **4.** F ____________________

5. Cu ____________________ **6.** Be ____________________

7. Ag ____________________ **8.** Br ____________________

9. Zn ____________________ **10.** Al ____________________

11. Ba ____________________ **12.** Li ____________________

Answers

1. magnesium	**2.** potassium	**3.** gold
4. fluorine	**5.** copper	**6.** beryllium
7. silver	**8.** bromine	**9.** zinc
10. aluminum	**11.** barium	**12.** lithium

3.3 The Periodic Table

- The periodic table is an arrangement of the elements into vertical columns and horizontal rows.
- Each vertical column contains a *group* of elements, which have similar properties.
- A horizontal row of elements is called a *period.*
- On the periodic table, the *metals* are located on the left of the heavy zigzag line, the *nonmetals* are to the right, and *metalloids* are next to the zigzag line.

◆ Learning Exercise 3.3A

Study Note

1. The periodic table consists of horizontal rows called *periods* and vertical columns called *groups.*
2. Elements in Group 1A (1) are the *alkali metals.* Elements in Group 2A (2) are the *alkaline earth metals*, and Group 7A (17) contains the *halogens.* Elements in Group 8A (18) are the *Noble gases.*

Indicate whether the following elements are in a group (G), period (P), or neither (N):

a. Li, C, and O ________________ **b.** Br, Cl, and F ________________

c. Al, Si, and Cl ________________ **d.** C, N, and O ________________

e. Mg, Ca, and Ba ________________ **f.** C, S, and Br ________________

g. Li, Na, and K ________________ **h.** K, Ca, and Br ________________

Answers **a.** P **b.** G **c.** P **d.** P
e. G **f.** N **g.** G **h.** P

◆ Learning Exercise 3.3B

Complete the list of elements, group numbers, and period numbers in the following table:

Element and Symbol	Group Number	Period Number
	2A (2)	3
Silicon, Si		
	5A (15)	2
Aluminum, Al		
	4A (14)	5
	1A (1)	6

Answers

Element Symbol	Group Number	Period Number
Magnesium, Mg	2A (2)	3
Silicon, Si	4A (14)	3
Nitrogen, N	5A (15)	2
Aluminum, Al	3A (13)	3
Tin, Sn	4A (14)	5
Cesium, Cs	1A (1)	6

◆ Learning Exercise 3.3C

Identify each of the following elements as a metal (M), metalloid (ML), or nonmetal (NM):

1. Cl _____	**2.** N _____	**3.** Fe _____	**4.** Si _____	**5.** Al _____
6. C _____	**7.** Ca _____	**8.** Zn _____	**9.** Sb _____	**10.** Mg _____

Answers					
	1. NM	**2.** NM	**3.** M	**4.** ML	**5.** M
	6. NM	**7.** M	**8.** M	**9.** ML	**10.** M

◆ Learning Exercise 3.3D

Match the names of the chemical groups with the elements K, Cl, He, Fe, Mg, Ne, Li, Cu, and Br.

1. Halogens ______________________

2. Noble gases ______________________

3. Alkali metals ______________________

4. Alkaline earth metals ______________________

5. Transition elements ______________________

Answers **1.** Cl, Br **2.** He, Ne **3.** K, Li **4.** Mg **5.** Fe, Cu

3.4 The Atom

- An atom is the smallest particle that retains the characteristics of an element.
- Atoms are composed of three subatomic particles. Protons have a positive charge (+), electrons carry a negative charge (–), and neutrons are electrically neutral.
- The protons and neutrons, each with a mass of about 1 amu, are found in the tiny, dense nucleus. The electrons are located outside the nucleus.

◆ Learning Exercise 3.4A

Indicate whether each of the following statements is consistent with the modern atomic theory (true or false):

1. All matter is composed of atoms.

2. All atoms of an element are identical.

3. Atoms combine to form compounds.

4. Most of the mass of the atom is in the nucleus.

Answers **1.** true **2.** false **3.** true **4.** true

◆ Learning Exercise 3.4B

Match the following terms with the correct statements:

a. proton **b.** neutron **c.** electron **d.** nucleus

1. _____ Found in the nucleus of an atom
2. _____ Has a –1 charge
3. _____ Found outside the nucleus
4. _____ Has a mass of 1 amu
5. _____ The small, dense center of the atom
6. _____ Is neutral

Answers **1.** a and b **2.** c **3.** c **4.** a and b **5.** d **6.** b

3.5 Atomic Number and Mass Number

- The *atomic number* is the number of protons in every atom of an element.
- In neutral atoms, the number of protons is equal to the number of electrons.
- The mass number is the total number of protons and neutrons in an atom.

◆ Learning Exercise 3.5A

Give the number of protons in each of the following neutral atoms:

a. An atom of carbon _______
b. An atom of the element with atomic number 15 _______
c. An atom with a mass number of 40 and atomic number 19 _______
d. An atom with 9 neutrons and a mass number of 19 _______
e. A neutral atom that has 18 electrons _______

Answers **a.** 6 **b.** 15 **c.** 19 **d.** 10 **e.** 18

◆ Learning Exercise 3.5B

Study Note

The *atomic number* is the number of protons in an atom. The *mass number* is the total number of neutrons and protons in the nucleus of an atom.
Example: How many protons and neutrons are in the nucleus of an isotope of silver (Ag) with a mass number of 109?
Solution: The atomic number of Ag is 47. Thus, an atom of Ag has 47 protons.
Mass number – atomic number = number of neutrons 109 – 47 = 62 neutrons

Determine the number of neutrons in each of the following atoms:

a. A mass number of 42 and atomic number 20 __________
b. A mass number of 10 and 5 protons __________
c. $^{30}_{14}Si$ __________
d. A mass number of 9 and atomic number 4 __________
e. A mass number of 22 and 10 protons __________
f. A zinc atom with a mass number of 66 __________

Answers **a.** 22 **b.** 5 **c.** 16 **d.** 5 **e.** 12 **f.** 36

◆ Learning Exercise 3.5C

Study Note

In the atomic symbol for a particular atom, the mass number appears in the upper left corner and the atomic number in the lower left corner.

Mass number → ^{32}S ^{26}Al
Atomic number → 16 13

Complete the following table for neutral atoms.

Symbol	Atomic Number	Mass Number	Number of Protons	Number of Neutrons	Number of Electrons
	12			12	
			20	22	
		55		27	
	35			45	
		35	17		
$^{120}_{50}Sn$					

Answers

Symbol	Atomic Number	Mass Number	Number of Protons	Number of Neutrons	Number of Electrons
$^{24}_{12}Mg$	12	24	12	12	12
$^{42}_{20}Ca$	20	42	20	22	20
$^{55}_{26}Fe$	26	55	26	29	26
$^{80}_{35}Br$	35	80	35	45	35
$^{35}_{17}Cl$	17	35	17	18	17
$^{120}_{50}Sn$	50	120	50	70	50

3.6 Isotopes and Atomic Mass

- Atoms that have the same number of protons, but different numbers of neutrons, are called *isotopes*.
- The atomic mass of an element is the average mass of all isotopes in a naturally occurring sample of that element.

◆ Learning Exercise 3.6A

Identify the sets of atoms that are isotopes.

A. $^{20}_{10}X$ **B.** $^{20}_{11}X$ **C.** $^{21}_{11}X$ **D.** $^{19}_{10}X$ **E.** $^{19}_{9}X$

Answer Atoms A and D are isotopes (At. No. 10); atoms B and C are isotopes (At. No. 11).

◆ Learning Check 3.6B

Essay Copper has two naturally occurring isotopes, ^{63}Cu and ^{65}Cu. If that is the case, why is the atomic mass of copper listed as 63.55 on the periodic table?

Answer Copper in nature consists of two isotopes with different atomic masses. The atomic mass is the average of the individual masses of the two isotopes and their percent abundance in the sample. The atomic mass does not represent the mass of any individual atom.

◆ Learning Check 3.6C

Of all the atoms in a sample of an element, 69.06% have an atomic mass of 62.93 amu. If there is only one other natural isotope of that element and its atomic mass is 64.93 amu, what is the atomic mass of the element? Using the periodic table, write the symbol and name of the element.

Answer: 100% – 69.06 = 30.94%

$$62.93 \text{ amu} \times \frac{69.06}{100} + 64.93 \text{ amu} \times \frac{30.94}{100} = 63.55 \text{ amu}$$

The element is copper (Cu).

Checklist for Chapter 3

You are ready to take the practice test for Chapter 3. Be sure you have accomplished the following learning goals for this chapter. If you are not sure, review the section listed at the end of the goal. Then apply your new skills and understanding to the practice test.

After studying Chapter 3, I can successfully:

____ Identify matter as a pure substance or mixture (3.1).

____ Write the correct symbol or name for an element (3.2).

____ Use the periodic table to identify the group and period of an element, and describe it as a metal or nonmetal (3.3).

____ State the electrical charge, mass, and location of the protons, neutrons, and electrons in an atom (3.4).

____ Given the atomic number and mass number of an atom, state the number of protons, neutrons, and electrons (3.5).

____ Identify an isotope and describe the atomic mass of an element (3.6).

Practice Test for Chapter 3

Write or select the correct answer for each of the following questions.
Classify the following as a pure substance (P) or a mixture (M).

1. toothpaste _____ **2.** platinum ______ **3.** chromium ______

4. mouthwash _____ **5.** bronze ______

Write the correct symbol for each of the elements listed:

6. potassium _____ **7.** phosphorus __________

8. calcium _____ **9.** carbon __________

10. sodium __________

Write the correct name for each of the symbols listed:

11. Fe ____________________ **12.** Cu ____________________

13. Cl ____________________ **14.** Pb ____________________

15. Ag ____________________

16. The elements C, N, and O are part of a
A. period **B.** family **C.** neither

17. The elements Li, Na, and K are part of a
A. period **B.** family **C.** neither

18. What is the classification of an atom with 15 protons and 17 neutrons?
A. metal **B.** nonmetal **C.** transition element **D.** noble gas **E.** halogen

19. What is the group number of the element with atomic number 3?
A. 1 **B.** 2 **C.** 3 **D.** 7 **E.** 8

For questions 20 through 23, consider an atom with 12 protons and 13 neutrons.

20. This atom has an atomic number of
A. 12 **B.** 13 **C.** 23 **D.** 24 **E.** 25

21. This atom has a mass number of
A. 12 **B.** 13 **C.** 23 **D.** 24 **E.** 25

22. This is an atom of
A. carbon **B.** sodium **C.** magnesium **D.** aluminum **E.** manganese

23. The number of electrons in this atom is
A. 12 **B.** 13 **C.** 23 **D.** 24 **E.** 25

For questions 24 through 27, consider an atom of calcium with a mass number of 42.

24. This atom of calcium has an atomic number of
A. 20 **B.** 22 **C.** 40 **D.** 41 **E.** 42

25. The number of protons in this atom of calcium is
A. 20 **B.** 22 **C.** 40 **D.** 41 **E.** 42

26. The number of neutrons in this atom of calcium is
A. 20 **B.** 22 **C.** 40 **D.** 41 **E.** 42

27. The number of electrons in this atom of calcium is
A. 20 **B.** 22 **C.** 40 **D.** 41 **E.** 42

28. Platinum, ^{195}Pt, has
A. 78 p^+, 78e^-, 78n **B.** 195 p^+, 195e^-, 195n **C.** 78p^+, 78e^-, 195n
D. 78p^+, 78e^-, 117n **E.** 78p^+, 117e^-, 117n

For questions 29 through 30, use the following list of atoms.

$^{14}_{7}V$ $^{16}_{8}W$ $^{19}_{9}X$ $^{16}_{7}Y$ $^{18}_{8}Z$

29. Which atom(s) is(are) isotopes of an atom with 8 protons and 9 neutrons?
A. W **B.** W, Z **C.** X, Y **D.** X **E.** Y

30. Which atom(s) are isotopes of an atom with 7 protons and 8 neutrons?
A. V **B.** W **C.** V, Y **D.** W, Z **E.** none

31. Which element would you expect to have properties most like oxygen?
A. nitrogen **B.** carbon **C.** chlorine **D.** argon **E.** sulfur

32. Which of the following is an isotope of nitrogen?
A. $^{14}_{8}N$ **B.** $^{7}_{3}N$ **C.** $^{10}_{5}N$ **D.** $^{4}_{2}He$ **E.** $^{15}_{7}N$

Answers for the Practice Test

1. M	**2.** P	**3.** P	**4.** M	**5.** M
6. K	**7.** P	**8.** Ca	**9.** C	**10.** Na
11. iron	**12.** copper	**13.** chlorine	**14.** lead	**15.** silver
16. A	**17.** B	**18.** B	**19.** A	**20.** A
21. E	**22.** C	**23.** A	**24.** A	**25.** A
26. B	**27.** A	**28.** D	**29.** B	**30.** C
31. E	**32.** E			

Answers and Solutions to Selected Text Problems

Section 3.1

3.1 A *pure substance* has a definite composition. A *mixture* has a variable composition.
a. pure substance **b.** mixture
c. pure substance **d.** pure substance

3.3 *Elements* are the simplest type of pure substance.
Compounds contain two or more elements in the same ratio.
a. element **b.** compound
c. element **d.** compound

3.5 A *homogeneous mixture* has a uniform composition; a *heterogeneous mixture* does not have a uniform composition throughout the mixture.
a. heterogeneous **b.** homogeneous
c. homogeneous **d.** heterogeneous

Section 3.2

3.7 **a.** Cu **b.** Si **c.** K **d.** N
e. Fe **f.** Ba **g.** Pb **h.** Sr

3.9 **a.** carbon **b.** chlorine **c.** iodine **d.** mercury
e. fluorine **f.** argon **g.** zinc **h.** nickel

3.11 **a.** sodium (Na) and chlorine (Cl)
b. calcium (Ca), sulfur (S), and oxygen (O)
c. carbon (C), hydrogen (H), chlorine (Cl), nitrogen (N), and oxygen (O)
d. calcium (Ca), carbon (C), and oxygen (O)

Section 3.3

3.13 **a.** C, N, and O are in Period 2.
b. He is the element at the top of Group 8A (18).
c. The alkali metals are the elements in Group 1A (1).
d. Period 2 is the horizontal row of elements that ends with neon (Ne).

3.15 **a.** alkaline earth metal **b.** transition element **c.** noble gas
d. alkali metal **e.** halogen

3.17 **a.** C **b.** He **c.** Na **d.** Ca **e.** Al

3.19 On the periodic table, *metals* are located to the left of the heavy zigzag line, *nonmetals* are elements to the right, and metalloids (B, Si, Ge, As, Sb, Te, Po, and At) are located along the line.
a. metal **b.** nonmetal **c.** metal **d.** nonmetal
e. nonmetal **f.** nonmetal **g.** metalloid **h.** metal

Section 3.4

3.21 **a.** electron **b.** proton **c.** electron **d.** neutron

3.23 The two most massive subatomic particles, protons and neutrons, are located in a very small region of the atom, which is called the nucleus.

3.25 Selection **b** (a proton and an electron) is the only one with a pair of particles having opposite charges.

3.27 In the process of brushing hair, like charges on the hair and brush repel each other.

Section 3.5

3.29 The atomic number is equal to the number of protons. The mass number is the sum of the protons and neutrons.
a. atomic number **b.** both **c.** mass number **d.** atomic number

3.31 **a.** lithium, Li **b.** fluorine, F **c.** calcium, Ca **d.** zinc, Zn
e. neon, Ne **f.** silicon, Si **g.** iodine, I **h.** oxygen, O

3.33 **a.** 12 **b.** 30 **c.** 53 **d.** 19

3.35

Name of Element	Symbol	Atomic Number	Mass Number	Number of Protons	Number of Neutrons	Number of Electrons
Aluminum	Al	13	27	13	14	13
Magnesium	Mg	12	24	12	12	12
Potassium	K	19	39	19	20	19
Sulfur	S	16	31	16	15	16
Iron	Fe	26	56	26	30	26

Section 3.6

3.37 **a.** Because the atomic number of aluminum is 13, every Al atom has 13 protons. An atom of aluminum (mass number 27) has 14 neutrons (27 – 13 = 14 n). Neutral atoms have the same number of protons and electrons—13 protons, 14 neutrons, and 13 electrons.

b. Because the atomic number of chromium is 24, every Cr atom has 24 protons. An atom of chromium (mass number 52) has 28 neutrons (52 – 24 = 28 n). Neutral atoms have the same number of protons and electrons—24 protons, 28 neutrons, and 24 electrons.
c. Because the atomic number of sulfur is 16, every S atom has 16 protons. An atom of sulfur (mass number 34) has 18 neutrons (34 – 16 = 18 n). Neutral atoms have the same number of protons and electrons—16 protons, 18 neutrons, and 16 electrons.
d. Because the atomic number of iron is 26, every Fe atom has 26 protons. An atom of iron (mass number 56) has 30 neutrons (56 – 26 = 30 n). Neutral atoms have the same number of protons and electrons—26 protons, 30 neutrons, and 26 electrons.

3.39 **a.** $^{31}_{15}P$ **b.** $^{80}_{35}Br$ **c.** $^{27}_{13}Al$ **d.** $^{35}_{17}Cl$

3.41 **a.** $^{32}_{16}S$ $^{33}_{16}S$ $^{34}_{16}S$ $^{36}_{16}S$
b. They all have the same atomic number (the same number of protons and electrons).
c. They have different numbers of neutrons, which is reflected in their mass numbers.
d. The atomic mass of sulfur on the periodic table is the average atomic mass of all naturally occurring isotopes of sulfur.

3.43 The mass of an isotope is the mass of an individual atom. The atomic mass is the weighted average of all the naturally occurring isotopes of that element.

3.45 Because the atomic mass of copper is closer to 63, there are more atoms of ^{63}Cu.

3.47 Because the atomic mass of iron is 55.85, the most abundant isotope is ^{56}Fe.

3.49 $68.926 \text{ amu} \times \frac{60.10}{100} + 70.925 \text{ amu} \times \frac{39.90}{100} = 69.72 \text{ amu}$

Additional Problems

3.57 **a.** element **b.** compound **c.** mixture
d. element **e.** mixture

3.59 Mixture **a** is homogeneous because it has the same composition everywhere.

3.61 Any element with a two-letter symbol has the first letter capitalized and the second letter in lower case. CO would indicate a compound made of the two elements carbon and oxygen.

3.63 **a.** Mg, magnesium **b.** Br, bromine **c.** Al, aluminum **d.** O, oxygen

3.65 Any two of the following in each part are correct responses:
a. fluorine, chlorine, bromine, iodine, and astatine
b. helium, neon, argon, krypton, xenon, and radon
c. lithium, sodium, potassium, rubidium, cesium, and francium
d. beryllium, magnesium, calcium, strontium, barium, and radium

3.67 **a.** False. A proton has a positive charge.
b. False. The neutron has about the same mass as a proton.
c. True.
d. False. The nucleus is the tiny, dense central core of an atom.
e. True

3.69 **a.** protons **b.** protons **c.** alkali metals

3.71 **a.** lithium, Li **b.** fluorine, F **c.** calcium, Ca **d.** arsenic, As
e. tin, Sn **f.** cesium, Cs **g.** gold, Au **h.** oxygen, O

3.73 **a.** 25 protons, 25 electrons **b.** 30 protons, 30 electrons
c. 53 protons, 53 electrons **d.** 12 protons, 12 electrons
e. 19 protons, 19 electrons

3.75 **a.** 13 protons, 14 neutrons, 13 electrons
b. 24 protons, 28 neutrons, 24 electrons
c. 16 protons, 18 neutrons, 16 electrons
d. 26 protons, 30 neutrons, 26 electrons
e. 54 protons, 82 neutrons, 54 electrons

3.77 **a.** ^{9}Be **b.** ^{26}Mg **c.** ^{46}Ca **d.** ^{70}Zn **e.** ^{63}Cu

3.79

Name	Nuclear Symbol	Number of Protons	Number of Neutrons	Number of Electrons
Sulfur	$^{34}_{16}S$	16	**18**	16
Zinc	$^{70}_{30}Zn$	30	40	30
Magnesium	$^{26}_{12}Mg$	12	14	**12**
Radon	$^{220}_{86}Rn$	86	134	86

3.81 **a.** 26 protons, 30 neutrons, 26 electrons
b. $^{51}_{26}Fe$ **c.** $^{51}_{24}Cr$

3.83 **a.** $^{16}_{8}X$ $^{17}_{8}X$ $^{18}_{8}X$ All have eight protons.

b. $^{16}_{8}X$ $^{17}_{8}X$ $^{18}_{8}X$ All are isotopes of oxygen.

c. $^{16}_{8}X$ $^{16}_{9}X$ Both have mass number of 16.

$^{18}_{10}X$ $^{18}_{8}X$ Both have mass number of 18.

d. $^{16}_{8}X$ $^{18}_{10}X$ Both have eight neutrons.

3.85 **a.** 82 protons, 126 neutrons, 82 electrons

b. ^{214}Pb

c. ^{214}Bi, bismuth

3.87 $27.977 \times \frac{92.23}{100} + 28.976 \times \frac{4.68}{100} + 29.974 \times \frac{3.09}{100}$

$= 25.80 + 1.36 + 0.9262$
$= 28.09$ amu

3.89 $1\ \cancel{\text{in.}} \times \frac{2.54\ \cancel{\text{cm}}}{1\ \cancel{\text{in.}}} \times \frac{1\ \text{atom}}{3.14 \times 10^{-8}\ \cancel{\text{cm}}} = 8.09 \times 10^{7}$ atoms

4

Electronic Structure and Periodic Trends

Study Goals

- Identify electromagnetic radiation as energy that travels as waves at the speed of light.
- Compare the wavelength of radiation with its frequency.
- Explain the unique atomic spectra of elements.
- Describe the sublevels and orbitals available in the principle energy levels.
- Write orbital diagrams and electron configurations for atoms and ions.
- Describe the changes in sizes of atoms and ionization energies going down a group and across a period.

Think About It

1. How does the energy of microwaves compare with the energy of radio waves?

2. How much of the electromagnetic spectrum can we see?

3. What causes the different colors seen in fireworks?

Key Terms

Match each the following key terms with the correct definition.

a. photon | **b.** wavelength | **c.** electron configuration
d. electromagnetic radiation | **e.** orbital | **f.** valence electrons

1.____ The distance between the peaks of two adjacent waves

2.____ The electrons in the outermost energy level of an atom

3.____ Energy that travels as waves at the speed of light

4.____ The smallest particle of light

5.____ The organization of electrons within an atom by orbitals of increasing energy

6.____ The region within an atom where an electron of a certain energy is most likely to be found

Answers **1.** b **2.** f **3.** d **4.** a **5.** c **6.** e

4.1 Electromagnetic Radiation

- Electromagnetic radiation is energy that travels as waves in space at the speed of light.
- The wavelength is the distance between the peaks of adjacent waves.
- The frequency is the number of waves that pass a certain point in one second.
- The electromagnetic spectrum is all forms of electromagnetic radiation in order of decreasing wavelength.

◆ Learning Exercise 4.1A

Calculate the wavelength in meters for electromagnetic radiation with the following frequencies.

a. A radio wave from an FM station that broadcasts at 105 MHz

b. Light in the infrared region at a frequency of $6.6 \times 10^{13}\ s^{-1}$

c. A police radar monitor that operates at 2.2×10^{10} Hz

Answers

$$\lambda = \frac{c}{\nu} = \frac{3.0 \times 10^8\ m\ s^{-1}}{\nu}$$

a. $105\ \cancel{MHz} \times \frac{1 \times 10^6\ \cancel{Hz}}{1\ \cancel{MHz}} \times \frac{1\ s^{-1}}{1\ \cancel{Hz}} = 1.05 \times 10^8\ s^{-1}$

$$\frac{3.0 \times 10^8\ m\ \cancel{s^{-1}}}{1.05 \times 10^8\ \cancel{s^{-1}}} = 2.9\ m$$

b. $\frac{3.0 \times 10^8\ m\ \cancel{s^{-1}}}{6.6 \times 10^{13}\ \cancel{s^{-1}}} = 4.5 \times 10^{-6}\ m$

c. $2.2 \times 10^{10}\ \cancel{Hz} \times \frac{1\ s^{-1}}{1\ \cancel{Hz}} = 2.2 \times 10^{10}\ s^{-1}$

$$\frac{3.0 \times 10^8\ m\ \cancel{s^{-1}}}{2.2 \times 10^{10}\ \cancel{s^{-1}}} = 1.4 \times 10^{-2}\ m$$

◆ Learning Exercise 4.1B

Calculate the frequency for electromagnetic radiation with the following wavelengths.

a. Radar with a wavelength of 10 cm

b. An X ray with a wavelength of 1.0×10^{-10} m

c. Blue light at 453 nm

Answers

$$v = \frac{c}{\lambda} = \frac{3.0 \times 10^8 \text{ m s}^{-1}}{\lambda}$$

a. $\frac{3.0 \times 10^8 \text{ \sout{m} s}^{-1}}{10. \text{ \sout{cm}}} \times \frac{100 \text{ \sout{cm}}}{1 \text{ \sout{m}}} = 3.0 \times 10^9 \text{ s}^{-1}$

b. $\frac{3.0 \times 10^8 \text{ \sout{m} s}^{-1}}{1.0 \times 10^{-10} \text{ \sout{m}}} = 3.0 \times 10^{18} \text{ s}^{-1}$

c. $\frac{3.0 \times 10^8 \text{ \sout{m} s}^{-1}}{453 \text{ \sout{nm}}} \times \frac{10^9 \text{ \sout{nm}}}{1 \text{ \sout{m}}} = 6.6 \times 10^{14} \text{ s}^{-1}$

◆ Learning Exercise 4.1C

Using the electromagnetic spectrum, identify the type of radiation that would have the shorter wavelength.

a. microwave or infrared ________________

b. radio waves or X rays ________________

c. gamma rays or radio waves ________________

d. ultraviolet or microwave ________________

Answers **a.** infrared **b.** X rays **c.** gamma rays **d.** ultraviolet

4.2 Atomic Spectra and Energy Levels

- An atomic spectrum is a series of colored lines that correspond to photons of specific energies emitted by a heated element.
- A photon is the smallest particle of electromagnetic radiation.
- Electrons in atoms exist in quantized energy levels.
- When electrons change energy levels, photons of specific energies are absorbed or emitted.

◆ Learning Exercise 4.2

Identify the photon in each pair with the greater energy.

a. ______ yellow light or green light **b.** ______ $\lambda = 10^9$ nm or $\lambda = 10^5$ nm

c. ______ purple light or red light **d.** ______ $\lambda = 10^{-3}$ nm or $\lambda = 10^2$ nm

Answers **a.** green light **b.** $\lambda = 10^5$ nm **c.** purple light **d.** $\lambda = 10^{-3}$ nm

4.3 Energy Levels, Sublevels, and Orbitals

- Energy levels indicated by the principal quantum numbers contain electrons of similar energies.
- Within each energy level, electrons with identical energy are grouped in *sublevels.* An *s* sublevel can accommodate 2 electrons; a *p* sublevel can accommodate 6 electrons; a *d* sublevel can accommodate 10 electrons; and an *f* sublevel can accommodate 14 electrons.
- An orbital is a region in an atom where there is the greatest probability of finding an electron of certain energy.
- An *s* orbital is spherical, and *p* orbitals have two lobes along an axis. The *d* and *f* orbitals have more complex shapes.
- Each sublevel consists of a set of orbitals: an *s* sublevel consists of one orbital; a *p* sublevel consists of three orbitals; a *d* sublevel consists of five orbitals; and an *f* sublevel consists of seven orbitals.
- An orbital can contain a maximum of $2e^-$, which have opposite spins.

◆ Learning Exercise 4.3

State the maximum number of electrons for each of the following:

a. 3*p* sublevel ______ **b.** 3*d* sublevel ______

c. 2*s* orbital ______ **d.** energy level 4 ______

e. 1s sublevel ______ **f.** 4*p* orbital ______

g. 5*p* sublevel ______ **h.** 4*f* sublevel ______

Answers **a.** 6 **b.** 10 **c.** 2 **d.** 32
e. 2 **f.** 2 **g.** 6 **h.** 14

4.4 Writing Orbital Diagrams and Electron Configurations

- An orbital diagram represents the orbitals in an atom that contain electrons.
- The electron configuration shows the number of electrons in each sublevel in order of increasing energy.

◆ Learning Exercise 4.4A

Write the orbital diagram for each of the following elements.

a. beryllium ______________________ **b.** carbon ______________________

c. sodium ______________________ **d.** nitrogen ______________________

e. fluorine ______________________ **f.** magnesium ______________________

Answers

a. 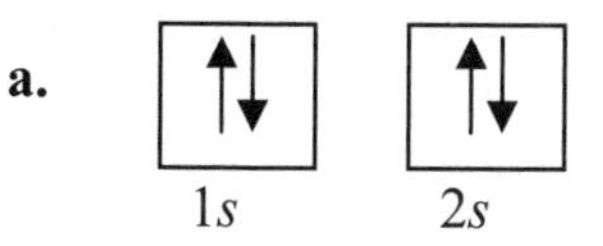

b. 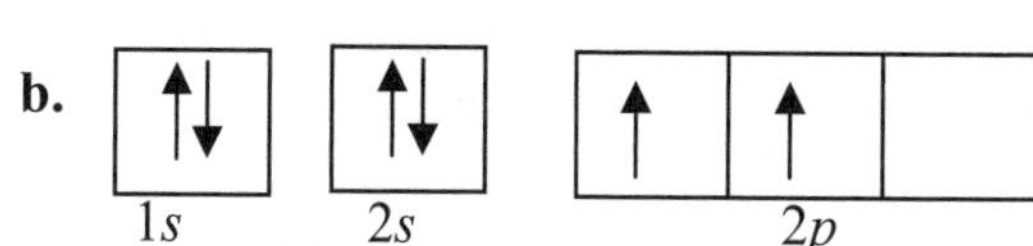

c. 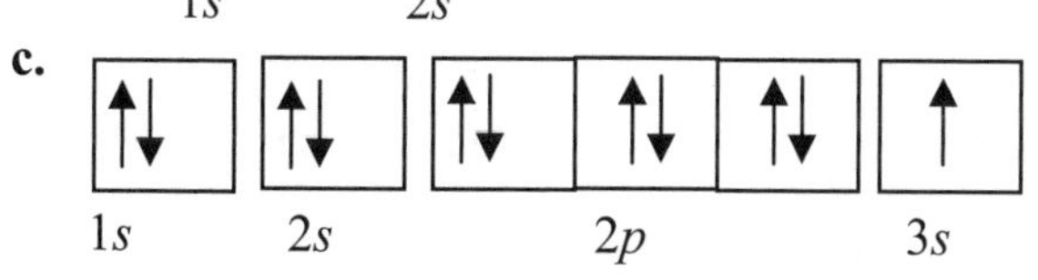

d. 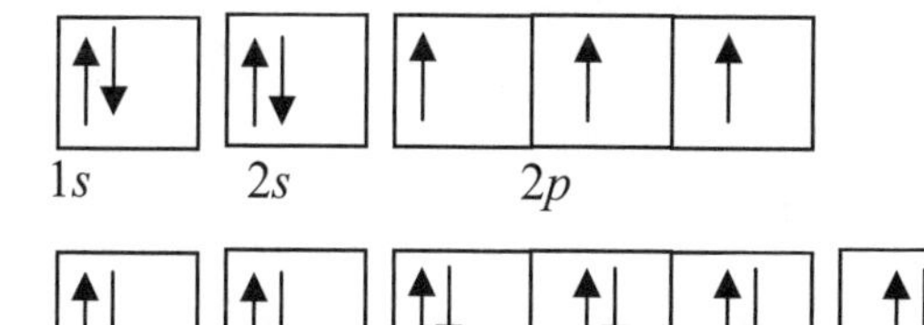

e 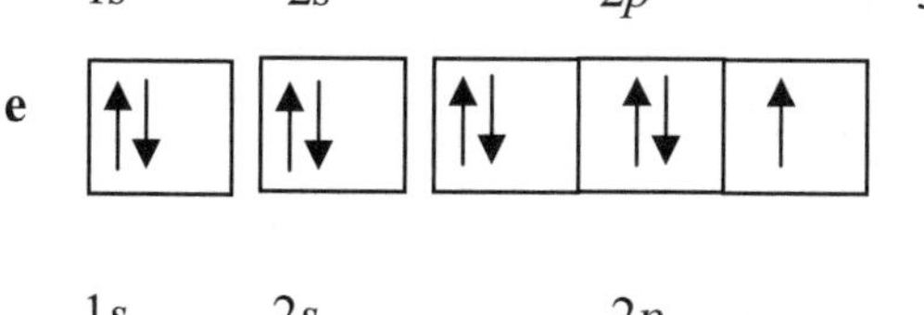
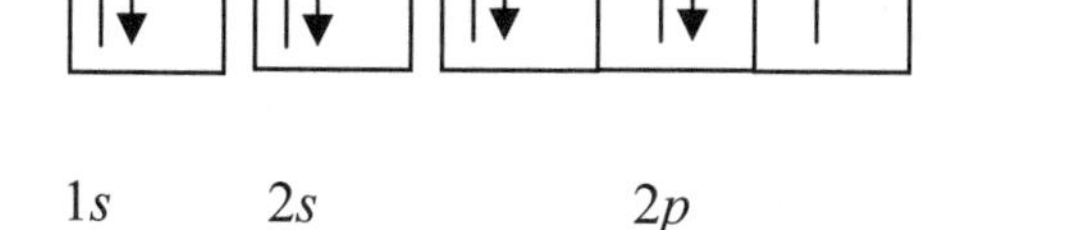

f. 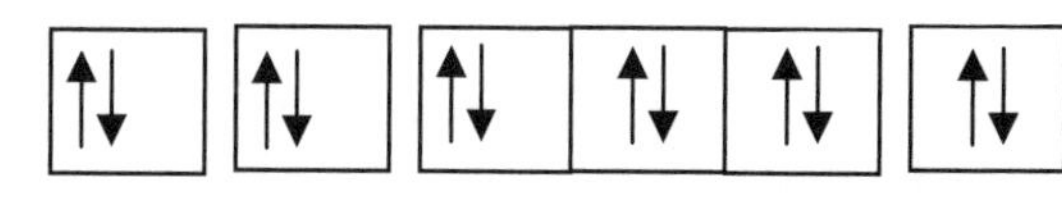

◆ Learning Exercise 4.4B

Write the electron configuration for each of the following elements:

a. carbon ______________________

b. magnesium ______________________

c. iron ______________________

d. silicon ______________________

e. chlorine ______________________

f. phosphorus ______________________

Answers

a. $1s^22s^22p^2$ **b.** $1s^22s^22p^63s^2$ **c.** $1s^22s^22p^63s^23p^64s^23d^6$

d. $1s^22s^22p^63s^23p^2$ **e.** $1s^22s^22p^63s^23p^5$ **f.** $1s^22s^22p^63s^23p^3$

◆ Learning Exercise 4.4C

Name the element with an electron configuration ending with each of the following notations.

a. $3p^5$ ______ **b.** $2s^1$ ______

c. $3d^8$ ______ **d.** $4p^1$ ______

e. $5p^5$ ______ **f.** $3p^2$ ______

g. $1s^1$ ______ **h.** $6s^2$ ______

Answers **a.** chlorine **b.** lithium **c.** nickel **d.** gallium
e. iodine **f.** silicon **g.** hydrogen **h.** barium

4.5 Electron Configurations and the Periodic Table

- The electron sublevels are organized as blocks on the periodic table. The *s* block corresponds to Groups 1A (1) and 2A (2), the *p* block extends from Group 3A (13) to 8A (18), the *d* block contains the transition elements, and the *f* block contains the lanthanides and actinides.
- In the abbreviated configuration, the electron configuration of the preceding noble gas is replaced by its symbol in square brackets.

◆ Learning Exercise 4.5A

Use the sublevel blocks on the periodic table to write the electron configuration for each of the following elements:

a. fluorine ______

b. sulfur ______

c. cadmium ______

d. strontium ______

Answers **a.** $1s^22s^22p^5$ **b.** $1s^22s^22p^63s^23p^4$
c. $1s^22s^22p^63s^23p^64s^23d^{10}4p^65s^24d^{10}$ **d.** $1s^22s^22p^63s^23p^64s^23d^{10}4p^65s^2$

◆ Learning Exercise 4.5B

Write the abbreviated electron configuration for the each of the following elements:

a. iodine ______ **b.** barium ______

c. zinc ______ **d.** tin ______

e. cesium ______ **f.** bromine ______

Answers **a.** $[Kr]5s^2\ 4d^{10}5p^5$ **b.** $[Xe]6s^2$ **c.** $[Ar]4s^2\ 3d^{10}$
d. $[Kr]5s^24d^{10}5p^2$ **e.** $[Xe]\ 6s^1$ **f.** $[Ar]\ 4s^2\ 3d^{10}4p^5$

◆ Learning Exercise 4.5C

Give the symbol of the element that has the following:

a. six 3*d* electrons ____ b. First element to completely fill four s orbitals ____

c. [Kr]$5s^1$ ____ d. [Ar]$4s^2 3d^{10} 4p^5$ ____

e. two 6*p* electrons ____ f. First to have 9 completely filled p orbitals ____

Answers **a.** Fe **b.** Ca **c.** Rb **d.** Br **e.** Pb **f.** Kr

4.6 Periodic Trends of the Elements

- The physical and chemical properties of elements change in a periodic manner going across each period and are repeated in each successive period.
- Representative elements in a group have similar behavior.
- The group number of an element gives the number of valence electrons.
- The atomic radius of representative elements generally increases going down a group and decreases going across a period.
- The ionization energy generally decreases going down a group and increases going across a period.

◆ Learning Exercise 4.6A

State the number of electrons in the outermost energy level and the group number of each element.

Element	Valence Electrons	Group Number (A/B)
a. sulfur	________	________
b. oxygen	________	________
c. magnesium	________	________
d. hydrogen	________	________
e. fluorine	________	________
f. aluminum	________	________

Answers

a. $6e^-$, Group 6A (16) **b.** $6e^-$, Group 6A (16) **c.** $2e^-$, Group 2A (2)

d. $1e^-$, Group 1A (1) **e.** $7e^-$, Group 7A (17) **f.** $3e^-$, Group 3A (13)

◆ Learning Exercise 4.6B

Indicate the element that has the larger atomic radius.

a. _____ Mg or Ca **b.** _____ Si or Cl

c. _____ Sr or Rb **d.** _____ Br or Cl

e. _____ Li or Cs **f.** _____ Li or N

g. _____ N or P **h.** _____ As or Ca

Answers	**a.** Ca	**b.** Si	**c.** Rb	**d.** Br
	e. Cs	**f.** Li	**g.** P	**g.** Ca

◆ Learning Exercise 4.6C

Indicate the element that has the lower ionization energy.

a. _____ Mg or Na **b.** _____ P or Cl

c. _____ K or Rb **d.** _____ Br or F

e. _____ Li or O **f.** _____ Sb or N

g. _____ K or Br **h.** _____ S or Na

Answers	**a.** Na	**b.** P	**c.** Rb	**d.** Br
	e. Li	**f.** Sb	**g.** K	**g.** Na

Checklist for Chapter 4

You are ready to take the practice test for Chapter 4. Be sure you have accomplished the following learning goals for this chapter. If you are not sure, review the section listed at the end of the goal. Then apply your new skills and understanding to the practice test.

After studying Chapter 4, I can successfully:

_____ Calculate the frequency or wavelength of electromagnetic radiation (4.1).

_____ Compare frequency, wavelength, and energy of radiation on the electromagnetic spectrum (4.1).

_____ Describe how atomic spectra correlates with the energy levels in atoms (4.2).

_____ Describe the shapes of orbitals and the number of each in a sublevel (4.3).

_____ Write the orbital diagrams for hydrogen to argon (4.4).

_____ Use the sublevel blocks on the periodic table to write electron configurations (4.5).

_____ Explain the trends in valence electrons, group numbers, atomic size, and ionization energy going down a group and across a period (4.6).

Practice Test for Chapter 4

Write or select the correct answer for each of the following questions.

1. Which of the following has the longest wavelength?
 A. microwave **B.** ultraviolet **C.** radio waves **D.** infrared **E.** visible

2. Which of the following has the highest frequency?
 A. microwave **B.** ultraviolet **C.** radio waves **D.** infrared **E.** visible

3. What color of visible light has the highest frequency?
 A. violet **B.** blue **C.** green **D.** yellow **E.** red

4. What color of visible light has the longest wavelength?
 A. violet **B.** blue **C.** green **D.** yellow **E.** red

5. Arrange the following in order of decreasing wavelength: infrared, ultraviolet, radio waves, X rays.
 A. X rays, infrared, ultraviolet, radio waves
 B. radio waves, ultraviolet, infrared, X rays
 C. ultraviolet, infrared, radio waves, X rays
 D. radio waves, X rays, infrared, ultraviolet
 E. radio waves, infrared, ultraviolet, X rays

6. The wavelength is
 A. the height to the peak of a wave
 B. the length of a wave
 C. the distance between two adjacent peaks of a wave
 D. the number of waves that pass a point in 1 s
 E. related directly to the frequency of a wave of electromagnetic radiation

7. If a microwave operates at a frequency of $3.0 \times 10^9 \text{ s}^{-1}$, the wavelength is
 A. 1.0×10^{-17} m **B.** 1.0×10^{-1} m **C.** 1.0×10^{1} m
 D. 3.0×10^{8} m **E.** 1.0×10^{17} m

8. Atomic spectra
 A. consist of lines of different colors
 B. are different for each of the elements
 C. occur when energy changes provide photons of certain wavelengths
 D. indicate that electrons in atoms have specific energy levels
 E. all of these

9. The maximum number of electrons that can be accommodated in the principal energy level $n = 4$ is
 A. 2 **B.** 4 **C.** 8 **D.** 18 **E.** 32

10. The sublevels that make up principal energy level n = 3 are
 A. 1*s*2*s*3*s* **B.** 3*s*3*p* **C.** 3*s*3*p*3*d* **D.** 3*s*3*p*3*d*3*f* **E.** 3*p*3*d*3*f*

11. A space within an atom that has a spherical shape is called a(n)
 A. *d* orbital **B.** *p* orbital **C.** *s* orbital **D.** *f* orbital **E.** *g* orbital

12. The number of orbitals in a 4*p* sublevel is
 A. one **B.** two **C.** three **D.** four **E.** five

13. The principal energy level that consists of one *s* orbital and three *p* orbitals has quantum number
 A. $n = 1$ **B.** $n = 2$ **C.** $n = 3$ **D.** $n = 4$ **E.** $n = 5$

14. The maximum number of electrons that the 5*d* sublevel can accommodate is
A. 2 **B.** 3 **C.** 6 **D.** 10 **E.** 14

15. In the orbital diagram of nitrogen, the 2*p* sublevel would be

A. [↑↓][ ][↑] **B.** [↑↑][↑][ ] **C.** [↑↓][↑↓][↑]

D. [↑][↑][↑] **E.** [↑][ ][↑↓]

16. The electron configuration for silicon is
A. $1s^22s^22p^63s^4$ **B.** $1s^22s^22p^63s^23p^2$ **C.** $1s^22s^22p^63s^23d^2$
D. $1s^22s^22p^63s^23p^4$ **E.** $1s^22s^22p^63p^4$

17. The electron configuration for an oxygen atom is
A. $2s^22p^4$ **B.** $1s^22s^42p^4$ **C.** $1s^22s^6$
D. $1s^22s^22p^23s^2$ **E.** $1s^2\ 2s^2\ 2p^4$

18. The electron configuration for aluminum is
A. $1s^22s^22p^9$ **B.** $1s^22s^22p^63p^5$ **C.** $1s^22s^22p^63s^23p^1$
D. $1s^22s^22p^83p^1$ **E.** $1s^22s^22p^63p^3$

For questions 19–22, match the final notation in the electron configuration with the following elements:
A. As **B.** Rb **C.** Na **D.** N **E.** Xe

19. $4p^3$ ______ **20.** $5s^1$ ______

21. $3s^1$ ______ **22.** $5p^6$ ______

23. The element that has an electron configuration that ends with $5p^2$ is

A. strontium **B.** germanium **C.** titanium
D. tin **E.** lead

24. The element that has an abbreviated electron configuration of $[Ar]4s^23d^6$ is
A. chromiun **B.** iron **C.** krypton
D. calcium **E.** zinc

25. The element that begins filling the 6*s* sublevel is
A. lithium **B.** rubidium **C.** cesium
D. scandium **E.** barium

26. The element that has 5 electrons in its principal energy level $n = 4$ is
A. boron **B.** phosphorus **C.** vanadium
D. bromine **E.** arsenic

27. The number of electrons in the 5*p* sublevel of iodine is
A. 2 **B.** 3 **C.** 5 **D.** 7 **E.** 15

28. The number of valence electrons in gallium is
A. 1 **B.** 2 **C.** 3 **D.** 13 **E.** 31

29. The atomic radius of oxygen is larger than
A. lithium **B.** sulfur **C.** fluorine **D.** boron **E.** argon

30. Of C, Si, Ge, Sn, and Pb, the element with the greatest ionization energy of is
A. C **B.** Si **C.** Ge **D.** Sn **E.** Pb

Answers for the Practice Test

1. C	**2.** B	**3.** A	**4.** E	**5.** E
6. C	**7.** B	**8.** E	**9.** E	**10.** C
11. C	**12.** C	**13.** B	**14.** D	**15.** D
16. B	**17.** E	**18.** C	**19.** A	**20.** B
21. C	**22.** E	**23.** D	**24.** B	**25.** C
26. E	**27.** C	**28.** C	**29.** C	**30.** A

Answers and Solutions to Selected Text Problems

Section 4.1

4.1 The wavelength of UV light is the distance between crests of the wave.

4.3 White light has all the colors and wavelength of the visible spectrum, including red and blue light. Red and blue light is visible light with specific wavelengths.

4.5 $\lambda = \dfrac{c}{\nu} = \dfrac{3.0 \times 10^{8}\ \text{m s}^{-1}}{\nu}$

$650\ \cancel{\text{kHz}} \times \dfrac{1 \times 10^{3}\ \cancel{\text{Hz}}}{1\ \cancel{\text{kHz}}} \times \dfrac{1\ \text{s}^{-1}}{1\ \cancel{\text{Hz}}} = 6.5 \times 10^{5}\ \text{s}^{-1}$

$\dfrac{3.0 \times 10^{8}\ \text{m}\ \cancel{\text{s}^{-1}}}{6.5 \times 10^{5}\ \cancel{\text{s}^{-1}}} = 4.6 \times 10^{2}\ \text{m}$

$980\ \cancel{\text{kHz}} \times \dfrac{1 \times 10^{3}\ \cancel{\text{Hz}}}{1\ \cancel{\text{kHz}}} \times \dfrac{1\ \text{s}^{-1}}{1\ \cancel{\text{Hz}}} = 9.8 \times 10^{5}\ \text{s}^{-1}$

$\dfrac{3.0 \times 10^{8}\ \text{m}\ \cancel{\text{s}^{-1}}}{9.8 \times 10^{5}\ \cancel{\text{s}^{-1}}} = 3.1 \times 10^{2}\ \text{m}$

4.7 $\lambda = \dfrac{c}{\nu} = \dfrac{3.0 \times 10^{8}\ \text{m}\ \cancel{\text{s}^{-1}}}{4.8 \times 10^{14}\ \cancel{\text{s}^{-1}}} = 6.3 \times 10^{-7}$ m or 630 nm.

4.9 Microwaves have a longer wavelength than UV light or X rays.

4.11 From shortest to longest wavelength: X rays, blue light, infrared, microwaves

Section 4.2

4.13 Atomic spectra consist of a series of lines separated by dark sections, indicating that the energy emitted by the elements is not continuous.

4.15 Electrons absorb a specific quantity of energy to jump to a higher energy level.

4.17 A photon in the infrared region of the spectrum may be emitted by an excited electron that drops to the third energy level.

4.19 The photon with greater energy is **a.** green light and **b.** blue light.

Section 4.3

4.21 **a.** A 1*s* orbital is spherical. **b.** A 2*p* orbital has two lobes.
c. A 5*s* orbital is spherical.

4.23 **a.** All *s* orbitals are spherical.
b. A 3*s* sublevel and a 3*p* sublevel are in the energy level $n = 3$.
c. All *p* sublevels contain 3 *p* orbitals.
d. The 3*p* orbitals all have two lobes and are in energy level $n = 3$.

4.25 **a.** There are a maximum of 5 orbitals in the 3*d* sublevel.
b. There is one sublevel in the $n = 1$ principal energy level.
c. There is one orbital in the 6*s* sublevel.
d. There are nine orbitals in the $n = 3$ energy level: one 3*s* orbital, three 3*p* orbitals, and five 3*d* orbitals.

4.27 **a.** Any orbital has a maximum of two electrons. Thus, a 2*p* orbital has a maximum of two electrons.
b. The 3*p* sublevel contains three *p* orbitals, each of which can hold a maximum of two electrons, which gives a maximum of six electrons in the 3*p* sublevel.
c. Using $2n^2$, the calculation for the maximum number of electrons in the $n = 4$ energy level is $2(4)^2 = 2\ (16) = 32$ electrons.
d. The 5*d* sublevel contains five *d* orbitals, each of which can hold a maximum of two electrons, which gives a maximum of ten electrons in the 5*d* sublevel.

Section 4.4

4.29 The electron configuration shows the number of electrons in each sublevel of an atom. The abbreviated electron configuration uses the symbol of the noble gas to show completed sublevels.

4.31

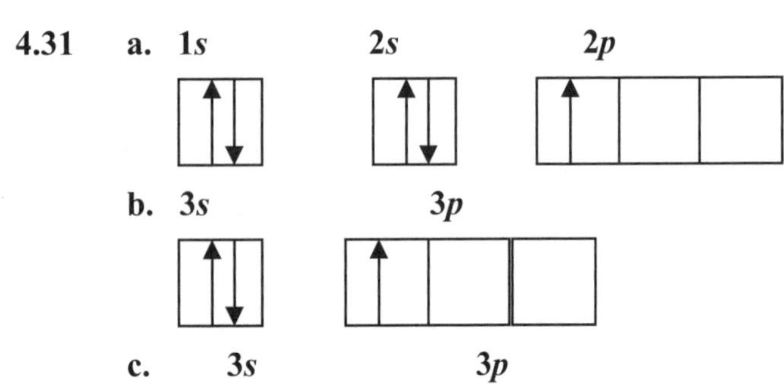

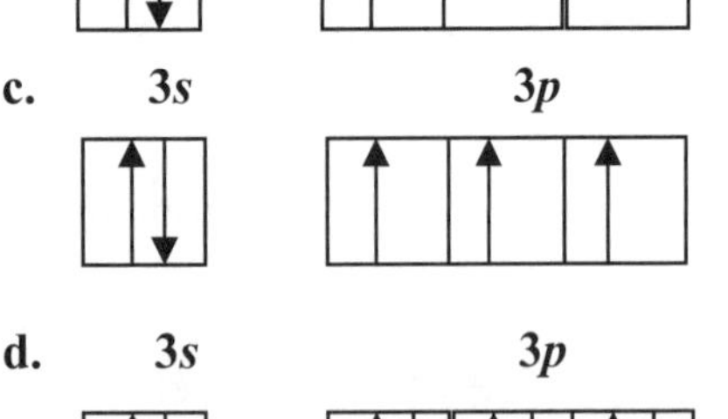

d. **3*s*** **3*p***

4.33 **a.** N $1s^2 2s^2 2p^3$ **b.** Na $1s^2 2s^2 2p^6 3s^1$
c. S $1s^2 2s^2 2p^6 3s^2 3p^4$ **d.** B $1s^2 2s^2 2p^1$

4.35 The abbreviated electron configuration consists of the symbol of the preceding noble gas followed by the electron configuration in the next period. [He] = $1s^2$ and [Ne] = $1s^2 2s^2 2p^6$.
a. Mg [Ne]$3s^2$ **b.** S [Ne]$3s^2 3p^4$
c. Al [Ne]$3s^2 3p^1$ **d.** N [He]$2s^2 2p^3$

4.37 **a.** Li has one electron in the 2*s* sublevel.
b. S has two electrons in the 3*s* and four electrons in the 3*p* sublevels.
c. Si has two electrons in the 3*s* and two electrons in the 3*p* sublevels.
d. F has two electrons in the 2*s* and five electrons in the 2*p* sublevels.

4.39 **a.** Al has three electrons in the third energy level $3s^23p^1$.
b. C has two 2*p* electrons.
c. Ar completes the 3*p* sublevel $3p^6$.
d. Be has two electrons in the 2*s* sublevel.

Section 4.5

4.41 Using the periodic table, the *s* sublevel block is on the left, the *p* sublevel block is on the right, and the *d* sublevel block is in the center between the *s* and *p* blocks.
a. As $1s^22s^22p^63s^23p^64s^23d^{10}4p^3$

b. Fe $1s^22s^22p^63s^23p^64s^23d^6$

c. Pd $1s^22s^22p^63s^23p^64s^23d^{10}4p^65s^24d^8$

d. I $1s^22s^22p^63s^23p^64s^23d^{10}4p^65s^24d^{10}5p^5$

4.43 Using the periodic table, the *s* sublevel block is on the left, the *p* sublevel block is on the right, and the *d* sublevel block is in the center between the *s* and *p* blocks. The abbreviated electron configuration consists of the symbol of the preceding noble gas followed by the electron configuration in the next period.
a. Ti [Ar] $4s^23d^2$
b. Sr [Kr] $5s^2$
c. Ba [Xe] $6s^2$
d. Pb [Xe] $6s^24f^{14}5d^{10}6p^2$

4.45 Use the final sublevel notation in the electron configuration to locate the element.

a. Li (ends in $2s^1$) **b.** Co (ends in $3d^7$)

c. Si (ends in $3p^2$) **d.** Br (ends in $4p^5$)

4.47 **a.** Ga has three electrons in energy level 4; two in the 4*s* block, and one in the 4*p* block.

b. C is the second element in the 2*p* block, it has two 2*p* electrons.

c. Xe is the final element (six electrons) in the 5*p* block.

d. Zr is the second element in the 4*d* block; it has two 4*d* electrons.

4.49 **a.** Zn is the tenth element in the 3*d* block; it has ten 3*d* electrons.

b. Na has an electron in the 3*s* block; the 2*p* block in Na is complete with six electrons.

c. As is the third element in the 4*p* block; it has three 4*p* electrons.

d. Rb is the first element in the 5*s* block; Rb has one 5*s* electron.

Section 4.6

4.51 The group numbers 1A–8A or the one's digit in 1, 2, and 13–18 indicate 1–8 valence electrons. The group numbers 3–12 give the electrons in the *s* and *d* sublevel. Group B indicates that the *d* sublevel is filling.

4.53 **a.** An element with two valence electrons is in Group 2A (2).

b. An element with five valence electrons is in Group 5A (15)

c. An element with two valence electrons and five electrons in the *d* block is in Group 7B(7).

d. An element with six valence electrons is in Group 6A(16).

4.55 **a.** Alkali metals, which are in Group 1A (1), have a valence electron configuration ns^1.
b. Elements in Group 4A (4) have a valence electron configuration ns^2np^2
c. Elements in Group 3A (13) have a valence electron configuration ns^2np^1
d. Elements in Group 5A (15) have a valence electron configuration ns^2np^3

4.57 **a.** Aluminum in Group 3A (13) has three valence electrons.
b. Any element in Group 5A (15) has five valence electrons.
c. The two valence electrons for nickel are $4s^2$.
d. Each halogen in Group 7A (17) has seven valence electrons.

4.59 Mg and Ca both have two valence electrons: Mg is $[Ne]3s^2$ and Ca is $[Ar]\ 4s^2$.

4.61 **a.** The atomic radius of representative elements decrease from Group 1A to 8A: Mg, Al, Si.
b. The atomic radius of representative elements increase going down a group: I, Br, Cl.
c. The atomic radius of representative elements decrease from Group 1A to 8A: Sr, Sb, I.
d. The atomic radius of representative elements decrease from Group 1A to 8A: Na, Si, P.

4.63 The atomic radius of representative elements decreases going across a period from Group 1A to 8A and increases going down a group.
a. In Period 3, Na, which is on the left, is larger than O.
b. In Group 1A (1), Rb, which is further down the group, is larger than Na.
c. In Period 3, Na, which is on the left, is larger than Mg.
d. In Period 3, Na, which is on the left, is larger than Cl.

4.65 **a.** The ionization energy decreases going down a group: Br, Cl, F.
b. Going across a period from left to right, the ionization energy generally increases: Na, Al, Cl.
c. The ionization energy decreases going down a group: Cs, K, Na.
d. Going across a period from left to right, the ionization energy generally increases. The ionization energy decreases going down a group as atoms become larger: Sn, Sb, As.

4.67 **a.** Br, which is above I in Group 7A, has a higher ionization energy than I.
b. Ionization energy decreases from Group 2A to 3A, which gives Mg a higher ionization energy than Al.
c. Ionization energy decreases from Group 5A to 6A, which gives P a higher ionization energy than S.
d. The noble gases have the higher ionization energy in each period, which gives Xe a higher ionization energy than I.

Additional Problems

4.77 $$1.5 \times 10^8\ \cancel{\text{km}} \times \frac{1000\ \cancel{\text{m}}}{1\ \cancel{\text{km}}} \times \frac{1\ \cancel{\text{s}}}{3.0 \times 10^8\ \cancel{\text{m}}} \times \frac{1\ \text{min}}{60\ \cancel{\text{s}}} = 8.3\ \text{min}$$

4.79 $$v = \frac{c}{\lambda} = \frac{3.0 \times 10^8\ \text{m s}^{-1}}{\lambda}$$

a. $$\frac{3.0 \times 10^8\ \cancel{\text{m}}\ \text{s}^{-1}}{590\ \cancel{\text{nm}}} \times \frac{10^9\ \cancel{\text{nm}}}{1\ \cancel{\text{m}}} = 5.1 \times 10^{14}\ \text{s}^{-1}$$

b. $$\frac{3.0 \times 10^8\ \cancel{\text{m}}\ \text{s}^{-1}}{4.5 \times 10^{-7}\ \cancel{\text{m}}} = 6.7 \times 10^{14}\text{s}^{-1}$$

c. $$\frac{3.0 \times 10^8\ \cancel{\text{m}}\ \text{s}^{-1}}{1.0 \times 10^{-1}\ \cancel{\text{nm}}} \times \frac{10^9\ \cancel{\text{nm}}}{1\ \cancel{\text{m}}} = 3.0 \times 10^{18}\ \text{s}^{-1}$$

4.81 A continuous spectrum from white light contains wavelengths of all energies. Atomic spectra are line spectra in which a series of lines correspond to energy emitted when electrons drop from a higher energy level to a lower level.

4.83 **a.** An orbital with two lobes is a *p* orbital.
b. A spherical orbitals is an *s* orbital.
c. An orbital with two lobes is a *p* orbital.

4.85 The Pauli exclusion principle states that two electrons in the same orbital must have opposite spins.

4.87 **a.** A 2*p* and a 3*p* orbital have the same spatial shape with two lobes, and each *p* orbital can hold up to two electrons with opposite spins. However, the 3*p* orbital is larger because the 3*p* electron has a higher energy level and is most likely to be found further from the nucleus.

b. A 2*s* and a 2*p* orbital are found in the same energy level, $n = 2$, and each can hold up to two electrons with opposite spins. However, the shapes of a 2*s* orbital and a 2*p* orbital are different.

c. The orbitals in the 4*p* sublevel all have the same energy level and shape. However, there are three 4*p* orbitals directed along the *x, y,* and *z*-axes around the nucleus.

4.89 A 4*p* orbital is possible because $n = 4$ has four sublevels, including a *p* sublevel. A 2*d* orbital is not possible because $n = 2$ has only *s* and *p* sublevels. There are no 3*f* orbitals because only *s*, *p*, and *d* sublevels are allowed for $n = 3$. A 5*f* sublevel is possible in $n = 5$ because five sublevels are allowed.

4.91 **a.** On the periodic table, the 3*p* sublevel block follows the 3*s* sublevel block.
b. On the periodic table, the 5*s* sublevel block follows the 4*p* sublevel block.
c. On the periodic table, the 4*p* sublevel block follows the 3*d* sublevel block.
d. On the periodic table, the 4*s* sublevel block follows the 3*p* sublevel block.

4.93 **a.** Iron is the sixth element in the 3*d* block; iron has six 3*d* electrons.
b. Barium has a completely filled 5*p* sublevel, which is six 5*p* electrons.
c. Iodine has a completely filled 4*d* sublevel, which is ten 4*d* electrons.
d. Barium has a filled 6*s* sublevel or 6*s* block, which is two 6*s* electrons.

4.95 Ca, Sr, and Ba all have two valence electrons ns^2, which places them in Group 2A (2).

4.97 **a.** X is a metal; Y and Z are nonmetals.
b. X has the largest atomic radius.
c. Y and Z have six valence electrons and are in Group 6A (16).
d. Y has the highest ionization energy.
e. Y has the smallest atomic radius.

4.99 **a.** Phosphorus in Group 5A has an electron configuration that ends with $3s^23p^3$.
b. Lithium is the alkali metal that is highest in Group 1A (1) and has the smallest atomic radius. (H in Group 1A (1) is a nonmetal.)
c. Cadmium in Period 5 has a complete 4*d* sublevel with ten electrons.
d. Nitrogen at the top of Group 5A has the highest ionization energy in that group.
e. Sodium, the first element in Period 3, has the largest atomic radius of that period.

4.101 Calcium has a greater net nuclear charge than K. The least tightly bound electron in Ca is further from the nucleus than in Mg and needs less energy to remove.

4.103 In Group 3A (13), ns^2np^1, the *p* electron is further from the nucleus and easier to remove.

4.105 a. Na is on the far left of the heavy zigzag line. Na is a metal.
b. Na at the beginning of Group 3 has the largest atomic radius.
c. F at the top of Group 7A (17) and to the far right in Period 2 has the highest ionization energy.
d. Na has the lowest ionization energy and loses an electron most easily.
e. Cl is found in Period 3 in Group 7A.

4.107 a. [Ne] $3s^23p^2$; Group 4A (14)
b. [Ar] $4s^23d^{10}4p^4$; Group 6A (16)
c. [Ar] $4s^23d^5$ Group 7B (7)
d. [Kr] $5s^24d^{10}5p^3$; Group 5A (15)

4.109 a. In a group, the atomic radius increases going down a group, which gives O the smallest atomic radius in Group 6A.
b. In a period, the atomic radius generally decreases going from left to right, which gives Ar the smallest atomic radius in Period 3.
c. In a group, the ionization energy decreases going down a group, which gives N the highest ionization energy in Group 15.
d. In a period, the ionization energy generally increases going left to right, which gives Na the lowest ionization energy in Period 3.
e. Ru in Period 5 has six electrons in $4d$.

5
Ionic Compounds

Study Goals

- Write an electron-dot symbol for an atom of a representative element.
- Use the octet rule to determine the ionic charge of ions for representative elements.
- Use charge balance to write an ionic formula.
- Write the correct names for ionic compounds.
- Write formulas and names of compounds with polyatomic ions.

Think About It

1. What are the valence electrons in an atom?

2. How does a compound differ from an element?

3. What makes salt an ionic compound?

Key Terms

Match each the following key terms with the correct definition.
a. valence electrons **b.** ion **c.** ionic bond
d. polyatomic ion **e.** octet

1. _____ An atom with a positive or negative charge

2. _____ An arrangement of eight valence electrons

3. _____ The attraction between positively and negatively charged particles

4. _____ The electrons that make up the outermost energy level of an atom

5. _____ A group of atoms with a positive or negative charge

Answers **1.** b **2.** e **3.** c **4.** a **5.** d

5.1 Valence Electrons and Electron-Dot Symbols

- The electrons located in the outermost energy level of an atom play a major role in determining its chemical properties.
- An electron-dot symbol represents the valence electrons in an atom. For example, the electron configuration of potassium, $1s^22s^22p^63s^23p^64s^1$, shows one valence electron, which gives it an electron-dot symbol of K$^{\bullet}$.

◆ Learning Exercise 5.1A

Write the electron-dot symbol for each of the following atoms:

1. O **2.** Cl **3.** Na **4.** Ca **5.** Li

6. H **7.** P **8.** S **9.** Mg **10.** C

Answers

1. :Ö· **2.** :C̈l· **3.** Na· **4.** Ċa· **5.** Li·

6. H· **7.** ·P̈· **8.** :S̈· **9.** Ṁg· **10.** ·Ċ·

◆ Learning Exercise 5.1B

For each of the following elements, write the electron configuration and the number of valence electrons. Indicate the elements that have octets.

Element	Electron Configuration	Number of Valence Electrons	Octet? (Yes/No)
C			
Ne			
Ca			
Ar			
N			

Answers

Element	Electron Arrangement	Number of Valence Electrons	Octet? (Yes/No)
C	$1s^22s^22p^2$	4	No
Ne	$1s^22s^22p^6$	8	Yes
Ca	$1s^22s^22p^63s^23p^64s^2$	2	No
Ar	$1s^22s^22p^63s^23p^6$	8	Yes
N	$1s^22s^22p^3$	5	No

5.2 Octet Rule and Ions

- The stability of the noble gases is associated with an electron configuration of eight valence electrons (ns^2np^6), an octet, except helium, which is stable with two valence electrons.

He	$1s^2$	Ne	$1s^22s^22p^6$
Ar	$1s^22s^22p^63s^23p^6$	Kr	$1s^22s^22p^63s^23p^64s^23d^{10}4p^6$

- Atoms of elements other than the noble gases achieve stability by losing, gaining, or sharing valence electrons with other atoms in the formation of compounds.
- A metal of the representative elements in Groups 1A (1), 2A (2), and 3A (13) achieves an octet by losing its valence electrons to form a cation 1+, 2+, or 3+.
- When a nonmetal in Groups 5A (15), 6A (16), and 7A (17) forms an ion, electrons add to the outermost energy level to give an octet and form an anion 3–, 2–, or 1–.

◆ Learning Exercise 5.2A

Study Note

When an atom loses or gains electrons, it acquires the electron configuration of the nearest noble gas. For example, sodium loses one electron, which gives the Na^+ ion an electron configuration of neon. Oxygen gains two electrons to give an oxide ion O^{2-} an electron configuration of neon.

Write the electron configurations of the following atoms and their ions. For each ion, indicate the noble gas that has the same electron configuration.

	Atom	Ion		Noble gas
a. Ca	________	Ca^{2+}	________	____
b. N	________	N^{3-}	________	____
c. Cl	________	Cl^-	________	____
d. Na	________	Na^+	________	____
e. S	________	S^{2-}	________	____

Answers

	Atom	Ion		Noble gas
a. Ca	$1s^22s^22p^63s^23p^64s^2$	Ca^{2+}	$1s^22s^22p^63s^23p^6$	Ar
b. N	$1s^22s^22p^3$	N^{3-}	$1s^22s^22p^6$	Ne
c. Cl	$1s^22s^22p^63s^23p^5$	Cl^-	$1s^22s^22p^63s^23p^6$	Ar
d. Na	$1s^22s^22p^63s^1$	Na^+	$1s^22s^22p^6$	Ne
e. S	$1s^22s^22p^63s^23p^4$	S^{2-}	$1s^22s^22p^63s^23p^6$	Ar

◆ Learning Exercise 5.2B

The following elements lose electrons when they form ions. Indicate the group number, the number of electrons lost, and the ion (symbol and charge) for each of the following:

Element	Group Number	Electrons Lost	Ion Formed
magnesium			
sodium			
calcium			
potassium			
aluminum			

Answers

Element	Group Number	Electrons Lost	Ion Formed
magnesium	2 (2A)	2	Mg^{2+}
sodium	1 (12A)	1	Na^{+}
calcium	2 (2A)	2	Ca^{2+}
potassium	1 (1A)	1	K^{+}
aluminum	13 (3A)	3	Al^{3+}

◆ Learning Exercise 5.2C

Study Note

The valence electrons are the electrons in the outermost energy level of an atom. For representative elements, the number of valence electrons is obtained from the group number.

The following elements gain electrons when they form ions. Indicate the group number, the number of electrons gained, and the ion (symbol and charge) for each of the following:

Element	Group Number	Electrons Gained	Ion Formed
chlorine			
oxygen			
nitrogen			
fluorine			
sulfur			

Answers

Element	Group Number	Electrons Gained	Ion Formed
chlorine	17 (7A)	1	Cl^{-}
oxygen	16 (6A)	2	O^{2-}
nitrogen	15 (5A)	3	N^{3-}
fluorine	17 (7A)	1	F^{-}
sulfur	16 (6A)	2	S^{2-}

◆ Learning Exercise 5.2D

Which is smaller in each of the following?

a. Mg or Mg^{2+} ______ **b.** Al^{3+} or Al ______ **c.** S^{2-} or S ______

d. N or N^{3+} ______ **e.** Cl^- or Br^- ______ **f.** K^+ or Cs^+ ______

Answers

a. Mg or Mg^{2+} Mg^{2+} **b.** Al^{3+} or Al Al^{3+} **c.** S^{2-} or S S

d. Cl^- or Cl Cl **e.** Cl^- or Br^- Cl^- **f.** K^+ or Cs^+ K^+

5.3 Ionic Compounds

- In the formulas of ionic compounds, the total positive charge is equal to the total negative charge. For example, the compound magnesium chloride, $MgCl_2$, contains Mg^{2+} and 2 Cl^-. The sum of the charges is zero: $(2+) + 2(-) = 0$.
- When two or more ions are needed for charge balance, that number is indicated by subscripts in the formula.

◆ Learning Exercise 5.3A

For this exercise, you may want to cut pieces of paper that represent typical positive and negative ions as shown. To determine an ionic formula, place the positive and negative pieces together to complete a geometric shape. Write the number of positive ions and negative ions as the subscripts for the formula.

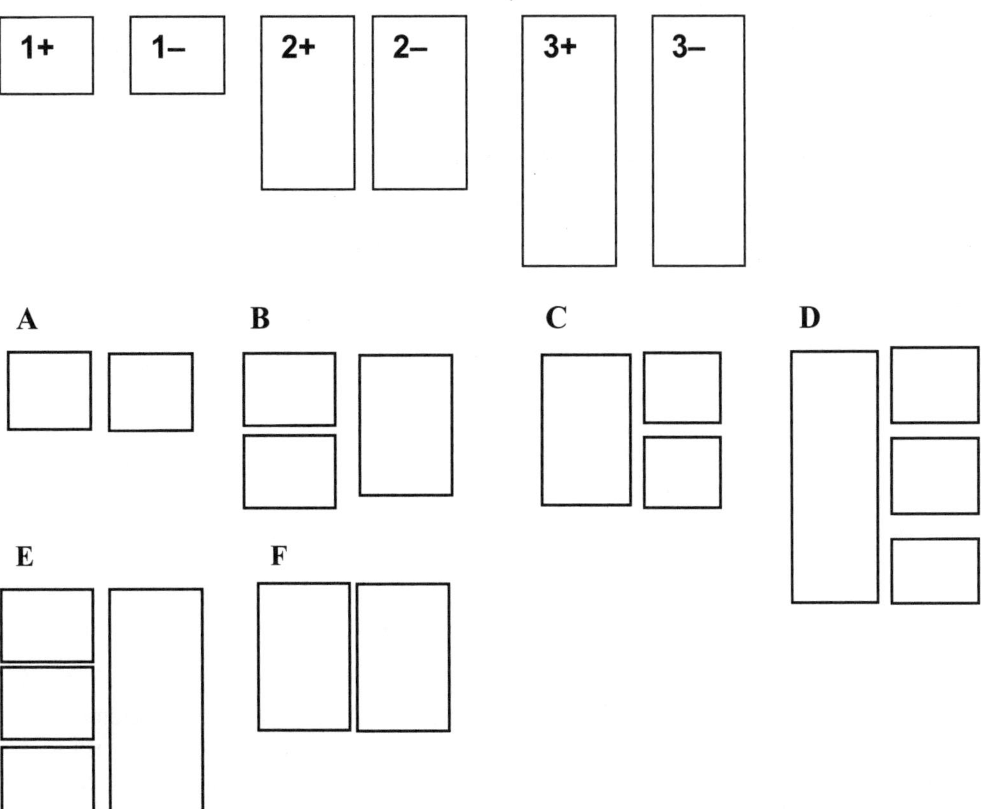

Give the letter (A–F) that matches the arrangement of ions in the following compounds:

Compound	Combination	Compound	Combination
1. $MgCl_2$	______	**2.** Na_2S	______
3. LiCl	______	**4.** CaO	______
5. K_3N	______	**6.** $AlBr_3$	______
7. MgS	______	**8.** $BaCl_2$	______

Answers **1.** C **2.** B **3.** A **4.** F
5. E **6.** D **7.** F **8.** C

◆ Learning Exercise 5.3B

Study Note

In a formula, the overall charge is zero; the total positive charge is equal to the total negative charge. You can check that the formula is electrically neutral by multiplying each ionic charge by its subscript. When added together, the sum should equal zero.

Example: Show the charge balance in the formula Na_2O.

$Na_2O = 2Na^+ + 1O^{2-}$

$2(1+) + 1(2-) = (2+) + (2-) = 0$ (electrically neutral)

Write the correct ionic formula for the compound formed from the following pairs of ions:

1. Na^+ and Cl^- ____________	**2.** K^+ and S^{2-} ____________
3. Al^{3+} and O^{2-} ____________	**4.** Mg^{2+} and Cl^- ____________
5. Ca^{2+} and S^{2-} ____________	**6.** Al^{3+} and Cl^- ____________
7. Li^+ and N^{3-} ____________	**8.** Ba^{2+} and P^{3-} ____________

Answers **1.** NaCl **2.** K_2S **3.** Al_2O_3 **4.** $MgCl_2$
5. CaS **6.** $AlCl_3$ **7.** Li_3N **8.** Ba_3P_2

5.4 Naming and Writing Ionic Compounds

- In naming ionic compounds, the positive ion is named first, followed by the name of the negative ion. The name of a representative metal ion (Group 1, 2, or 3) is the same as its elemental name. The name of a nonmetal ion is obtained by replacing the end of its element name with *ide.*
- Most transition metals form cations with two or more ionic charges. Then the ionic charge must be written as a Roman numeral after the name of the metal. For example, the cations of iron, Fe^{2+} and Fe^{3+}, are named iron(II) and iron(III). The ions of copper are Cu^+, copper(I), and Cu^{2+}, copper(II).
- The only transition elements with fixed charges are zinc, Zn^{2+}; silver, Ag^+; and cadmium, Cd^{2+}.

◆ Learning Exercise 5.4A

Write the name of each of the following ions:

1. Cl^- ____________
2. Fe^{2+} ____________
3. Cu^+ ____________
4. Ag^+ ____________
5. O^{2-} ____________
6. Ca^{2+} ____________
7. S^{2-} ____________
8. Al^{3+} ____________
9. Fe^{3+} ____________
10. Ba^{2+} ____________
11. Cu^{2+} ____________
12. N^{3-} ____________

Answers **1.** chloride **2.** iron(II) **3.** copper(I) **4.** silver **5.** oxide **6.** calcium **7.** sulfide **8.** aluminum **9.** iron(III) **10.** barium **11.** copper(II) **12.** nitride

◆ Learning Exercise 5.4B

Write the symbol of each of the following:

	Name	Symbol		Name	Symbol
1.	iron(III) ion	_______	2.	cobalt(II) ion	_______
3.	zinc ion	_______	4.	lead(IV) ion	_______
5.	copper(I) ion	_______	6.	silver ion	_______
7.	potassium ion	_______	8.	nickel(III) ion	_______

Answers **1.** Fe^{3+} **2.** Co^{2+} **3.** Zn^{2+} **4.** Pb^{4+} **5.** Cu^+ **6.** Ag^+ **7.** K^+ **8.** Ni^{3+}

◆ Learning Exercise 5.4C

Write the ions and the correct ionic formula for the following ionic compounds:

Compound	Positive Ion	Negative Ion	Formula of Compound
aluminum sulfide			
copper(II) chloride			
magnesium oxide			
gold(III) bromide			
silver oxide			

Answers

Compound	Positive Ion	Negative Ion	Formula of Compound
aluminum sulfide	Al^{3+}	S^{2-}	Al_2S_3
copper(II) chloride	Cu^{2+}	Cl^-	$CuCl_2$
magnesium oxide	Mg^{2+}	O^{2-}	MgO
gold(III) bromide	Au^{3+}	Br^-	$AuBr_3$
silver oxide	Ag^+	O^{2-}	Ag_2O

◆ Learning Exercise 5.4D

Study Note

The ionic charge of a metal that forms more than one positive ion is determined from the total negative charge in the formula. For example, in $FeCl_3$, the 3 Cl^- = 3(–). Therefore, this particular iron ion has an ionic charge of 3+ or Fe^{3+}, which is named iron(III).

Write the ions and a correct name for each of the following ionic compounds:

Formula	Ions		Name
1. $BaCl_2$	______	______	________________________
2. $SnBr_4$	______	______	________________________
3. Na_3P	______	______	________________________
4. Al_2O_3	______	______	________________________
5. CuO	______	______	________________________
6. Mg_3N_2	______	______	________________________

Answers

1. Ba^{2+}, Cl^-, barium chloride
2. Sn^{4+}, Br^-, tin(IV) bromide
3. Na^+, P^{3-}, sodium phosphide
4. Al^{3+}, O^{2-}, aluminum oxide
5. Cu^{2+}, O^{2-}, copper(II) oxide
6. Mg^{2+}, N^{3-}, magnesium nitride

5.5 Polyatomic Ions

- A polyatomic ion is a group of nonmetal atoms that carries an electrical charge, usually negative, 1–, 2–, or 3–. The polyatomic ion NH_4^+ has a positive charge.
- Polyatomic ions cannot exist alone, but are combined with an ion of the opposite charge.
- Ionic compounds containing three elements (polyatomic ions) end with *-ate* or *-ite.*

Study Note

Learn the most common polyatomic ions: nitrate NO_3^-, carbonate CO_3^{2-}, sulfate SO_4^{2-}, chlorate ClO_3^-, and phosphate PO_4^{3-}. From these, you can derive the related polyatomic ions. For example, the nitrite ion, NO_2^-, has one oxygen atom less than the nitrate.

NO_3^- nitrate $\qquad$ NO_2^- nitrite

◆ Learning Exercise 5.5A

Write the polyatomic ion (symbol and charge) for each of the following:

1. sulfate ion	_______________	**2.** hydroxide ion	_______________
3. carbonate ion	_______________	**4.** sulfite ion	_______________
5. ammonium ion	_______________	**6.** phosphate ion	_______________
7. nitrate ion	_______________	**8.** nitrite ion	_______________

Answers: **1.** SO_4^{2-} **2.** OH^- **3.** CO_3^{2-} **4.** SO_3^{2-}
5. NH_4^+ **6.** PO_4^{3-} **7.** NO_3^- **8.** NO_2^-

Study Note

Writing Formulas and Names of Ionic Compounds

- In ionic compounds containing *two* different elements, the name of the element written first is named as the element. The suffix "*ide*" is used for the ending of the name of the second element.
  $BaCl_2$ *barium chloride*
- If the metal forms two or more positive ions, a Roman numeral follows its name to indicate the ionic charge.
  $FeCl_3$ *iron(III) chloride*
- The names of most compounds containing polyatomic ions end in *-ate* or *-ite*, except for hydroxide.
  Na_2SO_4 *sodium sulfate*
- When a polyatomic ion occurs two or more times in a formula, its formula is placed inside parenthesis and the number of ions are shown as a subscript after the parenthesis.
  calcium nitrate $Ca(NO_3)_2$

◆ Learning Exercise 5.5B

Write the formula of each ion or polyatomic ion, and the correct formula for each of the following compounds:

Compound	Positive Ion	Negative Ion	Formula
sodium phosphate			
iron(II) hydroxide			
ammonium carbonate			
silver bicarbonate			
chromium(III) sulfate			
lead(II) nitrate			
potassium sulfite			
barium phosphate			

Answers

Compound	Positive Ion	Negative Ion	Formula
sodium phosphate	Na^+	PO_4^{3-}	Na_3PO_4
iron(II) hydroxide	Fe^{2+}	OH^-	$Fe(OH)_2$
ammonium carbonate	NH_4^+	CO_3^{2-}	$(NH_4)_2CO_3$
silver bicarbonate	Ag^+	HCO_3^-	$AgHCO_3$
chromium(III) sulfate	Cr^{3+}	SO_4^{2-}	$Cr_2(SO_4)_3$
lead(II) nitrate	Pb^{2+}	NO_3^-	$Pb(NO_3)_2$
potassium sulfite	K^+	SO_3^{2-}	K_2SO_3
barium phosphate	Ba^{2+}	PO_4^{3-}	$Ba_3(PO_4)_2$

Checklist for Chapter 5

You are ready to take the self-test for Chapter 5. Be sure you have accomplished the following learning goals for this chapter. If you are not sure, review the section listed at the end of the goal. Then apply your new skills and understanding to the practice test.

After studying Chapter 5, I can successfully:

_______ Write the electron-dot symbol for the representative elements (5.1).

_______ Illustrate the octet rule for the formation of ions (5.2).

_______ Write the formulas of ionic compounds containing the ions of metals and nonmetals of representative elements (5.3).

_______ Use charge balance to write an ionic formula (5.4).

_______ Write the name of an ionic compound (5.4).

_______ Write the formula of a compound containing a polyatomic ion (5.5).

Practice Test for Chapter 5

For questions 1 through 4, consider an atom of phosphorus.

1. It is in group

A. 2A **B.** 3A **C.** 5A **D.** 7A **E.** 8A

2. How many valence electrons does it have?

A. 2 **B.** 3 **C.** 5 **D.** 8 **E.** 15

3. To achieve an octet, the phosphorus atom will

A. lose one electron **B.** lose two electrons **C.** lose five electrons
D. gain two electrons **E.** gain three electrons

4. As an ion, it has an ionic charge (valence) of

A. 1+ **B.** 2+ **C.** 5+ **D.** 2– **E.** 3–

5. To achieve an octet, a calcium atom

A. loses one electron **B.** loses two electrons **C.** loses three electrons
D. gains one electron **E.** gains two electrons

6. To achieve an octet, a chlorine atom

A. loses one electron **B.** loses two electrons **C.** loses three electrons
D. gains one electron **E.** gains two electrons

7. Another name for a positive ion is

A. anion **B.** cation **C.** proton **D.** positron **E.** sodium

8. The correct ionic charge (valence) for calcium ion is

A. 1+ **B.** 2+ **C.** 1– **D.** 2– **E.** 3–

9. The silver ion has a charge of

A. 1+ **B.** 2+ **C.** 1– **D.** 2– **E.** 3–

10. The correct ionic charge (valence) for phosphate ion is

A. 1+ **B.** 2+ **C.** 1– **D.** 2– **E.** 3–

11. The correct ionic charge (valence) for fluoride is

A. 1+ **B.** 2+ **C.** 1– **D.** 2– **E.** 3–

12. The correct ionic charge (valence) for sulfate ion ($SO_4^{?}$) is

A. 1+ **B.** 2+ **C.** 1– **D.** 2– **E.** 3–

13. When the elements magnesium and sulfur are mixed,

A. An ionic compound forms.
B. A covalent compound forms.
C. No reaction occurs.
D. The two repel each other and will not combine.
E. None of the above.

14. An ionic bond typically occurs between

A. Two different nonmetals
B. Two of the same type of nonmetals
C. Two noble gases
D. Two different metals
E A metal and a nonmetal

15. The formula for a compound between sodium and sulfur is

A. SoS **B.** NaS **C.** Na_2S **D.** NaS_2 **E.** Na_2SO_4

16. The formula for a compound between aluminum and oxygen is

A. AlO **B.** Al_2O **C.** AlO_3 **D.** Al_2O_3 **E.** Al_3O_2

17. The formula for a compound between barium and sulfur is

A. BaS **B.** Ba_2S **C.** BaS_2 **D.** Ba_2S_2 **E.** $BaSO_4$

18. The correct formula for iron(III) chloride is

A. FeCl **B.** $FeCl_2$ **C.** Fe_2Cl **D.** Fe_3Cl **E.** $FeCl_3$

19. The correct formula for ammonium sulfate is

A. AmS **B.** $AmSO_4$ **C.** $(NH_4)_2S$ **D.** NH_4SO_4 **E.** $(NH_4)_2SO_4$

20. The correct formula for copper(II) chloride is

A. CoCl **B.** CuCl **C.** $CoCl_2$ **D.** $CuCl_2$ **E.** Cu_2Cl

21. The correct formula for lithium phosphate is

A. $LiPO_4$ **B.** Li_2PO_4 **C.** Li_3PO_4 **D.** $Li_2(PO_4)_3$ **E.** $Li_3(PO_4)_2$

22. The correct formula for silver oxide is

A. AgO **B.** Ag_2O **C.** AgO_2 **D.** Ag_3O_2 **E.** Ag_3O

23. The correct formula for magnesium carbonate is

A. $MgCO_3$ **B.** Mg_2CO_3 **C.** $Mg(CO_3)_2$ **D.** MgCO **E.** $Mg_2(CO_3)_3$

24. The correct formula for copper(I) sulfate is

A. $CuSO_3$ **B.** $CuSO_4$ **C.** Cu_2SO_3 **D.** $Cu(SO_4)_2$ **E.** Cu_2SO_4

25. The name of $Al_3(HPO_4)_2$ is
A. aluminum hydrogen phosphite
B. aluminum hydrogen phosphate
C. aluminum hydrogen phosphorus
D. aluminum hydrogen phosphorus oxide
E. trialuminum diphosphate

26. The name of CoS is

A. copper sulfide **B.** cobalt(II) sulfate **C.** cobalt(I) sulfide
D. cobalt sulfide **E.** cobalt(II) sulfide

27. The name of $MnCl_2$ is

A. magnesium chloride **B.** manganese(II) chlorine **C.** manganese(II) chloride
D. manganese chlorine **E.** manganese(III) chloride

28. The name of $ZnCO_3$ is

A. zinc(III) carbonate **B.** zinc(II) carbonate **C.** zinc bicarbonate
D. zinc carbon trioxide **E.** zinc carbonate

29. The name of Al_2O_3 is

A. aluminum oxide **B.** aluminum(II) oxide **C.** aluminum trioxide
D. dialuminum trioxide **E.** aluminum oxygenate

30. The name of $Cr_2(SO_3)_3$ is

A. chromium sulfite **B.** dichromium trisulfite **C.** chromium(III) sulfite
D. chromium(III) sulfate **E.** chromium sulfate

Answers to the Practice Test

1. C	**2.** C	**3.** E	**4.** E	**5.** B
6. D	**7.** B	**8.** B	**9.** A	**10.** E
11. C	**12.** D	**13.** A	**14.** E	**15.** C
16. D	**17.** A	**18.** E	**19.** E	**20.** D
21. C	**22.** B	**23.** A	**24.** E	**25.** B
26. E	**27.** C	**28.** E	**29.** A	**30.** C

Answers and Solutions to Selected Text Problems

Section 5.1

5.1 The valence electrons are found in the *s* and *p* orbitals of the outermost energy level in an atom.

5.3 The electron-dot symbol is written by placing the valence electrons around the symbol of the element.

a. $1s^2\ 2s^2\ 2p^3$ $\cdot\ddot{\underset{\cdot}{N}}\cdot$

b. $1s^2$ $\mathbf{2s^2}$ $\mathbf{2p^4}$ $\quad$ $:\ddot{O}\cdot$ (with one dot below)

c. $1s^2\ 2s^2\ 2p^6$ $\mathbf{3s^2}$ $\mathbf{3p^6}$ $\quad$ $:\ddot{\underset{\cdot\cdot}{Ar}}:$

d. $1s^2\ 2s^2\ 2p^6\ 3s^2\ 3p^6$ $\mathbf{4s^1}$ $\quad$ $K\cdot$

e. $1s^2\ 2s^2\ 2p^6$ $\mathbf{3s^2}$ $\mathbf{3p^4}$ $\quad$ $:\ddot{S}\cdot$ (with one dot below)

5.5 The group number gives the number of valence electrons for the electron-dot symbol.

a. Sulfur in Group 6A (16) has six valence electrons $:\ddot{S}\cdot$ (with one dot below)

b. Nitrogen in Group 5A (15) has five valence electrons $\cdot\ddot{N}\cdot$ (with one dot below)

c. Calcium in Group 2A (2) has two valence electrons $\dot{Ca}\cdot$

d. Sodium in Group 1A (1) has 1 valence electron $Na\cdot$

e. Potassium in Group 1A (1) has one valence electron $K\cdot$

5.7 **a.** A metal in Group 1A (1) has one valence electron $M\cdot$
b. A metal in Group 2A (2) has two valence electrons $\cdot M\cdot$

5.9 Alkali metals are the elements below H in Group 1A (1), and each has one valence electron.

Section 5.2

5.11 **a.** When a sodium atom loses its valence electron, its second energy level has a complete octet.

b. Group 1A (1) and 2A (2) elements can lose one or two electrons to attain a noble gas configuration. Group 8A (18) elements already have an octet of valence electrons, so they do not lose or gain electrons and are not normally found in compounds.

5.13 Atoms with one, two, or three valence electrons lose those electrons to form ions.
a. one **b.** two **c.** three **d.** one **e.** two

5.15 Atoms form ions by losing or gaining electrons to achieve the same electron configuration of their nearest noble gas.
a. Na^+ has an electron configuration $1s^22s^22p^6$, which is the same as neon (Ne).

b. Mg^{2+} has an electron configuration $1s^22s^22p^6$, which is the same as neon (Ne).

c. K^+ has an electron configuration $1s^22s^22p^62s^23p^6$, which is the same as argon (Ar).

d. O^{2-} has an electron configuration $1s^22s^22p^6$, which is the same as neon (Ne).

e. F^- has an electron configuration $1s^22s^22p^6$, which is the same as neon (Ne).

5.17 Atoms form ions by losing or gaining electrons to achieve the same electron configuration of their nearest noble gas. Elements in Groups 1A(1), 2A(2), and 3A(13) lose valence electrons, whereas elements in Groups 5A (15), 6A (16), and 7A (17) gain valence electrons to complete octets.

a. Mg loses $2e^-$ **b.** P gains $3e^-$ **c.** Group 7A (17) gains $1e^-$

d. Na loses $1e^-$ **e.** Al loses $3e^-$

5.19 **a.** Li^+ (3+, 2- = 1+) **b.** F^- (9+, 10- = 1-) **c.** Mg^{2+} (12+, 10- = 2+)

d. Fe^{3+} (26+, 23- = 3+) **e.** Zn^{2+} (30+, 28- = 2+)

5.21 When a potassium ion is formed, it loses the only valence electron in its outermost energy level, which makes the potassium ion smaller than a potassium atom.

5.23 **a.** A Na atom with a valence electron in energy level $n = 3$ is larger than Na^+, which has lost that valence electron.

b. A bromide ion (Br^-) is larger that a Br atom because the addition of a valence electron increases repulsion between electrons, which increases the size.

c. A sulfide ion (S^{2-}) is larger that an S atom because the addition of two valence electrons increases repulsion between electrons, which increases the size.

Section 5.3

5.25 A metal and a nonmetal are most likely to form an ionic compound.

a. (Li and Cl) and **c.** (K and O) would form ionic compounds

5.27 **a.** Potassium loses $1e^-$ and chlorine gains $1e^-$.

$$K\cdot + \cdot\underset{\cdot\cdot}{\ddot{Cl}}: \rightarrow K^+ + [:\underset{\cdot\cdot}{\ddot{Cl}}:]^- \rightarrow KCl$$

b. Calcium loses $2e^-$ and two chlorine atoms each gain $1e^-$.

$$\cdot Ca\cdot + \cdot\underset{\cdot\cdot}{\ddot{Cl}}: + \cdot\underset{\cdot\cdot}{\ddot{Cl}}: \rightarrow Ca^{2+} + 2[:\underset{\cdot\cdot}{\ddot{Cl}}:]^- \rightarrow CaCl_2$$

c. Each of three sodium atoms lose $1e^-$ and the nitrogen gains $3e^-$.

$$Na\cdot + Na\cdot + Na\cdot + \cdot\underset{\cdot}{\ddot{N}}\cdot \rightarrow 3\,Na^+ + [:\underset{\cdot\cdot}{\ddot{N}}:]^{3-} \rightarrow Na_3N$$

5.29

a. Na_2O Check: $2Na^+$ and O^{2-} = 2(+) + 1(2-) = 0

b. $AlBr_3$ Check: $1Al^{3+}$ and $3Br^-$ = 1(3+) + 3(-) = 0

c. BaO Check: Ba^{2+} and O^{2-} = 1(2+) + 1(2-) = 0

d. $MgCl_2$ Check: Mg^{2+} and $2Cl^-$ = 1(2+) + 2(1-) = 0

e. Al_2S_3 Check: $2Al^{3+}$ and $3S^{2-}$ = 2(3+) + 3(2-) = 0

5.31 **a.** Ions: Na^+ and S^{2-} $\rightarrow Na_2S$ Check: $2Na^+$ and S^{2-} = 2(+) + 1(2-) = 0

b. Ions: K^+ and N^{3-} $\rightarrow K_3N$ Check: $3K^+$ and N^{3-} = 3(+) + 1(3-) = 0

c. Ions: Al^{3+} and I^- $\rightarrow AlI_3$ Check: Al^{3+} and I^- = 1(3+) + 3(1-) = 0

d. Ions: Li and O^{2-} $\rightarrow Li_2O$ Check: $2Li^+$ and O^{2-} = 2(+) + 1(2-) = 0

Section 5.4

5.33 **a.** Chlorine in Group 7A (17) gains one electron to form chloride ion Cl^-.
b. Potassium in Group 1A (1) loses one electron to form potassium ion K^+.
c. Oxygen in Group 6A (16) gains two electrons to form oxide ion O^{2-}.
d. Aluminum in Group 1A (1) loses three electrons to form aluminum ion Al^{3+}.

5.35 **a.** potassium ion **b.** sulfide ion **c.** calcium ion **d.** nitride ion

5.37 In naming an ionic compound, the metal ion is named first, followed by the nonmetal ion name ending in *-ide*.
a. Ions: Al^{3+} aluminum and O^{2-} oxide $\rightarrow$ aluminum oxide
b. Ions: Ca^{2+} calcium and chloride Cl^- $\rightarrow$ calcium chloride
c. Ions: Na^+ sodium and O^{2-} oxide $\rightarrow$ sodium oxide
d. Ions: Mg^{2+} magnesium and nitride N^{3-} $\rightarrow$ magnesium nitride
e. Ions: K^+ potassium and I^- iodide $\rightarrow$ potassium iodide
f. Ions: Ba^{2+} barium and fluoride F^- $\rightarrow$barium fluoride

5.39 The Roman numeral is used to specify the positive charge on the transition metal in the compound. It is necessary on most transition metal compounds because many transition metals can exist as more than one cation; transition metals have variable ionic charges.

5.41 **a.** iron(II) **b.** copper(II) **c.** zinc
d. lead(IV) **e.** chromium(III) **f.** manganese(II)

5.43 For metal ions with variable charge, determine the ionic charge and use as a Roman numeral following the name of the metal.
a. Sn^{2+} and $2Cl^-$ $\rightarrow$ tin(II) chloride
b. Fe^{2+} and O^{2-} $\rightarrow$ iron(II) oxide
c. Cu^+ and S^{2-} $\rightarrow$ copper(I) sulfide
d. Cu^{2+} and S^{2-} $\rightarrow$ copper(II) sulfide
e. Cd^{2+} and Br^- $\rightarrow$ cadmium bromide
f. Hg^{2+} and Cl^- $\rightarrow$ mercury(II) chloride

5.45 **a.** $? + 3(-1) = 0$ $? = 3+$ $\rightarrow$ Au^{3+}
b. $2? + 3(-2) = 0$ $2? = 6+$ $? = 3+$ $\rightarrow$ Fe^{3+}
c. $? + 4(-1) = 0$ $? = 4+$ $\rightarrow$ Pb^{4+}
d. $? + 2(-1) = 0$ $? = 2+$ $\rightarrow$ Sn^{2+}

5.47 **a.** Ions: Mg^{2+} and Cl^- $\rightarrow$ $MgCl_2$
b. Ions: Na^+ and S^{2-} $\rightarrow$ Na_2S
c. Ions: Cu^+ and O^{2-} $\rightarrow$ Cu_2O
d. Ions: Zn^{2+} and P^{3-} $\rightarrow$ Zn_3P_2
e. Ions: Au^{3+} and N^{3-} $\rightarrow$ AuN

5.49 **a.** Ions: Co^{3+} and Cl^- $\rightarrow$ $CoCl_3$
b. Ions: Pb^{4+} and O^{2-} $\rightarrow$ PbO_2
c. Ions: Ag^+ and Cl^- $\rightarrow$ AgCl
d. Ions: Ca^{2+} and N^{3-} $\rightarrow$ Ca_3N_2
e. Ions: Cu^+ and P^{3-} $\rightarrow$ Cu_3P
f. Ions: Cr^{2+} and Cl^- $\rightarrow$ $CrCl_2$

Section 5.5

5.51 The most common forms of negatively charged polyatomic ions end in *-ate*; one O less end in *-ite*. A hydrogen in front is named as hydrogen or bi-.

a. bicarbonate → H and CO_3 → HCO_3^-
b. ammonium is positively charged NH_4^+
c. phosphate is the most common polyatomic ion of P → PO_4^{3-}
d. bisulfate → H and SO_4 → HSO_4^-
e. hypo- indicates there is one O less than the *–ite* (ClO_2^-) form of ion → ClO^-
$HClO_3$ chlorate (most common)
$HClO_2$ chlorite (one O less)
HClO (one O less than *ite*)

5.53 **a.** The common polyatomic ion of sulfur, SO_4^{2-}, is named sulfate.
b. The common polyatomic ion of carbon, CO_3^{2-}, is named carbonate.
c. The common polyatomic ion of phosphorus, PO_4^{3-}, is named phosphate.
d. The common polyatomic ion of nitrogen, NO_3^-, is named nitrate.
e. The polyatomic ion with one more oxygen than chlorate (ClO_3^-) is named perchlorate.

5.55

	OH^-	**NO_2**	**CO_3^{2-}**	**HSO_4^-**	**PO_4^{3-}**
Li^+	lithium hydroxide LiOH	lithium nitrite $LiNO_3$	lithium carbonate Li_2CO_3	lithium hydrogen sulfate $LiHSO_4$	lithium phosphate Li_3PO_4
Cu^{2+}	copper (II) hydroxide $Cu(OH)_2$	copper(II) nitrite $Cu(NO_3)_2$	copper(II) carbonate $CuCO_3$	copper(II) hydrogen sulfate $Cu(HSO_4)_2$	copper(II) phosphate $Cu_3(PO_4)_2$
Ba^{2+}	barium hydroxide $Ba(OH)_2$	barium nitrite $Ba(NO_3)_2$	barium carbonate $BaCO_3$	barium hydrogen sulfate $Ba(HSO_4)_2$	barium phosphate $Ba_3(PO_4)_2$

5.57 **a.** The polyatomic ion is CO_3^{2-} ; the compound is sodium carbonate.
b. The polyatomic ion is NH_4^+; the compound is ammonium chloride.
c. The polyatomic ion is PO_4^{3-}; the compound is lithium phosphate.
d. The polyatomic ion is NO_2^-; the compound is copper(II) nitrite.
e. The polyatomic ion is SO_3^{2-}; the compound is iron(II) sulfite.
f. The polyatomic ion is $C_2H_3O_2^-$; the compound is potassium acetate.

5.59 Write the positive and negative ions first, and then use charge balance to write the formula.
a. Ions: Ba^{2+} and $2OH^-$ → $Ba(OH)_2$ **b.** Ions: $2Na^+$ and SO_4^{2-} → Na_2SO_4
c. Ions: Fe^{2+} and $2NO_3^-$ → $Fe(NO_3)_2$ **d.** Ions: $3Zn^{2+}$ and $2PO_4^{3-}$ → $Zn_3(PO_4)_2$
e. Ions: Fe^{3+} and CO_3^{3-} → $Fe_2(CO_3)_3$

5.61 **a.** This is an ionic compound with Al^{3+} ion and the sulfate SO_4^{2-} polyatomic ion. The correct name is aluminum sulfate.
b. This is an ionic compound with Ca^{2+} ion and the carbonate CO_3^{2-} polyatomic ion. The correct name is calcium carbonate.
c. This is an ionic compound with Cr^{3+} and O^{2-}. Because chromium has variable valences, a Roman numeral is used to indicate the 3+ charge. It is named chromium(III) oxide.
d. This is an ionic compound with sodium ion Na^+ and the PO_4^{3-} polyatomic ion. The correct name is sodium phosphate.

e. This ionic compound contains two polyatomic ions ammonium NH_4^+ and sulfate SO_4^{2-}. It is named ammonium sulfate.

f. This is an ionic compound containing the variable metal ion Fe^{3+} and oxide ion O^{2-}. It is named using the Roman numeral as iron(III) oxide.

Answers to Additional Problems

5.69 The valence electrons are the *s* and *p* electrons in the highest energy level.

a. B in Group 3A (13) has three valence electrons.
b. Sn in Group 4A (14) has four valence electrons.
c. Ca in Group 2A (2) has two valence electrons.
d. Mg in Group 2A (2) has two valence electrons.

5.71 **a.** Ba in Group 2A (2) has two valence electrons.

```
 •
Ba •
```

b. Ge in Group 4A (14) has four valence electrons.

```
  •
• Ge •
  •
```

c. As in Group 5A (15) has five valence electrons.

```
  ••
• As •
  •
```

d. Sr in Group 2A (2) has two valence electrons.

```
 •
Sr •
```

5.73 **a.** P in Period 3 has five valence electrons.
b. Na in Period 3 has one valence electron.
c. Al in Period 3 has three valence electrons.
d. Si in Period 3 has four valence electrons.

5.75 **a.** $1s^22s^22p^6$ **b.** $1s^22s^22p^6$ **c.** $1s^22s^22p^6$
d. $1s^22s^22p^6$ **e.** $1s^2$

5.77 **a.** An element that forms an ion with a 2+ charge would be in Group 2A (2).
b. The electron-dot symbol for an element in Group 2A (2) is • X •.
c. Be is the Group 2A (2) element in Period 2.
d. Three ions each with a 2+ charge are needed to balance two N^{3-}, which give a formula X_3N_2.

5.79 **a.** Lithium, the metal in Period 2 with the largest atomic size, has an electron configuration $1s^22s^1$.
b. Zinc, the transition element in Period 4 with the higher atomic number, has an electron configuration of $1s^22s^22p^63s^23p^64s^2\,3d^{10}$.

5.81 When two electrons are added to the outermost electron level in an oxygen atom, there is an increase in electron repulsion that pushes the electrons apart and increases the size of the oxide ion compared with that of the oxygen atom.

5.83 **a.** A positive ion Sr^{2+} is smaller than its corresponding atom Sr.
b. The Se atom is smaller than its corresponding ion Se^{2-}.
c. Because Br is above I in Group 7A (17), Br^- is smaller than I^-.

5.85 **a.** Tin(IV) indicates the Sn^{4+} ion.
b. The Sn^{4+} ion has 50 protons and 46 electrons.
c. The Sn^{4+} ion is balanced with two O^{2-} ions to give the formula SnO_2.
d. Three Sn^{4+} ions are needed to balance four PO_4^{3-} ions to give the formula $Sn_3(PO_4)_4$.

5.87 **a.** X as a X^{3+} ion would be in Group 3A (13).
b. X as a X^{2-} ion would be in Group 6A (16).
c. X as a X^{4+} ion would be in Group 4A (14).

5.89 **a.** Fe^{3+} is the iron(III) ion; iron(III) chloride
b. calcium phosphate
c. aluminum carbonate
d. Pb^{4+} is the lead(IV) ion; lead(IV) chloride
e. magnesium carbonate
f. Sn^{2+} is the tin(II) ion; tin(II) sulfate
g. Cu^{2+} is the copper(II) ion: copper(II) sulfide

5.91 **a.** Copper(I) is Cu^+ and nitride is N^{3-}; formula is Cu_3N.
b. Potassium ion is K^+ and hydrogen sulfite is HSO_3^-; formula is $KHSO_3$.
c. Lead(IV) is Pb^{4+} and sulfide is S^{2-}; formula is PbS_2.
d. Gold(III) is Au^{3+} and carbonate is CO_3^{2-}; formula is $Au_2(CO_3)_3$.
e. Zinc is always Zn^{2+} and perchlorate is ClO_4^-; formula is $Zn(ClO_4)_2$.

5.93 **a.** magnesium oxide
b. $Cr(HCO_3)_3$ is chromium(III) hydrogen carbonate or chromium(III) bicarbonate.
c. manganese(III) chromate

5.95 Na_2S has two Na^+ ions to every S^{2-} ion.

$$4.8 \times 10^{22}\ \cancel{Na^+\ ions} \times \frac{1\ S^{2-}\ ion}{2\ \cancel{Na^+\ ions}} = 2.4 \times 10^{22}\ S^{2-}\ ions$$

6
Molecules and Covalent Compounds

Study Goals

- Write the correct names and formulas for covalent compounds.
- Draw the electron-dot formulas with single and multiple covalent bonds.
- Write resonance structures when two or more electron-dot formulas are possible.
- Use electronegativity values to identify polar covalent, nonpolar covalent, and ionic bonds.
- Use the valence-shell electron-pair repulsion (VSEPR) theory to determine the shape and bond angles of a molecule.
- Identify a covalent molecule as polar or nonpolar.

Think About It

1. How is a covalent bond different from an ionic bond?

2. When is an electron-dot formula written with multiple bonds?

3. How does the VSPER theory predict the bond angles in a molecule of a covalent compound?

Key Terms

Match each the following key terms with the correct definition.

a. polar covalent bond **b.** multiple bond **c.** VSEPR theory
d. nonpolar covalent bond **e.** resonance structures

1. _____ Equal sharing of valence electrons by two atoms

2. _____ Occurs when two or more electron-dot formulas can be written for the same compound

3. _____ The unequal attraction for shared electrons in a covalent bond

4. _____ The atoms in a molecule are arranged to minimize repulsion between electrons

5. _____ The sharing of two or three pairs of electrons by two atoms

Answers **1.** d **2.** e **3.** a **4.** c **5.** b

6.1 Names and Formulas of Covalent Compounds

- Covalent compounds are composed of nonmetals bonded together to give discrete units called *molecules.*

- The formula of a covalent compound is written using the order of the symbols of the elements in the name, followed by subscripts indicated by prefixes.

◆ Learning Exercise 6.1A

Study Note

Two nonmetals can form two or more different covalent compounds. In the names, prefixes indicate the number of each atom. Some typical prefixes are *mono-* (1), *di-* (2), *tri-* (3), *tetra-* (4), and *penta-* (5). The ending of the second nonmetal is changed to *-ide.*

Use the appropriate prefixes in naming the following covalent compounds:

1. CS_2 ____________ **2.** CCl_4 ____________

3. CO ____________ **4.** SO_3 ____________

5. N_2O_4 ____________ **6.** PCl_3 ____________

7. P_4S_6 ____________ **8.** IF_7 ____________

9. ClO_2 ____________ **10.** S_2O ____________

Answers

1. carbon disulfide
2. carbon tetrachloride
3. carbon monoxide
4. sulfur trioxide
5. dinitrogen tetroxide
6. phosphorus trichloride
7. tetraphosphorus hexasulfide
8. iodine heptafluoride
9. chlorine dioxide
10. disulfur monoxide

◆ Learning Exercise 6.2B

Write the formula of each of the following covalent compounds:

1. dinitrogen oxide ____________ **2.** silicon tetrabromide ____________

3. nitrogen trichloride ____________ **4.** carbon dioxide ____________

5. sulfur hexafluoride ____________ **6.** oxygen difluoride ____________

7. phosphorus trifluoride ____________ **8.** dinitrogen tetroxide ____________

9. iodine trifluoride ____________ **10.** sulfur dioxide ____________

Answers

1. N_2O **2.** $SiBr_4$ **3.** NCl_3 **4.** CO_2 **5.** SF_6
6. OF_2 **7.** PF_3 **8.** N_2O_4 **9.** IF_3 **10.** SO_2

6.2 Covalent Bonds and Electron-Dot Formulas

- In a covalent bond, atoms of nonmetals share electrons to achieve an octet.
- For example, oxygen with six valence electrons shares electrons with two hydrogen atoms to form

the covalent compound water (H_2O).

```
    ..
H :O:
   ..
   H
```

◆ Learning Exercise 6.2A

List the number of bonds typically formed by the following atoms in covalent compounds:

a. N ______ **b.** S ______ **c.** P ______ **d.** C ______

e. Cl ______ **f.** O ______ **g.** H ______ **h.** F ______

Answers **a.** 3 **b.** 2 **c.** 3 **d.** 4
e. 1 **f.** 2 **g.** 1 **h.** 1

◆ Learning Exercise 6.2B

Study Note

An electron-dot formula for SCl_2 can be written as follows:
STEP 1: Arrange atoms around the central atom.
Cl S Cl
STEP 2: Determine the total number of valence electrons.
1 S and 2 Cl = 1 (6e) + 2(7e) = 20 valence electrons
STEP 3: Attach the central atom to each bonded atom by one pair of electrons (single bond).
Cl– C– Cl 20 – 4 e = 16 remaining valence electrons (8 pairs)
STEP 4: Arrange other valence electrons as lone pairs to complete octets.

```
 ..   ..   ..
:Cl– C– Cl:
 ..   ..   ..
```

Write the electron-dot formulas for each of the following covalent compounds:

H_2 NCl_3 HCl

Cl_2 H_2S CCl_4

Answers H:H :C̤̈l:N̈:C̤̈l: / :C̤̈l: H:C̤̈l: :C̤̈l:C̤̈l: H:S̤̈: / H :C̤̈l:C̤̈:C̤̈l: (with :C̤̈l: above and below C)

6.3 Multiple Covalent Bonds and Resonance

- In a double bond, two pairs of electrons are shared between the same two atoms to complete octets.
- In a triple bond, three pairs of electrons are shared to complete octets.

- When two or more electron-dot formulas can be written for the same compound, the resulting formulas are called *resonance structures*.

Study Note

An electron-dot formula for CO_2 can be written as follows:
STEP 1: Arrange atoms around the central atom.
O C O
STEP 2: Determine the total number of valence electrons.
1 C and 2 O = 1 (4e) + 2(6e) = 16 valence electrons
STEP 3: Attach the central atom to each bonded atom by one pair of electrons (single bond).
O– C–O 16 – 4 e = 12 remaining valence electrons (6 pairs)
STEP 4: Arrange other valence electrons as lone pairs to complete octets.
:O– C– O: (with lone pairs above and below each O)
STEP 5: When octets cannot be completed with available valence electrons, one or more lone pairs are shared between the central atom and bonded atoms.
:O=C=O: (with lone pairs above each O)

◆ Learning Exercise 6.3A

Each of the following compounds contains a multiple bond. Write the electron-dot formulas.

a. CS_2

b. HCN

c. H_2CCH_2

d. HONO

Answers

a. : S :: C :: S : (with lone pairs above each S)

b. H : C ::: N :

c. H : C :: C : H (with H bonded above each C)

d. H:O: N:: O : (with lone pairs above and below O, above N, and above the terminal O)

◆ Learning Exercise 6.3B

Write two or more resonance structures for each of the following:

a. SO_2

b. CO_3^{2-}

c. NCO^-

d. NO_3^-

Answers

a. :Ö– S =Ö: :Ö=S– Ö:

b. $\left[\text{:Ö}-\text{C(–:Ö:)}=\text{Ö:}\right]^{2-}$ $\left[\text{:Ö}-\text{C(=Ö:)}-\text{Ö:}\right]^{2-}$ $\left[\text{:Ö}=\text{C(–:Ö:)}-\text{Ö:}\right]^{2-}$

c. $[\text{:N̈}-\text{C}\equiv\text{O:}]^-$ $[\text{:N̈}=\text{C}=\text{Ö:}]^-$ $[\text{:N}\equiv\text{C}-\text{Ö:}]^-$

d. $\left[\text{:Ö}=\text{N(–:Ö:)}-\text{Ö:}\right]^-$ $\left[\text{:Ö}-\text{N(=Ö:)}-\text{Ö:}\right]^-$ $\left[\text{:Ö}-\text{N(–:Ö:)}=\text{Ö:}\right]^-$

6.4 Shapes of Molecules and Ions (VSEPR Theory)

- The VSEPR theory predicts the geometry of a molecule by placing the electron groups around a central atom as far apart as possible.
- A central atom with two electron groups has a linear geometry (180°); three electron groups gives a trigonal planar geometry (120°); and four electron pairs gives a tetrahedral geometry (109°).
- A linear molecule has a central atom bonded to two atoms and no lone pairs.
- A trigonal planar molecule has a central atom bonded to three atoms and no lone pairs. A bent molecule at 120° has a central atom bonded to two atoms and one lone pair.
- A tetrahedral molecule has a central atom bonded to four atoms and no lone pairs. In a trigonal pyramidal molecule, a central atom is bonded to three atoms and one lone pair. In a bent molecule at 109°, a central atom is bonded to two atoms and two lone pairs.

◆ Learning Exercise 6.4A

Match the shape of a molecule with the following descriptions of the electron groups around the central atoms and the number of bonded atoms.

A. linear **B.** trigonal planar **C.** tetrahedral
D. trigonal pyramidal **E.** bent (120°) **F.** bent (109°)

1. three electron groups with three bonded atoms _______

2. two electron groups with two bonded atoms _______

3. four electron groups with three bonded atoms _______

4. three electron groups with two bonded atoms _______

5. four electron groups with four bonded atoms _______

6. four electron groups with two bonded atoms _______

Answers **1.** B **2.** A **3.** D **4.** E **5.** C **6.** F

◆ Learning Exercise 6.4B

Study Note

Guidelines for predicting the shapes of molecules:

STEP 1. Write the electron-dot formula.

STEP 2. Arrange the electron groups around the central atom to minimize repulsion.

STEP 3. Use the atoms around the central atom to determine shape.

For each of the following, write the electron-dot formula, state thc number of electron groups and bonded atoms, and predict the shape and angles of the molecule or ion:

Molecule or Ion	Electron-Dot Formula	Number of Electron Groups	Number of Bonded Atoms	Shape and Angle
CH_4				
PCl_3				
SO_3				
H_2S				
NO_2^-				

Answers

Molecule or Ion	Electron-Dot Formula	Number of Electron Groups	Number of Bonded Atoms	Shape and Angle
CH_4	H H:C:H H	4	4	Tetrahedral, 109°
PCl_3	:C̤̈l: P̈ :C̤̈l: :C̤̈l:	4	3	Trigonal pyramidal, 109°
SO_3	:Ö̤: S: :O: :Ö̤:	3	3	Trigonal planar, 120°
H_2S	H:S̤̈: H	4	2	Bent, 109°
NO_2^-	:Ö̤:N̈::O̤:	3	2	Bent, 120°

6.5 Electronegativity and Bond Polarity

- Electronegativity values indicate the ability of an atom to attract electrons. In general, metals have low electronegativity values and nonmetals have high values.
- When atoms sharing electrons have the same or similar electronegativity values, electrons are shared equally and the bond is *nonpolar covalent.*
- Electrons are shared unequally in *polar covalent* bonds because they are attracted to the more electronegative atom.
- An electronegativity difference of 0 to 0.4 indicates a nonpolar covalent bond, whereas a difference of 0.5 to 1.7 indicates a polar covalent bond.
- An electronegativity difference of 1.8 or greater indicates a bond that is ionic.

◆ Learning Exercise 6.5

Using the electronegativity values, determine the following:
1. the electronegativity difference for each pair
2. the type of bonding as (I) ionic, (PC) polar covalent, or (NC) nonpolar covalent

Elements	Electronegativity Difference	Bonding	Elements	Electronegativity Difference	Bonding
a. H and O	_______	_______	**b.** N and S	_______	_______
c. Al and O	_______	_______	**d.** Li and F	_______	_______
e. H and Cl	_______	_______	**f.** Cl and Cl	_______	_______
g. S and F	_______	_______	**h.** H and C	_______	_______

Answers

a. 1.4, PC	**b.** 0.5, PC	**c.** 2.0, I	**d.** 3.0, I
e. 0.9, PC	**f.** 0, NP	**g.** 1.5, PC	**h.** 0.4, NP

6.6 Polarity of Molecules

- A polar bond with its charge separation is called a dipole; the positive end is marked as δ^+ and the negative end as δ^-.
- Nonpolar molecules can have polar bonds when the dipoles are in a symmetric arrangement.
- In polar molecules, the dipoles do not cancel each other.

◆ Learning Exercise 6.6A

Write the symbols δ^+ and δ^- over the atoms in polar bonds.

1. H—O **2.** N—H **3.** C—Cl

4. O—F **5.** N—F **6.** P—Cl

Answers

1. $\overset{\delta^+}{\text{H}}—\overset{\delta^-}{\text{O}}$ **2.** $\overset{\delta^-}{\text{N}}—\overset{\delta^+}{\text{H}}$ **3.** $\overset{\delta^+}{\text{C}}—\overset{\delta^-}{\text{Cl}}$

4. $\overset{\delta^+}{O}—\overset{\delta^-}{F}$ **5.** $\overset{\delta^+}{N}—\overset{\delta^-}{F}$ **6.** $\overset{\delta^+}{P}—\overset{\delta^-}{Cl}$

◆ Learning Exercise 6.6B

Indicate the dipoles in each of the following and determine whether the molecule is polar or nonpolar:

1. CF_4 **2.** HCl

3. NH_3 **4.** OF_2

Answers

1. CF_4 F ← C → F (with C → F up and C → F down) dipoles cancel, nonpolar

2. HCl $\overset{\delta^+}{H} \rightarrow \overset{\delta^-}{Cl}$ ⟶ dipole does not cancel, polar

3. NH_3 H → N̈ ← N (with H → N from below) ↑ dipoles do not cancel, polar

4. OF_2 :Ö → F (with O → F down) ↘ dipoles do not cancel, polar

Checklist for Chapter 6

You are ready to take the self-test for Chapter 6. Be sure you have accomplished the following learning goals for this chapter. If you are not sure, review the section listed at the end of the goal. Then apply your new skills and understanding to the practice test.

After studying Chapter 6, I can successfully:

_______ Write the name and formula of a covalent compound (6.1).

_______ Write the electron-dot formula of a covalent compound or polyatomic ion (6.2).

_______ Write an electron-dot formula with multiple bonds (6.3).

_______ Write resonance structures for when two or more electron-dot formulas are possible (6.3).

_______ Predict the shape and bond angles for a molecule (6.4).

_______ Determine the electronegativity difference for two atoms in a compound (6.5).

_______ Classify a bond as nonpolar covalent, polar covalent, or ionic (6.5).

_______ Classify a molecule as polar or nonpolar (6.6).

Practice Test for Chapter 6

1. A covalent bond (nonpolar) always occurs between

   A. Two different nonmetals
   B. Two atoms of the same nonmetal
   C. Two noble gases
   D. Two different metals
   E. A metal and a nonmetal

2. The name of NCl_3 is

   A. nitrogen chloride **B.** nitrogen trichloride **C.** trinitrogen chloride
   D. nitrogen chlorine three **E.** nitrogen trichlorine

3. The name of CO is

   A. carbon monoxide **B.** carbonic oxide **C.** carbon oxide
   D. carbonious oxide **E.** carboxide

4. The formula for a compound between carbon and chlorine is
   A. Cl **B.** CCl_2 **C.** C_4Cl **D.** CCl_4 **E.** C_4Cl_2

5. A polar covalent bond typically occurs between

   A. Two different nonmetals
   B. Two of the same type of nonmetals
   C. Two noble gases
   D. Two different metals
   E. A metal and a nonmetal

For questions 6 through 11, indicate the type of bonding expected between the following elements:

A. ionic **B.** nonpolar covalent **C.** polar covalent

6. ______ silicon and oxygen **7.** ______ barium and chlorine

8. ______ aluminum and fluorine **9.** ______ chlorine and chlorine

10. ______ sulfur and oxygen **11.** ______ nitrogen and oxygen

Match the following shapes with the description:

A. linear **B.** trigonal planar **C.** tetrahedral
D. trigonal pyramidal **E.** bent (120°) **F.** bent (109°)

12. Has a central atom with three electron groups with three bonded atoms ______

13. Has a central atom with two electron groups with two bonded atoms ______

14. Has a central atom with four electron groups with three bonded atoms ______

15. Has a central atom with three electron groups with two bonded atoms ______

16. Has a central atom with four electron groups with four bonded atoms ______

17. Has a central atom with four electron groups with two bonded atoms ______

Determine the shape and angles of each of the following molecules:

A. linear, 180° **B.** trigonal planar, 120° **C.** bent, 120°
D. tetrahedral, 109° **E.** trigonal pyramidal, 109° **F.** bent, 109°

18. PCl_3 **19.** CBr_4 **20.** H_2S

21. BCl_3 **22.** $BeBr_2$

Answers to the Practice Test

1. B	**2.** B	**3.** A	**4.** D	**5.** A
6. C	**7.** A	**8.** A	**9.** B	**10.** C
11. C	**12.** B	**13.** A	**14.** D	**15.** E
16. C	**17.** F	**18.** E	**19.** D	**20.** F
21. B	**22.** A			

Answers and Solutions to Selected Text Problems

6.1 When naming covalent compounds, prefixes are used to indicate the number of each atom as shown in the subscripts of the formula. The first nonmetal is named the same as the element; the second nonmetal changes the ending of the element name to *-ide*.

- **a.** one (mono-omitted) phosphorus atom and three (tri) bromine atoms = phosphorus tribromide
- **b.** one (mono-omitted) carbon atom and four (tetra) bromine atoms = carbon tetrabromide
- **c.** one (mono-omitted) silicon atom and two (di) oxygen atoms = silicon dioxide
- **d.** one (mono-omitted) hydrogen atom and one(mono) fluorine atom = hydrogen monofluoride or hydrogen fluoride
- **e.** one (mono-omitted) nitrogen atom and three (tri) iodine atoms = nitrogen triiodide

6.3 When naming covalent compounds, prefixes are used to indicate the number of each atom as shown in the subscripts of the formula. The first nonmetal is named the same as the element; the second nonmetal changes the ending of the element name to *-ide*.

- **a.** two (di) nitrogen atoms and three (tri) oxygen atoms = dinitrogen trioxide
- **b.** one (mono-omitted) nitrogen atom and three (tri) chlorine atoms = nitrogen trichloride
- **c.** one(mono-omitted) silicon atom and four (tetra) bromine atoms = silicon tetrabromide
- **d.** one (mono-omitted) phosphorus atom and five (penta) chlorine atoms = phosphorus pentachloride
- **e.** one (mono-omitted) sulfur atom and three(tri) oxygen atoms =sulfur trioxide

6.5 The prefixes in the names of covalent compounds indicate the number of each type of atom, which is placed as a subscript in the formula. When there is no prefix because *mono-* is understood, there is one atom in the formula.

- **a.** carbon (1 C) and tetrachloride (4 Cl) = CCl_4
- **b.** carbon (1 C) and monooxide (1 O) =CO
- **c.** phosphorus (1 P) and trichloride (3 Cl) = PCl_3
- **d.** dinitrogen (2 N) and tetroxide (4 O) = N_2O_4

6.7 The prefixes in the names of covalent compounds indicate the number of each type of atom, which is placed as a subscript in the formula. When there is no prefix because *mono-* is understood, there is one atom in the formula.

- **a.** oxygen (1 O) and difluoride (2 F) = OF_2
- **b.** boron (1 B) and trifluoride (3F) = BF_3
- **c.** dinitrogen (2 N) and trioxide (3 O) = N_2O_3
- **d.** sulfur (1S) and hexafluoride (6 F) = SF_6

6.9 The nonmetallic elements that are not noble gases are likely to form covalent bonds.

6.11 Nonmetal atoms form octets for their valence electrons by sharing valence electrons. The valence electrons of the nonmetals are the only electrons available for bonding.

6.13 **a.** When two H atoms share, each has two valence electrons. In H_2, there is one bonding pair and no lone pair.

b. The Br atom achieves an octet by sharing a valence electron with one H atom to give eight valence electrons, one bonding pair, and three lone pairs on the Br atom.

c. Each Br atom achieves an octet by sharing one valence electron to give a total of 14 valence electrons, one bonding pair between the Br atoms, and six lone pairs (three lone pairs for each Br atom).

6.15 **a.** 2 H + 1 S = 2(1e) + 1(6e) = 8 valence electrons

b. 2 I = 2(7e) = 14 valence electrons

c. 1 C + 4 Cl; = 1(4e) + 4(7e) = 4 + 28 = 32 valence electrons

d. 1 O + 1 H = 1(6e) + 1(1e) + 1e (negative charge) = 8 valence electrons

6.17 **a.** HF ($8e^-$)

```
      ..              ..
    H : F :    or   H—F :
      ..              ..
```

b. SF_2 ($20\ e^-$)

```
  ..  ..  ..          ..  ..  ..
: F : S : F :   or  : F — S — F :
  ..  ..  ..          ..  ..  ..
```

c. NBr_3 ($26e^-$)

```
            ..                       ..
          : Br :                   : Br :
  ..   ..   ..                ..     |     ..
: Br : N : Br :      or     : Br  —  N  —  Br :
  ..   ..   ..                ..     ..    ..
```

d. BH_4^- ($8\ e^-$)

```
 (     H     )-        (     H     )-
 (     ..    )         (     |     )
 (  H : B : H )   or   (  H—B—H    )
 (     ..    )         (     |     )
 (     H     )         (     H     )
```

e. CH_3OH ($14\ e^-$)

```
     H                    H
     ..  ..               |  ..
  H : C : O : H    or  H—C—O—H
     ..  ..               |  ..
     H                    H
```

f. N_2H_4 ($14\ e^-$)

```
     H   H              H   H
     ..  ..             |   |
  H : N : N : H   or  H—N—N—H
     ..  ..             ..  ..
```

6.19 When using all the valence electrons does not give complete octets, it is necessary to write multiple bonds.

6.21 Resonance occurs when we can write two or more formulas for the same molecule or ion.

6.23 **a.** CO ($10\ e^-$)

```
:C:::O:   or   :C≡O:
```

b. H_2CCH_2 (12 e^-)

```
  H    H              H  H
  ..   ..             |  |
H : C : : C : H   or   H—C=C—H
```

c. H_2CO (12 e^-)

```
   :O:            :O:
   ::             ||
H : C : H    or H—C—H
```

6.25 **a.** $ClNO_2$

```
        :O:                      ..
   ..   ||  ..                  :O:
 : Cl—N—O:      <——>       ..   |   ..
   ..       ..             :Cl—N =O:
                             ..
```

b. OCN^-

```
  ..    ..   -                 ..   -          ..          -
[ :O=C=N: ]     <——>   [ :O≡C—N: ]     <——>  [ :O—C≡N: ]
                               ..              ..
```

6.27 **a.** linear

b. Four electron groups around a central atom have a tetrahedral electron structure. When three electron groups are bonded to the central atom, the structure is trigonal pyramidal.

6.29 The four electron pairs in PCl_3 have tetrahedral arrangement, but three bonded atoms and one lone pair around a central atom give a trigonal pyramidal shape.

6.31 In BF_3, the central atom B has three bonded atoms and no lone pairs, which gives BF_3 a trigonal planar shape. In NF_3, the central atom N has three bonded atoms and one lone pair, which give NF_3 a trigonal pyramidal shape.

6.33 **a.** Three electron groups and three bonded have a trigonal planar shape.

b. The central oxygen atom has four electron pairs, but only two are bonded to fluorine atoms. Its shape is bent with 109° angles.

c. The central atom C has two electron groups bonded to two atoms; HCN is linear.

d. The central atom C has four electron pairs bonded to four chlorine atoms; CCl_4 has a tetrahedral shape.

e. The central atom Se has three electron groups with two bonded atoms and a lone pair, which gives SeO_2 a bent shape with 120° angles.

6.35 To find the total valence electrons for an ion, add the total valence electrons for each atom and add the number of electrons indicated by a negative charge.

a. C (4 valence electrons) + 3 O (3 x 6 valence electrons) + charge (2 electrons) = $4e^- + 18e^- + 2e^- = 24\ e^-$ total for the electron-dot formula

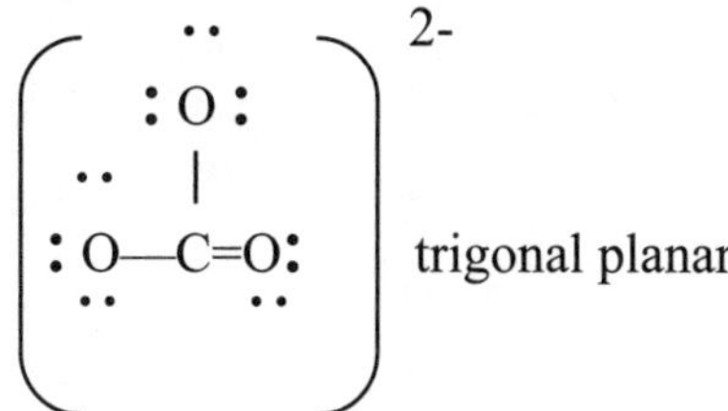

trigonal planar

b. S (6 valence electrons) + 4 O (4 x 6 valence electrons) + charge (2 electrons) = $6e^- + 24e^- + 2e^- = 32\ e^-$ total for the electron-dot formula

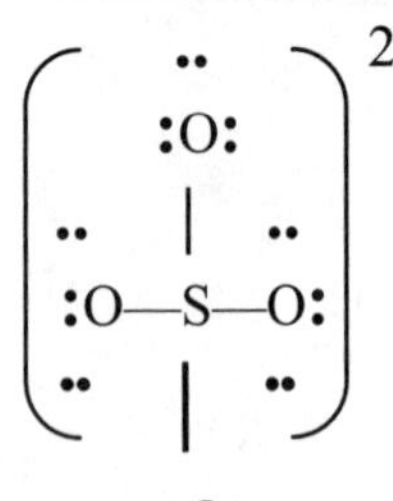

4 electron pairs around S; tetrahedral shape

c. BH_4^- (8 e^-) [H—B(H)(H)—H]$^-$ tetrahedral

d. NO_2^+ (16 e^-) [:O=N=O:]$^+$ linear

6.37 The electronegativity increases going across a period.

6.39 A nonpolar covalent bond would have an electronegativity difference of 0.0 to 0.4.

6.41 **a.** Electronegativity increases going up a group: K, Na, Li.
b. Electronegativity increases going across a period: Na, P, Cl.
c. Electronegativity increases going across a period and at the top of a group: Ca, Br, O.

6.43 **a.** Ca(1.0), Al(1.5), P(2.1), Br(2.8)
b. K(0.8), Se(2.4), Br(2.8), F(4.0)
c. Cs(0.7), Sn(1.8), B(2.0), S(2.5)

6.45 **a.** $\overset{\delta^+}{N}$—$\overset{\delta^-}{F}$ (dipole arrow $\mapsto$ toward F)

b. $\overset{\delta^+}{Si}$—$\overset{\delta^-}{P}$ (dipole arrow toward P)

c. $\overset{\delta^+}{C}$—$\overset{\delta^-}{O}$ (dipole arrow toward O)

d. $\overset{\delta^+}{P}$—$\overset{\delta^-}{Br}$ (dipole arrow toward Br)

e. $\overset{\delta^+}{B}$—$\overset{\delta^-}{Cl}$ (dipole arrow toward Cl)

6.47 **a.** Si—Br electronegavity difference 1.0, polar covalent
b. Li—F electronegavity difference 3.0, ionic
c. Br—F electronegavity difference 1.2, polar covalent
d. Br—Br electronegavity difference 0, nonpolar covalent
e. N—P electronegavity difference 0.9, polar covalent
f. C—P electronegavity difference 0.4, nonpolar covalent

6.49 Electrons are shared equally between two identical atoms and unequally between most nonidentical atoms.

6.51 **a.** two dipoles cancel; nonpolar **b.** dipoles do not cancel; polar
c. four dipoles cancel; nonpolar **d.** three dipoles cancel; nonpolar

Answers to Additional Questions

6.59 **a.** 1 N and 3 Cl → nitrogen trichloride
b. 1 S and 2 Cl → sulfur dichloride
c. 2 N and 1 O → dinitrogen monoxide
d. 2 F → fluorine (named as the element)
e. 1 P and 5 Cl → phosphorus pentachloride
f. 2 P and 5 O → diphosphorus pentoxide

6.61 **a.** 1 C and 1 O → CO
b. di (2) and penta (5) → P_2O_5
c. di (2) and 1 S → H_2S
d. 1 S and di (2) Cl → SCl_2

6.63 To find the total valence electrons for an ion, add the total valence electrons for each atom and add the number of valence electrons indicated by a negative charge. If charge is positive, remove one or more valence electrons.
a. 1 C(4e) + 2S(6e) = 4 + 12 = 16 valence electrons
b. 2C(4e) + 4H(1e) + 1 O(6e) = 8 + 4 + 6 = 18 valence electrons
c. 1P(5e) + 4H(1e) – 1e (positive charge) = 5 + 4 -1 = 8 valence electrons
d. 1B(3e) + 3Cl(7e) = 3 + 21 = 24 valence electrons
e. 1S(6e) + 3 O(6e) + 2e (negative charge) = 6 + 18 + 2 = 26 valence electrons

6.65

a. BF_4^- (32 e^-)

```
   ( ..      )-         ( ..      )-
   (  F      )          (  F      )
   ( .. .. ..)          ( .. | .. )
   (:F : B : F :)   or  (:F—B—F:  )
   ( .. .. ..)          ( ..  | ..)
   ( : F :   )          ( : F :   )
   (   ..    )          (   ..    )
```

b. Cl_2O (20 e^-)

```
 ..  ..  ..           ..  ..  ..
:Cl :O :Cl :    or   :Cl—O—Cl :
 ..  ..  ..           ..  ..  ..
```

c. H_2NOH (14 e^-)

```
      H                  H
     ..  ..              |  ..
  H : N : O : H   or  H—N— O— H
     ..  ..              ..  ..
```

d. NO_2^+ (16 e^-)

```
 (  ..      ..  )+        ( ..   .. )+
 ( :O::N::O:    )    or   ( :O=N=O: )
```

e. H_2CCl_2 (24 e^-)

```
          ..                 ..
      H  :Cl :            H  :Cl :
     ..   ..  ..          |   |  ..
  H : C ::C : Cl :   or  H—C = C—Cl :
              ..                 ..
```

6.67 **a.** 16 valence electrons :N=N=O: ⟷ :N≡N—O:

b. 16 valence electrons $[:O=N=O:]^+$ ⟷ $[:O≡N—O:]^+$ ⟷ $[:O—N≡O:]^+$

c. 16 valence electrons $[:C≡N—S:]^-$ ⟷ $[:C=N=S:]^-$ ⟷ $[:C—N≡S:]^-$

6.69 **a.** NF_3 :F—N—F: (with a third :F: bonded to N) trigonal pyramidal

b. $SiBr_4$:Br—Si—Br: (with :Br: above and below Si) tetrahedral

c. $BeCl_2$:Cl—Be—Cl: linear

d. SO_2 [: O=S—O :] ⟷ [: O—S=O:] bent (120°)

6.71 Arrange the elements in order of increasing electronegativity values:
a. Electronegativity is higher at the top of a group: I, Cl, F.
b. Electronegativity increases left to right across a period: K, Li, S, Cl.
c. Electronegativity is higher at the top of a group: Ba, Sr, Mg, Be.

6.73 Determine the difference in electronegativity values:

a. C—O (1.0)	C—N is less (0.5).
b. N—F (1.0)	N—Br is less (0.2).
c. S—Cl (0.5)	Br—Cl is less (0.2).
d. Br—I (0.3)	Br—Cl is less (0.2).
e. C—O (1.0)	C—S is less (0).

6.75 A dipole arrow points from the atom with the lower electronegativity value (more positive) to the atom in the bond that has the higher electronegativity value (more negative).

a. Si has the lower electronegativity value of 1.8, making Si the positive end of the dipole. The Cl atom has a higher electronegativity value of 3.0.

Si—Cl
⟼

b. C has the lower electronegativity value of 2.5, making C the positive end of the dipole. The N atom has a higher electronegativity value of 3.0.

c. Cl has the lower electronegativity value of 3.0, making Cl the positive end of the dipole. The F atom has a higher electronegativity value of 4.0.

F—Cl
←+

d. C has the lower electronegativity value of 2.5, making C the positive end of the dipole. The F atom has a higher electronegativity value of 4.0.

C—F
+→

e. N has the lower electronegativity value of 3.0, making N the positive end of the dipole. The O atom has a higher electronegativity value of 3.5.

N—O
+→

6.77 **a.** polar covalent (Cl 3.0 – Si 1.8 = 1.2)
b. nonpolar covalent (C 2.5 – C 2.5 = 0.0)
c. ionic (Cl 3.0 – Na 0.9 = 2.1)
d. nonpolar covalent (C 2.5 – H 2.1 = 0.4)
e. nonpolar covalent (F 4.0 – F 4.0 = 0.0)

6.79

a. BrO_2^- [: O—Br—O :]$^-$ (with lone pairs •• above and below each atom) 4 electron groups, 2 bonded atoms, bent (109°)

b. H_2O H—:O—H (O with lone pairs) 4 electron groups, 2 bonded atoms, bent (109°)

c. CO_3^{2-} [:O=C—O: with a third :O: bonded above C]$^{2-}$ (lone pairs shown) 3 electron groups, 3 bonded atoms, trigonal planar

d. CF_4 :F—C—F: with :F: above and below C (lone pairs shown) 4 electron groups, 4 bonded atoms, tetrahedral

e. CS_2 : S=C=S : (lone pairs shown) 2 electron groups, 2 bonded atoms, linear

f. PO_3^{3-} [:O—P—O: with :O: bonded above P, lone pair on P]$^{3-}$ 4 electron groups, 3 bonded atoms, trigonal pyramidal

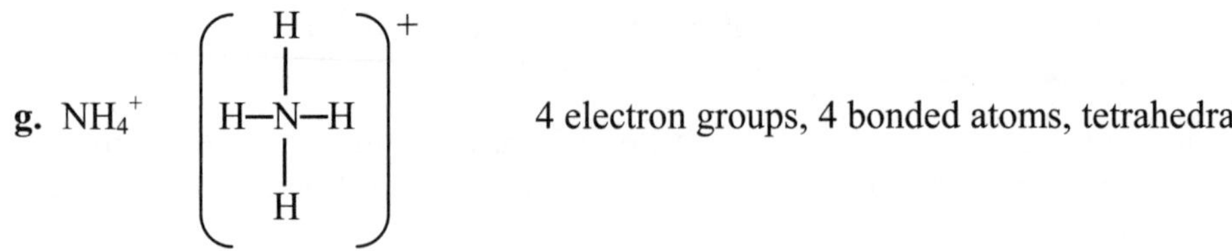

g. NH_4^+ 4 electron groups, 4 bonded atoms, tetrahedral

6.81 **a.** Polar. A single polar bond makes the Br end more negative than the H end.

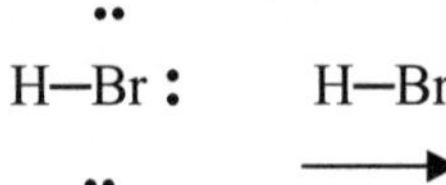

b. Nonpolar. In a linear molecular, two equal dipoles directed away from each other at 180 ° will cancel.

:O=Si=O: O—Si—O

c. Nonpolar. There are three nonpolar N-Cl bonds (no dipoles) in a trigonal pyramidal shape.

:Cl:
:Cl—N—Cl:

d. Polar. In a tetrahedral, a Cl provides a polar C-Cl bond that gives a negative end (Cl) to the CH_3Cl molecules.

:Cl:
:Cl—C—H:
: Cl:

e.

:F:
:F—N—F: Polar, trigonal pyramidal with one lone pair; dipoles do not cancel.

f. Polar. Two polar bonds do not oppose each other in the bent H_2O molecule. Both O-H bonds make the O end of the molecule more negative than the H end.

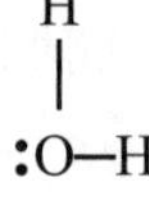

6.83 **a.** Tin(II) is Sn^{2+}; carbonate is CO_3^{2-}. With charges balanced, the formula is $SnCO_3$.
b. Lithium is Li^+; phosphide is P^{3-}. Using three Li^+ for charge balance, the formula is Li_3P.
c. Silicon has four valence electrons to share with four chlorine atoms to give $SiCl_4$.
d. Iron(III) is Fe^{3+}; sulfide is S^{2-}. Charge is balanced with two Fe^{3+} and three S^{2-} to write the formula Fe_2S_3.
e. Carbon has four valence electrons to form two double bonds with two oxygen atoms to give the formula CO_2.
f. Calcium is Ca^{2+}; bromide is Br^-. With charges balanced, the formula is $CaBr_2$.

6.85 **a.** In a molecule that has a trigonal planar shape, the dipoles cancel, making the molecule nonpolar.
b. In a molecule with a bent shape and one lone pair, the dipoles do not cancel. The molecule is polar.
c. In a linear molecule with identical atoms, any dipoles cancel, making the molecule nonpolar.

7
Chemical Quantities

Study Goals

- Use Avogadro's number to determine the number of particles in a given number of moles.
- Determine the formula mass and molar mass of a compound from its formula.
- Use molar mass to convert between the grams and moles of a substance.
- Use the formula of a compound to calculate its percent composition.
- From percent composition, determine the empirical formula of a compound.
- Using molar mass and the empirical formula, determine the molecular formula.

Think About It

1. How is a mole analogous to a term for a collection such as one dozen?

2. How are the atomic masses of elements in a compound used to calculate its percent composition?

3. What is the difference between the empirical formula and molecular formula of a compound?

Key Terms

Match the following terms with the statements below:

a. mole　　**b.** Avogadro's number　　**c.** empirical formula
d. molar mass　　**e.** molecular formula

1. _____ The formula that gives the actual number of atoms of each element in a compound.

2. _____ The number of items in one mol equal to 6.022×10^{23}.

3. _____ The smallest whole-number ratio of atoms in a formula.

4. _____ The amount of a substance that contains 6.022×10^{23} particles of that substance.

5. _____ The mass in grams of an element or compound that is equal numerically to its atomic or sum of atomic masses.

Answers **1.** e **2.** b **3.** c **4.** a **5.** d

7.1 Atomic Mass and Formula Mass

- The atomic mass unit (amu) is one-twelfth (1/12) the mass of a carbon-12 atom (^{12}C), which has a mass of exactly 12 amu.
- In a sample of atoms of any elements, each atom is assigned the atomic mass on the periodic table.

◆ Learning Exercise 7.1A

Calculate the mass in amu of each of the following:

a. 2500 atoms of Zn

b. 4.8×10^5 atoms of S

c. 765 atoms of Br

Answers **a.** 1.6×10^5 amu **b.** 1.5×10^7 amu **c.** 6.112×10^4 amu

◆ Learning Exercise 7.1B

Calculate the number of atoms in each of the following:

a. 8400 amu P

b. 2.24×10^4 amu Mn

c. 8620 amu C

Answers **a.** 2.7×10^2 atoms P **b.** 408 atoms Mn **c.** 718 atoms C

◆ Learning Exercise 7.1C

Determine the formula mass of each of the following compounds:

a. N_2O_4

b. $Mg(NO_3)_2$

c. $Al_2(CO_3)_3$

Answers **a.** 92.02 amu **b.** 148.33 amu **c.** 234.0 amu

7.2 The Mole

- A mole of any element contains Avogadro's number, 6.022×10^{23}, of atoms; a mole of any compound contains 6.022×10^{23} molecules or formula units.

◆ Learning Exercise 7.2A

Use Avogadro's number to calculate the particles or moles of particles in each of the following:

a. How many atoms of calcium are in 3.00 mol Ca?

b. How many atoms of zinc are in 0.250 mol zinc?

c. How many molecules of SO_2 are in 0.118 mol SO_2?

d. How many moles of silver are in 4.88×10^{23} atoms Ag?

e. How many moles of ammonia are in 7.52×10^{23} molecules NH_3?

Answers

a. 1.81×10^{24} atoms Ca
b. 1.51×10^{23} atoms Zn
c. 7.11×10^{22} molecules SO_2
d. 0.810 mol Ag
e. 1.25 mol NH_3

◆ Learning Exercise 7.2B

Study Note

The subscripts in the formula of a compound indicate the number of moles of each element in one mol of that compound. For example, consider the formula Mg_3N_2:

$$1 \text{ mol } Mg_3N_2 = 3 \text{ mol Mg atoms and } 2 \text{ mol N atoms}$$

Some conversion factors for the moles of elements can be written as

$$\frac{3 \text{ mol Mg atoms}}{1 \text{ mol } Mg_3N_2} \text{ and } \frac{1 \text{ mol } Mg_3N_2}{3 \text{ mol Mg atoms}} \qquad \frac{2 \text{ mol N atoms}}{1 \text{ mol } Mg_3N_2} \text{ and } \frac{1 \text{ mol } Mg_3N_2}{2 \text{ mol N atoms}}$$

For the compound ibuprofen used in Advil™ and Motrin™ ($C_{13}H_{18}O_2$), determine the particles or moles of each of the following:

a. Moles of carbon (C) atoms in 2.20 mol ibuprofen

b. Moles of hydrogen (H) in 4.4×10^{24} molecules of ibuprofen

c. Atoms of oxygen (O) in 0.750 mol ibuprofen

d. Molecules of ibuprofen that contain 15 mol hydrogen (H)

e. Molecules of ibuprofen that contain 8.50×10^{24} atoms of hydrogen (H)

Answers

a. 28.6 mol C
b. 132 mol H
c. 9.03×10^{23} atoms O
d. 5.0×10^{23} molecules ibuprofen
e. 4.72×10^{23} molecules ibuprofen

7.3 Molar Mass

- The molar mass (g/mol) of an element is numerically equal to its atomic mass in grams.
- The molar mass (g/mol) of a compound is the mass in grams equal numerically to the sum of the mass for each element in the formula.

Study Note

The molar mass of an element or compound is determined as follows:

1. Determine the moles of each element (from subscripts) in the compound.
2. Calculate the total mass contributed by each element.
3. Total the masses of all the elements.

Example: What is the molar mass of silver nitrate, $AgNO_3$?

1 mol Ag	×	107.9 g/mol	=	107.9 g
1 mol N	×	14.01 g/mol	=	14.01 g
3 mol O	×	16.00 g/mol	=	48.00 g
		molar mass $AgNO_3$	=	169.9 g

◆ Learning Exercise 7.3

Determine the molar mass for each of the following:

a. K_2O

b. $AlCl_3$

c. $C_{13}H_{18}O_2$ ibuprofen

d. C_4H_{10}

e. $Ca(NO_3)_2$

f. Mg_3N_2

g. $FeCO_3$

h. $(NH_4)_3PO_4$

Answers
a. 94.20 g/mol **b.** 133.33 g/mol **c.** 206.27 g/mol **d.** 58.12 g/mol
e. 164.10 g/mol **f.** 100.95 g/mol **g.** 115.86 g/mol **h.** 149.10 g/mol

7.4 Calculations Using Molar Mass

The molar mass is useful as a conversion factor to change a given quantity in moles to grams.

$$\text{~~mol~~} \times \underset{\text{molar mass}}{\frac{\text{grams}}{1\ \text{~~mol~~}}} = \text{grams}$$

◆ Learning Exercise 7.4A

Study Note

When the number of moles is given, molar mass is used as a conversion factor to determine the mass in grams.

Example: What is the mass in grams of 0.254 mol Na_2CO_3?

$$0.254\ \text{~~mol~~}\ \text{~~Na}_2\text{CO}_3\text{~~} \times \underset{\text{Molar mass}}{\frac{106.0\ \text{g}\ Na_2CO_3}{1\ \text{~~mol Na}_2\text{CO}_3\text{~~}}} = 26.9\ \text{g}$$

Calculate the number of grams in each of the following:

a. 0.75 mol S

b. 3.18 mol K_2SO_4

c. 2.50 mol NH_4Cl

d. 1.25×10^{24} molecules O_2

e. 3.2×10^{23} atoms Pb

f. 4.08 mol $FeCl_3$

g. 2.28 mol PCl_3

h. 0.815 mol $Mg(NO_3)_2$

Answers **a.** 24 g **b.** 554 g **c.** 134 g **d.** 66.4 g
e. 110 g **f.** 662 g **g.** 313 g **h.** 121 g

◆ Learning Exercise 7.4B

When the amount of a substance is given, molar mass is used to calculate the number of moles of substance present.

$$\cancel{\text{grams}} \times \frac{1\text{ mol}}{\cancel{\text{grams}}} = \text{mol}$$

molar mass(inverted)

Study Note

Example: How many moles of NaOH are in 84.5 g NaOH?

$$84.5\ \cancel{\text{g NaOH}} \times \frac{1\text{ mol NaOH}}{40.00\ \cancel{\text{g NaOH}}} = 2.11\text{ mol NaOH}$$

molar mass (inverted)

Calculate the number of moles in each of the following quantities:

a. 108 g CH_4

b. 6.12 g CO_2

c. 38.7 g $CaBr_2$

d. 236 g Cl_2

e. 128 g $Mg(OH)_2$

f. 172 g Al_2O_3

g. The methane burned in a gas heater has a formula of CH_4. If 725 g methane are used in 1 month, how many moles of methane were burned?

h. There is 18 mg iron in a vitamin tablet. If there are 100 tablets in a bottle, how many moles of iron are contained in the vitamins in the bottle?

Answers

Answers	**a.** 6.73 mol	**b.** 0.139 mol	**c.** 0.194 mol	**d.** 3.33 mol
	e. 2.19 mol	**f.** 1.69 mol	**g.** 45.2 mol	**h.** 0.032 mol

7.5 Percent Composition and Empirical Formulas

- A mole of any compound contains a definite proportion by mass of its elements.
- Percent composition is the percent by mass of each element in a compound.
- An empirical formula gives the simplest or lowest whole number ratio of atoms in a compound.

Study Note

When the formula of a substance is given, the percent composition is determined as follows:

1. Determine the molar mass.
2. Calculate the percent by mass of each element.

$$\frac{\text{grams of element}}{\text{molar mass}} \times 100 = \%\text{ by mass element}$$

Example: What is the percent Na in NaOH?

$$\frac{22.99\text{ g Na}}{40.00\text{ g NaOH}} \times 100\% = 57.48\%$$

◆ Learning Exercise 7.5A

Calculate the percent composition by mass for the following compounds:

a. C_3H_6O

b. $BaSO_4$

c. $Ca(NO_3)_2$

d. NaOCl

e. $(NH_4)_3PO_4$

Answers
a. C 62.04%, H 10.41%, O 27.55%
b. Ba 58.83%, S 13.74%, O 27.42%
c. Ca 24.42%, N 17.07%, O 58.50%
d. Na 30.88%, O 21.49%, Cl 47.62%
e. N 28.19%, H 8.11%, P 20.77%, O 42.92%

◆ Learning Exercise 7.5B

Study Note

When the percent composition or grams of the elements in a compound are given, the empirical formula is determined as follows:

1. Calculate the moles of each element.
2. Divide each number of moles by the smaller number of moles.
3. Write the whole numbers as subscripts in the formula.
4. If fractions are obtained, multiply by an integer that gives whole number ratios.

Example: What is the empirical formula of a compound containing 27.3%C and 72.7%O by mass. In 100 g of compound, there is 27.3 g C and 72.7 g O.

1. Moles of each element

$27.3 \text{ g C} \times \frac{1 \text{ mol C}}{12.01 \text{ g C}} = 2.27 \text{ mol C}$ (smaller number of moles) $72.7 \text{ g C} \times \frac{1 \text{ mol O}}{16.00 \text{ g O}} = 4.54 \text{ mol O}$

2. Divide each by the smaller number of moles

$\frac{2.27 \text{ mol C}}{2.27} = 1.00 \text{ mol C}$ $\frac{4.54 \text{ mol O}}{2.27} = 2.00 \text{ mol O}$

Empirical formula = $C_{1.00}O_{2.00}$ = CO_2

Determine the empirical formula of each of the following compounds:

a. A compound that is 75.7% by mass tin (Sn) and 24.3% by mass fluorine (F)

b. A compound that is 20.2% by mass magnesium (Mg), 26.7 % sulfur (S), and 53.2% oxygen (O)

c. A 4.58 sample of a compound that contains 2.00 g phosphorus (P) and the rest is oxygen (O)

d. A compound that contains 1.00 g C, 0.168 g H, and 0.890 g O

Answers **a.** SnF_2 **b.** $MgSO_4$ **c.** P_2O_5 **d.** $C_3H_6O_2$

7.6 Molecular Formulas

- A molecular formula gives the actual number of atoms of each element in the compound.
- The molecular formula is obtained using the empirical formula and molar mass of the compounds.

Study Note

When the empirical formula and molar mass of a compound are given, the molecular formula is obtained as follows:

1. Calculate the mass of the empirical formula.
2. Divide the molar mass by the mass of the empirical formula to obtain an integer.
3. Multiply the empirical formula by the integer to obtain the molecular formula.

Example: Lactic acid has the empirical formula CH_2O. If the molar mass of lactic acid is 90.08, what is the molecular formula of lactic acid?

1. mass of CH_2O = 12.01 g C + 2(1.008) g H + 16.00 g = 30.03 g

2. $\frac{\text{molar mass}}{\text{mass of empirical formula}} = \frac{90.08\text{ g}}{30.03\text{ g}} = 3$ (small integer)

3. molecular formula = 3 x (CH_2O) = $C_3H_6O_3$ = lactic acid

◆ Learning Exercise 7.6A

Determine the molecular formula of each empirical formula and molar mass:

a. NS, 184 g/mol

b. KH_4O, 118.3 g/mol

c. HIO_3, 175.93 g/mol

d. NaO_3P, 305.9 g/mol

e. $C_7H_8O_3$, 420.4 g/mol

f. C_3H_5O, 228.3 g/mol

Answers

a. N_4S_4 **b.** $K_2H_8O_2$ **c.** HIO_3
d. $Na_3O_9P_3$ **e.** $C_{21}H_{24}O_9$ **f.** $C_{12}H_{20}O_4$

◆ Learning Exercise 7.6B

Determine the molecular formula for each of the following:

a. Pyrogallol with a composition of C 57.14%, H 4.80%, and O 38.06% and a molar mass of 126.1

b. Triazaborane with a composition B 40.31%, H 7.51%, and N 52.18% and a molar mass of 80.5

c. A substance used to tan leather with a composition K 26.58%, Cr 35.36%, and O 38.07% and a molar mass of 294.2

d. Pyrocatechol, a topic anesthetic with a composition of C 65.44%, H 5.49%, and O 29.06% and a molar mass of 110.1

Answers **a.** $C_6H_6O_3$ **b.** $B_3H_6N_3$ **c.** $K_2Cr_2O_7$ **d.** $C_6H_6O_2$

Checklist for Chapter 7

You are ready to take the practice test for Chapter 7. Be sure you have accomplished the following learning goals for this chapter. If you are not sure, review the section listed at the end of the goal. Then apply your new skills and understanding to the practice test.

After studying Chapter 7, I can successfully:

_____ Determine the atomic mass of an element or formula mass of a compound (7.1).

_____ Determine the number of particles in a mole of a substance (7.2).

_____ Calculate the molar mass given the formula of a substance (7.3).

_____ Convert the grams of a substance to moles, and moles to grams (7.4).

_____ Calculate the percent composition of a compound (7.5).

_____ Determine the empirical formula for a compound (7.5).

_____ Determine the molecular formula for a compound (7.6).

Practice Test for Chapter 7

1. The mass in amu of 125 atoms of Ne atoms is
A. 0.161 amu **B.** 20.28 amu **C.** 125.0 amu
D. 2522 amu **E.** 1.22×10^{25} amu

2. The number of Cu atoms in 3.50×10^4 amu Cu is
A. 350 atoms **B.** 222 atoms **C.** 551 atoms
D. 2.22×10^6 atoms **E.** 3.50×10^4 atoms

3. The number of carbon atoms in 2.0 mol C is
A. 6.0 **B.** 12 **C.** 6.0×10^{23}
D. 3.0×10^{23} **E.** 1.2×10^{24}

4. The number of molecules in 0.25 molNH_3 is
A. 0.25 **B.** 2.5×10^{23} **C.** 4.2×10^{-25}
D. 1.5×10^{23} **E.** 2.4×10^{24}

5. The number of moles in 8.8×10^{24} molecules SO_3 is
A. 0.068 **B.** 2.6 **C.** 1.5 **D.** 15 **E.** 53

6. The moles of oxygen (O) in 2.0 mol of $Al(OH)_3$ is
A. 1 **B.** 2 **C.** 3 **D.** 4 **E.** 6

7. The number of atoms of phosphorus in 1.00 mol Be_3P_2 is
A. 3.01×10^{23} **B.** 6.02×10^{23} **C.** 1.20×10^{23}
D. 9.03×10^{23} **E.** 1.20×10^{24}

8. What is the molar mass of Li_2SO_4?
A. 55.1 g **B.** 62.1 g **C.** 100.1 g **D.** 120.0 g **E.** 103.1 g

9. What is the molar mass of $NaNO_3$?
A. 34.0 g **B.** 37.0 g **C.** 53.0 g **D.** 75.0 g **E.** 85.0 g

10. The number of grams in 0.600 mol Cl_2 is
A. 71.0 g **B.** 21.3 g **C.** 42.5 g **D.** 84.5 g **E.** 4.30 g

11. How many grams are in 4.00 mol NH_3?
A. 4.00 g **B.** 17.0 g **C.** 34.0 g **D.** 68.1 g **E.** 0.240 g

12. How many grams are in 4.50 mol N_2?
A. 6.22 g **B.** 28.0 g **C.** 56.0 g **D.** 112 g **E.** 126 g

13. How many moles is 8.00 g NaOH?
A. 0.100 mol **B.** 0.200 mol **C.** 0.400 mol **D.** 2.00 mol **E.** 4.00 mol

14. The number of moles of aluminum in 54.0 g of Al is
A. 0.500 mol **B.** 1.00 mol **C.** 2.00 mol **D.** 3.00 mol **E.** 4.00 mol

15. The number of moles of water in 3.60 g of H_2O is
A. 0.0500 mol **B.** 0.100 mol **C.** 0.200 mol **D.** 0.300 mol **E.** 0.400 mol

16. What is the number of moles in 2.20 g CO_2?
A. 2.00 mol **B.** 1.00 mol **C.** 0.200 mol **D.** 0.0500 mol **E.** 0.0100 mol

17. 0.200 g H_2 = _____ mol H_2
A. 0.100 mol **B.** 0.200 mol **C.** 0.400 mol **D.** 0.0400 mol **E.** 0.0100 mol

18. The percent by mass of carbon in C_3H_8 is
A. 18.2% **B.** 27.3% **C.** 33.3% **D.** 44.0% **E.** 81.8%

19. What is the empirical formula of a compound that is 27.3% C and 72.7% O?
A. CO **B.** CO_2 **C.** C_2O **D.** C_2O_3 **E.** CO_3

20. What is the empirical formula of a compound that has 3.88 g Cl and 6.12 g O?
A. ClO **B.** Cl_2O_7 **C.** Cl_3O **D.** Cl_2O_3 **E.** ClO_4

Answers to the Practice Test

1. D	**2.** C	**3.** E	**4.** D	**5.** D
6. E	**7.** E	**8.** D	**9.** E	**10.** C
11. D	**12.** E	**13.** B	**14.** C	**15.** C
16. D	**17.** A	**18.** E	**19.** B	**20.** B

Answers and Solutions to Selected Text Problems

Section 7.1

7.1 **a.** $25\ \cancel{\text{O atoms}} \times \frac{16.00\ \text{amu}}{1\ \cancel{\text{O atom}}} = 400.0\ \text{amu}\ (4.000 \times 10^2\ \text{amu})$

b. $1.50 \times 10^5\ \cancel{\text{Cr atoms}} \times \frac{52.00\ \text{amu}}{1\ \cancel{\text{Cr atom}}} = 7.80 \times 10^6\ \text{amu}$

c. $6.24 \times 10^{20}\ \cancel{\text{F atoms}} \times \frac{19.00\ \text{amu}}{1\ \cancel{\text{F atom}}} = 1.19 \times 10^{22}\ \text{amu}$

7.3 **a.** $540\ \cancel{\text{amu Al}} \times \frac{1\ \text{atom Al}}{26.98\ \cancel{\text{amu Al}}} = 20\ \text{atoms Al}$

b. $2.95\ \cancel{\text{amu Ag}} \times \frac{1\ \text{atom Ag}}{107.9\ \cancel{\text{amu Ag}}} = 2.73 \times 10^2\ \text{atoms Ag}$

c. $35\,000\ \cancel{\text{amu Ne}} \times \frac{1\ \text{atom Ne}}{20.18\ \cancel{\text{amu Ne}}} = 1.7 \times 10^3\ \text{atoms Ne}$

7.5 **a.**

$$1\ \cancel{\text{atom S}} \times \frac{32.07\text{ amu}}{1\ \cancel{\text{atom S}}} = 32.07\text{ amu}$$

$$6\ \cancel{\text{atoms F}} \times \frac{19.00\text{ amu}}{1\ \cancel{\text{atom F}}} = \underline{114.0\text{ amu}}$$

146.1 amu (formula mass)

b.

$$1\ \cancel{\text{atom Ca}} \times \frac{40.08\text{ amu}}{1\ \cancel{\text{atom Ca}}} = 40.08\text{ amu}$$

$$2\ \cancel{\text{atoms N}} \times \frac{14.01\text{ amu}}{1\ \cancel{\text{atom N}}} = 28.02\text{ amu}$$

$$6\ \cancel{\text{atoms O}} \times \frac{16.00\text{ amu}}{1\ \cancel{\text{atom O}}} = \underline{96.00\text{ amu}}$$

164.10 amu (formula mass)

c.

$$2\ \cancel{\text{atoms C}} \times \frac{12.01\text{ amu}}{1\ \cancel{\text{atom C}}} = 24.02\text{ amu}$$

$$6\ \cancel{\text{atoms H}} \times \frac{1.008\text{ amu}}{1\ \cancel{\text{atom H}}} = 6.048\text{ amu}$$

$$1\ \cancel{\text{atoms O}} \times \frac{16.00\text{ amu}}{1\ \cancel{\text{atom O}}} = \underline{16.00\text{ amu}}$$

46.07 amu (formula mass)

d.

$$6\ \cancel{\text{atom C}} \times \frac{12.01\text{ amu}}{1\ \cancel{\text{atom C}}} = 72.06\text{ amu}$$

$$12\ \cancel{\text{atoms H}} \times \frac{1.008\text{ amu}}{1\ \cancel{\text{atom H}}} = 12.10\text{ amu}$$

$$6\ \cancel{\text{atoms O}} \times \frac{16.00\text{ amu}}{1\ \cancel{\text{atom O}}} = \underline{96.00\text{ amu}}$$

180.16 amu (formula mass)

7.7 **a.**

$$2\ \cancel{\text{atoms Na}} \times \frac{22.99\text{ amu}}{1\ \cancel{\text{atom Na}}} = 45.98\text{ amu}$$

$$1\ \cancel{\text{atoms S}} \times \frac{32.07\text{ amu}}{1\ \cancel{\text{atom S}}} = 32.07\text{ amu}$$

$$3\ \cancel{\text{atoms O}} \times \frac{16.00\text{ amu}}{1\ \cancel{\text{atom O}}} = \underline{48.00\text{ amu}}$$

126.05 amu (formula mass)

b.

$$1\ \cancel{\text{atom Al}} \times \frac{26.98\text{ amu}}{1\ \cancel{\text{atom Al}}} = 26.98\text{ amu}$$

$$3\ \cancel{\text{atoms O}} \times \frac{16.00\text{ amu}}{1\ \cancel{\text{atom O}}} = 48.00\text{ amu}$$

$$3\ \cancel{\text{atoms H}} \times \frac{1.008\text{ amu}}{1\ \cancel{\text{atom H}}} = \underline{3.024\text{ amu}}$$

78.00 amu (formula mass)

c.

$$1\ \cancel{\text{atom Fe}} \times \frac{55.85\text{ amu}}{1\ \cancel{\text{atom Fe}}} = 55.85\text{ amu}$$

$$1\ \cancel{\text{atom S}} \times \frac{32.07\text{ amu}}{1\ \cancel{\text{atom S}}} = 32.07\text{ amu}$$

$$4\ \cancel{\text{atoms O}} \times \frac{16.00\text{ amu}}{1\ \cancel{\text{atom O}}} = \underline{64.00\text{ amu}}$$

151.92 amu (formula mass)

d.

$$3\ \cancel{\text{atoms Ca}} \times \frac{40.08\text{ amu}}{1\ \cancel{\text{atom Ca}}} = 120.2\text{ amu}$$

$$2\ \cancel{\text{atom P}} \times \frac{30.97\text{ amu}}{1\ \cancel{\text{atom P}}} = 61.94\text{ amu}$$

$$8\ \cancel{\text{atoms O}} \times \frac{16.00\text{ amu}}{1\ \cancel{\text{atom O}}} = \underline{128.0\text{ amu}}$$

310.1 amu (formula mass)

Section 7.2

7.9 The mole is a unit that contains 6.022×10^{23} particles (atoms, molecules of a covalent substance, ions, or formula units of an ionic substance).

7.11 1 mol chlorine atoms contains 6.022×10^{23} atoms of chlorine; 1 mol chlorine molecules contains 6.022×10^{23} molecules of chlorine, which is $2 \times 6.022 \times 10^{23}$ or 1.204×10^{24} atoms of chlorine.

7.13 **a.** $0.500\ \cancel{\text{mol C}} \times \dfrac{6.022 \times 10^{23}\text{ atoms C}}{1\ \cancel{\text{mol C}}} = 3.01 \times 10^{23}\text{ C atoms}$

b. $1.28\ \cancel{\text{mol SO}_2} \times \dfrac{6.022 \times 10^{23}\text{ molecules SO}_2}{1\ \cancel{\text{mol SO}_2}} = 7.71 \times 10^{23}\text{ SO}_2\text{ molecules}$

c. $5.22 \times 10^{22}\ \cancel{\text{atoms Fe}} \times \dfrac{1\text{ mol Fe}}{6.022 \times 10^{23}\ \cancel{\text{atoms Fe}}} = 0.0867\text{ mol Fe}$

d. $8.50 \times 10^{24}\ \cancel{\text{atoms C}_2\text{H}_5\text{OH}} \times \dfrac{1\text{ mol C}_2\text{H}_5\text{OH}}{6.022 \times 10^{23}\ \cancel{\text{atoms C}_2\text{H}_5\text{OH}}} = 14.1\text{ mol C}_2\text{H}_5\text{OH}$

7.15 1 mol H_3PO_4 molecules contains 3 mol H atoms, 1 mol P atoms, and 4 mol O atoms.

a. $2.00\ \cancel{\text{mol H}_3\text{PO}_4} \times \dfrac{3\text{ mol H}}{1\ \cancel{\text{mol H}_3\text{PO}_4}} = 6.00\text{ mol H}$

b. $2.00\ \cancel{\text{mol H}_3\text{PO}_4} \times \dfrac{4\text{ mol O}}{1\ \cancel{\text{mol H}_3\text{PO}_4}} = 8.00\text{ mol O}$

c. $2.00\ \cancel{\text{mol H}_3\text{PO}_4} \times \dfrac{1\ \cancel{\text{mol P}}}{1\ \cancel{\text{mol H}_3\text{PO}_4}} \times \dfrac{6.022 \times 10^{23}\text{ atoms P}}{\cancel{1\text{ mol P}}} = 1.20 \times 10^{24}\text{ P atoms}$

d. $2.00\ \cancel{\text{mol H}_3\text{PO}_4} \times \dfrac{4\ \cancel{\text{mol O}}}{1\ \cancel{\text{mol H}_3\text{PO}_4}} \times \dfrac{6.022 \times 10^{23}\text{ atoms O}}{\cancel{1\text{ mol O}}} = 4.82 \times 10^{24}\text{ O atoms}$

Section 7.3

7.17 **a.** $1\ \cancel{\text{mol Na}} \times \dfrac{22.99\text{ g Na}}{1\ \cancel{\text{mol Na}}} = 22.99\text{ g Na}$

$1\ \cancel{\text{mol Cl}} \times \dfrac{35.45\text{ g Cl}}{1\ \cancel{\text{mol Cl}}} = \underline{35.45\text{ g Cl}}$

58.44 g NaCl (molar mass)

b. $2\ \cancel{\text{mol Fe}} \times \dfrac{55.85\text{ g Fe}}{1\ \cancel{\text{mol Fe}}} = 111.7\text{ g Fe}$

$3\ \cancel{\text{mol O}} \times \dfrac{16.00\text{ g O}}{1\ \cancel{\text{mol O}}} = \underline{48.00\text{ g O}}$

159.7 g Fe_2O_3 (molar mass)

c. $2\ \cancel{\text{mol Li}} \times \dfrac{6.941\text{ g Li}}{1\ \cancel{\text{mol Li}}} = 13.88\text{ g Li}$

$1\ \cancel{\text{mol C}} \times \dfrac{12.01\text{g C}}{1\ \cancel{\text{mol C}}} = 12.01\text{ g C}$

$3\ \cancel{\text{mol O}} \times \dfrac{16.00\text{ g O}}{1\ \cancel{\text{mol O}}} = \underline{48.00\text{ g O}}$

73.89 g Li_2CO_3 (molar mass)

d. 1 mol $Al_2(SO_4)_3$ contains 2 mol Al, 3 mol S, and 12 mol O.

$2\ \cancel{\text{mol Al}} \times \dfrac{26.98\text{ g Al}}{1\ \cancel{\text{mol Al}}} = 53.96\text{ g Al}$

$3\ \cancel{\text{mol S}} \times \dfrac{32.07\text{ g S}}{1\ \cancel{\text{mol S}}} = 96.21\text{ g S}$

$12\ \cancel{\text{mol O}} \times \dfrac{16.00\text{ g O}}{1\ \cancel{\text{mol O}}} = \underline{192.0\text{ g O}}$

342.2 g $Al_2(SO_4)_3$

e. $1\ \cancel{\text{mol Mg}} \times \frac{24.31\text{ g Mg}}{1\ \cancel{\text{mol Mg}}} = 24.31\text{ g Mg}$

$2\ \cancel{\text{mol O}} \times \frac{16.00\text{g O}}{1\ \cancel{\text{mol O}}} = 32.00\text{ g O}$

$2\ \cancel{\text{mol H}} \times \frac{1.008\text{ g H}}{1\ \cancel{\text{mol H}}} = \underline{48.00\text{ g H}}$

58.33 g Mg(OH)_2

f. 1 mol $C_{16}H_{19}N_3O_5S$ contains 16 mol C, 19 mol H, 3 mol N, 5 mol O, and 1 mol S.

$16\ \cancel{\text{mol C}} \times \frac{12.01\text{g C}}{1\ \cancel{\text{mol C}}} = 192.2\text{ g C}$

$19\ \cancel{\text{mol H}} \times \frac{1.008\text{ g H}}{1\ \cancel{\text{mol H}}} = 19.15\text{ g H}$

$3\ \cancel{\text{mol N}} \times \frac{14.01\text{ g N}}{1\ \cancel{\text{mol N}}} = 42.03\text{ g N}$

$5\ \cancel{\text{mol O}} \times \frac{16.00\text{g O}}{1\ \cancel{\text{mol O}}} = 80.00\text{ g O}$

$1\ \cancel{\text{mol S}} \times \frac{32.07\text{ g S}}{1\ \cancel{\text{mol S}}} = \underline{32.07\text{ g S}}$

$365.5\text{ g }C_{16}H_{19}N_3O_5S$

Section 7.4

7.19 **a.** $1\ \cancel{\text{mol Cl}_2} \times \frac{70.90\text{ g Cl}_2}{1\ \cancel{\text{mol Cl}_2}} = 70.90\text{ g Cl}_2$

b. $3\ \cancel{\text{mol C}} \times \frac{12.01\text{ g C}}{1\ \cancel{\text{mol C}}} = 36.03\text{ g C}$

$6\ \cancel{\text{mol H}} \times \frac{1.008\text{ g H}}{1\ \cancel{\text{mol H}}} = 6.048\text{ g H}$

$3\ \cancel{\text{mol O}} \times \frac{16.00\text{ g O}}{1\ \cancel{\text{mol O}}} = \underline{48.00\text{ g O}}$

$90.08\text{ g }C_3H_6O_3$

c. $3\ \cancel{\text{mol Mg}} \times \frac{24.31\text{ g Mg}}{1\ \cancel{\text{mol Mg}}} = 72.93\text{ g Mg}$

$2\ \cancel{\text{mol P}} \times \frac{30.97\text{ g P}}{1\ \cancel{\text{mol P}}} = 61.94\text{ g P}$

$8\ \cancel{\text{mol O}} \times \frac{16.00\text{ g O}}{1\ \cancel{\text{mol O}}} = \underline{128.0\text{ g O}}$

$262.9\text{ g }C_3H_6O_3$

d. $1\ \cancel{\text{mol Al}} \times \frac{26.98\text{ g Al}}{1\ \cancel{\text{mol Al}}} = 26.98\text{ g Al}$

$3\ \cancel{\text{mol F}} \times \frac{19.00\text{ g F}}{1\ \cancel{\text{mol F}}} = \underline{57.00\text{ g O}}$

83.98 g AlF_3

e. $2\ \cancel{\text{mol C}} \times \frac{12.01\text{ g C}}{1\ \cancel{\text{mol C}}} = 24.02\text{ g C}$

$4\ \cancel{\text{mol H}} \times \frac{1.008\text{ g H}}{1\ \cancel{\text{mol H}}} = 4.032\text{ g H}$

$2\ \cancel{\text{mol Cl}} \times \frac{35.45\text{ g Cl}}{1\ \cancel{\text{mol Cl}}} = \underline{70.90\text{ g Cl}}$

$98.95\text{ g }C_2H_4Cl_2$

f. $2\ \cancel{\text{mol Al}} \times \frac{26.98\text{ g Al}}{1\ \cancel{\text{mol Al}}} = 53.96\text{ g Al}$

$3\ \cancel{\text{mol S}} \times \frac{32.07\text{ g S}}{1\ \cancel{\text{mol S}}} = 96.21\text{ g S}$

$12\ \cancel{\text{mol O}} \times \frac{16.00\text{ g O}}{1\ \cancel{\text{mol O}}} = \underline{192.0\text{ g O}}$

$342.2\text{ g }Al_2(SO_4)_3$

7.21 **a.** $1.50\ \cancel{\text{mol Na}} \times \frac{22.99\text{ g Na}}{1\ \cancel{\text{mol Na}}} = 34.5\text{ g Na}$

b. $2.80\ \cancel{\text{mol Ca}} \times \frac{40.08\text{ g Ca}}{1\ \cancel{\text{mol Ca}}} = 112\text{ g Ca}$

c. $0.125\ \cancel{\text{mol }CO_2} \times \frac{44.01\text{ g }CO_2}{1\ \cancel{\text{mol }CO_2}} = 5.50\text{ g }CO_2$

d. $0.0485\ \cancel{\text{mol }Na_2CO_3} \times \frac{105.99\text{ g }Na_2CO_3}{1\ \cancel{\text{mol }Na_2CO_3}} = 5.14\text{ g }Na_2CO_3$

e. $7.14 \times 10^2\ \cancel{\text{mol }PCl_3} \times \frac{137.32\text{ g }PCl_3}{1\ \cancel{\text{mol }PCl_3}} = 9.80 \times 10^4\text{ g }PCl_3$

7.23 **a.** $0.150\ \cancel{\text{mol Ne}} \times \frac{20.18\text{ g Ne}}{1\ \cancel{\text{mol Ne}}} = 3.03\text{ g Ne}$

b. $0.150\ \cancel{\text{mol }I_2} \times \frac{253.8\text{ g }I_2}{1\ \cancel{\text{mol }I_2}} = 38.1\text{ g }I_2$

c. $0.150\ \cancel{\text{mol }Na_2O} \times \frac{61.98\text{ g }Na_2O}{1\ \cancel{\text{mol }Na_2O}} = 9.30\text{ g }Na_2O$

d. $0.150\ \cancel{\text{mol }Ca(NO_3)_2} \times \frac{164.10\text{ g }Ca(NO_3)_2}{1\ \cancel{\text{mol }Ca(NO_3)_2}} = 24.6\text{ g }Ca(NO_3)_2$

e. $0.150\ \cancel{\text{mol }C_6H_{14}} \times \frac{86.17\text{ g }C_6H_{14}}{1\ \cancel{\text{mol }C_6H_{14}}} = 12.9\text{ g }Ca(NO_3)_2$

7.25 **a.** $82.0\ \cancel{\text{g Ag}} \times \frac{1\text{ mol Ag}}{107.9\ \cancel{\text{g Ag}}} = 0.760\text{ mol Ag}$

b. $0.188\ \cancel{\text{g C}} \times \frac{1\text{ mol C}}{12.01\ \cancel{\text{g C}}} = 0.0240\text{ mol C}$

c. $15.0\ \cancel{\text{g }NH_3} \times \frac{1\text{mol }NH_3}{17.03\ \cancel{\text{g }NH_3}} = 0.881\text{ mol }NH_3$

d. $7.25\ \cancel{\text{g }C_3H_8} \times \frac{1\text{ mol }C_3H_8}{44.09\ \cancel{\text{g }C_3H_8}} = 0.164\text{ mol }C_3H_8$

e. $245\ \cancel{\text{g }Fe_2O_3} \times \frac{1\text{ mol }Fe_2O_3}{159.7\ \cancel{\text{g }Fe_2O_3}} = 1.53\text{ mol }Fe_2O_3$

7.27 **a.** $25.0\ \cancel{\text{g He}} \times \frac{1\text{ mol He}}{4.003\ \cancel{\text{g He}}} = 6.25\text{ mol He}$

b. $25.0\ \cancel{\text{g }O_2} \times \frac{1\text{ mol }O_2}{32.00\ \cancel{\text{g }O_2}} = 0.781\text{ mol }O_2$

c. $25.0\ \cancel{\text{g }Al(OH)_3} \times \frac{1\text{ mol }Al(OH)_3}{78.00\ \cancel{\text{g }Al(OH)_3}} = 0.320\text{ mol }Al(OH)_3$

d. $25.0\ \cancel{\text{g }Ga_2S_3} \times \frac{1\text{ mol }Ga_2S_3}{235.65\ \cancel{\text{g }Ga_2S_3}} = 0.106\text{ mol }Ga_2S_3$

e. $25.0\ \cancel{\text{g }C_4H_{10}} \times \frac{1\text{ mol }C_4H_{10}}{58.12\ \cancel{\text{g }C_4H_{10}}} = 0.430\text{ mol }C_4H_{10}$

7.29 **a.** $25.0\ \text{g C} \times \frac{1\ \text{mol C}}{12.01\ \text{g C}} \times \frac{6.022 \times 10^{23}\ \text{C atoms}}{1\ \text{mol C}} = 1.25 \times 10^{24}\ \text{C atoms}$

b. $0.688\ \text{mol C} \times \frac{6.022 \times 10^{23}\ \text{C atoms}}{1\ \text{mol C}} = 4.14 \times 10^{24}\ \text{C atoms}$

c. $275\ \text{g } C_3H_8 \times \frac{1\ \text{mol } C_3H_8}{44.09\ \text{g } C_3H_8} \times \frac{3\ \text{mol C}}{1\ \text{mol } C_3H_8} \times \frac{6.022 \times 10^{23}\ \text{C atoms}}{1\ \text{mol C}} = 1.13 \times 10^{25}\ \text{C atoms}$

d. $1.84\ \text{mol } C_2H_6O \times \frac{2\ \text{mol C}}{1\ \text{mol } C_2H_6O} \times \frac{6.022 \times 10^{23}\ \text{C atoms}}{1\ \text{mol C}} = 2.22 \times 10^{24}\ \text{C atoms}$

e. $7.5 \times 10^{24}\ \text{molecules } CH_4 \times \frac{1\ \text{atom C}}{1\ \text{molecule } CH_4} = 7.5 \times 10^{24}\ \text{C atoms}$

7.31 **a.** $1.50\ \text{mol } C_3H_8 \times \frac{44.09\ \text{g } C_3H_8}{1\ \text{mol } C_3H_8} = 6.61\ \text{g propane } (C_3H_8)$

b. $34.0\ \text{g } C_3H_8 \times \frac{1\ \text{mol } C_3H_8}{44.09\ \text{g } C_3H_8} = 0.771\ \text{mol propane } (C_3H_8)$

c. $0.771\ \text{mol } C_3H_8 \times \frac{3\ \text{mol C}}{1\ \text{mol } C_3H_8} \times \frac{12.01\ \text{g C}}{1\ \text{mol C}} = 27.8\ \text{g C}$

d. $0.254\ \text{g } C_3H_8 \times \frac{1\ \text{mol } C_3H_8}{44.09\ \text{g } C_3H_8} \times \frac{8\ \text{mol H}}{1\ \text{mol } C_3H_8} \times \frac{6.022 \times 10^{23}\ \text{atoms H}}{1\ \text{mol H}} = 2.78 \times 10^{22}\ \text{atoms H}$

Section 7.5

7.33 **a.** $1\ \text{mol Mg} \times \frac{24.31\ \text{g Mg}}{1\ \text{mol Mg}} = 24.31\ \text{g Mg}$

$2\ \text{mol F} \times \frac{19.00\ \text{g F}}{1\ \text{mol F}} = \frac{38.00\ \text{g F}}{62.31\ \text{g } MgF_2}$

$\frac{24.31\ \text{g Mg}}{62.31\ \text{g } MgF_2} \times 100\% = 39.01\%\ \text{Mg}$

$\frac{38.00\ \text{g F}}{62.31\ \text{g } MgF_2} \times 100\% = 60.99\%\ \text{F}$

b. $1\ \text{mol Ca} \times \frac{40.08\ \text{g Ca}}{1\ \text{mol Ca}} = 40.08\ \text{g Ca}$

$2\ \text{mol O} \times \frac{16.00\ \text{g O}}{1\ \text{mol O}} = 32.00\ \text{g O}$

$2\ \text{mol H} \times \frac{1.008\ \text{g H}}{1\ \text{mol H}} = \frac{2.016\ \text{g H}}{74.10\ \text{g } Ca(OH)_2}$

$\frac{40.08\ \text{g Ca}}{74.10\ \text{g } Ca(OH)_2} \times 100\% = 54.09\%\ \text{Ca}$

$\frac{32.00\ \text{g O}}{74.10\ \text{g } Ca(OH)_2} \times 100\% = 42.18\%\ \text{O}$

$\frac{2.016\ \text{g H}}{74.10\ \text{g } Ca(OH)_2} \times 100\% = 2.72\%\ \text{H}$ (rounded to 0.01%)

c. $4\ \cancel{\text{mol C}} \times \frac{12.01\text{ g C}}{1\ \cancel{\text{mol C}}} = 48.04\text{ g C}$

$8\ \cancel{\text{mol H}} \times \frac{1.008\text{ g H}}{1\ \cancel{\text{mol H}}} = 8.06\text{ g H}$ (rounded to 0.01%)

$4\ \cancel{\text{mol O}} \times \frac{16.00\text{ g O}}{1\ \cancel{\text{mol O}}} = \underline{64.00\text{ g O}}$

$120.10\text{ g } C_4H_8O_4$

$\frac{48.04\text{ g C}}{120.10\text{ g } C_4H_8O_4} \times 100\% = 40.00\%\text{ C}$

$\frac{8.064\text{ g H}}{120.10\text{ g } C_4H_8O_4} \times 100\% = 6.71\%\text{ H}$ (rounded to 0.01%)

$\frac{64.00\text{ g O}}{120.10\text{ g } C_4H_8O_4} \times 100\% = 53.29\%\text{ O}$

d. $3\ \cancel{\text{mol N}} \times \frac{14.01\text{ g N}}{1\ \cancel{\text{mol N}}} = 42.03\text{ g N}$

$12\ \cancel{\text{mol H}} \times \frac{1.008\text{ g H}}{1\ \cancel{\text{mol H}}} = 12.10\text{ g H}$

$1\ \cancel{\text{mol P}} \times \frac{30.97\text{ g P}}{1\ \cancel{\text{mol P}}} = 30.97\text{ g P}$

$4\ \cancel{\text{mol O}} \times \frac{16.00\text{ g O}}{1\ \cancel{\text{mol O}}} = \underline{64.00\text{ g O}}$

$149.10\text{ g } C_4H_8O_4$

$\frac{43.03\text{ g N}}{149.10\text{ g } C_4H_8O_4} \times 100\% = 28.19\%\text{ N}$

$\frac{12.10\text{ g H}}{149.10\text{ g } C_4H_8O_4} \times 100\% = 8.12\%\text{ H}$ (rounded to 0.01%)

$\frac{30.97\text{ g P}}{149.10\text{ g } C_4H_8O_4} \times 100\% = 20.77\%\text{ P}$

$\frac{64.00\text{ g O}}{149.10\text{ g } C_4H_8O_4} \times 100\% = 42.92\%\text{ O}$

e. $17\ \cancel{\text{mol C}} \times \frac{12.01\text{ g C}}{1\ \cancel{\text{mol C}}} = 204.2\text{ g C}$

$19\ \cancel{\text{mol H}} \times \frac{1.008\text{ g H}}{1\ \cancel{\text{mol H}}} = 19.15\text{ g H}$

$1\ \cancel{\text{mol N}} \times \frac{14.01\text{ g N}}{1\ \cancel{\text{mol N}}} = 14.01\text{ g N}$

$3\ \cancel{\text{mol O}} \times \frac{16.00\text{ g O}}{1\ \cancel{\text{mol O}}} = \underline{48.00\text{ g O}}$

$285.3\text{ g } C_{17}H_{19}NO_3$

$\frac{204.2\text{ g C}}{285.3\text{ g } C_{17}H_{19}NO_3} \times 100\% = 71.57\%\text{ C}$

$\frac{19.15\text{ g H}}{285.3\text{ g } C_{17}H_{19}NO_3} \times 100\% = 6.71\%\text{ H}$ (rounded to 0.01%)

$\frac{14.01\text{ g N}}{285.3\text{ g } C_{17}H_{19}NO_3} \times 100\% = 4.91\%\text{ N}$ (rounded to 0.01%)

$\frac{48.00\text{ g O}}{285.3\text{ g } C_{17}H_{19}NO_3} \times 100\% = 16.82\%\text{ O}$

7.35 **a.** $2 \text{ mol N} \times \frac{14.01 \text{ g N}}{1 \text{ mol N}} = 28.02 \text{ g N}$

$5 \text{ mol O} \times \frac{16.00 \text{ g O}}{1 \text{ mol O}} = \frac{80.00 \text{ g O}}{108.20 \text{ g } N_2O_5}$

$\frac{28.02 \text{ g N}}{108.20 \text{ g } N_2O_5} \times 100\% = 25.94\% \text{ N}$

b. $2 \text{ mol N} \times \frac{14.01 \text{ g N}}{1 \text{ mol H}} = 28.02 \text{ g N}$

$4 \text{ mol H} \times \frac{1.008 \text{ g H}}{1 \text{ mol H}} = 4.032 \text{ g H}$

$3 \text{ mol O} \times \frac{16.00 \text{ g O}}{1 \text{ mol O}} = \frac{48.00 \text{ g O}}{80.05 \text{ g } NH_4NO_3}$

$\frac{28.02 \text{ g N}}{80.05 \text{ g } NH_4NO_3} \times 100\% = 35.00\% \text{ N}$

c. $2 \text{ mol C} \times \frac{12.01 \text{ g C}}{1 \text{ mol C}} = 24.02 \text{ g C}$

$8 \text{ mol H} \times \frac{1.008 \text{ g H}}{1 \text{ mol H}} = 8.064 \text{ g H}$

$3 \text{ mol N} \times \frac{14.01 \text{ g N}}{1 \text{ mol N}} = \frac{28.02 \text{ g N}}{60.10 \text{ g } C_2H_8N_2}$

$\frac{28.02 \text{ g N}}{60.10 \text{ g } C_2H_8N_2} \times 100\% = 46.62\% \text{ N}$

d. $9 \text{ mol C} \times \frac{12.01 \text{ g C}}{1 \text{ mol C}} = 108.0 \text{ g C}$

$15 \text{ mol H} \times \frac{1.008 \text{ g H}}{1 \text{ mol H}} = 15.12 \text{ g H}$

$5 \text{ mol N} \times \frac{14.01 \text{ g N}}{1 \text{ mol N}} = 70.05 \text{ g N}$

$1 \text{ mol O} \times \frac{16.00 \text{ g O}}{1 \text{ mol O}} = \frac{16.00 \text{ g O}}{209.3 \text{ g } C_9H_{15}N_5O}$

$\frac{70.05 \text{ g N}}{209.3 \text{ g } C_9H_{15}N_5O} \times 100\% = 33.48\% \text{ N}$

e. $14 \text{ mol C} \times \frac{12.01 \text{ g C}}{1 \text{ mol C}} = 168.1 \text{ g C}$

$22 \text{ mol H} \times \frac{1.008 \text{ g H}}{1 \text{ mol H}} = 22.18 \text{ g H}$

$2 \text{ mol N} \times \frac{14.01 \text{ g N}}{1 \text{ mol N}} = 28.02 \text{ g N}$

$1 \text{ mol O} \times \frac{16.00 \text{ g O}}{1 \text{ mol O}} = \frac{16.00 \text{ g O}}{234.3 \text{ g } C_{14}H_{22}N_2O}$

$\frac{28.02 \text{ g N}}{234.3 \text{ g } C_{14}H_{22}N_2O} \times 100\% = 11.96\% \text{ N}$

7.37 **a.** $3.57 \cancel{\text{g N}} \times \dfrac{1 \text{ mol N}}{14.01 \cancel{\text{g N}}} = 0.255 \text{ mol N}$

$2.04 \cancel{\text{g O}} \times \dfrac{1 \text{ mol O}}{16.00 \cancel{\text{g O}}} = 0.128 \text{ mol O}$ (smallest number of moles)

$\dfrac{0.255 \text{ mol N}}{0.128} = 1.99 \text{ mol N} \rightarrow 2$ $\dfrac{0.128 \text{ mol O}}{0.128} = 1.00 \text{ mol O}$

Empirical formula = $\mathbf{N_2O}$

b. $7.00 \cancel{\text{g C}} \times \dfrac{1 \text{ mol C}}{12.01 \cancel{\text{g C}}} = 0.583 \text{ mol C}$ (smallest number of moles)

$1.75 \cancel{\text{g H}} \times \dfrac{1 \text{ mol H}}{1.008 \cancel{\text{g H}}} = 1.74 \text{ mol H}$

$\dfrac{0.583 \text{ mol C}}{0.583} = 1.00 \text{ mol C}$ $\dfrac{1.74 \text{ mol H}}{0.583} = 2.98 \text{ mol H} \rightarrow 3$

Empirical formula = $\mathbf{CH_3}$

c. $0.175 \cancel{\text{g H}} \times \dfrac{1 \text{ mol H}}{1.008 \cancel{\text{g H}}} = 0.174 \text{ mol H}$

$2.44 \cancel{\text{g N}} \times \dfrac{1 \text{ mol N}}{14.01 \cancel{\text{g N}}} = 0.174 \text{ mol N}$ (smallest number of moles)

$8.38 \cancel{\text{g O}} \times \dfrac{1 \text{ mol O}}{16.00 \cancel{\text{g O}}} = 0.524 \text{ mol O}$

$\dfrac{0.174 \text{ mol H}}{0.174} = 1.00 \text{ mol H}$ $\dfrac{0.174 \text{ mol N}}{0.174} = 1.00 \text{ mol O}$

$\dfrac{0.524 \text{ mol O}}{0.174} = 3.01 \text{ mol O}$ Empirical formula = $\mathbf{HNO_3}$

d. $2.06 \cancel{\text{g Ca}} \times \dfrac{1 \text{ mol Ca}}{1.008 \cancel{\text{g Ca}}} = 0.0514 \text{ mol Ca}$

$2.66 \cancel{\text{g Cr}} \times \dfrac{1 \text{ mol Cr}}{52.00 \cancel{\text{g Cr}}} = 0.0512 \text{ mol Cr}$ (smallest number of moles)

$3.28 \cancel{\text{g O}} \times \dfrac{1 \text{ mol O}}{16.00 \cancel{\text{g O}}} = 0.205 \text{ mol O}$

$\dfrac{0.0514 \text{ mol Ca}}{0.0512} = 1.00 \text{ mol Ca}$ $\dfrac{0.0512 \text{ mol Cr}}{0.0512} = 1.00 \text{ mol Cr}$

$\dfrac{0.205 \text{ mol O}}{0.0512} = 4.00 \text{ mol O}$ Empirical formula = $\mathbf{CaCrO_4}$

7.39 11.44 g compound (S and F) – 2.51 g S = 8.93 g F

$2.51 \cancel{\text{g S}} \times \dfrac{1 \text{ mol S}}{32.07 \cancel{\text{g S}}} = 0.0783 \text{ mol S}$ (smallest number of moles)

$8.93 \cancel{\text{g F}} \times \dfrac{1 \text{ mol F}}{19.00 \cancel{\text{g F}}} = 0.470 \text{ mol F}$

$\dfrac{0.0783 \text{ mol S}}{0.0783 \text{ mol}} = 1.00 \text{ mol S}$ $\dfrac{0.470 \text{ mol F}}{0.0783} = 6.00 \text{ mol F}$

Empirical formula = $\mathbf{SF_6}$

7.41 **a.** $70.9\ \cancel{g\ K} \times \frac{1\ mol\ K}{39.01\ \cancel{g\ K}} = 1.81\ mol\ K$

$29.1\ \cancel{g\ S} \times \frac{1\ mol\ S}{32.07\ \cancel{g\ S}} = 0.907\ mol\ S$ (smallest number of moles)

$\frac{1.81\ mol\ K}{0.907} = 2.00\ mol\ K$ $\qquad \frac{0.907\ mol\ S}{0.907} = 1.00\ mol\ S$

Empirical formula = $\mathbf{K_2S}$

b. $55.0\ \cancel{g\ Ga} \times \frac{1\ mol\ Ga}{69.72\ \cancel{g\ Ga}} = 0.789\ mol\ Ga$ (smallest number of moles)

$45.0\ \cancel{g\ F} \times \frac{1\ mol\ F}{19.00\ \cancel{g\ F}} = 2.36\ mol\ F$

$\frac{0.789\ mol\ S}{0.789} = 1.00\ mol\ Ga$ $\qquad \frac{2.36\ mol\ F}{0.789} = 2.99\ mol\ F \rightarrow 3\ F$

Empirical formula = $\mathbf{GaF_3}$

c. $31.0\ \cancel{g\ B} \times \frac{1\ mol\ B}{10.81\ \cancel{g\ B}} = 2.87\ mol\ B$ (smallest number of moles)

$69.0\ \cancel{g\ O} \times \frac{1\ mol\ O}{16.00\ \cancel{g\ O}} = 4.31\ mol\ O$

$\frac{2.87\ mol\ B}{2.87} = 1.00\ mol\ B$ $\qquad \frac{4.31\ mol\ O}{2.87} = 1.50\ mol\ O$

$1.00\ mol\ B \times 2 = 2.00\ mol\ B$ $\qquad 1.50\ mol\ O \times 2 = 3.00\ mol\ O$

Empirical formula = $\mathbf{B_2O_3}$

d. $18.8\ \cancel{g\ Li} \times \frac{1\ mol\ Li}{6.941\ \cancel{g\ Li}} = 2.71\ mol\ Li$

$16.3\ g\ \cancel{g\ C} \times \frac{1\ mol\ C}{12.01\ \cancel{g\ C}} = 1.36\ mol\ C$ (smallest number of moles)

$64.9\ \cancel{g\ O} \times \frac{1\ mol\ O}{16.00\ \cancel{g\ O}} = 4.06\ mol\ O$

$\frac{2.71\ mol\ Li}{1.36} = 1.99\ mol\ Li \rightarrow 2\ Li$ $\qquad \frac{1.36\ mol\ C}{1.36} = 1.00\ mol\ C$

$\frac{4.06\ mol\ O}{1.36} = 2.98\ mol \rightarrow 3\ O$

Empirical formula = Li_2CO_3

e. $51.7\ \cancel{g\ C} \times \frac{1\ mol\ C}{12.01\ \cancel{g\ C}} = 4.31\ mol\ C$ $\qquad 6.90\ \cancel{g\ H} \times \frac{1\ mol\ H}{1.008\ \cancel{g\ H}} = 6.85\ mol\ H$

$41.3\ \cancel{g\ O} \times \frac{1\ mol\ O}{16.00\ \cancel{g\ O}} = 2.58\ mol\ O$ (smallest number of moles)

$\frac{4.31\ mol\ C}{2.58} = 1.67\ mol\ C$ $\qquad \frac{6.85\ mol\ H}{2.58} = 2.66\ mol\ H$

$\frac{2.58\ mol\ O}{2.58} = 1.00\ mol\ O$

$1.67\ mol\ C \times 3 = 5.01\ mol\ C \rightarrow 5\ C$ $\qquad 2.66\ mol\ H \times 3 = 7.98\ mol\ H \rightarrow 8\ H$

$1.00\ mol\ O \times 3 = 3.00\ mol\ O$ $\qquad$ Empirical formula = $\mathbf{C_5H_8O_3}$

Section 7.6

7.43 **a.** HO $2\ H \div 2 = 1\ H$ and $2\ O \div 2 = 1\ O$

b. C_3H_2 $18\ C \div 6 = 3\ C$ and $12\ H \div 6 = 2$

c. C_5H_8O $10\ C \div 2 = 5\ C$ $16\ H \div 2 = 8\ H$ $2\ O \div 2 = 1\ O$

d. $C_3H_6N_2$ $9\ C \div 3 = 3\ C$ $18\ H \div 3 = 6\ H$ $6\ N \div 3 = 2\ N$

e. CH_2NO $2\ C \div 2 = 1\ C$ $4\ H \div 2 = 2\ H$ $2\ N \div 2 = 1\ N$ $2\ O \div 2 = 1\ O$

7.45 mass of CH_2O = 12.01 + 2(1.008) + 16.00 = 30.03 g

$\frac{180 \text{ g (molar mass)}}{30.03 \text{ g (empirical mass)}} = 6$ $CH_2O \times 6 = C_6H_{12}O_6$

7.47 mass of empirical formula CH = 12.01 + 1.008 = 13.02 g

benzene $\frac{78 \text{ g (molar mass)}}{13.02 \text{ g (empirical mass)}} = 6.0$ $CH \times 6 = C_6H_6$

acetylene $\frac{26 \text{ g (molar mass)}}{13.02 \text{ g (mass of empirical formula)}} = 2.0$ $CH \times 2 = C_2H_2$

7.49 In 100 g compound, there is 48.64 g C, 8.16 g H, and 43.20 g O.

moles of C = $48.64\ \cancel{g\ C} \times \frac{1 \text{ mol C}}{12.01\ \cancel{g\ C}}$ = 4.050 mol C

moles of H = $8.16\ \cancel{g\ H} \times \frac{1 \text{ mol H}}{1.008\ \cancel{g\ H}}$ = 8.10 mol H

moles of O = $43.20\ \cancel{g\ O} \times \frac{1 \text{ mol O}}{16.00\ \cancel{g\ O}}$ = 2.70 mol O (smallest number of moles)

$\frac{4.050 \text{ mol C}}{2.70}$ = 1.50 mol C $\frac{8.10 \text{ mol H}}{2.70}$ = 3.00 mol H

$\frac{2.70 \text{ mol O}}{2.70}$ = 1.00 mol O

1.50 mol C x 2 = 3.00 mol C 3.00 mol O x 2 = 6.00 mol H 1.00 mol O x 2 = 2.00 mol O

empirical formula $C_3H_6O_2$

mass of $C_3H_6O_2$ = 3 x 12.01 + 6 x 1.008 + 2 x 16.00 = 74.08 g

$\frac{148 \text{ g (molar mass)}}{74.08 \text{ g (mass of empirical formula)}} = 2.00$

2 x (empirical formula $C_3H_6O_2$) = molecular formula $C_6H_{12}O_4$

7.51 In 100 g compound, there are 54.14 g C, 4.80 g H, and 38.06 g O.

moles of C = $54.14\ \cancel{g\ C} \times \frac{1 \text{ mol C}}{12.01\ \cancel{g\ C}}$ = 4.758 mol C

moles of H = $4.80\ \cancel{g\ H} \times \frac{1 \text{ mol H}}{1.008\ \cancel{g\ H}}$ = 4.76 mol H

moles of O = $38.06\ \cancel{g\ O} \times \frac{1 \text{ mol O}}{16.00\ \cancel{g\ O}}$ = 2.379 mol O (smallest number of moles)

$\frac{4.758 \text{ mol C}}{2.379}$ = 2.00 mol C $\frac{4.76 \text{ mol H}}{2.379}$ = 2.00 mol H

$\frac{2.379 \text{ mol O}}{2.379}$ = 1.00 mol O

empirical formula $C_2H_2O_1$

mass of $C_2H_2O_1$ = 2 x 12.01 + 2 x 1.008 + 1 x 16.00 = 42.04 g

$\frac{168.1 \text{ g (molar mass)}}{42.08 \text{ g (mass of empirical formula)}}$ = 3.99 → 4.00

4 x (empirical formula C_2H_2O) = molecular formula $C_8H_8O_4$

7.53 In 100 g compound, there are 74.0 g C and 8.7 g H. 100 g – (74.0 g + 8.7 g) = 17.3 g N

moles of C = 74.0 $\cancel{\text{g C}}$ x $\frac{1 \text{ mol C}}{12.01 \cancel{\text{g C}}}$ = 6.16 mol C

moles of H = 8.7 $\cancel{\text{g H}}$ x $\frac{1 \text{ mol H}}{1.008 \cancel{\text{g H}}}$ = 8.6 mol H

moles of N = 17.3 $\cancel{\text{g N}}$ x $\frac{1 \text{ mol N}}{14.01 \cancel{\text{g N}}}$ = 1.23 mol N (smallest number of moles)

$\frac{6.16 \text{ mol C}}{1.23}$ = 5.01 mol C $\frac{8.6 \text{ mol H}}{1.23}$ = 7.0 mol H

$\frac{1.23 \text{ mol N}}{1.23}$ = 1.00 mol N

empirical formula $C_5H_7N_1$

mass of $C_5H_7N_1$ = 5 x 12.01 + 7 x 1.008 + 1 x 14.01 = 81.12 g

$\frac{162 \text{ g (molar mass)}}{81.12 \text{ g (mass of empirical formula)}}$ = 2.00

2 x (empirical formula C_5H_7N) = molecular formula $C_{10}H_{14}N_2$

Answers to Additional Questions and Problems

7.59 **a.** 1 $\cancel{\text{Fe atom}}$ x $\frac{55.85 \text{ amu}}{1 \cancel{\text{Fe atom}}}$ = 55.85 amu

1 $\cancel{\text{S atom}}$ x $\frac{32.07 \text{ amu}}{1 \cancel{\text{S atom}}}$ = 32.07 amu

4 $\cancel{\text{O atoms}}$ x $\frac{16.00 \text{ amu}}{1 \cancel{\text{O atom}}}$ = $\underline{64.00 \text{ amu}}$
151.92 amu

b. 1 $\cancel{\text{Ca atom}}$ x $\frac{40.08 \text{ amu}}{1 \cancel{\text{Ca atom}}}$ = 40.08 amu

2 $\cancel{\text{I atoms}}$ x $\frac{126.9 \text{ amu}}{1 \cancel{\text{I atom}}}$ = 253.8 amu

6 $\cancel{\text{O atoms}}$ x $\frac{16.00 \text{ amu}}{1 \cancel{\text{O atom}}}$ = $\underline{96.00 \text{ amu}}$
389.9 amu

c. 5 $\cancel{\text{C atoms}}$ x $\frac{12.01 \text{ amu}}{1 \cancel{\text{C atom}}}$ = 60.05 amu

8 $\cancel{\text{H atom}}$ x $\frac{1.008 \text{ amu}}{1 \cancel{\text{H atom}}}$ = 8.064amu

1 $\cancel{\text{N atom}}$ x $\frac{14.01 \text{ amu}}{1 \cancel{\text{N atom}}}$ = 14.01 amu

1 $\cancel{\text{Na atom}}$ x $\frac{22.99 \text{ amu}}{1 \cancel{\text{Na atom}}}$ = 22.99 amu

4 $\cancel{\text{O atom}}$ x $\frac{16.00 \text{ amu}}{1 \cancel{\text{O atom}}}$ = $\underline{64.00 \text{ amu}}$
169.11 amu

d. $6\ \cancel{\text{C atoms}} \times \dfrac{12.01\ \text{amu}}{1\ \cancel{\text{C atom}}} = 72.06\ \text{amu}$

$12\ \cancel{\text{H atom}} \times \dfrac{1.008\ \text{amu}}{1\ \cancel{\text{H atom}}} = 12.10\text{amu}$

$2\ \cancel{\text{O atom}} \times \dfrac{16.00\ \text{amu}}{1\ \cancel{\text{O atom}}} = \underline{32.00\ \text{amu}}$

116.16 amu

7.61 **a.** $2\ \cancel{\text{mol K}} \times \dfrac{39.10\ \text{g K}}{1\ \cancel{\text{mol K}}} = 78.20\ \text{g K}$

$1\ \cancel{\text{mol Cr}} \times \dfrac{52.00\ \text{g Cr}}{1\ \cancel{\text{mol Cr}}} = 52.00\ \text{g Cr}$

$4\ \cancel{\text{mol O}} \times \dfrac{16.00\ \text{g O}}{1\ \cancel{\text{mol O}}} = \underline{64.00\ \text{g O}}$

194.20 g K_2CrO_4

$\dfrac{78.20\ \text{g K}}{194.20\ \text{g}\ K_2CrO_4} \times 100\% = 40.27\%\ \text{K}$

$\dfrac{52.00\ \text{g Cr}}{194.20\ \text{g}\ K_2CrO_4} \times 100\% = 26.78\%\ \text{Cr}$

$\dfrac{64.00\ \text{g O}}{194.20\ \text{g}\ K_2CrO_4} \times 100\% = 32.96\%\ \text{O}$

b. $1\ \cancel{\text{mol Al}} \times \dfrac{26.98\ \text{g Al}}{1\ \cancel{\text{mol Al}}} = 26.98\ \text{g Al}$

$3\ \cancel{\text{mol H}} \times \dfrac{1.008\ \text{g H}}{1\ \cancel{\text{mol H}}} = 3.024\ \text{g H}$

$3\ \cancel{\text{mol C}} \times \dfrac{12.01\ \text{g C}}{1\ \cancel{\text{mol C}}} = 36.03\ \text{g C}$

$9\ \cancel{\text{mol O}} \times \dfrac{16.00\ \text{g O}}{1\ \cancel{\text{mol O}}} = \underline{144.0\ \text{g O}}$

210.0 g $Al(HCO_3)_3$

$\dfrac{26.98\ \text{g Al}}{210.0\ \text{g}\ Al(HCO_3)_3} \times 100\% = 12.85\%\ \text{Al}$

$\dfrac{3.024\ \text{g H}}{210.0\ \text{g}\ Al(HCO_3)_3} \times 100\% = 1.44\%\ \text{H}$ (rounded to 0.01%)

$\dfrac{36.03\ \text{g C}}{210.0\ \text{g}\ Al(HCO_3)_3} \times 100\% = 17.16\%\ \text{C}$

$\dfrac{144.0\ \text{g O}}{210.0\ \text{g}\ Al(HCO_3)_3} \times 100\% = 68.57\%\ \text{O}$

c. $6\ \cancel{\text{mol C}} \times \dfrac{12.01\ \text{g C}}{1\ \cancel{\text{mol C}}} = 72.06\ \text{g}$ $\quad 12\ \cancel{\text{mol H}} \times \dfrac{1.008\ \text{g H}}{1\ \cancel{\text{mol H}}} = 12.10\ \text{g}$

$6\ \cancel{\text{mol O}} \times \dfrac{16.00\ \text{amu}}{1\ \cancel{\text{O atom}}} = \underline{96.00\ \text{g}}$

180.16 g

$\dfrac{72.06\ \text{g C}}{180.16\ \text{g}\ C_6H_{12}O_6} \times 100\% = 40.00\%\ \text{C}$

$\dfrac{96.00\ \text{g O}}{180.16\ \text{g}\ C_6H_{12}O_6} \times 100\% = 6.71\%\ \text{H}$ (rounded to 0.01%)

$\dfrac{96.00\ \text{g O}}{180.16\ \text{g}\ C_6H_{12}O_6} \times 100\% = 53.29\%\ \text{O}$

7.63 **a.** $C_{10}H_8N_2O_2S_2 \div 2 = C_5H_4NOS$ (empirical formula)

b.

$10\ \cancel{mol\ C} \times \frac{12.01\ g\ C}{1\ \cancel{mol\ C}} = 120.1\ g\ C$

$8\ \cancel{mol\ H} \times \frac{1.008\ g\ H}{1\ \cancel{mol\ H}} = 8.064\ g\ H$

$2\ \cancel{mol\ N} \times \frac{14.01\ g\ N}{1\ \cancel{mol\ N}} = 28.02\ g\ N$

$2\ \cancel{mol\ O} \times \frac{16.00\ g\ O}{1\ \cancel{mol\ O}} = 32.00\ g\ O$

$2\ \cancel{mol\ S} \times \frac{32.07\ g\ S}{1\ \cancel{mol\ S}} = \underline{64.14\ g\ S}$

$252.3\ g\ C_{10}H_8N_2O_2S_2$

$\frac{120.1\ g\ C}{252.3\ g\ C_{10}H_8N_2O_2S_2} \times 100 = 47.60\%\ C$

$\frac{8.064\ g\ H}{252.3\ g\ C_{10}H_8N_2O_2S_2} \times 100 = 3.20\%\ H$ (rounded to 0.01%)

$\frac{28.04\ g\ N}{252.3\ g\ C_{10}H_8N_2O_2S_2} \times 100 = 11.10\%\ N$

$\frac{32.00\ g\ O}{252.3\ g\ C_{10}H_8N_2O_2S_2} \times 100 = 12.68\%\ O$

$\frac{64.14\ g\ S}{252.3\ g\ C_{10}H_8N_2O_2S_2} \times 100 = 25.42\%\ S$

d. $25.0\ g\ C_{10}H_8N_2O_2S_2 \times \frac{1\ \cancel{mol\ C_{10}H_8N_2O_2S_2}}{252.3\ \cancel{g\ C_{10}H_8N_2O_2S_2}} \times \frac{10\ \cancel{mol\ C}}{1\ \cancel{mol\ C_{10}H_8N_2O_2S_2}} \times \frac{6.022 \times 10^{23}\ C\ atoms}{1\ \cancel{mol\ C}}$

$= 5.97 \times 10^{23}$ C atoms

e. $8.2 \times 10^{24}\ \cancel{N\ atoms} \times \frac{1\ \cancel{mol\ N}}{6.022 \times 10^{23}\ \cancel{N\ atoms}} \times \frac{1\ mol\ C_{10}H_8N_2O_2S_2}{2\ \cancel{mol\ N}} = 6.8\ mol\ C_{10}H_8N_2O_2S_2$

7.65 a.

$3\ \cancel{mol\ C} \times \frac{12.01\ g\ C}{1\ \cancel{mol\ C}} = 36.03\ g\ C$

$6\ \cancel{mol\ H} \times \frac{1.008\ g\ H}{1\ \cancel{mol\ H}} = 6.048\ g\ H$

$3\ \cancel{mol\ O} \times \frac{16.00\ g\ O}{1\ \cancel{mol\ O}} = \underline{48.00\ g\ O}$

$90.08\ g\ C_3H_6O_3$

$\frac{48.00\ g\ O}{90.08\ g\ C_3H_6O_3} \times 100 = 53.29\%\ O$

b. $125\ \cancel{g\ C_3H_6O_3} \times \frac{1\ \cancel{mol\ C_3H_6O_3}}{90.08\ \cancel{g\ C_3H_6O_3}} \times \frac{3\ \cancel{mol\ C}}{1\ \cancel{mol\ C_3H_6O_3}} \times \frac{6.022 \times 10^{23}\ C\ atoms}{1\ \cancel{mol\ C}}$

$= 2.51 \times 10^{24}$ C atoms

c. $3.50\ \cancel{g\ H} \times \frac{1\ \cancel{mol\ H}}{1.008\ \cancel{g\ H}} \times \frac{1\ \cancel{mol\ C_3H_6O_3}}{6\ \cancel{mol\ H}} \times \frac{90.08\ g\ C_3H_6O_3}{1\ \cancel{mol\ C_3H_6O_3}} = 52.1\ g\ C_3H_6O_3$

d. $C_3H_6O_3 \div 3 = CH_2O$ (empirical formula)

7.67 a.

$9\ \cancel{mol\ C} \times \frac{12.01\ g\ C}{1\ \cancel{mol\ C}} = 108.1\ g\ C$

$8\ \cancel{mol\ H} \times \frac{1.008\ g\ H}{1\ \cancel{mol\ H}} = 8.064\ g\ H$

$4\ \cancel{mol\ O} \times \frac{16.00\ g\ O}{1\ \cancel{mol\ O}} = \underline{64.00\ g\ O}$

$180.2\ g\ C_3H_6O_3$

$$\frac{108.1 \text{ g C}}{180.2 \text{ g } C_9H_8O_4} \times 100 = 59.99\% \text{ O}$$

$$\frac{8.064 \text{ g H}}{180.2 \text{ g } C_9H_8O_4} \times 100 = 4.48\% \text{ H (rounded to 0.01\%)}$$

$$\frac{64.00 \text{ g O}}{180.2 \text{ g } C_9H_8O_4} \times 100 = 35.52\% \text{ O}$$

b. $5.00 \times 10^{24} \cancel{\text{C atoms}} \times \frac{1 \cancel{\text{mol C}}}{6.022 \times 10^{23} \cancel{\text{C atoms}}} \times \frac{1 \cancel{\text{mol } C_9H_8O_4}}{9 \cancel{\text{mol C}}} = 0.923 \text{ mol } C_9H_8O_4 \text{ (aspirin)}$

c. $7.50 \cancel{\text{g } C_9H_8O_4} \times \frac{1 \cancel{\text{mol } C_9H_8O_4}}{90.08 \cancel{\text{g } C_9H_8O_4}} \times \frac{4 \cancel{\text{mol O}}}{1 \cancel{\text{mol } C_9H_8O_4}} \times \frac{6.022 \times 10^{23} \text{ O atoms}}{1 \cancel{\text{mol O}}}$

$= 1.00 \times 10^{23}$ O atoms

d. $2.50 \cancel{\text{g H}} \times \frac{1 \cancel{\text{mol H}}}{1.008 \cancel{\text{g H}}} \times \frac{1 \cancel{\text{mol } C_9H_8O_4}}{8 \cancel{\text{mol H}}} \times \frac{6.022 \times 10^{23} \text{ molecules } C_9H_8O_4}{1 \cancel{\text{mol } C_9H_8O_4}}$

$= 1.87 \times 10^{23}$ molecules aspirin

7.69 a. $0.250 \cancel{\text{mol } Mn_2O_3} \times \frac{3 \cancel{\text{mol O}}}{1 \cancel{\text{mol } Mn_2O_3}} = 0.750 \text{ mol O}$

$20.0 \cancel{\text{g } MnO_2} \times \frac{1 \cancel{\text{mol } MnO_2}}{86.94 \cancel{\text{g } MnO_2}} \times \frac{2 \text{ mol O}}{1 \cancel{\text{mol } MnO_2}} = 0.460 \text{ mol O}$

0.750 mol O + 0.460 mol O = 1.210 mol O

$1.210 \cancel{\text{mol O}} \times \frac{6.022 \times 10^{23} \text{ O atoms}}{1 \cancel{\text{mol O}}} = 7.287 \times 10^{23}$ O atoms or 7.29×10^{23} O atoms

b. $20.0 \cancel{\text{g } MnO_2} \times \frac{1 \cancel{\text{mol } MnO_2}}{86.94 \cancel{\text{g } MnO_2}} \times \frac{1 \cancel{\text{mol Mn}}}{1 \cancel{\text{mol } MnO_2}} \times \frac{54.94 \text{ g Mn}}{1 \cancel{\text{mol Mn}}} = 12.6 \text{ g Mn}$

$0.250 \cancel{\text{mol } Mn_2O_3} \times \frac{2 \cancel{\text{mol Mn}}}{1 \cancel{\text{mol } Mn_2O_3}} \times \frac{54.94 \text{ g Mn}}{1 \cancel{\text{mol Mn}}} = 27.5 \text{ g Mn}$

12.6 g Mn + 27.5 g Mn = 40.1 g Mn

7.71 **a.** $C_5H_5N_5 \div 5 = CHN$ (empirical formula)

b. $FeC_2O_4 \div 1 = FeC_2O_4$ (empirical formula)

c. $C_{16}H_{16}N_4 \div 4 = C_4H_4N$ (empirical formula)

d. $C_6H_{14}N_2O_2 \div 2 = C_3H_7NO$ (empirical formula)

7.73 **a.** $2.20 \cancel{\text{g S}} \times \frac{1 \text{ mol S}}{32.07 \cancel{\text{g S}}} = 0.0686 \text{ mol S}$ (smaller number of moles)

$7.81 \cancel{\text{g F}} \times \frac{1 \text{ mol F}}{19.00 \cancel{\text{g F}}} = 0.411 \text{ mol F}$

$\frac{0.0686 \text{ mol S}}{0.0686} = 1.00 \text{ mol S}$ $\quad \frac{0.411 \text{ mol F}}{0.0686} = 5.99 \text{ mol F} \rightarrow 6 \text{ mol F}$

empirical formula = SF_6

b. moles of Ag = 6.35 ~~g Ag~~ x $\frac{1 \text{ mol Ag}}{107.9 \text{ g Ag}}$ = 0.0589 mol Ag (smallest number of moles)

moles of N = 0.825 ~~g N~~ x $\frac{1 \text{ mol N}}{14.01 \text{ g N}}$ = 0.0589 mol N

moles of O = 2.83 ~~g O~~ x $\frac{1 \text{ mol O}}{16.00 \text{ g O}}$ = 0.177 mol O

$\frac{0.0589 \text{ mol Ag}}{0.0589}$ = 1.00 mol Ag $\frac{0.0589 \text{ mol N}}{0.0589}$ = 1.00 mol N

$\frac{0.177 \text{ mol O}}{0.0589}$ = 3.01 mol O

empirical formula = $AgNO_3$

c. 89.2 ~~g Au~~ x $\frac{1 \text{ mol Au}}{197.0 \text{ g Au}}$ = 0.453 mol Au (smallest number of moles)

10.9 ~~g O~~ x $\frac{1 \text{ mol O}}{16.00 \text{ g O}}$ = 0.681 mol O

$\frac{0.453 \text{ mol Au}}{0.453}$ = 1.00 mol Au × 2 = 2.00 mol Au

$\frac{0.681 \text{ mol O}}{0.453}$ = 1.50 mol O × 2 = 3.00 mol O

empirical formula = Au_2O_3

7.75 a. In 100 g compound, there are 76.54 g C, 12.13 g H, and 11.33 g O.

moles of C = 76.54 ~~g C~~ x $\frac{1 \text{ mol C}}{12.01 \text{ g C}}$ = 6.373 mol C

moles of H = 12.13 ~~g H~~ x $\frac{1 \text{ mol H}}{1.008 \text{ g H}}$ = 12.03 mol H

moles of O = 11.33 ~~g O~~ x $\frac{1 \text{ mol O}}{16.00 \text{ g O}}$ = 0.7081 mol O (smallest number of moles)

$\frac{6.373 \text{ mol C}}{0.7081}$ = 9.000 mol C $\frac{12.03 \text{ mol H}}{0.7081}$ = 16.99 → 17 mol H

$\frac{0.7081 \text{ mol O}}{0.7081}$ = 1.000 mol O

empirical formula $C_9H_{17}O$ = 9 x 12.01 + 17 x 1.008 + 1 x 16.00 = 141.2 g

$\frac{282 \text{ g (molar mass)}}{141.2 \text{ g (mass of empirical formula)}}$ = 2.00

2 x (empirical formula $C_9H_{17}O$) = molecular formula $C_{18}H_{34}O_2$

b. 3.00 ~~mL~~ x $\frac{0.895 \text{ g } C_{18}H_{34}O_2}{1 \text{ mL}}$ x $\frac{1 \text{ mol } C_{18}H_{34}O_2}{282.4 \text{ g } C_{18}H_{34}O_2}$ x $\frac{6.022 \times 10^{23} \text{ molecules}}{1 \text{ mol } C_{18}H_{34}O_2}$

= 5.73×10^{21} molecules of oleic acid

7.77 In 100 g compound, there are 40.7 g C, 5.12 g H, and 54.2 g O.

moles of C = $40.7\ \cancel{g\,C} \times \frac{1\ \text{mol C}}{12.01\ \cancel{g\,C}} = 3.39\ \text{mol C}$

moles of H = $5.12\ \cancel{g\,H} \times \frac{1\ \text{mol H}}{1.008\ \cancel{g\,H}} = 5.08\ \text{mol H}$

moles of O = $54.2\ \cancel{g\,O} \times \frac{1\ \text{mol O}}{16.00\ \cancel{g\,O}} = 3.39\ \text{mol O}$ (smallest number of moles)

$\frac{3.39\ \text{mol C}}{3.39} = 1.00\ \text{mol C}$ $\frac{5.08\ \text{mol H}}{3.39} = 1.50\ \text{mol H}$

$\frac{3.39\ \text{mol O}}{3.39} = 1.00\ \text{mol O}$

1.00 mol C x 2 = 2.00 mol C 1.50 mol H x 2 = 3.00 mol H 1.00 mol O x 2 = 2.00 mol O

empirical formula = $C_2H_3O_2$ = 2 x 12.01 + 3 x 1.008 + 2 x 16.00 = 59.04 g

$\frac{118\ \text{g (molar mass)}}{59.04\ \text{g (mass of empirical formula)}} = 2.00$

2 x (empirical formula $C_2H_3O_2$) = molecular formula $C_4H_6O_4$

7.79

moles of C = $1.65 \times 10^{23}\ \cancel{\text{atoms C}} \times \frac{1\ \text{mol C}}{6.022 \times 10^{23}\ \cancel{\text{atoms C}}} = 0.274\ \text{mol C}$

moles of H = $0.552\ \cancel{g\,H} \times \frac{1\ \text{mol H}}{1.008\ \cancel{g\,H}} = 0.548\ \text{mol H}$

moles of O = $4.39\ \cancel{g\,O} \times \frac{1\ \text{mol O}}{16.00\ \cancel{g\,O}} = 0.274\ \text{mol O}$ (smallest number of moles)

$\frac{0.274\ \text{mol C}}{0.274} = 1.00\ \text{mol C}$ $\frac{0.548\ \text{mol H}}{0.274} = 2.00\ \text{mol H}$

$\frac{0.274\ \text{mol O}}{0.274} = 1.00\ \text{mol O}$

empirical formula = CH_2O

molecular formula = CH_2O x 4 = $C_4H_8O_4$

molar mass = 4 x 12.01 + 8 x 1.008 + 4 x 16.00 = 120.10 g

8
Chemical Reactions

Study Goals

- Classify a change in matter as a chemical change or a physical change.
- Show that a balanced equation has an equal number of atoms of each element on the reactant side and the product side.
- Write a balanced equation for a chemical reaction when given the formulas of the reactants and products.
- Classify an equation as a combination, decomposition, replacement, and/or combustion reaction.
- Given the quantity in grams of a substance in a reaction, calculate the quantity of another substance in the reaction.
- Determine the amount of product in a limiting reactant problem.
- Given the actual quantity of product, determine the percent yield for the reaction.

Think About It

1. Why is boiling water a physical change, whereas the formation of rust is a chemical change?

2. How is a recipe like a chemical equation?

3. What is a limiting reactant?

Key Terms

Match the following terms with the following statements:

a. chemical change **b.** chemical equation **c.** combination reaction
d. mole–mole factor **e.** theoretical yield **f.** percent yield

1. ___ The relationship between the number of moles of two substances in an equation
2. ___ A change that alters the composition of a substance producing a new substance with new properties
3. ___ The maximum amount of product that can be produced for a given amount of reactant
4. ___ The type of reaction in which reactants combine to form a single product
5. ___ A shorthand method of writing a chemical reaction with the formulas of the reactants written on the left side of an arrow and the formulas of the products on the right side
6.___ The ratio of the amount of product actually produced compared with the theoretical yield

Answers **1.** d **2.** a **3.** e **4.** c **5.** b **6.** f

8.1 Chemical Reactions

- A chemical change occurs when the atoms of the initial substances rearrange to form new substances.
- Chemical change is indicated by a change in properties of the reactants. For example, a rusting nail, souring milk, and a burning match are all chemical changes.
- When new substances form, a chemical reaction has taken place.

◆ Learning Exercise 8.1

Identify each of the following as a chemical (C) or a physical (P) change:

1. _____ tearing a piece of paper **2.** _____ burning paper

3. _____ rusting iron **4.** _____ digestion of food

5. _____ dissolving salt in water **6.** _____ boiling water

7. _____ chewing gum **8.** _____ removing tarnish with silver polish

Answers	**1.** P	**2.** C	**3.** C	**4.** C
	5. P	**6.** P	**7.** P	**8.** C

8.2 Chemical Equations

- A chemical equation shows the formulas of thc reactants on the left side of the arrow and the formulas of the products on the right side.
- In a balanced equation, *coefficients* in front of the formulas provide the same number of atoms for each kind of element on the reactant and product sides.

◆ Learning Exercise 8.2

State the number of atoms of each element on the reactant side and on the product side for each of the following balanced equations:

a. $CaCO_3(s) \longrightarrow CaO(g) + CO_2(g)$

Element	Atoms on Reactant Side	Atoms on Product Side
Ca		
C		
O		

b. $2Na(s) + H_2O(l) \longrightarrow Na_2O(s) + H_2(g)$

Element	Atoms on Reactant Side	Atoms on Product Side
Na		
H		
O		

c. $C_5H_{12}(g) + 8O_2(g) \longrightarrow 5CO_2(g) + 6H_2O(g)$

Element	Atoms on Reactant Side	Atoms on Product Side
C		
H		
O		

d. $2AgNO_3(aq) + K_2S(aq) \longrightarrow 2KNO_3(aq) + Ag_2S(s)$

Element	Atoms on Reactant Side	Atoms on Product Side
Ag		
N		
O		
K		
S		

e. $2Al(OH)_3(aq) + 3H_2SO_4(aq) \longrightarrow Al_2(SO_4)_3(s) + 6H_2O(l)$

Element	Atoms on Reactant Side	Atoms on Product Side
Al		
O		
H		
S		

Answers

a. $CaCO_3(s) \longrightarrow CaO(g) + CO_2(g)$

Element	Atoms on Reactant Side	Atoms on Product Side
Ca	1	1
C	1	1
O	3	3

b. $2Na(s) + H_2O(l) \longrightarrow Na_2O(s) + H_2(g)$

Element	Atoms on Reactant Side	Atoms on Product Side
Na	2	2
H	2	2
O	1	1

c. $C_5H_{12}(g) + 8O_2(g) \longrightarrow 5CO_2(g) + 6H_2O(g)$

Element	Atoms on Reactant Side	Atoms on Product Side
C	5	5
H	12	12
O	16	16

d. $2AgNO_3(aq) + K_2S(aq) \longrightarrow 2KNO_3(aq) + Ag_2S(s)$

Element	Atoms on Reactant Side	Atoms on Product Side
Ag	2	2
N	2	2
O	6	6
K	2	2
S	1	1

e. $2Al(OH)_3(aq) + 3H_2SO_4\,(aq) \longrightarrow Al_2(SO_4)_3(s) + 6H_2O(l)$

Element	Atoms on Reactant Side	Atoms on Product Side
Al	2	2
O	18	18
H	12	12
S	3	3

8.3 Balancing a Chemical Equation

- A chemical equation is balanced by placing coefficients in front of the symbols or formulas in the equation.

  Example: Balance the following equation:

  $N_2(g) + H_2(g) \longrightarrow NH_3(g)$

  1. Count the atoms of N and H on the reactant side and on the product side.

  $N_2(g) + H_2(g) \longrightarrow NH_3(g)$

  2N, 2H   1N, 3H

  2. Balance the N atoms by placing a coefficient of 2 in front of NH_3. (This increases the H atoms, too.) Recheck the number of N atoms and the number of H atoms.

  $N_2(g) + H_2(g) \longrightarrow \mathbf{2}NH_3(g)$

  3. Balance the H atoms by placing a coefficient of 3 in front of H_2. Recheck the number of N atoms and the number of H atoms.

  $N_2(g) + \mathbf{3}H_2(g) \longrightarrow \mathbf{2}NH_3(g)$

  2N, 6H   2 N, 6H   *The equation is balanced.*

◆ Learning Exercise 8.3

Balance each of the following equations by placing appropriate coefficients in front of the formulas as needed:

a. ____ $MgO(s) \longrightarrow$ ____ $Mg(s)$ + ____ $O_2(g)$

b. ____ $Zn(s)$ + ____ $HCl(aq) \longrightarrow$ ____ $ZnCl_2(aq)$ + ____ $H_2(g)$

c. ____ $Al(s)$ + ____ $CuSO_4(aq) \longrightarrow$ ____ $Cu(s)$ + ____ $Al_2(SO_4)_3(aq)$

d. ____ $Al_2S_3(s)$ + ____ $H_2O(l) \longrightarrow$ ____ $Al(OH)_3(aq)$ + ____ $H_2S(aq)$

e. ____ $BaCl_2(aq)$ + ____ $Na_2SO_4(aq) \longrightarrow$ ____ $BaSO_4(s)$ + ____ $NaCl(aq)$

f. ____ $CO(g)$ + ____ $Fe_2O_3(s) \longrightarrow$ ____ $Fe(s)$ + ____ $CO_2(g)$

g. ____ $K(s)$ + ____ $H_2O(l) \longrightarrow$ ____ $K_2O(aq)$ + ____ $H_2(g)$

h. ____ $Fe(OH)_3\,(aq) \longrightarrow$ ____ $Fe_2O_3(s)$ + ____ $H_2O(l)$

Answers

a. $2MgO(s) \rightarrow 2Mg(s) + O_2(g)$ **b.** $Zn(s) + 2HCl(aq) \rightarrow ZnCl_2(aq) + H_2(g)$
c. $2Al(s) + 3CuSO_4(aq) \rightarrow 3Cu(s) + Al_2(SO_4)_3(aq)$
d. $Al_2S_3 + 6H_2O(l) \rightarrow 2Al(OH)_3 + 3H_2S(aq)$
e. $BaCl_2(aq) + Na_2SO_4(aq) \rightarrow BaSO_4(s) + 2NaCl(aq)$ **f.** $3CO(g) + Fe_2O_3(s) \rightarrow 2Fe(s) + 3CO_2(g)$
g. $2K(s) + H_2O(l) \rightarrow K_2O(aq) + H_2(g)$ **h.** $2Fe(OH)_3(aq) \rightarrow Fe_2O_3(s) + 3H_2O(l)$

8.4 Types of Reactions

- Reactions are classified as combination, decomposition, replacement, and combustion.
- In a *combination* reaction, reactants are combined. In a *decomposition* reaction, a reactant splits into simpler products.
- In *single (or double) replacement* reactions, one (or two) elements in the reacting compounds are replaced with the element(s) from the other reactant(s).
- In a *combustion* reaction, oxygen combines with a reactant to form an oxide product. Compounds of carbon and hydrogen react with oxygen to produce CO_2 and H_2O.

◆ Learning Exercise 8.4A

Study Note

Combination reactions combine reactants. *Decomposition* splits compounds into simpler products. In *replacement*, elements in the reacting compounds are replaced with the element(s) from the other reactant (s). In *combustion*, oxygen combines with a reactant to form an oxide product.

Match each of the following reactions with the type of reaction:

a. combination **b.** decomposition **c.** single replacement
d. double replacement **e.** combustion

1.______ $N_2(g) + 3H_2(g) \longrightarrow 2NH_3(g)$

2.______ $BaCl_2(aq) + K_2CO_3(aq) \longrightarrow BaCO_3(s) + 2KCl(aq)$

3.______ $2H_2O_2(aq) \longrightarrow 2H_2O(l) + O_2(g)$

4.______ $CuO(s) + H_2(g) \longrightarrow Cu(s) + H_2O(l)$

5.______ $N_2(g) + 2O_2(g) \longrightarrow 2NO_2(g)$

6.______ $2NaHCO_3(aq) \longrightarrow Na_2O(aq) + 2CO_2(g) + H_2O(l)$

7.______ $PbCO_3(s) \longrightarrow PbO(s) + CO_2(g)$

8.______ $Al(s) + Fe_2O_3(aq) \longrightarrow Fe(s) + Al_2O_3(aq)$

Answers **1.** a **2.** d **3.** b **4.** c
5. a, e **6.** b **7.** b **8.** c

◆ Learning Exercise 8.4B

1. One way to remove tarnish from silver is to place the silver object on a piece of aluminum foil and add boiling water and some baking soda. The unbalanced equation is the following:

$$Al(s) + Ag_2S(s) \longrightarrow Ag(s) + Al_2S_3(s)$$

a. What is the balanced equation?

b. What type of reaction takes place?

2. Octane C_8H_{18}, a compound in gasoline, burns in oxygen to produce carbon dioxide and water.
a. What is the balanced equation for the reaction?

b. What type of reaction takes place?

Answers
1a. $2Al(s) + 3Ag_2S(s) \rightarrow 6Ag(s) + Al_2S_3(s)$ **1b.** single replacement
2a. $2C_8H_{18}(g) + 25O_2(g) \rightarrow 16CO_2(g) + 18H_2O(g)$ **2b.** combustion

8.5 Mole Relationships in Chemical Equations

- The coefficients in a balanced chemical equation describe the moles of reactants and products in the reactions.
- Using the coefficients, mole–mole conversion factors are written for any two substances in the equation.
- For the reaction of oxygen-forming ozone, $3O_2(g) \longrightarrow 2O_3(g)$, the mole–mole conversion factors are the following:

$$\frac{3 \text{ mol } O_2}{2 \text{ mol } O_3} \text{ and } \frac{2 \text{ mol } O_3}{3 \text{ mol } O_2}$$

◆ Learning Exercise 8.5A

Write the conversion factors that are possible from the following equation:

$$N_2(g) + O_2(g) \longrightarrow 2NO(g)$$

Answers

$$\frac{1 \text{ mol } N_2}{1 \text{ mol } O_2} \text{ and } \frac{1 \text{ mol } O_2}{1 \text{ mol } N_2}; \quad \frac{1 \text{ mol } N_2}{2 \text{ mol NO}} \text{ and } \frac{2 \text{ mol NO}}{1 \text{ mol } N_2}$$

$$\frac{1 \text{ mol } O_2}{2 \text{ mol NO}} \text{ and } \frac{2 \text{ mol NO}}{1 \text{ mol } O_2}$$

◆ Learning Exercise 8.5B

Study Note

The appropriate mole factor is used to change the number of moles of the given substance to moles of the desired products.

Example: Using the equation, $N_2(g) + O_2(g) \longrightarrow 2NO(g)$, calculate the moles of NO obtained from 3.0 mol N_2.

$$3.0 \text{ ~~mol N}_2\text{~~} \times \frac{2 \text{ mol NO}}{1 \text{ ~~mol N}_2\text{~~}} = 6.0 \text{ mol NO}$$

Mole–mole factor

Use this equation to answer the following questions:

$$C_3H_8(g) + 5O_2(g) \longrightarrow 3CO_2(g) + 4\ H_2O(g)$$

a. How many moles of O_2 are needed to react with 2.00 mol C_3H_8?

b. How many moles CO_2 are produced when 4.00 mol O_2 react?

c. How many moles of C_3H_8 react with 3.00 mol O_2?

d. How many molecules of H_2O are produced from 0.500 mol C_3H_8?

Answers

a. 10.0 mol O_2 **b.** 2.40 mol CO_2

c. 0.600 mol C_3H_8 **d.** 1.20×10^{24} molecules H_2O

8.6 Mass Calculations for Reactions

- The grams or moles of one substance in an equation are converted to another using their respective molar masses and mole–mole factors.
- Suppose that a problem asks for the number of grams of O_3 (ozone) produced from 8.00 g O_2.

	Step 1 Use molar mass of O_2		Step 2 Use mole factor from coefficients		Step 3 Use molar mass of O_3	
g O_2	$\longrightarrow$	mol O_2	$\longrightarrow$	mol O_3	$\longrightarrow$	g O_3

$$8.00\ \cancel{\text{g } O_2} \times \frac{1\ \cancel{\text{mol } O_2}}{32.00\ \cancel{\text{g } O_2}} \times \frac{2\ \cancel{\text{mol } O_2}}{3\ \cancel{\text{mol } O_2}} \times \frac{48.00\ \text{g } O_3}{1\ \cancel{\text{mol } O_3}} = 8.00\ \text{g } O_3$$

◆ Learning Exercise 8.6

Consider the equation for the following questions:

$$2C_2H_6(g) + 7O_2(g) \longrightarrow 4CO_2(g) + 6H_2O(g)$$

a. How many grams of oxygen (O_2) are needed to react with 4.00 mol of C_2H_6?

b. How many grams of C_2H_6 are needed to react with 115 g of O_2?

c. How many grams of C_2H_6 react if 2.00 L of CO_2 gas are produced at STP?

d. How many grams of CO_2 are produced when 2.00 mol of C_2H_6 react with sufficient oxygen?

e. How many grams of water are produced when 82.5 g O_2 react with sufficient C_2H_6?

f. How many molecules of H_2O are produced when 25.0 g of O_2 react?

Answers

a. 448 g O_2	**b.** 30.8 g C_2H_6	**c.** 1.34 g C_2H_6
d. 176 g CO_2	**e.** 39.8 g H_2O	**f.** 4.03×10^{23} molecules H_2O

8.7 Limiting Reactants

- In a limiting reactant problem, the availability of one of the reactants limits the amount of product.
- The reactant that is used up is the limiting reactant; the reactant that remains is the excess reactant.
- The limiting reactant produces the smallest number of moles of product.

◆ Learning Exercise 8.7

Study Note

The amount of product possible from a mixture of two reactants is determined by calculating the moles of product each will produce. The limiting reactant produces the smallest amount of product. In the reaction, $S(l) + 3F_2(g) \rightarrow SF_6(g)$, how many grams of SF_6 are possible when 5.00 mol S is mixed with 12.0 mol F_2?

Find the limiting reactant:

$$5.00\ \cancel{\text{mol S}} \times \frac{1\ \text{mol } SF_6}{1\ \cancel{\text{mol S}}} = 5.00\ \text{mol } SF_6$$

$$12.0\ \cancel{\text{mol } F_2} \times \frac{1\ \text{mol } SF_6}{3\ \cancel{\text{mol } F_2}} = 4.00\ \text{mol } SF_6$$ limiting reactant (smallest number of moles)

Calculate the grams of 4.0 mol SF_6 produced by the limiting reactant:

$$4.00\ \cancel{\text{mol } SF_6} \times \frac{146.07\ \text{g } SF_6}{1\ \cancel{\text{mol } SF_6}} = 584\ \text{g } SF_6$$

a. How many grams of Co_2S_3 can be produced from the reaction of 2.20 mol Co and 3.60 mol S?

$2Co(s) + 3S(s) \rightarrow Co_2S_3(s)$

b. How many grams of NO_2 can be produced from the reaction of 32.0 g NO and 24.0 g O_2?

$2NO(g) + O_2(g) \rightarrow 2NO_2(g)$

Answers **a.** 235 g **b.** 49.1 g

8.8 Percent Yield

- Theoretical yield is the maximum amount of product calculated for a given amount of a reactant.
- Percent yield is the ratio of the actual amount (yield) of product obtained to the theoretical yield.

◆ Learning Exercise 8.8

Study Note

The percent yield is the ratio of the actual yield obtained to the theoretical yield, which is calculated for a given amount of starting reactant. If we calculate that the reaction of 35.5 g N_2 can theoretically produce 43.1 g NH_3, but the actual yield is 26.0 g NH_3, the percent yield is

$$\frac{26.0\ NH_3\ \text{(actual)}}{43.1\ g\ NH_3\ \text{(theoretical)}} \times 100 = 60.3\% \quad \text{Percent yield}$$

Consider the following reaction: $2H_2S(g) + 3O_2(g) \longrightarrow 2SO_2(g) + 2H_2O(g)$

a. If 60.0 g H_2S reacts with sufficient oxygen and produces 45.5 g SO_2, what is the percent yield for SO_2?

b. If 25.0 g O_2 reacting with H_2S produces 18.6 g SO_2, what is the percent yield for SO_2?

Consider the reaction $\underset{\text{ethane}}{2C_2H_6(g)} + 7O_2(g) \longrightarrow 4CO_2(g) + 6H_2O(g)$

c. If 125 g C_2H_6 reacting with sufficient oxygen produces 175 g CO_2, what is the percent yield for CO_2?

d. When 35.0 g O_2 reacts with sufficient ethane to produce 12.5 g H_2O, what is the percent yield of water?

Answers **a.** 40.3% **b.** 55.7% **c.** 47.8% **d.** 74.0%

Checklist for Chapter 8

You are ready to take the practice test for Chapter 8. Be sure you have accomplished the following learning goals for this chapter. If you are not sure, review the section listed at the end of the goal. Then apply your new skills and understanding to the practice test.

After studying Chapter 8, I can successfully:

____ Identify a chemical and physical change (8.1).

____ State a chemical equation in words and calculate the total atoms of each element in the reactants and products (8.2).

____ Write a balanced equation for a chemical reaction from the formulas of the reactants and products (8.3).

____ Identify a reaction as a combination, decomposition, replacement, or combustion reaction (8.4).

____ Use mole–mole factors for the mole relationships in an equation to calculate the moles of another substance in an equation for a chemical reaction (8.5).

____ Calculate the mass of a substance in an equation using mole factors and molar masses (8.6).

____ Determine the mass of product in a reaction with a limiting reactant in a reaction (8.7).

____ Calculate the percent yield for a reaction given the actual yield (8.8).

Practice Test for Chapter 8

Indicate whether each change is a (A) physical change or a (B) chemical change:

1.____A melting ice cube **2.**____Breaking glass **3.**____Bleaching a stain

4.____A burning candle **5.**____Milk turning sour

For each of the *unbalanced equations* in questions 6 to 10, balance and indicate the correct coefficient for the component in the equation written in boldface type.

A. 1 **B.** 2 **C.** 3 **D.** 4 **E.** 5

6. ____ $Sn(s) + \mathbf{Cl_2}(g) \longrightarrow SnCl_4(s)$

7. ____ $Al(s) + H_2O(l) \longrightarrow Al_2O_3(s) + \mathbf{H_2}(g)$

8. ____ $C_3H_8(g) + \mathbf{O_2}(g) \longrightarrow CO_2(g) + H_2O(g)$

9. ____ $\mathbf{NH_3}(g) + O_2(g) \longrightarrow N_2(g) + H_2O(g)$

10. ____ $N_2O(g) \longrightarrow N_2(g) + \mathbf{O_2}(g)$

For questions 11 to 15, classify each reaction as one of the following:
A. combination **B.** decomposition **C.** single replacement **D.** double replacement

11. ____ $S(s) + O_2(g) \longrightarrow SO_2(g)$

12. ____ $Fe_2O_3(s) + 3C(s) \longrightarrow 2Fe(s) + 3CO(g)$

13. ____ $CaCO_3(s) \longrightarrow CaO(s) + CO_2(g)$

14. ____ $Mg(s) + 2AgNO_3(aq) \longrightarrow Mg(NO_3)_2(aq) + 2Ag(s)$

15. ____ $Na_2S(aq) + Pb(NO_3)_2(aq) \longrightarrow PbS(s) + 2NaNO_3(aq)$

For questions, 16 to 21, use the reaction: $C_2H_5OH(g)$ + $3O_2(g)$ $\longrightarrow$ $2CO_2(g)$ + $3H_2O(g)$
Ethanol

16. How many grams of oxygen are needed to react with 1.00 mol ethanol?
A. 8.00 g **B.** 16.0 g **C.** 32.0 g **D.** 64.0 g **E.** 96.0 g

17. How many moles of water are produced when 12.0 mol oxygen react?
A. 3.00 mol **B.** 6.00 mol **C.** 8.00 mol **D.** 12.0 mol **E.** 36.0 mol

18. How many grams of carbon dioxide are produced when 92.0 g ethanol react?
A. 22.0 g **B.** 44.0 g **C.** 88.0 g **D.** 92.0 g **E.** 176 g

19. How many moles of oxygen would be needed to produce 44.0 g CO_2?
A. 0.670 mol **B.** 1.00 mol **C.** 1.50 mol **D.** 2.00 mol **E.** 3.00 mol

20. How many grams of water will be produced if 23.0 g ethanol react?
A. 54.0 g **B.** 27.0 g **C.** 18.0 g **D.** 9.00 g **E.** 6.00 g

21. How many grams of water will be produced if 3.00 mol ethanol and 5.00 mol O_2 react?
A. 3.60 g **B.** 18.0 g **C.** 54.1 g **D.** 90.1 g **E.** 162 g

22. How many grams of water will be produced if 5.00 mol ethanol and 12.0 mol O_2 react?
A. 270 g **B.** 216 g **C.** 54.1 g **D.** 36.0 g **E.** 18.0 g

23. In an experiment, 36.0 g NO are produced from 20.0 g N_2. What is the percent yield?
$N_2(g) + O_2(g) \longrightarrow 2NO(g)$
A. 42.9% **B.** 55.6% **C.** 71.4% **D.** 84.0% **E.** 93.4%

Answers to the Practice Test

1. A	**2.** A	**3.** B	**4.** B	**5.** B
6. B	**7.** C	**8.** E	**9.** D	**10.** A
11. A	**12.** C	**13.** B	**14.** C	**15.** D
16. E	**17.** D	**18.** E	**19.** C	**20.** B
21. D	**22.** B	**23.** D		

Answers and Solutions to Selected Text Problems

Section 8.1

8.1 A chemical change occurs when the atoms of the initial substances rearrange to form new substances. Chemical change is indicated by a change in properties of the reactants. For example, a rusting nail, souring milk, and a burning match are all chemical changes.
a. physical: the shape changes, but not the substance.
b. chemical: new substances form.
c. physical: water evaporates forming gaseous water.
d. chemical: the composition of the substances change to give new substances.

8.3 **a.** There is no evidence of a chemical reaction when water forms snowflakes.
b. Light, heat, and the formation of a gas are all evidence of a chemical reaction.
c. There is no evidence of a change in the properties of the bread.
d. The change in color during toasting a marshmallow is evidence of a chemical reaction.

Section 8.2

8.5 **a.** On the reactant side, there are two nitrogen atoms and four oxygen atoms. On the product side, there are two nitrogen atoms (2NO) and four oxygen atoms ($2NO + O_2$)

b. On the reactant side, there are five carbon atoms (5C), two sulfur atoms ($2SO_2$), and four oxygen atoms ($2SO_2$). On the product side, there are five carbon atoms, two sulfur atoms, and four oxygen atoms

c. On the reactant side, there are four carbon atoms, four hydrogen atoms, and ten oxygen atoms. On the product side, there are four carbon atoms, four hydrogen atoms, and ten oxygen atoms.

d. On the reactant side, there are two nitrogen atoms, eight hydrogen atoms, and four oxygen atoms. On the product side, there are two nitrogen atoms, eight hydrogen atoms, and four oxygen atoms

8.7 An equation is balanced when there is an equal number of atoms of each element on the reactant side and on the product side.

a. not balanced **b.** balanced **c.** not balanced **d.** balanced

8.9 **a.** There are two sodium atoms and two chlorine atoms on each side of the equation.

b. There are one phosphorus atom, three chlorine atoms, and six hydrogen atoms on each side of the equation.

c. There are 4 phosphorus atoms, 16 oxygen atoms, and 12 hydrogen atoms on each side of the equation.

Section 8.3

8.11 Place coefficients in front of formulas until you make the atoms of each element equal on each side of the equation. Try starting with the formula that has subscripts.

a. $N_2(g) + O_2(g) \rightarrow 2NO(g)$ **b.** $2HgO(s) \rightarrow 2Hg(l) + O_2(g)$

c. $4Fe(s) + 3O_2(g) \rightarrow 2Fe_2O_3(s)$ **d.** $2Na(s) + Cl_2(g) \rightarrow 2NaCl(s)$

e. $2Cu_2O(s) + O_2(g) \rightarrow 4CuO(s)$

8.13 **a.** There are two NO_3 in the product. Balance by placing a 2 before $AgNO_3$.

$Mg(s) + 2AgNO_3(aq) \rightarrow Mg(NO_3)_2(aq) + 2Ag(s)$

b. $CuCO_3(s) \rightarrow CuO(s) + CO_2(g)$

c. Start with the formula $Al_2(SO_4)_3$. Balance the Al by writing 2 Al and balance the SO_4 by writing 3 $CuSO_4$.

$2Al(s) + 3CuSO_4(aq) \rightarrow 3Cu(s) + Al_2(SO_4)_3(aq)$

d. $Pb(NO_3)_2(aq) + 2NaCl(aq) \rightarrow PbCl_2(s) + 2NaNO_3(aq)$

e. $2Al(s) + 6HCl(aq) \rightarrow 2AlCl_3(aq) + 3H_2(g)$

8.15 **a.** $Fe_2O_3(s) + 3CO(g) \rightarrow 2Fe(s) + 3CO_2(g)$

b. $2Li_3N(s) \rightarrow 6Li(s) + N_2(g)$

c. $2Al(s) + 6HBr(aq) \rightarrow 2AlBr_3(aq) + 3H_2(g)$

d. $3Ba(OH)_2(aq) + 2Na_3PO_4(aq) \rightarrow Ba_3(PO_4)_2(s) + 6NaOH(aq)$

e. $As_4S_6(s) + 9O_2(g) \rightarrow As_4O_6(s) + 6SO_2(g)$

8.17 **a.** $2Li(s) + 2H_2O(l) \rightarrow H_2(g) + 2LiOH(aq)$

b. $2P(s) + 5Cl_2(g) \rightarrow 2PCl_5(s)$

c. $FeO(s) + CO(g) \rightarrow Fe(s) + CO_2(g)$

d. $2C_5H_{10}(l) + 15O_2(g) \rightarrow 10CO_2(g) + 10H_2O(g)$

e. $3H_2S(g) + 2FeCl_3(s) \rightarrow Fe_2S_3(s) + 6HCl(g)$

Section 8.4

8.19 **a.** Decomposition. A single reactant splits into two simpler substances (elements).
b. This is a single replacement reaction. I_2 in BaI_2 is replaced by Br_2.

8.21 **a.** combination and combustion **b.** single replacement **c.** decomposition
d. double replacement **e.** combustion **f.** decomposition
g. double replacement **h.** combination and combustion

8.23 **a.** Combine the reactants to form a large compound: $Mg(s) + Cl_2(g) \rightarrow MgCl_2(s)$
b. Split the reactant to give simpler substances: $2\ HBr(g) \rightarrow H_2(g) + Br_2(g)$
c. Replace the Zn with Mg: $Mg(s) + Zn(NO_3)_2(aq) \rightarrow Mg(NO_3)_2(aq) + Zn(s)$
d. Switch metals placing K^+ with NO_3^- and Pb^{2+} with S^{2-}:
$K_2S(aq) + Pb(NO_3)_2(aq) \rightarrow 2KNO_3(aq) + PbS(s)$
e. Write the products CO_2 and H_2O and balance: $2C_2H_6(g) + 7O_2(g) \rightarrow 4CO_2(g) + 6H_2O(g)$

Section 8.5

8.25 **a.** Two SO_2 molecules react with one O_2 molecule to produce two SO_3 molecules.
Two mol SO_2 react with one mol O_2 to produce two mol SO_3.
b. Four P atoms react with five O_2 molecules to produce two P_2O_5 molecules.
Four mol P react with five mol O_2 to produce two mol P_2O_5.

8.27 **a.** Reactants: 2 mol SO_2 plus 1 mol O_2 =
2 mol (64.07 g/mol) + 1 mol (32.00 g/mol) = 160.14 g
Products: 2 mol SO_3 = 2 mol (80.07 g/mol) = 160.14 g

b. Reactants: 4 mol P and 5 mol O_2 =
4 mol (30.97 g/mol) + 5 mol (32.00 g/mol) = 283.88 g
Products: 2 mol P_2O_5 = 2 mol (141.94 g/mol) = 283.88 g

8.29 **a.** $\frac{2\text{ mol }SO_2}{1\text{ mol }O_2}$ and $\frac{1\text{ mol }O_2}{2\text{ mol }SO_2}$ $\frac{2\text{ mol }SO_2}{2\text{ mol }SO_3}$ and $\frac{2\text{ mol }SO_3}{2\text{ mol }SO_2}$

$\frac{1\text{ mol }O_2}{2\text{ mol }SO_3}$ and $\frac{2\text{ mol }SO_3}{1\text{ mol }O_2}$

b $\frac{4\text{ mol P}}{5\text{ mol }O_2}$ and $\frac{5\text{ mol }O_2}{4\text{ mol P}}$ $\frac{4\text{ mol P}}{2\text{ mol }P_2O_5}$ and $\frac{2\text{ mol }P_2O_5}{4\text{ mol P}}$

$\frac{5\text{ mol }O_2}{2\text{ mol }P_2O_5}$ and $\frac{2\text{ mol }P_2O_5}{5\text{ mol }O_2}$

8.31 **a.** $2.0\ \cancel{\text{mol }H_2} \times \frac{1\text{ mol }O_2}{2\ \cancel{\text{mol }H_2}} = 1.0\text{ mol }O_2$

b. $5.0\ \cancel{\text{mol }O_2} \times \frac{2\text{ mol }H_2}{1\ \cancel{\text{mol }O_2}} = 10.\text{ mol }H_2$

c. $2.5\ \cancel{\text{mol }O_2} \times \frac{2\text{ mol }H_2O}{1\ \cancel{\text{mol }O_2}} = 5.0\text{ mol }H_2O$

8.33 **a.** $0.500\ \cancel{\text{mol }SO_2} \times \frac{5\text{ mol C}}{2\ \cancel{\text{mol }SO_2}} = 1.25\text{ mol C}$

b. $1.2\ \cancel{\text{mol C}} \times \frac{4\text{ mol CO}}{5\ \cancel{\text{mol C}}} = 0.96\text{ mol CO}$

c. $0.50\ \cancel{\text{mol }CS_2} \times \frac{2\text{ mol }SO_2}{1\ \cancel{\text{mol }CS_2}} = 1.0\text{ mol }SO_2$

d. $2.5\ \cancel{\text{mol C}} \times \frac{1\ \text{mol CS}_2}{5\ \cancel{\text{mol C}}} = 0.50\ \text{mol CS}_2$

Section 8.6

8.35 **a.** $2.50\ \cancel{\text{mol Na}} \times \frac{2\ \cancel{\text{mol Na}_2\text{O}}}{4\ \cancel{\text{mol Na}}} \times \frac{61.98\ \text{g Na}_2\text{O}}{1\ \cancel{\text{mol Na}_2\text{O}}} = 77.5\ \text{g Na}_2\text{O}$

b. $18.0\ \cancel{\text{g Na}} \times \frac{1\ \cancel{\text{mol Na}}}{22.99\ \cancel{\text{g Na}}} \times \frac{1\ \cancel{\text{mol O}_2}}{4\ \cancel{\text{mol Na}}} \times \frac{32.0\ \text{g O}_2}{1\ \cancel{\text{mol O}_2}} = 6.26\ \text{g O}_2$

c. $75.0\ \cancel{\text{g Na}_2\text{O}} \times \frac{1\ \cancel{\text{mol Na}_2\text{O}}}{61.98\ \cancel{\text{g Na}_2\text{O}}} \times \frac{1\ \cancel{\text{mol O}_2}}{2\ \cancel{\text{mol Na}_2\text{O}}} \times \frac{32.00\ \text{g O}_2}{1\ \cancel{\text{mol O}_2}} = 19.4\ \text{g O}_2$

8.37 **a.** $8.00\ \cancel{\text{mol NH}_3} \times \frac{3\ \cancel{\text{mol O}_2}}{4\ \cancel{\text{mol NH}_3}} \times \frac{32.00\ \text{g O}_2}{1\ \cancel{\text{mol O}_2}} = 192\ \text{g O}_2$

b. $6.50\ \cancel{\text{g O}_2} \times \frac{1\ \cancel{\text{mol O}_2}}{32.00\ \cancel{\text{g O}_2}} \times \frac{2\ \cancel{\text{mol N}_2}}{3\ \cancel{\text{mol O}_2}} \times \frac{28.02\ \text{g N}_2}{1\ \cancel{\text{mol N}_2}} = 3.79\ \text{g N}_2$

c. $34.0\ \cancel{\text{g NH}_3} \times \frac{1\ \cancel{\text{mol NH}_3}}{17.03\ \cancel{\text{g NH}_3}} \times \frac{6\ \cancel{\text{mol H}_2\text{O}}}{4\ \cancel{\text{mol NH}_3}} \times \frac{18.02\ \text{g H}_2\text{O}}{1\ \cancel{\text{mol H}_2\text{O}}} = 54.0\ \text{g H}_2\text{O}$

8.39 **a.** $28.0\ \cancel{\text{g NO}_2} \times \frac{1\ \cancel{\text{mol NO}_2}}{46.01\ \cancel{\text{g NO}_2}} \times \frac{1\cancel{\text{mol H}_2\text{O}}}{3\ \cancel{\text{mol NO}_2}} \times \frac{18.02\ \text{g H}_2\text{O}}{1\ \cancel{\text{mol H}_2\text{O}}} = 3.66\ \text{g H}_2\text{O}$

b. $15.8\ \cancel{\text{g NO}_2} \times \frac{1\ \cancel{\text{mol NO}_2}}{46.01\cancel{\text{g NO}_2}} \times \frac{1\ \cancel{\text{mol NO}}}{3\ \cancel{\text{mol NO}_2}} \times \frac{30.01\ \text{g NO}}{1\ \cancel{\text{mol NO}}} = 3.44\ \text{g NO}$

c. $8.25\ \cancel{\text{g NO}_2} \times \frac{1\ \cancel{\text{mol NO}_2}}{46.01\cancel{\text{g NO}_2}} \times \frac{2\ \cancel{\text{mol HNO}_3}}{3\ \cancel{\text{mol NO}_2}} \times \frac{63.01\ \text{g HNO}_3}{1\ \cancel{\text{mol HNO}_3}} = 7.53\ \text{g NO}$

8.41 **a.** $2\text{PbS}(s) + 3\text{O}_2(g) \rightarrow 2\text{PbO}(s) + 2\text{SO}_2(g)$

b. $0.125\ \cancel{\text{mol PbS}} \times \frac{3\ \cancel{\text{mol O}_2}}{2\ \cancel{\text{mol PbS}}} \times \frac{32.00\ \text{g O}_2}{1\ \cancel{\text{mol O}_2}} = 6.00\ \text{g O}_2$

c. $65.0\ \cancel{\text{g PbS}} \times \frac{1\ \cancel{\text{mol PbS}}}{239.3\cancel{\text{g PbS}}} \times \frac{2\ \cancel{\text{mol SO}_2}}{2\ \cancel{\text{mol PbS}}} \times \frac{64.07\ \text{g SO}_2}{1\ \cancel{\text{mol SO}_2}} = 17.4\ \text{g SO}_2$

d. $128\ \cancel{\text{g PbO}} \times \frac{1\ \cancel{\text{mol PbO}}}{223.2\cancel{\text{g PbO}}} \times \frac{2\ \cancel{\text{mol PbS}}}{2\ \cancel{\text{mol PbO}}} \times \frac{239.3\ \text{g PbS}}{1\ \cancel{\text{mol PbS}}} = 137\ \text{g PbS}$

Section 8.7

8.43 **a.** With eight drivers available, only eight taxis can be used to pick up passengers.
b. Seven taxis are in working condition to be driven.

8.45 **a.** $3.0\ \cancel{\text{mol N}_2} \times \frac{2\ \text{mol NH}_3}{1\ \cancel{\text{mol N}_2}} = 6.0\ \text{mol NH}_3$

$5.0\ \cancel{\text{mol H}_2} \times \frac{2\ \text{mol NH}_3}{3\ \cancel{\text{mol H}_2}} = 3.3\ \text{mol NH}_3$ (smallest moles of product)

The limiting reactant is 5.0 mol H_2.

b. $8.0\ \cancel{\text{mol N}_2} \times \frac{2\ \text{mol NH}_3}{1\ \cancel{\text{mol N}_2}} = 16\ \text{mol NH}_3$

$4.0\ \cancel{\text{mol H}_2} \times \frac{2\ \text{mol NH}_3}{3\ \cancel{\text{mol H}_2}} = 2.7\ \text{mol NH}_3$ (smallest moles of product)

The limiting reactant is 4.0 mol H_2.

c. $3.0\ \cancel{\text{mol } N_2} \times \dfrac{2 \text{ mol } NH_3}{1\ \cancel{\text{mol } N_2}} = 6.0 \text{ mol } NH_3$ (smallest moles of product)

$12.0\ \cancel{\text{mol } H_2} \times \dfrac{2 \text{ mol } NH_3}{3\ \cancel{\text{mol } N_2}} = 8.0 \text{ mol } NH_3$

The limiting reactant is 3.0 mol N_2.

8.47 **a.** $2.00\ \cancel{\text{mol } SO_2} \times \dfrac{2 \text{ mol } SO_3}{2\ \cancel{\text{mol } SO_2}} = 2.00 \text{ mol } SO_3$ (smallest moles of product)

$2.00\ \cancel{\text{mol } O_2} \times \dfrac{2 \text{ mol } SO_3}{1\ \cancel{\text{mol } O_2}} = 4.00 \text{ mol } SO_3$

b. $2.00\ \cancel{\text{mol Fe}} \times \dfrac{1 \text{ mol } Fe_3O_4}{3\ \cancel{\text{mol Fe}}} = 0.667 \text{ mol } Fe_3O_4$

$2.00\ \cancel{\text{mol } H_2O} \times \dfrac{1 \text{ mol } Fe_3O_4}{4\ \cancel{\text{mol } H_2O}} = 0.500 \text{ mol } Fe_3O_4$ (smallest moles of product)

c. $2.00\ \cancel{\text{mol } C_7H_{16}} \times \dfrac{7 \text{ mol } CO_2}{1\ \cancel{\text{mol } C_7H_{16}}} = 14.0 \text{ mol } CO_2$

$2.00\ \cancel{\text{mol } O_2} \times \dfrac{7 \text{ mol } CO_2}{11\ \cancel{\text{mol } O_2}} = 1.27 \text{ mol } CO_2$ (smallest moles of product)

8.49 **a.** $20.0\ \cancel{\text{g Al}} \times \dfrac{1\ \cancel{\text{mol Al}}}{26.98\ \cancel{\text{g Al}}} \times \dfrac{2 \text{ mol } AlCl_3}{2\ \cancel{\text{mol Al}}} = 0.741 \text{ mol } AlCl_3$

$20.0\ \cancel{\text{g } Cl_2} \times \dfrac{1\ \cancel{\text{mol } Cl_2}}{70.90\ \cancel{\text{g } Cl_2}} \times \dfrac{2 \text{ mol } AlCl_3}{3\ \cancel{\text{mol } Cl_2}} = \mathbf{0.188 \text{ mol } AlCl_3}$ (smallest moles of product)

b. $20.0\ \cancel{\text{g } NH_3} \times \dfrac{1\ \cancel{\text{mol } NH_3}}{17.03\ \cancel{\text{g } NH_3}} \times \dfrac{6 \text{ mol } H_2O}{4\ \cancel{\text{mol } NH_3}} = 1.76 \text{ mol } H_2O$

$20.0\ \cancel{\text{g } O_2} \times \dfrac{1\ \cancel{\text{mol } O_2}}{32.00\ \cancel{\text{g } O_2}} \times \dfrac{6 \text{ mol } H_2O}{5\ \cancel{\text{mol } O_2}} = \mathbf{0.750 \text{ mol } AlCl_3}$ (smallest moles of product)

c. $20.0\ \cancel{\text{g } CS_2} \times \dfrac{1\ \cancel{\text{mol } CS_2}}{76.14\ \cancel{\text{g } CS_2}} \times \dfrac{2 \text{ mol } SO_2}{1\ \cancel{\text{mol } CS_2}} = 0.525 \text{ mol } SO_2$

$20.0\ \cancel{\text{g } O_2} \times \dfrac{1\ \cancel{\text{mol } O_2}}{32.00\ \cancel{\text{g } O_2}} \times \dfrac{2 \text{ mol } SO_2}{3\ \cancel{\text{mol } O_2}} = \mathbf{0.417 \text{ mol } SO_2}$ (smallest moles of product)

Section 8.8

8.51 **a.** $40.0\ \cancel{\text{g C}} \times \dfrac{1\ \cancel{\text{mol C}}}{12.01\ \cancel{\text{g C}}} \times \dfrac{1\cancel{\text{mol } CS_2}}{5\ \cancel{\text{mol C}}} \times \dfrac{76.14 \text{ g } CS_2}{1\ \cancel{\text{mol } CS_2}} = 50.7 \text{ g } CS_2$

$\dfrac{36.0 \text{ g } CS_2 \text{ (actual)}}{50.7 \text{ g } CS_2 \text{ (theoretical)}} \times 100 = 71.0\%$

b. $32.0\ \cancel{\text{g } SO_2} \times \dfrac{1\ \cancel{\text{mol } SO_2}}{64.07\ \cancel{\text{g } SO_2}} \times \dfrac{1\cancel{\text{mol } CS_2}}{2\ \cancel{\text{mol } SO_2}} \times \dfrac{76.14 \text{ g } CS_2}{1\ \cancel{\text{mol } CS_2}} = 19.0 \text{ g } CS_2$

$\dfrac{12.0 \text{ g } CS_2 \text{ (actual)}}{19.0 \text{ g } CS_2 \text{ (theoretical)}} \times 100 = 63.1\%$

8.53 $50.0\ \cancel{g\ Al} \times \frac{1\ \cancel{mol\ Al}}{26.98\ \cancel{g\ Al}} \times \frac{2\ \cancel{mol\ Al_2O_3}}{4\ \cancel{mol\ Al}} \times \frac{101.96\ g\ Al_2O_3}{1\ \cancel{mol\ Al_2O_3}} = 94.5\ g\ Al_2O_3$

Use the percent yield to convert theoretical to actual:

$94.5\ \cancel{g\ Al_2O_3} \times \frac{75.0\ g\ Al_2O_3}{100\ \cancel{g\ Al_2O_3}} = 70.9\ g\ Al_2O_3\ (actual)$

8.55 $30.0\ \cancel{g\ C} \times \frac{1\ \cancel{mol\ C}}{12.01\ \cancel{g\ C}} \times \frac{2\ \cancel{mol\ CO}}{3\ \cancel{mol\ C}} \times \frac{28.01\ g\ CO}{1\ \cancel{mol\ CO}} = 46.6\ g\ CO$

$\frac{28.2\ g\ CO\ (actual)}{46.6\ g\ CO\ (theoretical)} \times 100 = 60.5\%$

Answers to Additional Problems

8.61
a. combination
b. combustion
c. double replacement
d. decomposition
e. single replacement

8.63

a.	$NH_3(g) + HCl(g) \rightarrow NH_4Cl(s)$	combination
b.	$Fe_3O_4(s) + 4H_2(g) \rightarrow 3\ Fe(s) + 4H_2O(g)$	single replacement
c.	$2Sb(s) + 3Cl_2(g) \rightarrow 2SbCl_3(s)$	combination
d.	$2\ NI_3(s) \rightarrow N_2(g) + 3I_2(g)$	decomposition
e.	$2\ KBr(aq) + Cl_2(aq) \rightarrow 2KCl(aq) + Br_2(l)$	single replacement
f.	$2Fe(s) + 3H_2SO_4(aq) \rightarrow Fe_2(SO_4)_3 + 3H_2$	single replacement
g.	$Al_2(SO_4)_3(aq) + 6\ NaOH(aq) \rightarrow 3\ Na_2SO_4(aq) + 2\ Al(OH)_3(s)$	double replacement

8.65
a. $Zn(s) + 2\ HCl(aq) \rightarrow ZnCl_2(aq) + H_2(g)$
b. $BaCO_3(s) \rightarrow BaO(s) + CO_2(g)$
c. $NaOH(aq) + HCl(aq) \rightarrow NaCl(aq) + H_2O(l)$
d. $2Al(s) + 3F_2(g) \rightarrow 2AlF_3(s)$

8.67

a.	$2KClO_3(s) \rightarrow 2KCl(s) + 3O_2(g)$	decomposition
b.	$NaCl(aq) + AgNO_3(aq) \rightarrow AgCl(s) + NaNO_3(aq)$	double replacement

8.69 **a.** $124\ \cancel{g\ C_2H_6O} \times \frac{1\ \cancel{mol\ C_2H_6O}}{46.07\ \cancel{g\ C_2H_6O}} \times \frac{1\ mol\ C_6H_{12}O_6}{2\ \cancel{mol\ C_2H_6O}} = 1.35\ mol\ C_6H_{12}O_6$

b. $0.240\ \cancel{kg\ C_6H_{12}O_6} \times \frac{1000\ \cancel{g}}{1\ \cancel{kg}} \times \frac{1\ \cancel{mol\ C_6H_{12}O_6}}{180.0\ \cancel{g\ C_6H_{12}O_6}} \times \frac{2\ \cancel{mol\ C_2H_6O}}{1\ \cancel{mol\ C_6H_{12}O_6}} \times \frac{46.0\ g\ C_2H_6O}{1\ \cancel{mol\ C_2H_6O}}$

$= 123\ g\ C_2H_6O$

8.71 $2NH_3(g) + 5F_2(g) \rightarrow N_2F_4(g) + 6HF(g)$

a. $4.00\ \cancel{mol\ HF} \times \frac{2\ mol\ NH_3}{6\ \cancel{mol\ HF}} = 1.33\ mol\ NH_3$

$4.00\ \cancel{mol\ HF} \times \frac{5\ mol\ F_2}{6\ \cancel{mol\ HF}} = 3.33\ mol\ F_2$

b. $1.50\ \cancel{mol\ NH_3} \times \frac{5\ \cancel{mol\ F_2}}{2\ \cancel{mol\ NH_3}} \times \frac{38.0\ g\ F_2}{1\ \cancel{mol\ F_2}} = 143\ g\ F_2$

c. $3.40\ \cancel{g\ NH_3} \times \frac{1\ \cancel{mol\ NH_3}}{17.03\ \cancel{g\ NH_3}} \times \frac{1\ \cancel{mol\ N_2F_4}}{2\ \cancel{mol\ NH_3}} \times \frac{104.01\ g\ N_2F_4}{1\ \cancel{mol\ N_2F_4}} = 10.4\ g\ N_2F_4$

8.73 $12.8\ \text{g Na} \times \frac{1\ \text{mol Na}}{22.99\ \text{g Na}} \times \frac{2\ \text{mol NaCl}}{2\ \text{mol Na}} = 0.557\ \text{mol NaCl}$

$10.2\ \text{g}\ Cl_2 \times \frac{1\ \text{mol}\ Cl_2}{70.90\ \text{g}\ Cl_2} \times \frac{2\ \text{mol NaCl}}{1\ \text{mol}\ Cl_2} = 0.288\ \text{mol NaCl}$ (smallest moles of product)

$0.288\ \text{mol NaCl} \times \frac{58.44\ \text{g NaCl}}{1\ \text{mol NaCl}} = 16.8\ \text{g NaCl}$

8.75 **a.** $4.0\ \text{mol}\ H_2O \times \frac{1\ \text{mol}\ C_5H_{12}}{6\ \text{mol}\ H_2O} \times \frac{72.15\ \text{g}\ C_5H_{12}}{1\ \text{mol}\ C_5H_{12}} = 48\ \text{g}\ C_5H_{12}$

b. $32.0\ \text{g}\ O_2 \times \frac{1\ \text{mol}\ O_2}{32.00\ \text{g}\ O_2} \times \frac{5\ \text{mol}\ CO_2}{8\ \text{mol}\ O_2} \times \frac{44.01\ \text{g}\ CO_2}{1\ \text{mol}\ CO_2} = 27.5\ \text{g}\ CO_2$

c. $44.5\ \text{g}\ C_5H_{12} \times \frac{1\ \text{mol}\ C_5H_{12}}{72.15\ \text{g}\ C_5H_{12}} \times \frac{5\ \text{mol}\ CO_2}{1\ \text{mol}\ C_5H_{12}} = 3.08\ \text{mol}\ CO_2$

$108\ \text{g}\ O_2 \times \frac{1\ \text{mol}\ O_2}{32.00\ \text{g}\ O_2} \times \frac{5\ \text{mol}\ CO_2}{8\ \text{mol}\ O_2} = 2.11\ \text{mol}\ CO_2$ (smallest moles of product)

$2.11\ \text{mol}\ CO_2 \times \frac{44.01\ \text{g}\ CO_2}{1\ \text{mol}\ CO_2} = 92.8\ \text{g}\ CO_2$

8.77 $2C_2H_2(g) + 5O_2(g) \longrightarrow 4CO_2(g) + 2H_2O(g)$

$22.5\ \text{g}\ C_2H_2 \times \frac{1\ \text{mol}\ C_2H_2}{26.04\ \text{g}\ C_2H_2} \times \frac{4\ \text{mol}\ CO_2}{2\ \text{mol}\ C_2H_2} \times \frac{44.01\ \text{g}\ CO_2}{1\ \text{mol}\ CO_2} = 76.1\ \text{g}\ CO_2$ (theoretical)

$\frac{62.0\ \text{g (actual)}}{76.06\ \text{g (theoretical)}} \times 100 = 81.5\%$ (percent yield)

8.79 Theoretical yield would be

$30.0\ \text{g}\ NH_3\ \text{(actual)} \times \frac{100.0\ \text{g}\ NH_3\ \text{(theoretical)}}{65.0\ \text{g}\ NH_3\ \text{(actual)}} = 46.2\ \text{g}\ NH_3$ (theoretical)

$46.2\ \text{g}\ NH_3 \times \frac{1\ \text{mol}\ NH_3}{17.03\ \text{g}\ NH_3} \times \frac{1\ \text{mol}\ N_2}{2\ \text{mol}\ NH_3} \times \frac{38.01\ \text{g}\ N_2}{1\ \text{mol}\ N_2} = 38.0\ \text{g}\ N_2$ (reacted)

8.81 **a.** $22.0\ \text{g}\ C_2H_2 \times \frac{1\ \text{mol}\ C_2H_2}{26.04\ \text{g}\ C_2H_2} \times \frac{5\ \text{mol}\ O_2}{2\ \text{mol}\ C_2H_2} \times \frac{6.022 \times 10^{23}\ \text{molecules}\ O_2}{1\ \text{mol}\ O_2}$

$= 1.27 \times 10^{24}$ molecules O_2

b. $22.0\ \text{g}\ C_2H_2 \times \frac{1\ \text{mol}\ C_2H_2}{26.04\ \text{g}\ C_2H_2} \times \frac{4\ \text{mol}\ CO_2}{2\ \text{mol}\ C_2H_2} \times \frac{44.0\ \text{g}\ CO_2}{1\ \text{mol}\ CO_2} = 74.4\ \text{g}\ CO_2$ (theoretical)

c. $\frac{64.0\ \text{g (actual)}}{74.4\ \text{g (theoretical)}} \times 100 = 86.0\%$ (percent yield)

9

Energy and States of Matter

Study Goals

- Describe some forms of energy.
- Calculate the energy lost or gained by a specific amount of a substance for a specific temperature change.
- Determine the energy lost or gained during a change of state at the melting or boiling point.
- Identify the states of matter.
- Describe the types of forces that hold particles together in liquids and solids.
- Calculate the energy involved in a change of state.
- Draw a heating or cooling curve for a substance when heated or cooled.
- Given the heat of reaction, describe a reaction as an exothermic reactions or endothermic reaction.

Think About It

1. What are some of the forms of energy you use in your home?

2. Why is the energy in your breakfast cereal called *potential* energy?

3. Why is the high specific heat of water important to our survival?

4. During a rain or snowfall, temperature rises? Why?

5. What is the difference between an exothermic and an endothermic reaction?

Key Terms

Match the following terms with the statements:

a. potential energy	**b.** specific heat	**c.** dipole-dipole attraction
d. change of state	**e.** exothermic	**f.** endothermic

1. ____ The amount of energy needed to raise the temperature of 1 g water by 1°C

2. ____ A reaction that gives off heat

3. ____ Interaction between the positive end of a polar molecule and the negative end of another

4. ____ A reaction that absorbs heat

5. ____ Stored energy

6.____ The boiling of water

Answers: **1.** b **2.** e **3.** c **4.** f **5.** a **6.** d

9.1 Heat and Energy

- Energy is the ability to do work.
- Potential energy is stored energy; kinetic energy is the energy of motion.
- Some forms of energy include heat, mechanical, radiant, solar, electrical, chemical, and nuclear.

◆ Learning Exercise 9.1A

Match the words in column A with the descriptions in column B.

A	B
1.____kinetic energy	**a.** Inactive or stored energy
2.____potential energy	**b.** The ability to do work
3.____chemical energy	**c.** The energy of motion
4.____energy	**d.** The energy available in the bonds of chemical compounds

Answers: **1.** c **2.** a **3.** d **4.** b

◆ Learning Exercise 9.2B

State whether the following statements describe potential (P) or kinetic (K) energy:

1. ____ A potted plant sitting on a ledge	**2.** ____ Your breakfast cereal
3. ____ Logs sitting in a fireplace	**4.** ____ A piece of candy
5. ____ An arrow shot from a bow	**6.** ____ A ski jumper at the top of the ski jump
7. ____ A jogger running	**8.** ____ A sky diver waiting to jump
9. ____ Water flowing down a stream	**10.** ____ A bowling ball striking the pins

Answers:					
	1. P	**2.** P	**3.** P	**4.** P	**5.** K
	6. P	**7.** K	**8.** P	**9.** K	**10.** K

9.2 Units of Energy and Specific Heat

- The SI unit of energy is the joule (J).
- Specific heat is the amount of energy required to raise the temperature of 1 g of a substance by 1°C.
- The specific heat for liquid water is 4.184 J/g°C.

◆ Learning Exercise 9.2A

Match the words in column A with the descriptions in column B.

A	B
1. _____calorie	**a.** 1000 joules
2. _____specific heat	**b.** The heat needed to raise 1 g of water by 1°C
3. _____kilojoule	**c.** A measure of the ability of a substance to absorb heat

Answers: **1.** b **2.** c **3.** a

◆ Learning Exercise 9.2B

Calculate the specific heat for each of the following:

a. A 15.2-g sample of a metal that absorbs 231 J when its temperature rises from 84.5°C to 125.3°C.

b. A 31.8-g sample of a metal that absorbs 816 J when its temperature rises from 23.7°C to 56.2°C.

c. A 38.2-g sample of a metal that absorbs 125 J when its temperature rises from 62.1°C to 68.4°C.

***Answers*:** **a.** 0.372 J/g°C **b.** 0.790 J/g°C **c.** 0.52 J/g°C

9.3 Calculations Using Specific Heat

- The heat lost or gained can be calculated using the mass of the substance, temperature difference, and its specific heat.
- A substance that loses heat has a negative sign for heat (–q); heat flows out.
- A substance that gains heat has a positive sign (+q); heat flows in.
- A nutritional calorie is the same amount of energy as 1 kcal or 1000 calories.
- When a substance is burned in a calorimeter, the water that surrounds the reaction chamber absorbs the heat given off. The calories absorbed by the water are calculated, and the caloric value (energy per gram) is determined for the substance.

◆ Learning Exercise 9.3A

Study Note

The heat lost or gained by a substance is calculated from the mass, temperature change, and specific heat of the substance.

Heat (joules) = **mass** (g) x **temperature change** (ΔT) x **specific heat** (J/g°C)

Calculate the joules (J) and calories (cal) gained or released during the following:

1. Heating 20.0 g water from 22°C to 77°C.

2. Heating 10.0 g water from 12.4°C to 67.5°C.

3. Cooling 0.400 kg water from 80.0°C to 35.0°C.

4. Cooling 125 g water from 45.0°C to 72.0°C.

Answers: **1.** 4600 J; 1100 cal; **2.** 2310 J; 551 cal **3.** –75 300 J; –18 000 cal **4.** –14 100 J; –3380 cal

◆ Learning Exercise 9.3B

Study Note

The mass of a substance is calculated by rearranging the heat equation.

Heat (joules) = **mass** (g) x (ΔT) x SH (J/g°C)

$$\textbf{mass}\ (g) = \frac{\text{Heat (joules)}}{(\Delta T) \times \text{SH (J/g°C)}}$$

The temperature change (ΔT) for a substance is calculated by rearranging the heat equation.

$$\Delta T = \frac{\text{Heat (joules)}}{\text{mass(g)} \times \text{SH (J/g°C)}}$$

a. Copper has a specific heat of 0.386 J/g°C. When 1250 J are added to a copper sample, its temperature rises from 24.6°C to 61.3°C. What is the mass of the copper sample?

b. A sample of aluminum has a specific heat of 0.897 J/g°C. When 785 J are added to an aluminum sample, its temperature rises from 14°C to 106°C. What is the mass of the aluminum sample?

c. Silver has a specific heat of 0.235 J/g°C. What is the temperature change of a 15.2 g piece of silver at 10.0°C when 426 J is added?

d. What is the final temperature of 15.0 g water initially at 5.5°C when 1140 J is added? (Hint: Determine the ΔT first.)

e. A 25.6-g sample of a metal heated to 100.0°C is placed in 48.2 g of water initially at 14.5°C. If the final temperature of the water (and metal) is 18.6°C, what is the specific heat of the metal?

Answers:

a. 88.2 g — **b.** 9.5 g

c. 119°C — **d.** ΔT = 18.2°C; T_f = 23.7°C

e. H_2O 530 J: SH = 830 J/(25.6 g)(81.4°C) = 0.405 J/g °C

◆ Learning Exercise 9.3C

Study Note

The caloric content of a food is the sum of calories from carbohydrate, fat, and protein. It is calculated by using the number of grams of each in a food and the caloric values of 17 kJ/g (4 kcal/g) for carbohydrate and protein, and 38 kJ/g (9 kcal/g) for fat.

Calculate the kilojoules (kJ) and kilocalories (kcal) for the following foods using the following data:

Food	Carbohydrate	Fat	Protein	kJ	kcal
a. Peas, green, cooked	19 g	1 g	9 g	_______	_______
b. Potato chips, 10 chips	10 g	8 g	1 g	_______	_______
c. Cream cheese, 8 oz	5 g	86 g	18 g	_______	_______
d. Hamburger, lean, 3 oz	0	10 g	23 g	_______	_______
e Banana, 1	26 g	0	1 g	_______	_______

Answers: **a.** 510 kJ; 120 kcal **b.** 490 kJ; 120 kcal **c.** 3700 kJ; 870 kcal
d. 770 kJ; 180 kcal **e.** 460 kJ; 110 kcal

9.4 States of Matter

- Matter is anything that has mass and occupies space.
- The three states of matter are solid, liquid, and gas.
- Physical properties such as shape, state, or color can change without affecting the identity of a substance.

◆ Learning Exercise 9.4

State whether the following statements describe a gas (G), a liquid (L), or a solid (S).

1.______ There are no attractions among the molecules.

2.______ Particles are held close together in a definite pattern.

3.______ The substance has a definite volume, but no definite shape.

4.______ The particles are moving extremely fast.

5.______ This substance has no definite shape and no definite volume.

6.______ The particles are very far apart.

7.______ This material has its own volume, but takes the shape of its container.

8.______ The particles of this material bombard the sides of the container with great force.

9.______ The particles in this substance are moving very, very slowly.

10.______ This substance has a definite volume and a definite shape.

Answers: **1.** G **2.** S **3.** L **4.** G **5.** G
6. G **7.** L **8.** G **9.** S **10.** S

9.5 Attractive Forces Between Particles

- The interactions between particles in solids and liquids determine their melting and boiling points.
- Ionic solids have high melting points due to strong ionic interactions between positive and negative ions.
- In polar substances, dipole–dipole attractions occur between the positive end of one molecule and the negative end of another.
- Hydrogen bonding, a type of dipole–dipole interaction, occurs between partially positive hydrogen atoms and strongly electronegative atoms of F, O, or N.
- Dispersion forces occur when temporary dipoles form within the nonpolar molecules, causing attractions to other nonpolar molecules.

◆ Learning Exercise 9.5A

Indicate the major type of interactive force that occurs in each of the following substances:

A. ionic **B.** dipole–dipole **C.** hydrogen bond **D.** dispersion forces

1. _____ KCl

2. _____ NCl_3

3. _____ SBr_2

4. _____ Cl_2

5. _____ HF

6. _____ H_2O

7. _____ C_4H_{10}

8. _____ Na_2O

Answers: **1.** A **2.** B **3.** B **4.** D
5. C **6.** C **7.** D **8.** A

◆ Learning Exercise 9.5B

Identify the substance that would have the higher boiling point in each pair:

1. NaCl or HCl ___________
2. Br_2 or HBr ___________
3. H_2O or H_2S ___________
4. C_2H_6 or C_8H_{18} ___________
5. $MgCl_2$ or OCl_2 ___________
6. NH_3 or PH_3 ___________

Answers:
1. NaCl (ionic)
2. HBr (dipole–dipole)
3. H_2O (hydrogen bonding)
4. C_8H_{18} (dispersion forces larger molecule)
5. $MgCl_2$ (ionic)
6. NH_3 (hydrogen bonding)

9.6 Changes of State

- A substance melts and freezes at it melting (freezing) point. During the process of melting or freezing, the temperature remains constant.
- The *heat of fusion* is the energy heat required to change 1 g solid to liquid. For water to freeze at 0°C, the heat of fusion is 334 joules. This is also the amount of heat lost when 1 g water freezcs at 0°C.
- When water boils at 100°C, 2260 joules, the heat of vaporization, is required to change 1 g liquid to gas (steam); it is also the amount of heat released when 1 g water vapor condenses at 100°C.
- Sublimation is the change of state from a solid directly to a gas.
- A heating or cooling curve illustrates the changes in temperature and states as heat is added to or removed from a substance.
- The heat given off or gained by a substance undergoing temperature changes, as well as changes of state, is the sum of two or more energy calculations.

◆ Learning Exercise 9.6A

Identify each of the following as **1.** melting **2.** freezing **3.** sublimation.

a._______ A liquid changes to a solid.

b._______ Ice forms on the surface of a lake in winter.

c._______ Dry ice in an ice cream cart changes to a gas.

d._______ Butter in a hot pan turns to liquid.

Answers: **a.** 2 **b.** 2 **c.** 3 **d.** 1

◆ Learning Exercise 9.6B

Study Note

The amount of heat needed or released during melting or freezing can be calculated using the heat of fusion: Heat (cal) = mass (g) x heat of fusion

Calculate the energy required or released when the following substances melt or freeze:

a. How many joules are needed to melt 24.0 g ice at 0°C?

b. How much heat in kilojoules is released when 325 g water freezes at 0°C?

c. How many joules of heat are required to melt 125 g ice at 0°C?

d. How many grams of ice would melt when 1680 J heat were absorbed?

Answers: **a.** 8020 J **b.** −109 kJ **c.** 41 800 J **d.** 5.03 g

◆ Learning Exercise 9.6C

Calculate the energy required or released for the following substances undergoing boiling or condensation:

a. How many joules are needed to completely change 5.00 g water to vapor at 100°C?

b. How many kilojoules are released when 515 g steam at 100°C condense to form liquid water at 100°C?

c. How many grams of water can be converted to steam at 100°C when 155 kJ energy are absorbed?

d. How many grams of steam condense if 24 800 J are released at 100°C?

Answers: **a.** 11 300 J **b.** –1160 kJ **c.** 68.6 g **d.** 11.0 g

◆ Learning Exercise 9.6D

On each heating or cooling curve, indicate the portion that corresponds to a solid, liquid, gas, and the changes in state.

1. Draw a heating curve for water that begins at –20°C and ends at 120°C. Water has a melting point of 0°C and a boiling point of 100°C.

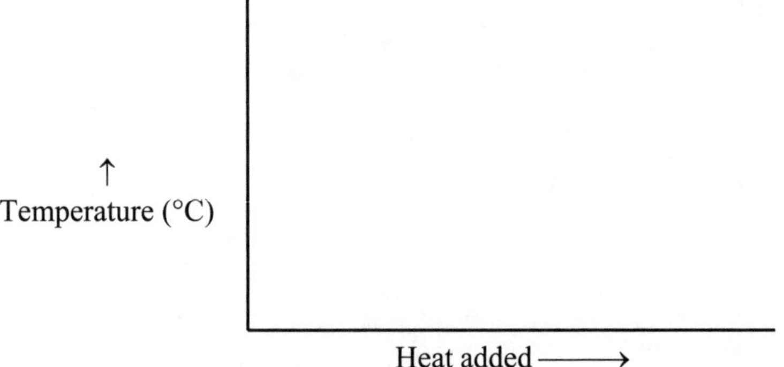

2. Draw a heating curve for bromine from –25° to 75°C. Bromine has a melting point of –7°C and a boiling point of 59°C.

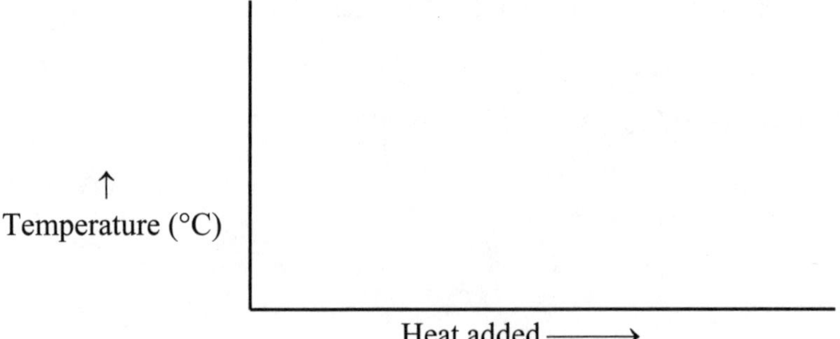

3. Draw a cooling curve for sodium from 1000°C to 0°C. Sodium has a freezing point of 98°C and a boiling (condensation) point of 883°C.

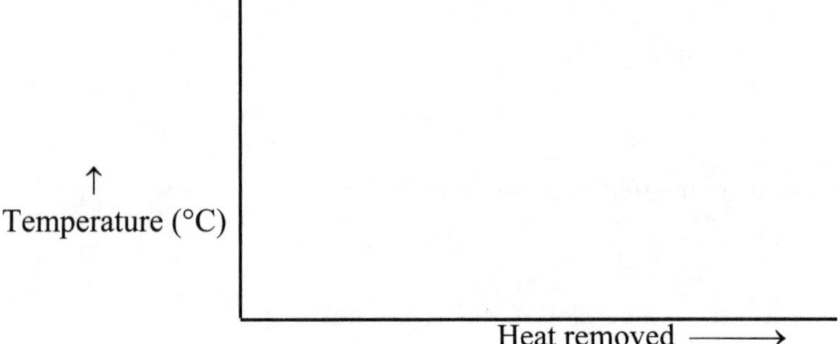

Answers:

1.

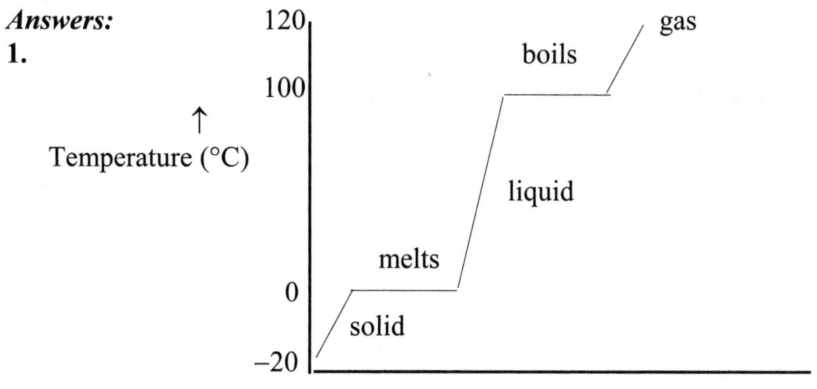

120
100
0
–20
↑
Temperature (°C)
gas
boils
liquid
melts
solid
Heat added ⟶

2.

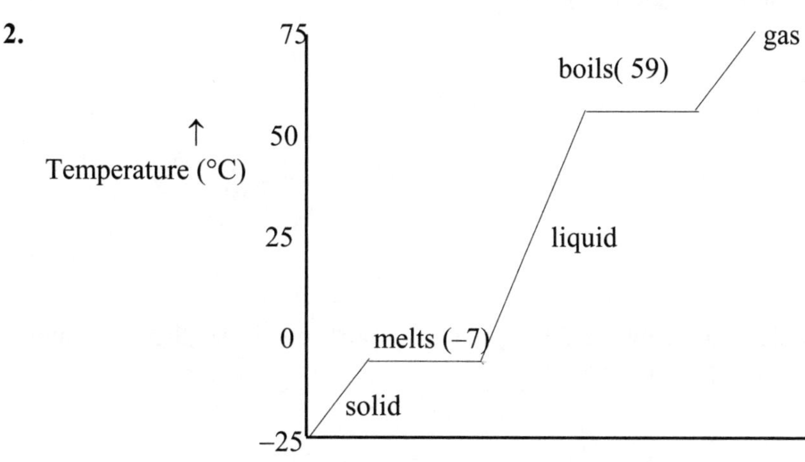

75
50
25
0
–25
↑
Temperature (°C)
gas
boils(59)
liquid
melts (–7)
solid
Heat added ⟶

3.

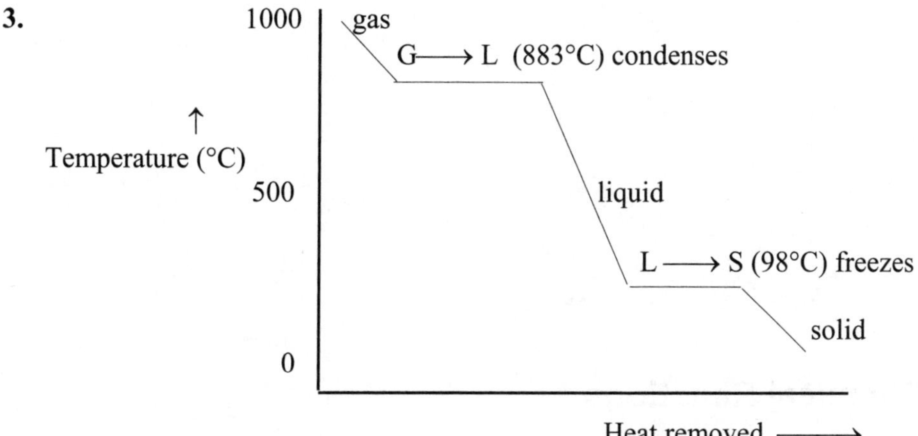

1000
500
0
↑
Temperature (°C)
gas
G ⟶ L (883°C) condenses
liquid
L ⟶ S (98°C) freezes
solid
Heat removed ⟶

◆ Learning Check 9.6E

a. How many kilojoules are released when 35.0 g water at 65.0°C are cooled to 0°C and frozen? (Hint: Two steps are needed.)

b. How many kilojoules are needed to melt 15.0 g ice at 0°C, heat the water to 100°C, and convert the water to gas at 100°C? (Hint: Three steps are needed.)

c. Calculate the number of kilojoules released when 25.0 g steam at 100°C condense, then cool, and finally freeze at 0°C. (Hint: Three steps are needed.)

Answers: **a.** –21.9 kJ **b.** 45.5 kJ **c.** –75.9 kJ

9.7 Energy in Chemical Reactions

- In a reaction, molecules (or atoms) must collide with energy equal to or greater than the energy of activation.
- The heat of reaction is the energy difference between the energy of the reactants and the products.
- In exothermic reactions, the heat of reaction is the energy released. In endothermic reactions, the heat of reaction is the energy absorbed.
- The rate of a reaction (the speed at which products form) can be increased by adding more reacting molecules, raising the temperature of the reaction, or adding a catalyst.

◆ Learning Exercise 9.6

Indicate whether each of the following is an endothermic or exothermic reaction:

1. $2H_2(g) + O_2(g) \longrightarrow 2H_2O(g) + 582\text{ kJ}$ ________________
2. $C_2H_4(g) + 176\text{ kJ} \longrightarrow H_2(g) + C_2H_2(g)$ ________________
3. $2C(s) + O_2(g) \longrightarrow 2CO(g) + 220\text{ kJ}$ ________________
4. $C_6H_{12}O_6(s) + 6\,O_2(g) \longrightarrow 6CO_2(g) + 6\,H_2O(l) + 1350\text{ kcal}$ ________________
   glucose
5. $C_2H_4(g) + H_2O(g) \longrightarrow C_2H_5OH(l) + 21\text{ kcal}$ ________________

Answers: **1.** exothermic **2.** endothermic **3.** exothermic **4.** exothermic **5.** exothermic

Checklist for Chapter 9

You are ready to take the self-test for Chapter 9. Be sure you have accomplished the following learning goals for this chapter. If you are not sure, review the section listed at the end of the goal. Then apply your new skills and understanding to the self-test.

After studying Chapter 9, I can successfully:

____ Describe some forms of energy (9.1).
____ Calculate the specific heat of a substance.
____ Given the mass of a sample, specific heat, and the temperature change, calculate the heat lost or gained (9.3).
____ Calculate the energy of a food sample (9.3).
____ Identify the physical state of a substance as a solid, liquid, or gas (9.4).
____ Identify the attractive forces between particles in a liquid or solid (9.5).
____ Calculate the heat change for a change of state for a specific amount of a substance (9.6).
____ Draw heating and cooling curves using the melting and boiling points of a substance (9.6).
____ Calculate the heat change for a specific amount of a substance in a chemical reaction (9.7).

Practice Test for Chapter 9

1. Which of the following would be described as potential energy?
   A. A car going around a racetrack **B.** A rabbit hopping
   C. Oil in an oil well **D.** A moving merry-go-round
   E. A bouncing ball

2. Which of the following would be described as kinetic energy?
   A. A car battery **B.** A can of tennis balls
   C. Gasoline in a car fuel tank **D.** A box of matches
   E. A tennis ball crossing over the net

3. When an electrical fan is working, electrical energy is converted to
   A. Heat energy **B.** Light energy
   C. Mechanical energy **D.** Chemical energy
   E. Electrical energy

4. The number of joules needed to raise the temperature of 5.0 g water from 25°C to 55°C is
A. 5.0 J **B.** 36 J **C.** 5.0J **D.** 335 J **E.** 630 J

5. The number of kilojoules (kJ) released when 15 g water cools from 58°C to 22°C.
A. –0.13 kJ **B.** –0.54 kJ **C.** –2.3 kJ **D.** –63 kJ **E.** –150 kJ

For questions 6 to 9, consider a cup of milk that is 3.5% butterfat with a caloric value of 690 kJ. In the cup of milk, there are 9 g fat, 12 g carbohydrate, and some protein.

6. The number of kcal provided by the carbohydrate is
A. 4 kcal **B.** 9 kcal **C.** 36 kcal **D.** 48 kcal **E.** 81 kcal

7. The number of kJ provided by the fat is
A. 9.0 kJ **B.** 38 kJ **C.** 150 kJ **D.** 200 kJ **E.** 340 kJ

8. The number of kcal provided by the protein is
A. 4 kcal **B.** 9 kcal **C.** 36 kcal **D.** 48 kcal **E.** 81 kcal

9. Which of the following describes a liquid?
A. A substance that has no definite shape and no definite volume
B. A substance with particles that are far apart
C. A substance with a definite shape and a definite volume
D. A substance containing particles that are moving very fast
E. A substance that has a definite volume, but takes the shape of its container

10. Which of the following describes a solid?
A. A substance that has no definite shape and no definite volume.
B. A substance with particles that are far apart.
C. A substance with a definite shape and a definite volume.
D. A substance containing particles that are moving very fast.
E. A substance that has a definite volume, but takes the shape of its container.

Identify the statements in questions 11 to 15 as:
A. energy **B.** evaporation **C.** heat of fusion
D. heat of vaporization **E.** boiling

11.____The energy required to convert a gram of solid to liquid

12.____The heat needed to boil a liquid

13.____The conversion of liquid molecules to gas at the surface of a liquid

14.____The ability to do work

15.____The formation of a gas within the liquid as well as on the surface

16. Ice cools down a drink because
A. the ice is warmer than the drink and heat flows out of the ice cubes
B. heat is absorbed from the drink to melt the ice cubes
C. the heat of fusion of the ice is higher than the heat of fusion for water
D. Both A and B
E. None of the above

17. A can full of steam is tightly stoppered. As the can cools
A. nothing will happen
B. the steam will blow up the can
C. the steam condenses and the can collapses
D. the steam condenses and the water formed will expand and explode the can
E. None of the above

18. The number joules needed to convert 15.0 g ice to liquid at 0°C is
A. 73J **B.** 334 J **C.** 2260 J **D.** 4 670 J **E.** 5 310 J

19. The number of joules released when 2.0 g water at 50°C are cooled and frozen at 0°C is
A. 418 J **B.** 670 J **C.** 1100 J **D.** 2100 J **E.** 3400 J

20. What is the total number of kilojoules required to convert 25 g ice at 0°C to gas at 100°C?
A. 8.4 kJ **B.** 19 kJ **C.** 59 kJ **D.** 67 kJ **E.** 76 kJ

21. The kcal needed to convert 10 g ice at 0°C to steam at 100°C are
A. 0.8 kcal **B.** 1.8 kcal **C.** 6.2 kcal **D.** 6.4 kcal **E.** 7.2 kcal

For questions 22 to 25, consider the heating curve below for p-toluidine. Answer the following questions when heat is added to p-toluidine at 20°C, where toluidine is below its melting point.

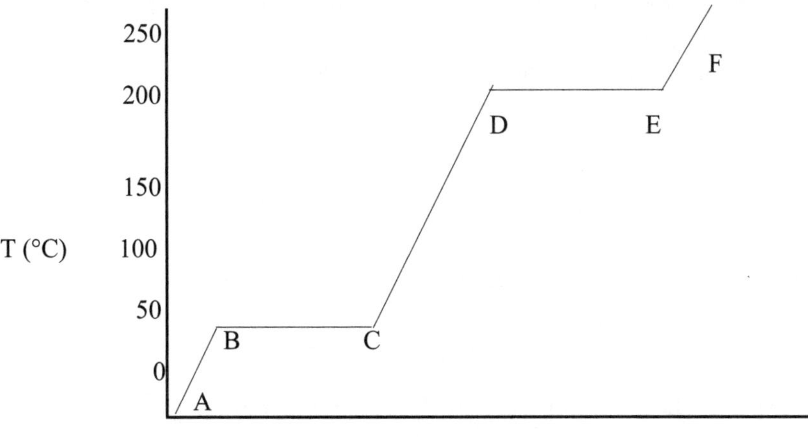

22. On the heating curve, segment BC indicates
A. solid **B.** melting **C.** liquid **D.** boiling **E.** gas

23. On the heating curve, segment CD shows toluidine as
A. solid **B.** melting **C.** liquid **D.** boiling **E.** gas

24. The boiling point of toluidine would be
A. 20°C **B.** 45°C **C.** 100°C **D.** 200°C **E.** 250°C

25. On the heating curve, segment EF shows toluidine as
A. solid **B.** melting **C.** a liquid **D.** boiling **E.** a gas

Answers to the Practice Test

1. C	**2.** E	**3.** C	**4.** E	**5** C
6. D	**7.** E	**8.** D	**9.** E	**10.** C
11. C	**12.** D	**13.** B	**14.** A	**15.** E
16. B	**17.** C	**18.** E	**19.** C	**20.** E
21. E	**22.** B	**23.** C	**24.** D	**25.** E

Answers and Solutions to Selected Text Problems

Section 9.1

9.1 At the top of the hill, all the energy of the car is in the form of potential energy. As it descends, potential energy is being converted into kinetic energy. When the car reaches the bottom, all its energy is in the form of motion (kinetic energy).

9.3 **a.** potential; stored energy **b.** kinetic; energy of motion
c. potential; stored energy **d.** potential; energy of motion

9.5 **a.** Using a hair dryer converts electrical energy into heat energy (the air is warmed) and mechanical energy.
b. Using a fan converts electrical energy into mechanical energy.
c. Burning gasoline converts chemical energy into mechanical energy as the car is propelled down the road, and heat energy as the engine warms up.
d. Radiant energy is converted into heat energy by the solar water heater.

9.7 **a.** Heat is transferred from the grill to the hamburger.
b. No heat is transferred.
c. No heat is transferred.

9.9 **a.** (2) light bulb
b. (3) hydroelectric power plant
c. (1) heater

Section 9.2

9.11 Copper, which has the lowest specific heat, would reach the highest temperature.

9.13 **a.** $3500\ \cancel{\text{cal}} \times \dfrac{1\ \text{kcal}}{1000\ \cancel{\text{cal}}} = 3.5\ \text{kcal}$

b. $415\ \cancel{\text{J}} \times \dfrac{1\ \text{cal}}{4.184\ \cancel{\text{J}}} = 99.2\ \text{cal}$

c. $28\ \cancel{\text{cal}} \times \dfrac{4.184\ \text{J}}{1\ \cancel{\text{cal}}} = 120\ \text{J}$

d. $4.5\ \cancel{\text{J}} \times \dfrac{1\ \cancel{\text{cal}}}{4.184\ \cancel{\text{J}}} \times \dfrac{1\ \text{kcal}}{1000\ \cancel{\text{cal}}} = 1100\ \text{cal}$

9.15 $\text{SH} = \dfrac{\text{J}}{\text{m} \times \Delta\text{T}}$

a. $\Delta\text{T} = 83.6°\text{C} - 24.2°\text{C} = 59.4°\text{C}$ $\quad \text{SH} = \dfrac{312\ \text{J}}{13.5\ \text{g} \times 59.4°\text{C}} = 0.389\ \text{J/g°C}$

b. $\Delta\text{T} = 57.9\ °\text{C} - 35.0°\text{C} = 22.9°\text{C}$ $\quad \text{SH} = \dfrac{345\ \text{J}}{48.2\ \text{g} \times 22.9°\text{C}} = 0.313\ \text{J/g°C}$

Section 9.3

9.17 The heat required is given by the relationship: Heat (q) = m x ΔT x SH.
If heat is added, q is +, if heat is lost g is –.

a. $q = m \times \Delta T \times SH = 25.0\text{ g} \times (25.7°C - 12.5°C) \times 4.184\text{ J/g°C} =$
$25.0\text{ g} \times 13.2°C \times 4.184\text{ J/g°C} = +1380\text{ J} \quad + \quad 1380\text{ J} \times \dfrac{1\text{ cal}}{4.184\text{ J}} = +330\text{ cal}$

b. $q = m \times \Delta T \times SH = 38.0\text{ g} \times (246°C - 122°C) \times 0.385\text{ J/g°C} =$
$38.0\text{ g} \times 124°C \times 0.385\text{ J/g°C} = +1810\text{ J} \quad + \quad 1810\text{ J} \times \dfrac{1\text{ cal}}{4.184\text{ J}} = +434\text{ cal}$

c. $q = m \times \Delta T \times SH = 15.0\text{ g} \times (-42.0°C - 65.0°C) \times 2.46\text{ J/g°C} =$
$15.0\text{ g} \times -107°C \times 2.46\text{ J/g°C} = -3780\text{ J} \quad - \quad 3780\text{ J} \times \dfrac{1\text{ cal}}{4.184\text{ J}} = -904\text{ cal}$

d. $q = m \times \Delta T \times SH = 125\text{ g} \times (55°C - 118°C) \times 0.450\text{ J/g°C} =$
$125\text{ g} \times -63°C \times 0.450\text{ J/g°C} = -3500\text{ J} \quad - \quad 3500\text{ J} \times \dfrac{1\text{ cal}}{4.184\text{ J}} = -850\text{ cal}$

9.19 **a.** $m = \dfrac{q}{\Delta T \times SH} = \dfrac{225\text{ J}}{(47.0°C - 15.0°C) \times 0.129\text{ J/g °C}} = \dfrac{225\text{ J}}{32.0°C \times 0.129\text{ J/g °C}} = 54.5\text{ g}$

b. $m = \dfrac{q}{\Delta T \times SH} = \dfrac{-8.40\text{ kJ}}{(82.0°C - 168.0°C) \times 0.45029\text{ J/g °C}} \times \dfrac{1000\text{ J}}{1\text{ kJ}}$

$\dfrac{-8400\text{ J}}{-86.0°C \times 0.450\text{ J/g °C}} = 217\text{ g}$

c. $m = \dfrac{q}{\Delta T \times SH} = \dfrac{8.80\text{ kJ}}{(26.8°C - 12.5°C) \times 0.897\text{ J/g °C}} \times \dfrac{1000\text{ J}}{1\text{ kJ}}$

$\dfrac{8800\text{ J}}{14.3°C \times 0.897\text{ J/g °C}} = 686\text{ g}$

d. $m = \dfrac{q}{\Delta T \times SH} = \dfrac{-14\,200\text{ J}}{(42°C - 185°C) \times 0.523\text{ J/g °C}} \times \dfrac{-14\,200\text{ J}}{-143°C \times 0.523\text{ J/g °C}} = 190\text{ g}$

9.21 **a.** $\Delta T = \dfrac{q}{m \times SH} = \dfrac{1580\text{ J}}{20.0\text{ g} \times 0.450\text{ J/g °C}} = 176\text{ °C}$

b. $\Delta T = \dfrac{q}{m \times SH} = \dfrac{7.10\text{ kJ}}{150.0\text{ g} \times 4.184\text{ J/g °C}} \times \dfrac{1000\text{ J}}{1\text{ kJ}} = 11.3°C$

c. $\Delta T = \dfrac{q}{m \times SH} = \dfrac{7680\text{ J}}{85.0\text{ g} \times 0.129\text{ J/g °C}} = 700°C$

d. $\Delta T = \dfrac{q}{m \times SH} = \dfrac{6.75\text{ kJ}}{50.0\text{ g} \times 0.385\text{ J/g °C}} \times \dfrac{1000\text{ J}}{1\text{ kJ}} = 351°C$

9.23 **a.** $505\ \cancel{g} \times \frac{4.184\ \cancel{J}}{\cancel{g\,^{\circ}C}} \times 10.5\ \cancel{^{\circ}C} \times \frac{1\ kJ}{1000\ \cancel{J}} = 22.2\ \cancel{kJ} \times \frac{1\ kcal}{4.184\ \cancel{kJ}} = 5.31\ kcal$

b. $4980\ \cancel{g} \times \frac{4.184\ \cancel{J}}{\cancel{g\,^{\circ}C}} \times 42\ \cancel{^{\circ}C} \times \frac{1\ kJ}{1000\ \cancel{J}} = 871\ \cancel{kJ} \times \frac{1\ kcal}{4.184\ \cancel{kJ}} = 208\ kcal$

c. $1250\ \cancel{g} \times \frac{4.184\ \cancel{J}}{\cancel{g\,^{\circ}C}} \times 25\ \cancel{^{\circ}C} \times \frac{1\ kJ}{1000\ \cancel{J}} = 132\ \cancel{kJ} \times \frac{1\ kcal}{4.184\ \cancel{kJ}} = 31.5\ kcal$

9.25 **a.** Because the orange juice contains both carbohydrate and protein, two calculations will be needed.

$26\ \cancel{g\ carbohydrate} \times \frac{17\ kJ}{\cancel{g\ carbohydrate}} = 442\ kJ$ (not rounded)

$2\ \cancel{g\ protein} \times \frac{17\ kJ}{\cancel{g\ protein}} = 34\ kJ$ (not rounded)

Total: 442 kJ + 34 kJ = 476 kJ (not rounded) = 480 kJ (rounded to tens)

$480\ \cancel{kJ} \times \frac{1\ kcal}{4.184\ \cancel{kJ}} = 110\ kcal$

b. $18\ \cancel{g\ carbohydrate} \times \frac{17\ kJ}{\cancel{g\ carbohydrate}} = 310\ kJ$

$18\ \cancel{g\ carbohydrate} \times \frac{4\ kcal}{\cancel{g\ carbohydrate}} = 70\ kcal$

c. $14\ \cancel{g\ fat} \times \frac{38\ kJ}{\cancel{g\ fat}} = 530\ kJ$

$14\ \cancel{g\ fat} \times \frac{9\ kcal}{\cancel{g\ fat}} = 130\ kcal$

d. Three calculations are needed:

$68\ \cancel{g\ carbohydrate} \times \frac{17\ kJ}{\cancel{g\ carbohydrate}} = 1156\ kJ$ (not rounded)

$150\ \cancel{g\ protein} \times \frac{17\ kJ}{\cancel{g\ protein}} = 2550\ kJ$ (not rounded)

$5.0\ \cancel{g\ fat} \times \frac{38\ kJ}{\cancel{g\ fat}} = 190\ kJ$

Total: 1156 kJ + 2550 kJ + 190 kJ = 3896 kJ (not rounded)
= 3900 kJ (rounded to tens place)

$3896\ \cancel{kJ}$ (not rounded) $\times \frac{1\ kcal}{4.184\ \cancel{kJ}} = 931\ kcal = 930\ kcal$ (rounded)

Section 9.4

9.27 **a.** A gas takes the shape and volume of its container. Thus, a gas has no definite volume or shape.
b. The particles in a gas have little attraction between them and do not interact.
c. A solid has a definite volume or shape.

Section 9.5

9.29 **a.** An attraction between the positive end of one polar molecule and the negative end of another polar molecule is called dipole–dipole attraction.
b. An ionic bond is an attraction between a positive and negative ion.
c. The weak attractions that occurs between temporary dipoles in nonpolar CCl_4 molecules are dispersion forces.
d. The attraction between H and F, O, or N in a dipole is a hydrogen bond.
e. The weak attractions that occurs between temporary dipoles in nonpolar Cl_2 molecules are dispersion forces.

9.31 **a.** Hydrogen bonding occurs between dipoles containing H and F, O, or N.
b. Dispersion forces occur between temporary dipoles in nonpolar molecules.
c. Dipole–dipole interactions occurs between dipoles in polar molecules.
d. Dispersion forces occur between temporary dipoles in nonpolar molecules.
e. Dispersion forces occur between temporary dipoles in nonpolar molecules.

9.33 **a.** HF; hydrogen bonds are stronger than dipole–dipole interactions of HBr.
b. NaF; ionic bonds are stronger than the hydrogen bonds in HF.
c. $MgBr_2$; ionic bonds are stronger than the dipole–dipole interactions in PBr_3.
d. C_4H_{10} has more electrons and therefore more dispersion forces than CH_4.

9.35 Both **b** (liquid water freezes) and **d** (solid butter melts) describe processes that involve a change of state.

Section 9.6

9.35 Both **b** (liquid water freezes) and **d** (solid butter melts) describe processes that involve a change of state.

9.37 **a.** melting (solid → liquid) **b.** melting (solid → liquid)
c. sublimation((solid → gas) **d.** freezing (solid → gas)

9.39 **a.** $65.0\ \cancel{\text{g ice}} \times \dfrac{334\ \text{J}}{1\ \cancel{\text{g ice}}} = 21700\ \text{J}$; absorbed

b. $17.0\ \cancel{\text{g ice}} \times \dfrac{334\ \text{J}}{1\ \cancel{\text{g ice}}} = 5680\ \text{J}$ absorbed

c. $225\ \cancel{\text{g water}} \times \dfrac{334\ \text{J}}{1\ \cancel{\text{g water}}} \times \dfrac{1\ \text{kJ}}{1000\ \cancel{\text{J}}} = 75.2\ \text{kJ}$; released

d. $50.0\ \cancel{\text{g water}} \times \dfrac{334\ \text{J}}{1\ \cancel{\text{g water}}} \times \dfrac{1\ \text{kJ}}{1000\ \cancel{\text{J}}} = 16.7\ \text{kJ}$; released

9.41 **a.** Vapor changing to liquid (rain) is condensation.
b. Liquid water changing to vapor is evaporation.
c. Steam forming from a lava flow into the ocean is boiling.
d. Water droplets form on a mirror after a shower as a result of condensation.

9.43 **a.** The liquid water in perspiration absorbs heat and changes to vapor. The heat needed for the change is removed from the skin.
b. On a hot day, there are more liquid water molecules in the damp clothing that have sufficient energy to become water vapor. Thus, water evaporates from the clothes more readily on a hot day.
c. Some water molecules evaporate, but they cannot escape from the sealed bag. The high humidity in the bag allows some of the gaseous water to condense back to liquid, so the clothes will not dry.

9.45 **a.** $10.0\ \cancel{\text{g water}} \times \dfrac{2260\ \text{J cal}}{1\ \cancel{\text{g water}}}$ = 22600 J; heat is absorbed

b. $50.0\ \cancel{\text{g water}} \times \dfrac{2260\ \text{J cal}}{1\ \cancel{\text{g water}}} \times \dfrac{1\ \text{kJ}}{1000\ \cancel{\text{J}}}$ =113 kJ; heat is absorbed

c. $8.0\ \cancel{\text{kg steam}} \times \dfrac{2260\ \text{J cal}}{1\ \cancel{\text{kg steam}}}$ = 1.81×10^{7} J; heat is released

d. $175\ \cancel{\text{g steam}} \times \dfrac{2260\ \text{J cal}}{1\ \cancel{\text{g water}}} \times \dfrac{1\ \text{kJ}}{1000\ \cancel{\text{J}}}$ = 396 kJ; heat is released

9.47

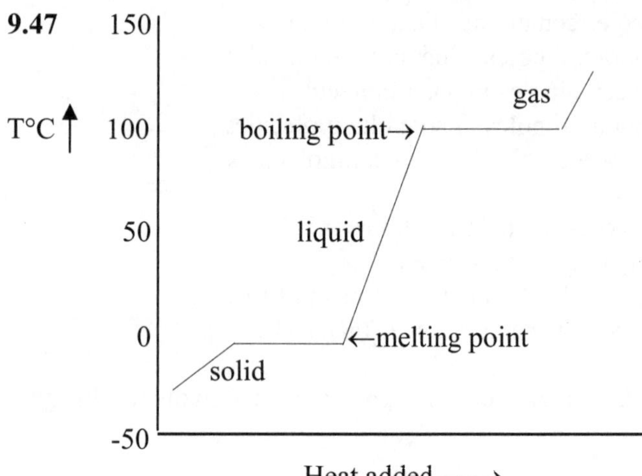

9.49 **a.** $20.0\ \cancel{\text{g}} \times 57\cancel{^{\circ}\text{C}} \times \dfrac{4.184\ \text{J}}{\cancel{\text{g}^{\circ}\text{C}}}$ = 4800 J

b. Two calculations are needed:

(1) $50.0\ \cancel{\text{g ice}} \times \dfrac{334\ \text{J}}{1\ \cancel{\text{g ice}}}$ = 16 700 J

(2) $50.0\ \cancel{\text{g ice}} \times 65\ \cancel{^{\circ}\text{C}} \times \dfrac{4.184\ \text{J}}{1\ \cancel{\text{g ice}}}$ = 13 600 J

Total: 16 700 J + 13 600 J = 30 300 J

c. Two calculations needed:

(1) $15.0\ \cancel{\text{g steam}} \times \dfrac{2260\ \cancel{\text{J}}}{1\ \cancel{\text{g steam}}} \times \dfrac{1\ \text{kJ}}{1000\ \cancel{\text{J}}}$ = 33.9 kJ

(2) $15.0\ \cancel{\text{g water}} \times 100\ \cancel{^{\circ}\text{C}} \times \dfrac{4.184\ \cancel{\text{J}}}{1\ \cancel{\text{g ice}}} \times \dfrac{1\ \text{kJ}}{1000\ \cancel{\text{J}}}$ = 6.28 kJ

Total: 33.9 kJ + 6.28 kJ = 40.2 kJ

d. Three ca1culations needed:

(1) $24.0\ \cancel{\text{g ice}} \times \dfrac{334\ \text{J}}{1\ \cancel{\text{g ice}}} \times \dfrac{1\ \text{kJ}}{1000\ \text{kJ}}$ = 8.016 kJ (not rounded)

(2) $24.0\ \cancel{\text{g water}} \times 100\ \cancel{^{\circ}\text{C}} \times \dfrac{4.184\ \cancel{\text{J}}}{1\ \cancel{\text{g ice}}} \times \dfrac{1\ \text{kJ}}{1000\ \cancel{\text{J}}}$ = 10.04 kJ (not rounded)

(3) $24.0\ \cancel{\text{g steam}} \times \dfrac{2260\ \cancel{\text{J}}}{1\ \cancel{\text{g steam}}} \times \dfrac{1\ \text{kJ}}{1000\ \cancel{\text{J}}}$ = 54.24 kJ (not rounded)

Total: 8.016 kJ + 10.04 kJ + 54.24 = 72.3 kJ (rounded to 0.1)

9.51 Two calculations are needed:

$$275 \text{ g ice} \times \frac{334 \text{ J}}{1 \text{ g ice}} \times \frac{1 \text{ kJ}}{1000 \text{ J}} = 91.9 \text{ kJ}$$

$$275 \text{ g wataer} \times 24.0^{\circ}\text{C} \times \frac{4.184 \text{ J}}{\text{g}^{\circ}\text{C}} \times \frac{1 \text{ kJ}}{1000 \text{ J}} = 27.6 \text{ kJ}$$

Total: 91.9 kJ + 27.6 kJ = 119.5 kJ

Section 9.7

9.53 In exothermic reactions, the energy of the products is lower than the reactants.

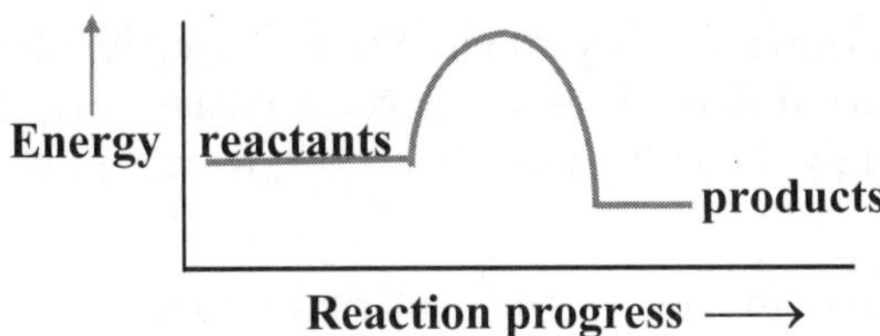

9.55 **a.** exothermic; heat loss **b.** endothermic; heat gain **c.** exothermic; heat loss

9.57 **a.** Heat is released, which makes the reaction exothermic with $\Delta H = -890$ kJ.
b. Heat is absorbed, which makes the reaction endothermic with $\Delta H = 65.3$ kJ.
c. Heat is released, which makes the reaction exothermic with $\Delta H = -853$ kJ.

9.59 $$125 \text{ g } Cl_2 \times \frac{1 \text{ mol } Cl_2}{70.90 \text{ g } Cl_2} \times \frac{657 \text{ kJ}}{2 \text{ mol } Cl_2} = 579 \text{ kJ}$$

Answer to Additional Questions and Problems

9.67 **a.** light bulb; light fixture **b.** generator; wind turbine
c. space heater; electric stove **d.** battery; coal-powered plant

9.69 $$50.0 \text{ g water} \times 9.4^{\circ}\text{C} \times \frac{4.183 \text{ J}}{\text{g }^{\circ}\text{C}} = 1970 \text{ J}$$

$$SH_{metal} = \frac{-1970 \text{ J}}{25.0 \text{ g } (-70.6^{\circ}\text{C})} = 1.1 \text{ J/g}^{\circ}\text{C}$$

9.71 $$8400 \text{ kJ} \times \frac{1000 \text{ J}}{1 \text{ kJ}} = 8\,400\,000 \text{ J}$$

Heat = mass x ΔT x SH

$$\Delta T = \frac{\text{Heat}}{\text{mass x SH}} = \frac{8\,400\,000 \text{ J}}{50\,000 \text{ g } (4.184 \text{ J/g }^{\circ}\text{C})} = 40^{\circ}\text{C}$$

Final T = 20°C + 40°C = 60°C

9.73 $$725 \text{ g} \times \frac{4.18 \text{ J}}{\text{g }^{\circ}\text{C}} \times 28^{\circ}\text{C} \times \frac{1 \text{ kJ}}{1000 \text{ J}} = 85 \text{ kJ}$$

9.75 The heat lost by the water is equal to the heat gained by the copper, for both: q = m x ΔT x SH.

For water. q = m x ΔT x SH = 50.0 g x (24.0°C – 16.0°C) x 4.184 J/g°C =
50.0 g x 8.0°C x 4.184 J/g°C = 1670 J (not rounded)

For copper: $$m = \frac{q}{\Delta T \times SH} = \frac{1670 \text{ J}}{(86.0^{\circ}\text{C} - 24.0^{\circ}\text{C}) \times 0.385 \text{ J/g }^{\circ}\text{C}} = \frac{1670 \text{ J}}{62.0^{\circ}\text{C} \times 0.385 \text{ J/g }^{\circ}\text{C}} = 70\text{g}$$

9.77 **a.** hydrogen bond (3) **b.** hydrogen bond (3) **c.** dispersion (4)
d. dipole–dipole (2) **e.** hydrogen bond (3) **f.** ionic (1)

9.79 **a.** HF. Hydrogen bonds are stronger and take more energy to break than dipole–dipole or nonpolar bonds.

b. H_2O. Hydrogen bonds are stronger and take more energy to break than dipole–dipole or nonpolar bonds.

c. KCl. Ionic bonds are stronger and take more energy to break than all types of covalent bonds.

d. NH_3. Hydrogen bonds are stronger and take more energy to break than nonpolar covalent bonds.

9.81 In nonpolar compounds, there are no dipoles. However, they do interact by dispersion forces from temporary dipoles that result from a momentary shift of electrons. Because octane C_8H_{18} has more electrons than ethane C_2H_6, octane can form larger temporary dipoles, which results in a higher melting point.

9.83 Heat is released (exothermic) as water vapor turn to rain or liquid water turns to snow. The heat released in either of these processes warms the surrounding air, so the air temperature is in fact raised.

9.85 $3.0\text{ kg} \times \frac{1000\text{ g}}{1\text{ kg}} \times \frac{0.13\text{ J}}{\text{g °C}} \times 300.\text{°C} = 117\,000\text{ J}$ (not rounded) available to melt ice

Because 334 J will melt 1 g ice, we can calculate the number of grams of ice that can melt.

$117\,000\text{ J} \times \frac{1\text{ g}}{334\text{ J}} = 350\text{ g}$ (rounded) ice will be melted

9.87 **a.** $3.00\text{ g NO} \times \frac{1\text{ mol NO}}{30.01\text{ g NO}} \times \frac{90.2\text{ kJ}}{2\text{ mol NO}} = 4.51\text{ kJ}$

b. $2\,NO(g) \rightarrow N_2(g) + O_2(g) + 90.2\text{ kJ}$

c. $5.00\text{ g NO} \times \frac{1\text{ mol NO}}{30.01\text{ g NO}} \times \frac{90.2\text{ kJ}}{2\text{ mol NO}} = 7.51\text{ kJ}$

9.89 (1) $5.00\text{ kg} \times \frac{1000\text{ g}}{1\text{ kg}} \times \frac{2260\text{ J}}{1\text{ g}} \times \frac{1\text{ kJ}}{1000\text{ J}} = 11\,300\text{ kJ}$

(2) $5.00\text{ kg} \times \frac{1000\text{ g}}{1\text{ kg}} \times 100\text{°C} \times \frac{4.184\text{ J}}{\text{g °C}} \times \frac{1\text{ kJ}}{1000\text{ J}} = 2\,092\text{ kJ}$

(3) $5.00\text{ kg} \times \frac{1000\text{ g}}{1\text{ kg}} \times \frac{334\text{ J}}{1\text{ g}} \times \frac{1\text{ kJ}}{1000\text{ J}} = 1\,670\text{ kJ}$

(4) $5.00\text{ kg} \times \frac{1000\text{ g}}{1\text{ kg}} \times 15\text{°C} \; \frac{2.03\text{ J}}{\text{g °C}} \times \frac{1\text{ kJ}}{1000\text{ J}} = 152\text{ kJ}$

Total: 11 300 kJ + 2092 kJ + 1670 kJ + 152 kJ = 15 200 kJ

10
Gases

Study Goals

- Describe the kinetic theory of gases.
- Use the gas laws to determine the new pressure, volume, or temperature of a specific amount of gas.
- Describe the relationship between the amount of a gas and its volume.
- Use the ideal gas law to solve for pressure, volume, temperature, or moles of gas when three of the four variables are given.
- Use partial pressures to calculate the total pressure of a gas mixture.
- Determine the mass or volume of a gas in a chemical reaction.

Think About It

1. How does a barometer work?

2. Why must the pressure of the inhaled gas mixture increase when a person is scuba diving?

3. Why are airplanes pressurized?

Key Terms

Match each of the following key terms with the correct definition.

a. kinetic theory **b.** pressure **c.** Boyle's law
d. Charles' law **e.** partial pressure

1. _____ The volume of a gas varies directly with the Kelvin temperature when pressure and amount of gas remain constant.

2. _____ Force exerted by gas particles that collide with the sides of a container.

3. _____ The pressure exerted by the individual gases in a gas mixture.

4. _____ The volume of a gas varies inversely with the pressure of a gas when temperature and amount of gas are constant.

5. _____ A model that explains the behavior of gaseous particles.

Answers **1.** d **2.** b **3.** e **4.** c **5.** a

10.1 Properties of Gases

- In a gas, particles are in constant motion and moving rapidly in straight lines until they collide.
- Particles in a gas are so far apart that they are not usually attracted to each other.
- A gas is described by the physical properties of pressure (P), volume (V), temperature (T), and amount in moles (n).

◆ Learning Exercise 10.1

True or false:

a. _____ Gases are composed of small particles.

b. _____ Gas molecules are usually close together.

c. _____ Gas molecules move rapidly because they are strongly attracted.

d. _____ The distances between gas molecules are great.

e. _____ Gas molecules travel in straight lines until they collide.

Answers **a.** T **b.** F **c.** F **d.** T **e.** T

10.2 Gas Pressure

- A gas exerts pressure, which is the force of the gas particles on the surface of a container.
- Units of gas pressure include torr, mm Hg, Pascal (Pa), kilopascal (kPa), and atm.

◆ Learning Exercise 10.2

Complete the following:

a. 1.50 atm = __________ mm Hg

b. 550 mm Hg = __________ atm

c. 0.725 atm = __________ kPa

d. 1520 mm Hg = __________ atm

e. 30.5 in. Hg = __________ mm Hg

f. During the weather report on TV, the pressure was given as 29.3 in. (of mercury). What is this pressure in mm Hg and in atm?

Answers **a.** 1140 mm Hg **b.** 0.72 atm **c.** 73.4 kPa
d. 2.00 atm **e.** 775 mm Hg **f.** 745 mm Hg; 0.980 atm

10.3 Pressure and Volume (Boyle's Law)

- According to Boyle's law, pressure increases if volume decreases and pressure decreases if volume increases.
- The volume (V) of a gas changes inversely with the pressure (P) of the gas when T and n are held constant: $P_1V_1 = P_2V_2$.

◆ Learning Exercise 10.3

Calculate the variable in each of the following gas problems using Boyle's law.

a. Four (4.0) liters of helium gas has a pressure of 1000. mm Hg. What will be the new pressure if the volume is reduced to 1.0 liter (n and T constant)?

b. A gas occupies a volume of 360 mL at 750 mm Hg. What volume does it occupy at a pressure of (1) 1500 mm Hg? (2) 375 mm Hg? (n and T constant)

c. A gas sample at a pressure of 5.00 atm has a volume of 3.00 L. If the gas pressure is changed to 760. mm Hg, what volume will the gas occupy (n and T constant)?

d. A sample of 250. mL of nitrogen is initially at a pressure of 2.50 atm. If the pressure changes to 1025 mm Hg, what is the new volume in mL?

Answers

a. 4000 mm Hg **b.** (1) 180 mL (2) 720 mL
c. 15.0 L **d.** 463 mL

10.4 Temperature and Volume (Charles' Law)

- The volume (V) of a gas is directly related to its Kelvin temperature (T) when there is no change in the pressure of the gas:

$$\frac{V_1}{T_1} = \frac{V_2}{T_2}$$

- According to Charles' law, temperature increases if the volume of the gas increases and temperature decreases if volume decreases.

◆ Learning Exercise 10.4

Solve the following gas law problems using Charles' law.

a. A large balloon has a volume of 2.5 L at a temperature of 0°C. What is the new volume of the balloon when the temperature rises to 120°C and the pressure remains constant?

b. Consider a balloon filled with helium to a volume of 6600 L at a temperature of 223°C. To what temperature must the gas be cooled to decrease the volume to 4100 L?
(P constant)

c. A sample of 750 mL of neon is heated from 120°C to 350°C. If pressure is kept constant, what is the new volume?

d. What is the final temperature of 350. mL of oxygen gas at 22°C if its volume decreases to 0.100 L?

Answers **a.** 3.6 L **b.** 308 K; 35°C **c.** 1200 mL **d.** 84 K, –189°C

10.5 Temperature and Pressure (Gay-Lussac's Law)

- The pressure (P) of a gas is directly related to its Kelvin temperature (T), when n and V are constant.

$$\frac{P_1}{T_1} = \frac{P_2}{T_2}$$

  This means that an increase in temperature increases the pressure of a gas or a decrease in temperature decreases the pressure, as long as the volume stays constant.
- Vapor pressure is the pressure of the gas that forms when a liquid evaporates. At the boiling point of a liquid, the vapor pressure equals the atmospheric pressure.

◆ Learning Exercise 10.5

Solve the following gas law problems using Gay-Lussac's law.

a. A sample of helium gas has a pressure of 1060 mm Hg at a temperature of 225 K. At what pressure (mm Hg) will the helium sample reach a temperature of 675 K? (*V* constant)

b. A balloon contains a gas with a pressure of 5100 mm Hg and a temperature of 227°C. What is the new pressure (mm Hg) of the gas when the temperature drops to 27°C? (*V* constant)

c. A spray can contains a gas with a pressure of 3.0 atm at a temperature of 17°C. What is the pressure (atm) inside the container if the temperature rises to 110°C? (*V* constant)

d. A gas has a pressure of 1200. mm Hg at 300.°C. What will the temperature (°C) be when the pressure falls to 1.10 atm? (*V* constant)

Answers

a. 3180 mm Hg **b.** 3100 mm Hg
c. 4.0 atm **d.** 126°C

10.6 The Combined Gas Law

- The gas laws can be combined into a relationship of pressure (*P*), volume (*V*), and temperature (*T*).

$$\frac{P_1V_1}{T_1} = \frac{P_2V_2}{T_2}$$

This expression is used to determine the effect of changes in two of the variables on the third.

◆ Learning Exercise 10.6

Solve the following using the combined gas laws:

a. A 5.0 L sample of nitrogen gas has a pressure of 1200 mm Hg at 220 K. What is the pressure of the sample when the volume increases to 20.0 L at 440 K?

b. A 25.0-mL bubble forms at the ocean depths where the pressure is 10.0 atm and the temperature is 5.0°C. What is the volume of that bubble at the ocean surface where the pressure is 760.0 mm Hg and the temperature is 25°C?

c. A 35.0 mL sample of argon gas has a pressure of 1.0 atm and a temperature of 15°C. What is the final volume if the pressure goes to 2.0 atm and the temperature to 45°C?

d. A 315-L weather balloon is launched at the earth's surface where the temperature is 12°C and the pressure is 0.930 atm. What is the volume of the balloon in the upper atmosphere if the pressure is 116 mm Hg and the temperature is –35°C?

Answers **a.** 600 mm Hg **b.** 268 mL **c.** 19 mL **d.** 1.60×10^3 L

10.7 Volume and Moles (Avogadro's Law)

- Avogadro's law states that equal volumes of gases at the same temperature and pressure contain the same number of moles. The volume (V) of a gas is directly related to the number of moles of the gas when the pressure and temperature of the gas do not change.

$$\frac{V_1}{n_1} = \frac{V_2}{n_2}$$

- At STP conditions, standard pressure (1 atm) and temperature (0°C), one mole of a gas occupies a volume of 22.4 L.

Study Note

At STP, the molar volume factor 22.4 L/mol converts between moles of a gas and volume.

Example: How many liters would 2.00 mol N_2 occupy at STP?

Solution: $2.00 \cancel{\text{mol } N_2} \times \frac{22.4 \text{ L}}{1 \cancel{\text{mol } N_2}} = 44.8 \text{ mol } N_2$

◆ Learning Exercise 10.7

Use Avogadro's law to solve the following gas problems:

a. A gas containing 0.50 mol helium has a volume of 4.00 L. What is the new volume when 1.0 mol nitrogen is added to the container when pressure and temperature remain constant?

b. A balloon containing 1.00 mol oxygen has a volume of 15 L. What is the new volume of the balloon when 2.00 mol helium are added (T and P constant)?

c. What is the volume occupied by 210. g nitrogen (N_2) at STP?

d. What is the volume (in liters) of a container that holds 6.40 g O_2 at STP?

Answers: **a.** 12 L **b.** 45 L **c.** 168 L **d.** 4.48 L

10.8 The Ideal Gas Law

- The ideal gas law $PV = nRT$ gives the relationship between the four variables: pressure, volume, mol, and temperature. When any three variables are given, the fourth can be calculated.
- R is the universal gas constant: 0.0821 L · atm/mol · K *or* 62.4 L · mm Hg/mol · K

Study Note

Identify the three known variables for the ideal gas law, and arrange the equation to solve for the unknown variable.

Example: Solve the ideal gas law for P.

$$PV = nRT \qquad P = \frac{nRT}{V}$$

◆ Learning Exercise 10.8

Use the ideal gas law to solve for the unknown variable in each of the following:

a. What volume (in liters) is occupied by 0.250 mol nitrogen gas (N_2) at 0°C and 1.50 atm?

b. What is the temperature (°C) of 0.500 mol helium that occupies a volume of 15.0 L at a pressure of 1250 mm Hg?

c. What is the pressure in atm of 1.50 mol neon in a 5.00 L steel container at a temperature of 125°C?

d. What is the pressure in atm of 10.0 g oxygen (O_2) that has a volume of 2450 mL at a temperature of 22°C?

Answers **a.** 3.74 L **b.** 328°C **c.** 9.80 atm **d.** 3.09 atm

10.9 Gas Laws and Chemical Reactions

- The ideal gas law or molar volume at STP is used to determine the mass or volume of a gas in a chemical reaction.

◆ Learning Exercise 10.9

Use gas laws to determine the quantity of a reactant or product in a chemical reaction.

a. How many liters of hydrogen gas at STP are produced when 12.5 g magnesium react?

$$Mg(s) + 2HCl(aq) \rightarrow MgCl_2(aq) + H_2(g)$$

b. How many grams of KNO_3 must decompose to produce 35.8 L O_2 at 28°C and 745 mm Hg?

$$2KNO_3(s) \rightarrow 2KNO_2(s) + O_2(g)$$

c. At a temperature of 325°C and a pressure of 1.20 atm, how many liters of CO_2 can be produced when 50.0 g propane undergo combustion?

$$C_3H_8(g) + 5O_2(g) \rightarrow 3CO_2(g) + 4H_2O(g)$$

Answers **a.** 11.5 L H_2 **b.** 287 g KNO_3 **c.** 139 L

10.10 Partial Pressures (Dalton's Law)

- In a mixture of two or more gases, the total pressure is the sum of the partial pressures of the individual gases.

$$P_{total} = P_1 + P_2 + P_3 + \cdots$$

- The partial pressure of a gas in a mixture is the pressure it would exert if it were the only gas in the container.

◆ Learning Exercise 10.10

Use Dalton's law to solve the following problems about gas mixtures:

a. What is the pressure in mm Hg of a sample of gases containing oxygen at 0.500 atm, nitrogen (N_2) at 132 torr, and helium at 224 mm Hg?

b. What is the pressure (atm) of a gas sample containing helium at 2105 mm Hg and oxygen (O_2) at 1.20 atm?

c. A gas sample containing nitrogen (N_2) and oxygen (O_2) has a pressure of 1500. mm Hg. If the partial pressure of the nitrogen is 0.900 atm, what is the partial pressure (mm Hg) of the oxygen gas in the mixture?

Answers **a.** 736 mm Hg **b.** 3.97 atm **c.** 816 mm Hg

Checklist for Chapter 10

You are ready to take the practice test for Chapter 10. Be sure you have accomplished the following learning goals for this chapter. If you are not sure, review the section listed at the end of the goal. Then apply your new skills and understanding to the practice test.

After studying Chapter 10, I can successfully:

_____ Describe the kinetic theory of gases (10.1).

_____ Change the units of pressure from one to another (10.2).

_____ Use the pressure–volume relationship (Boyle's law) to determine the new pressure or volume of a fixed amount of gas at constant temperature (10.3).

____ Use the temperature–volume relationship (Charles' law) to determine the new temperature or volume of a fixed amount of gas at a constant pressure (10.4).

____ Use the temperature–pressure relationship (Gay-Lussac's law) to determine the new temperature or pressure of a certain amount of gas at a constant volume (10.5).

____ Use the combined gas law to find the new pressure, volume, or temperature of a gas when changes in two of these properties are given (10.6).

____ Describe the relationship between the amount of a gas and its volume (Avogadro's law), and use this relationship in calculations (10.7).

____ Use the ideal gas law to solve for pressure, volume, temperature, or amount of a gas (10.8).

____ Use the gas laws to calculate the quantity of a reactant or product in a chemical reaction (10.9).

____ Calculate the total pressure of a gas mixture from the partial pressures (10.10).

Practice Test for Chapter 10

Answer questions 1 through 5 using T (true) or F (false):

1. ____ A gas does not have its own volume or shape.

2. ____ The molecules of a gas are moving extremely fast.

3. ____ The collisions of gas molecules with the walls of their container create pressure.

4. ____ Gas molecules are close together and move in straight-line patterns.

5. ____ We consider gas molecules to have no attractions between them.

6. When a gas is heated in a closed metal container, the

A. pressure increases. **B.** pressure decreases. **C.** volume increases.
D. volume decreases. **E.** number of molecules increases.

7. The pressure of a gas will increase when

A. the volume increases.
B. the temperature decreases.
C. more molecules of gas are added.
D. molecules of gas are removed.
E. none of these

8. If the temperature of a gas is increased,

A. the pressure will decrease.
B. the volume will increase.
C. the volume will decrease.
D. the number of molecules will increase.
E. none of these

9. The relationship that the volume of a gas is inversely related to its pressure at constant temperature is known as

A. Boyle's law **B.** Charles' law **C.** Gay-Lussac's law
D. Dalton's law **E.** Avogadro's law

10. What is the pressure (atm) of a gas with a pressure of 1200 mm Hg?

A. 0.63 atm **B.** 0.79 atm **C.** 1.2 atm
D. 1.6 atm **E.** 2.0 atm

11. A 6.00 L sample of oxygen has a pressure of 660. mm Hg. When the volume is reduced to 2.00 liters at constant temperature, it will have a new pressure of

A. 1980 mm Hg **B.** 1320 mm Hg **C.** 330. mm Hg
D. 220. mm Hg **E.** 110. mm Hg

12. A sample of nitrogen gas at 110 K has a pressure of 1.0 atm. When the temperature is increased to 360 K at constant volume, the new pressure will be

A. 0.50 atm **B.** 1.0 atm **C.** 1.5 atm
D. 3.3 atm **E.** 4.0 atm

13. If two gases have the same volume, temperature, and pressure, they also have the same

A. density **B.** number of molecules **C.** molar mass
D. speed **E.** size molecules

14. A gas sample with a volume of 4.0 L has a pressure of 750 mm Hg and a temperature of 77°C. What is its new volume at 277°C and 250 mm Hg?

A. 7.6 L **B.** 19 L **C.** 2.1 L
D. 0.00056 L **E.** 3.3 L

15. If the temperature of a gas does not change, but its volume doubles, its pressure will

A. double
B. triple
C. decrease to one-half the original pressure
D. decrease to one-fourth the original pressure
E. not change

16. A sample of oxygen with a pressure of 400 mm Hg contains 2.0 mol gas and has a volume of 4.0 L. What will the new pressure be when the volume expands to 5.0 L and 3.0 mol helium gas is added while temperature is constant?

A. 160 mm Hg **B.** 250 mm Hg **C.** 800 mm Hg
D. 1000 mm Hg **E.** 1560 mm Hg

17. A sample of 2.00 mol gas initially at STP is converted to a volume of 5.0 L and a temperature of 27°C. What is its new pressure in atm?

A. 0.12 atm **B.** 5.5 atm **C.** 7.5 atm
D. 9.8 atm **E.** 10. atm

18. The conditions for standard temperature and pressure (STP) are

A. 0 K, 1 atm **B.** 0°C, 10 atm **C.** 25°C, 1 atm
D. 273 K, 1 atm **E.** 273 K, 0.5 atm

19. The volume occupied by 1.50 mol CH_4 at STP is

A. 44.10 L **B.** 33.6 L **C.** 22.4 L
D. 11.2 L **E.** 5.60 L

20. How many grams of oxygen gas (O_2) are present in 44.1 L of oxygen at STP?

A. 10.0 g **B.** 16.0 g **C.** 32.0 g
D. 410.0 g **E.** 63.0 g

21. What is the volume in liters of 0.50 mol nitrogen gas (N_2) at 25°C and 2.0 atm?

A. 0.51 L **B.** 1.0 L **C.** 4.2 L
D. 6.1 L **E.** 24 L

22. A gas mixture contains helium with a partial pressure of 0.100 atm, oxygen with a partial pressure of 450 mm Hg, and nitrogen with a partial pressure of 230 mm Hg. What is the total pressure in atm for the gas mixture?

A. 0.995 atm **B.** 1.39 atm **C.** 1.69 atm
D. 2.00 atm **E.** 10.0 atm

23. A mixture of oxygen and nitrogen has a total pressure of 1040 mm Hg. If the oxygen has a partial pressure of 510 mm Hg, what is the partial pressure of the nitrogen?

A. 240 mm Hg **B.** 530 mm Hg **C.** 775 mm Hg
D. 1040 mm Hg **E.** 1350 mm Hg

24. 3.00 mol He in a steel container has a pressure of 12.0 atm. What is the new pressure when 4.00 moles more of He is added? (*T* is constant)
A. 5.14 atm **B.** 16.0 atm **C.** 28.0 atm
D. 32.0 atm **E.** 45.0 atm

25. 2.50 g $KClO_3$ decomposes by the equation: $2\ KClO_3(s) \rightarrow 2\ KCl(s) + 3\ O_2(g)$.
What volume of O_2 is produced at 25°C and a pressure of 750. mm Hg?

A. 0.00998 L **B.** 0.759 L **C.** 0.0636 L
D. 0.506 L **E.** 1.32 L

Answers to the Practice Test

1. T	**2.** T	**3.** T	**4.** F	**5.** T
6. A	**7.** C	**8.** B	**9.** A	**10.** D
11. A	**12.** D	**13.** B	**14.** B	**15.** C
16. C	**17.** D	**18.** D	**19.** B	**20.** E
21. D	**22.** A	**23.** B	**24.** C	**25.** B

Answers and Solutions to Selected Text Problems

10.1 a. Gaseous particles have greater kinetic energies at higher temperatures. Because kinetic energy is a measure of the energy of motion, the gaseous particles must be moving faster at higher temperatures than at lower values.

b. Because particles in a gas are very far apart, gases can be easily compressed without the particles bumping into neighboring gas particles. Neighboring particles are much closer together in solids and liquids, and they will "bump" into each other and repel each other if the sample is compressed.

c. Because the particles of a gas are very far apart, only a small amount of mass (due to the gas particles themselves) is found in a given volume of space.

10.3 **a.** temperature **b.** volume **c.** amount of gas **d.** pressure

10.5 Some units used to describe the pressure of a gas are pounds per square inch (lb/in.^{2}, which is also abbreviated as psi), atmospheres (abbreviated atm), torr, mm Hg, in. Hg, pascals (Pa), and kilopascals (kPa).

10.7 **a.** $2.00 \text{ atm} \times \dfrac{760 \text{ torr}}{1 \text{ atm}} = 1520 \text{ torr}$

b. $2.00 \text{ atm} \times \dfrac{14.7 \text{ lb/in.}^2}{1 \text{ atm}} = 29.4 \text{ lb/in.}^2$

c. $2.00 \text{ atm} \times \dfrac{760 \text{ mm Hg}}{1 \text{ atm}} = 1520 \text{ mm Hg}$

d. $2.00 \text{ atm} \times \dfrac{101.3 \text{ kPa}}{1 \text{ atm}} = 203 \text{ kPa}$

10.9 The gases in the diver's lungs (and dissolved in the blood) will expand because pressure decreases as the diver ascends. Unless the diver exhales, the expanding gases could rupture the membranes in the lung tissues. In addition, the formation of gas bubbles in the bloodstream could cause "the bends."

10.11 During expiration, the volume (capacity) of the lungs decreases as pressure increases.

10.13 **a.** According to Boyle's law, for the pressure to increase while temperature and quantity of gas remains constant, the gas volume must decrease. Thus, cylinder A would represent the final volume.

b. $P_1 = 650 \text{ mm Hg} \times \dfrac{1 \text{ atm}}{760 \text{ mm Hg}} = 0.86 \text{ atm}$ $\quad P_2 = 1.2 \text{ atm}$

$V_1 = 220 \text{ mL}$ $\quad V_2 = 160 \text{ mL}$

Because $P_1V_2 = P_2V_2$, then $V_2 = P_1V_1/P_2$

$V_2 = 220 \text{ mL} \times \dfrac{0.86 \text{ atm}}{1.2 \text{ atm}} = 160 \text{ mL}$

10.15 **a.** The pressure doubles when the volume is halved.

b. The pressure falls to one-third the initial pressure when the volume expands to three times its initial volume.

c. The pressure increases to ten times the original pressure when the volume decreases to 1/10 its initial volume.

10.17 From Boyle's law, we know that pressure is inversely related to volume. (For example, the pressure increases when the volume decreases.)

a. Volume increases; pressure must decrease.

$655 \text{ mm Hg} \times \dfrac{10.0 \text{ L}}{20.0 \text{ L}} = 328 \text{ mm Hg}$

b. Volume decreases; pressure must increase.

$655 \text{ mm Hg} \times \dfrac{10.0 \text{ L}}{2.50 \text{ L}} = 2620 \text{ mm Hg}$

c. The mL units must be converted to L for unit cancellation in the calculation, and because the volume decreases, pressure must increase.

$655 \text{ mm Hg} \times \dfrac{10.0 \text{ L}}{1500 \text{ mL}} \times \dfrac{1000 \text{ mL}}{1 \text{ L}} = 4400 \text{ mm Hg}$

d. The mL units must be converted to L for unit cancellation in the calculation, and because the volume decreases, pressure must increase.

$$120 \text{ mL} \times \frac{1 \text{ L}}{1000 \text{ mL}} = 0.12 \text{ L}$$

$$655 \text{ mm Hg} \times \frac{10.0 \text{ L}}{0.12 \text{ L}} \times = 55\,000 \text{ mm Hg}$$

10.19 $760 \text{ mm Hg} \times \frac{4.5 \text{ L}}{2.0 \text{ mL}} = 1700 \text{ mm Hg}$

10.21 From Boyle's law, we know that pressure is inversely related to volume. (For example, the pressure increases when the volume decreases.)

a. Pressure increases; volume must decrease.

$$50.0 \text{ L} \times \frac{760 \text{ mm Hg}}{1500 \text{ mm Hg}} = 25 \text{ L}$$

b. The mm Hg units must be converted to atm for unit cancellation in the calculation, and because the pressure increases, volume must decrease.

$$760 \text{ mm Hg} \times \frac{1 \text{ atm}}{760 \text{ mm Hg}} = 1.00 \text{ atm}$$

$$50.0 \text{ L} \times \frac{1.00 \text{ atm}}{2.0 \text{ atm}} = 25 \text{ L}$$

c. The mm Hg units must be converted to atm for unit cancellation in the calculation, and because the pressure decreases, volume must increase.

$$760 \text{ mm Hg} \times \frac{1 \text{ atm}}{760 \text{ mm Hg}} = 1.00 \text{ atm}$$

$$50.0 \text{ L} \times \frac{1.00 \text{ atm}}{0.500 \text{ atm}} = 100. \text{ L}$$

d. The mm Hg units must be converted to torr for unit cancellation in the calculation, and because the pressure increases, volume must decrease.

$$50.0 \text{ L} \times \frac{760 \text{ mm Hg}}{850 \text{ torr}} \times \frac{1 \text{ torr}}{1 \text{ mm Hg}} = 45 \text{ L}$$

10.23 According to Charles' law, there is a direct relationship between temperature and volume. For example, volume increases when temperature increases while the pressure and amount of gas remains constant.

a. Diagram C describes an increased volume corresponding to an increased temperature.
b. Diagram A describes a decreased volume corresponding to a decrease in temperature.
c. Diagram B shows no change in volume, which corresponds to no change in temperature.

10.25 Heating a gas in a hot air balloon increases the volume of gas, which reduces its density and allows the balloon to rise above the ground.

10.27 According to Charles' law, gas volume is directly proportional to Kelvin temperature when P and n are constant. In all gas law computations, temperatures must be in Kelvin units. (Temperatures in °C are converted to K by the addition of 273.)

a. When temperature decreases, volume must also decrease.

$75°\text{C} + 273 = 348 \text{ K}$ $\qquad$ $55°\text{C} + 273 = 328 \text{ K}$

$$2500 \text{ mL} \times \frac{328 \text{ K}}{348 \text{ K}} = 2400 \text{ mL}$$

b. When temperature increases, volume must also increase.

$$2500\text{ mL} \times \frac{680\text{ K}}{348\text{ K}} = 4900\text{ mL}$$

c. –25°C + 273 = 248 K

$$2500\text{ mL} \times \frac{248\text{ K}}{348\text{ K}} = 1800\text{ mL}$$

d. $2500\text{ mL} \times \frac{240\text{ K}}{348\text{ K}} = 1700\text{ mL}$

10.29 Because gas pressure increases with an increase in temperature, the gas pressure in an aerosol can may exceed the tolerance of the can when it is heated and cause it to explode.

10.31 According to Gay-Lussac's law, temperature is directly related to pressure. For example, the temperature increases when the pressure increases. In all gas law computations, temperatures must be in Kelvin units. (Temperatures in °C are converted to K by the addition of 273.)

a. When temperature decreases, pressure must also decrease.
P_1 = 1200 torr　　P_2 = ?
T_1 = 155°C + 273 = 428 K　　T_2 = 0°C + 273 = 273 K
$P_2 = 1200\text{ torr} \times \frac{273\text{ K}}{428\text{ K}} = 770\text{ torr}$

b. When temperature increases, pressure must also increase.
12°C + 273 = 285 K　　35°C + 273 = 308 K

$$1.40\text{ atm} \times \frac{308\text{ K}}{285\text{ K}} = 1.51\text{ atm}$$

10.33 **a.** boiling point　**b.** vapor pressure
c. atmospheric pressure　**d.** boiling point

10.35 **a.** Water boils at temperatures less than 100°C because the atmospheric pressure is less than one atmosphere on top of a mountain. The boiling point is the temperature at which the vapor pressure of a liquid becomes equal to the external (in this case, atmospheric) pressure.

b. The pressure inside a pressure cooker is greater than one atmosphere; therefore, water boils above 100°C. Foods cook faster at higher temperatures.

10.37 When Boyle's, Charles', and Gay-Lussac's laws are brought together, they form the combined gas law.

$$\frac{P_1V_1}{T_1} = \frac{P_2V_2}{T_2}$$

10.39 T_1 = 298 K; V_1 = 6.50 L; P_1 = 845 mm Hg (1.11 atm)

a. T_2 = 325 K; V_2 = 1.85 L

$$1.11\text{ atm} \times \frac{6.50\text{ L}}{1.85\text{ L}} \times \frac{325\text{ K}}{298\text{ K}} = 4.25\text{ atm}$$

b. T_2 = 12°C + 273 = 285 K; V_2 = 2.25 L

$$1.11\text{ atm} \times \frac{6.50\text{ L}}{2.25\text{ L}} \times \frac{285\text{ K}}{298\text{ K}} = 3.07\text{ atm}$$

c. $T_2 = 47°C + 273 = 320\text{ K}; V_2 = 12.8\text{ L}$

$$1.11\text{ atm} \times \frac{6.50\text{ }\cancel{L}}{12.8\text{ }\cancel{L}} \times \frac{320\text{ }\cancel{K}}{298\text{ }\cancel{K}} = 0.605\text{ atm}$$

10.41 $T_1 = 225°C + 273 = 498\text{ K}; P_1 = 1.80\text{ atm}; V_1 = 100.0\text{ mL}$

$T_2 = -25°C + 273 = 248\text{ K}; P_2 = 0.100\text{ atm}$

$$100.0\text{ mL} \times \frac{1.80\text{ }\cancel{atm}}{0.80\text{ }\cancel{atm}} \times \frac{248\text{ }\cancel{K}}{498\text{ }\cancel{K}} = 110\text{ mL}$$

10.43 Addition of more air molecules to a tire or basketball will increase its volume because more moles of gas are added.

10.45 According to Avogadro's law, the change in the gas volume is directly proportional to the change in the number of moles of gas.

a. When moles decrease, volume must also decrease. (One-half of 4.00 mol = 2.00 mol.)

$$8.00\text{ L} \times \frac{2.00\text{ }\cancel{mol}}{4.00\text{ }\cancel{mol}} = 4.00\text{ L}$$

b. When moles increase, volume must also increase.

$$25.0\text{ }\cancel{g\text{ Ne}} \times \frac{1\text{ mol Ne}}{20.18\text{ }\cancel{g\text{ Ne}}} = 1.24\text{ mol Ne added}$$

(1.24 mol + 1.50 mol = 2.74 mol)

$$8.00\text{ L} \times \frac{2.74\text{ }\cancel{mol}}{1.50\text{ }\cancel{mol}} = 14.6\text{ L}$$

b. 1.50 mol + 3.50 mol = 5.00 mol

$$8.00\text{ L} \times \frac{5.00\text{ }\cancel{mol}}{1.50\text{ }\cancel{mol}} = 26.7\text{ L}$$

10.47 At STP, the molar volume of any gas is 22.4 L/mol.

a. $44.8\text{ }\cancel{L\text{ }O_2} \times \frac{1\text{ mol }O_2}{22.4\text{ }\cancel{L}} = 2.00\text{ mol }CO_2$

b. $4.00\text{ }\cancel{L\text{ }CO_2} \times \frac{1\text{ mol }CO_2}{22.4\text{ }\cancel{L}} = 0.179\text{ mol }CO_2$

c. $6.40\text{ }\cancel{g\text{ }O_2} \times \frac{1\text{ }\cancel{mol\text{ }O_2}}{32.00\text{ }\cancel{g\text{ }O_2}} \times \frac{22.4\text{ L }O_2}{1\text{ }\cancel{mol\text{ }O_2}} = 4.48\text{ L }O_2$

d. $50.0\text{ }\cancel{g\text{ Ne}} \times \frac{1\text{ }\cancel{mol\text{ Ne}}}{20.18\text{ }\cancel{g\text{ Ne}}} \times \frac{22.4\text{ }\cancel{L\text{ Ne}}}{1\text{ }\cancel{mol\text{ Ne}}} \times \frac{1000\text{ mL}}{1\text{ }\cancel{L\text{ Ne}}} = 55\ 500\text{ mL Ne}$

10.49 At STP, the volume of any gas is 22.4 L/mol.

a. For F_2, the molar mass is 38.00 g/mol.

$$\frac{38.00\text{ g }F_2}{1\text{ }\cancel{mol\text{ }F_2}} \times \frac{1\text{ }\cancel{mol\text{ }F_2}}{22.4\text{ L}} = 1.70\text{ g }F_2/\text{L}$$

b. For CH_4, the molar mass is 16.04 g/mol.

$$\frac{16.04\text{ g }CH_4}{1\text{ }\cancel{mol\text{ }CH_4}} \times \frac{1\text{ }\cancel{mol\text{ }CH_4}}{22.4\text{ L}} = 0.716\text{ g }CH_4/\text{L}$$

c. For Ne, the molar mass is 20.18 g Ne/mol.

$$\frac{20.18\text{ g Ne}}{1\text{ }\cancel{mol\text{ Ne}}} \times \frac{1\text{ }\cancel{mol\text{ Ne}}}{22.4\text{ L}} = 0.901\text{ g Ne/L}$$

d. For SO_2, the molar mass is 64.06 g SO_2/mol.

$$\frac{64.06\text{ g }SO_2}{1\ \cancel{\text{mol }SO_2}} \times \frac{1\ \cancel{\text{mol }SO_2}}{22.4\text{ L}} = 2.86\text{ g }SO_2/\text{L}$$

10.51 $$P = \frac{nRT}{V} = \frac{(2.00\ \cancel{\text{mol}})(0.0821\ \cancel{\text{L}}\cdot\text{atm})(300\ \cancel{\text{K}})}{(10.0\ \cancel{\text{L}})(\cancel{\text{mol}}\cdot\cancel{\text{K}})} = 4.93\text{ atm}$$

10.53 $$n = \frac{PV}{RT} = \frac{(845\ \cancel{\text{mm Hg}})(20.0\ \cancel{\text{L}})}{\dfrac{(62.4\ \cancel{\text{L}}\cdot\cancel{\text{mm Hg}})(295\ \cancel{\text{K}})}{\text{mol}\cdot\cancel{\text{K}}}} \times \frac{32.00\text{ g }O_2}{1\ \cancel{\text{mol }O_2}} = 29.4\text{ g }O_2$$

10.55 25.0 g N_2 × 1 mol N_2/210.0 g = 0.1093 mol

$$T = \frac{PV}{nR} = \frac{(630.\ \cancel{\text{mm Hg}})(50.0\ \cancel{\text{L}})}{\dfrac{(0.893)(62.4\ \cancel{\text{L}}\cdot\cancel{\text{mm Hg}})}{\cancel{\text{mol}}\cdot\text{K}}} = 565\text{ K }(292°\text{C})$$

10.57 **a.** $$0.450\ \cancel{\text{L}} \times \frac{1\text{ mol}}{22.4\ \cancel{\text{L}}} = 0.0201\text{ mol}$$

$$\frac{0.84\text{ g}}{0.0201\text{ mol}} = 42\text{ g/mol}$$

b. $$\frac{1.28\text{ g}}{1\ \cancel{\text{L}}} \times \frac{22.4\ \cancel{\text{L}}}{1\text{ mol}} = 28.7\text{ g/mol}$$

c. $T = 295$ K $V = 1.00$ L $P = 685$ mm Hg

$$n = \frac{PV}{RT} = \frac{(685\ \cancel{\text{mm Hg}})(1.00\ \cancel{\text{L}})}{\dfrac{(62.4\ \cancel{\text{L}}\cdot\cancel{\text{mm Hg}})(295\ \cancel{\text{K}})}{\text{mol}\cdot\cancel{\text{K}}}} = 0.0372\text{ mol}$$

$$\text{Molar mass} = \frac{1.48\text{ g}}{0.372\text{ mol}} = 39.8\text{ g/mol}$$

d. $$n = \frac{PV}{RT} = \frac{(0.95\ \cancel{\text{atm}})(2.30\ \cancel{\text{L}})}{\dfrac{(0.0821\ \cancel{\text{L}}\cdot\cancel{\text{atm}})(297\ \cancel{\text{K}})}{\text{mol}\cdot\cancel{\text{K}}}} = 0.090\text{ mol}$$

$$\text{Molar mass} = \frac{2.96\text{ g}}{0.090\text{ mol}} = 33\text{ g/mol}$$

10.59 **a.** $$8.25\ \cancel{\text{g Mg}} \times \frac{1\text{ mol Mg}}{24.31\ \cancel{\text{g Mg}}} = 0.339\text{ mol Mg}$$

$$1\ \cancel{\text{mol Mg}} \times \frac{1\ \cancel{\text{mol }H_2}}{1\ \cancel{\text{mol Mg}}} \times \frac{22.4\text{ L}}{1\ \cancel{\text{mol }H_2}} = 7.60\text{ L }H_2\text{ released at STP}$$

b. $$n = \frac{PV}{RT} = \frac{(735\ \cancel{\text{mm Hg}})(5.00\ \cancel{\text{L}})}{\dfrac{(62.4\ \cancel{\text{L}}\cdot\cancel{\text{mm Hg}})(291\ \cancel{\text{K}})}{\text{mol}\cdot\cancel{\text{K}}}} = 0.202\text{ mol }H_2$$

$$0.202\ \cancel{\text{mol }H_2} \times \frac{1\ \cancel{\text{mol Mg}}}{1\ \cancel{\text{mol }H_1}} \times \frac{24.31\text{ g Mg}}{1\ \cancel{\text{mol Mg}}} = 4.92\text{ g Mg}$$

10.61 $$55.2\ \cancel{\text{g }C_4H_{10}} \times \frac{1\text{ mol }C_4H_{10}}{58.12\text{ g }C_4H_{10}} \times \frac{13\text{ mol }O_2}{2\text{ mol }C_4H_{10}} = 6.17\text{ mol }C_4H_{10}\text{ mol }O_2$$

$$V = \frac{nRT}{P} = \frac{(6.17\ \text{mol})(0.0821\ \text{L} \cdot \text{atm})(298\ \text{K})}{(0.850\ \text{atm})(\text{mol} \cdot \text{K})} = 179\ \text{L}$$

10.63 $5.4\ \text{g Al} \times \frac{1\ \text{mol Al}}{26.98\ \text{g Al}} \times \frac{3\ \text{mol } O_2}{4\ \text{mol Al}} = 0.15\ \text{mol } O_2$

$0.15\ \text{mol } O_2 \times \frac{22.4\ \text{L}}{1\ \text{mol } O_2} = 3.4\ \text{L } O_2$ (STP)

10.65 **a.** $P_{O2} = 765\ \text{mm Hg} - 22\ \text{mm Hg} = 743\ \text{mm Hg}$

b. $n = \frac{PV}{RT} = \frac{(743\ \text{mm Hg})(0.256\ \text{L})}{\left(62.4\ \frac{\text{L} \cdot \text{mm Hg}}{\text{mol} \cdot \text{K}}\right)(297\ \text{K})} = 0.0103\ \text{mol } O_2$

10.67 Each gas particle in a gas mixture exerts a pressure as it strikes the walls of the container. The total gas pressure for any gaseous sample is thus a sum of all the individual pressures. When the portion of the pressure due to a particular type of gaseous particle is discussed, it is only part of the total. Accordingly, these "portions" are referred to as "partial" pressures.

10.69 To obtain the total pressure in a gaseous mixture, add the partial pressures (provided each carries the same pressure unit).

$P_{\text{total}} = P_{\text{Nitrogen}} + P_{\text{Oxygen}} + P_{\text{Helium}}$
$= 425\ \text{torr} + 115\ \text{torr} + 225\ \text{torr} = 765\ \text{torr}$

10.71 Because the total pressure in a gaseous mixture is the sum of the partial pressures (provided each carries the same pressure unit), addition and subtraction is used to obtain the "missing" partial pressure.

$P_{\text{Nitrogen}} = P_{\text{total}} - (P_{\text{Oxygen}} + P_{\text{Helium}})$
$= 925\ \text{torr} - (425\ \text{torr} + 75\ \text{torr}) = 425\ \text{torr}$

Additional Questions and Problems

10.79 Gas particles move faster at higher temperatures. This causes the force that each particle exerts against the wall to increase. Pressure is the sum of these forces. Thus, pressure increases with an increase in temperature at constant volume.

10.81 $V_1 = 425\ \text{mL}$ $T_1 = 297\ \text{K}$ $P_1 = 745\ \text{mm Hg} \times \frac{1\ \text{atm}}{760\ \text{mm Hg}} = 0.980\ \text{atm}$

$V_2 = ?\ \text{L}$ $T_2 = 178\ \text{K}$ $P_2 = 0.115\ \text{atm}$

$$V_2 = \frac{(425\ \text{mL})(0.980\ \text{atm})(178\ \text{K})}{(297\ \text{K})(0.115\ \text{atm})} = 2170\ \text{mL}$$

10.83 **a.** A Volume decreases when temperature decreases.
b. C Volume increases when pressure decreases.
c. A Volume decreases when the moles of gas decrease.
d. B Doubling temperature doubles the volume, but losing half the gas particles decreases the volume by half. The two effects cancel, and no change in volume occurs.
e. C Increasing the moles increases the volume to keep T and P constant.

10.85 $T_1 = 15°\text{C} + 273 = 288\ \text{K}$; $P_1 = 745\ \text{mm Hg}$; $V_1 = 4250\ \text{mL}$

$P_2 = 1.20\ \text{atm} \times \frac{760\ \text{mm Hg}}{1\ \text{atm}} = 912\ \text{mm Hg}$; $V_2 = 2.50\ \text{L} \times \frac{1000\ \text{mL}}{1\ \text{L}} = 2.50 \times 10^3\ \text{mL}$

$288\ \text{K} \times \frac{2500\ \text{mL}}{4250\ \text{mL}} \times \frac{912\ \text{mm Hg}}{745\ \text{mm Hg}} = 207\ \text{K}$ $(207\ \text{K} - 273 = -66°\text{C})$

10.87 $n = \frac{PV}{RT} = \frac{(12\ \cancel{atm})(35.0\ \cancel{L})}{(0.0821\ \frac{\cancel{L}\cdot\cancel{atm}}{mol\cdot\cancel{K}})(278\ \cancel{K})} = 1.8\ mol\ CO_2$

$1.8\ \cancel{mol\ CO_2} \times \frac{6.022 \times 10^{23}\ molecules}{1\ \cancel{mol\ CO_2}} = 1.1 \times 10^{24}\ molecules\ CO_2$

10.89 $n = \frac{PV}{RT} = \frac{(2500\ \cancel{mm\ Hg})(2.00\ \cancel{L})}{(62.4\ \frac{\cancel{L}\cdot\cancel{mm\ Hg}}{mol\cdot\cancel{K}})(291\ \cancel{K})} = 0.275\ mol\ CH_4$

$0.275\ \cancel{mol\ CH_4} \times \frac{16.04\ g\ CH_4}{1\ \cancel{mol\ CH_4}} = 4.4\ g\ CH_4$

10.91 $T = 297\ K\quad V = 4.60\ L$

$1.00\ \cancel{g\ CO_2} \times \frac{1\ mol\ CO_2}{44.01\ \cancel{g\ CO_2}} = 0.0227\ mol\ CO_2$

$P = \frac{nRT}{V} = \frac{(0.0227\ \cancel{mol})(62.4\ \cancel{L}\cdot mm\ Hg)(297\ \cancel{K})}{(4.60\ \cancel{L})\quad(\cancel{mol}\cdot\cancel{K})} = mm\ Hg$

$= 91.5\ mm\ Hg$

10.93 $D = \frac{mass}{volume} = \frac{32.00\ g\ O_2}{1\ \cancel{mol}} \times \frac{1\ \cancel{mol}}{22.4\ L\ (STP)} = 1.43\ g/L$

10.95 $n = \frac{PV}{RT} = \frac{(749\ \cancel{torr})(0.941\ \cancel{L})}{(62.4\ \frac{\cancel{L}\cdot\cancel{mm\ Hg}}{mol\cdot\cancel{K}})(293\ \cancel{K})} = 0.0385\ mol\ CH_4$

$\text{Molar mass} = \frac{1.62\ g}{0.0385\ mol} = 42.1\ g/mol$

10.97 $25.0\ \cancel{g\ Zn} \times \frac{1\ mol\ Zn}{65.38\ \cancel{g\ Zn}} \times \frac{1\ \cancel{mol\ H_2}}{1\ \cancel{mol\ Zn}} \times \frac{22.4\ L\ H_2(STP)}{1\ \cancel{mol\ H_2}} = 8.57\ L\ H_2\ (STP)$

10.99 **a.** $2.5 \times 10^{23}\ \cancel{molecules\ NO_2} \times \frac{1\ mol\ NO_2}{6.022 \times 10^{23}\ \cancel{molecules\ NO_2}} = 0.415\ mol\ NO_2$

$0.415\ \cancel{mol\ NO_2} \times \frac{7\ \cancel{mol\ O_2}}{4\ \cancel{mol\ NO_2}} \times \frac{22.4\ L\ O_2}{1\ \cancel{mol\ O_2}} = 16\ L\ O_2$

b. $n(NH_3) = \frac{PV}{RT} = \frac{(725\ \cancel{mm\ Hg})(5.00\ \cancel{L})}{(62.4\ \frac{\cancel{L}\cdot\cancel{mm\ Hg}}{mol\cdot\cancel{K}})(648\ \cancel{K})} = 0.0897\ mol\ H_2O$

$0.0897\ \cancel{mol\ H_2O} \times \frac{4\ \cancel{mol\ NH_3}}{6\ \cancel{mol\ H_2O}} \times \frac{17.03\ g\ NH_3}{1\ \cancel{mol\ NH_3}} = 1.02\ g\ NH_3$

10.101 $n = \frac{PV}{RT} = \frac{(752\ \cancel{mm\ Hg}) \times (0.782\ \cancel{L})}{(62.4\ \frac{\cancel{L}\cdot\cancel{mm\ Hg}}{mol\cdot\cancel{K}})\ (296\ \cancel{K})} = 0.0318\ mol$

$\text{Molar mass} = g/mol = \frac{2.23\ g}{0.0318\ mol} = 70.1\ g/mol$

Empirical formula mass of $CH_2 = 14.0\ g/mol$

$70.1\ \cancel{g/mol} \div 14.0\ \cancel{g/mol} = 5.01\qquad CH_2 \times 5 = C_5H_{10}$

10.103 The partial pressure of each gas is proportional to the number of particles of each type of gas that is present. Thus, a ratio of partial pressure to total pressure is equal to the ratio of moles of that gas to the total number of moles of gases that are present:

$P_{\text{Helium}}/P_{\text{total}} = n_{\text{Helium}}/n_{\text{total}}$

Solving the equation for the partial pressure of helium yields:

$$P_{\text{Helium}} = 2400\ \cancel{\text{torr}} \times \frac{2.00\ \text{mol}}{760\ \cancel{\text{torr}}} = 600\ \text{torr}$$

And for oxygen:

$$P_{\text{Oxygen}} = 2400\ \cancel{\text{torr}} \times \frac{6.0\ \cancel{\text{mol}}}{8.0\ \cancel{\text{mol}}} = 1800\ \text{torr}$$

10.105 Because the partial pressure of nitrogen is to be reported in torr, the atm and mm Hg units (for oxygen and argon, respectively) must be converted to torr, as follows:

$$0.60\ \cancel{\text{atm}}\ \frac{760\ \text{torr}}{1\ \cancel{\text{atm}}} = 460\ \text{torr}\ (O_2)$$

$$425\ \cancel{\text{mm Hg}} \times \frac{1\ \text{torr}}{1\ \cancel{\text{mm Hg}}} = 425\ \text{torr}\ (\text{Ar})$$

and $P_{\text{Nitrogen}} = P_{\text{total}} - (P_{\text{Oxygen}} + P_{\text{Argon}})$
$= 1250\ \text{torr} - (460\ \text{torr} + 425\ \text{torr}) = 370\ \text{torr}$

10.107 a. $P_{\text{Hydrogen}} = P_{\text{total}} - P_{\text{Water vapor}} = 755\ \text{mm Hg} - 21\ \text{mm Hg} = 734\ \text{mm Hg}$

b. $$n = \frac{PV}{RT} = \frac{(734\ \cancel{\text{mm Hg}})(0.415\ \cancel{\text{L}})}{\frac{(62.4\ \cancel{\text{L}}\ \cancel{\text{mm Hg}})(296\ \cancel{\text{K}})}{\text{mole}\ \cancel{\text{K}}}} = 0.0165\ \text{mol}\ H_2$$

c. $$0.0165\ \cancel{\text{mol}\ H_2} \times \frac{2\ \cancel{\text{mol Al}}}{3\ \cancel{\text{mol}\ H_2}} \times \frac{26.98\ \text{g Al}}{1\ \cancel{\text{mol Al}}} = 0.297\ \text{g Al}$$

11
Solutions

Study Goals

- Identify the solute and solvent in a solution.
- Describe the formation of a solution.
- Define solubility and determine whether a salt will dissolve in water.
- Distinguish between strong electrolytes, weak electrolytes, and nonelectrolytes in solution.
- Calculate the percent (mass/mass) and percent (volume/volume) concentrations of a solution.
- Describe how to prepare a dilute solution.
- Calculate the molarity of a solution; use molarity to determine moles of solute or volume of solution.
- Calculate the quantities of reactants or products in reactions involving solutions.

Think About It

1. Why is tea called a solution, but the water used to make tea is a pure substance?

2. Sugar dissolves in water, but oil does not. Why?

3. Why does water in a big puddle evaporate faster than the same amount of water in a tall bucket?

Key Terms

Match each of the following key terms with the correct definition.

a. solution **b.** percent concentration (m/m) **c.** molarity
d. weak electrolyte **e.** strong electrolyte

1. _____ A substance that dissociates into ions when it dissolves in water.

2. _____ The grams of solute dissolved in 100 g solution.

3. _____ The number of moles of solute in 1 L solution.

4. _____ A solute that forms a few ions, but mostly molecules in water.

5. _____ A mixture of at least two components called a solute and a solvent.

Answers **1.** e **2.** b **3.** c **4.** d **5.** a

11.1 Solutions

- A solution forms when a solute dissolves in a solvent.
- A polar solute is soluble in a polar solvent; a nonpolar solute is soluble in a nonpolar solvent.
- Water molecules form hydrogen bonds because the partial positive charge of the hydrogen in one water molecule is attracted to the partial negative charge of oxygen in another water molecule.
- An ionic solute dissolves in water, a polar solvent, because the polar water molecules attract and pull the positive and negative ions into solution. In solution, water molecules surround the ions dues to a process called hydration.

◆ Learning Exercise 11.1A

Water is polar, and hexane is nonpolar. In which solvent is each of the following soluble?

a. Bromine, Br_2, nonpolar ________ **b.** HCl, polar ________

c. Cholesterol, nonpolar ________ **d.** Vitamin D, nonpolar ________

e. Vitamin C, polar ________

Answers **a.** hexane **b.** water **c.** hexane **d.** hexane **e.** water

◆ Learning Exercise 11.1B

Indicate the solute and solvent in each of the following:	**Solute**	**Solvent**
a. 10 g KCl dissolved in 100 g water.	________	________
b. Soda water: $CO_2(g)$ dissolved in water.	________	________
c. An alloy composed of 80% Zn and 20% Cu.	________	________
d. A mixture of O_2 (200 mm Hg) and He (500 mm Hg).	________	________
e. A solution of 40 mL CCl_4 and 2 mL Br_2.	________	________

Answers **a.** KCl; water **b.** CO_2; water **c.** Cu; Zn **d.** oxygen; helium **e.** Br_2; CCl_4

11.2 Electrolytes and Nonelectrolytes

- Electrolytes conduct an electrical current because they produce ions in aqueous solutions.
- Strong electrolytes are completely ionized, whereas weak electrolytes are slightly ionized.
- Nonelectrolytes do not form ions in solution but dissolve as molecules.
-

◆ Learning Exercise 11.2A

Write an equation for the formation of an aqueous solution of each of the following strong electrolytes:

a. LiCl ________________________________

b. $Mg(NO_3)_2$ ________________________________

c. Na_3PO_4 ________________________________

d. K_2SO_4 ________________________________

e. $MgCl_2$ ________________________________

Answers

a. $LiCl(s) \xrightarrow{H_2O} Li^+(aq) + Cl^-(aq)$

b. $Mg(NO_3)_2(s) \xrightarrow{H_2O} Mg^{2+}(aq) + 2NO_3^-(aq)$

c. $Na_3PO_4(s) \xrightarrow{H_2O} 3Na^+(aq) + PO_4^{3-}(aq)$

d. $K_2SO_4(s) \xrightarrow{H_2O} 2K^+(aq) + PO_4^{3-}(aq)$

e. $MgCl_2(s) \xrightarrow{H_2O} Mg^{2+}(aq) + 2Cl^-(aq)$

◆ Learning Exercise 11.2B

Indicate whether an aqueous solution of each of the following contains mostly ions, molecules only, or mostly molecules with some ions. Write an equation for the formation of the solution:

a. glucose, $C_6H_{12}O_6$, a nonelectrolyte

b. NaOH, a strong electrolyte

c. K_2SO_4, a strong electrolyte

d. HF, a weak electrolyte

Answers

a. $C_6H_{12}O_6(s) \longrightarrow C_6H_{12}O_6(aq)$ molecules only

b. $NaOH(s) \longrightarrow Na^+(aq) + OH^-(aq)$ mostly ions

c. $K_2SO_4(s) \longrightarrow 2K^+(aq) + SO_4^{2-}(aq)$ mostly ions

d. $HF(aq) + H_2O(aq) \longrightarrow H_3O^+(aq) + F^-(aq)$ mostly molecules and a few ions

11.3 Solubility

- The amount of solute that dissolves depends on the nature of the solute and solvent.
- Solubility describes the maximum amount of a solute that dissolves in 100 g solvent at a given temperature.
- A saturated solution contains the maximum amount of dissolved solute at a certain temperature.
- An increase in temperature increases the solubility of most solids, but decreases the solubility of gases in water.
- The solubility rules describe the kinds of ionic combinations that are soluble and insoluble in water. If a salt contains Li^+, Na^+, K^+, NO_3^-, or NH_4^+ ion, it is soluble in water. Most halides and sulfates are soluble.

◆ Learning Exercise 11.3A

Identify each of the following as a saturated solution (S) or an unsaturated solution (U):

1. A sugar cube dissolves when added to a cup of coffee. _______
2. A KCl crystal added to a KCl solution does not change in size. _______
3. A layer of sugar forms in the bottom of a glass of ice tea. _______
4. The rate of crystal formation equals the rate of solution. _______
5. Upon heating, all the sugar dissolves. _______

Answers **1.** U **2.** S **3.** S **4.** S **5.** U

◆ Learning Exercise 11.3B

Use the KNO_3 solubility chart for the following problems:

Temperature (°C)	Solubility of KNO_3 g KNO_3/100 g H_2O
0	15
20	30
40	65
60	110
80	170
100	250

a. How many grams of KNO_3 will dissolve in 100 g water at 40°C?

b. How many grams of KNO_3 will dissolve in 300 g water at 60°C?

c. A solution is prepared using 200 g water and 360 g KNO_3 at 80°C. Will all the solute dissolve?

d. Will 200 g KNO_3 dissolve when added to 100 g water at 100°C?

Answers **a.** 65 g **b.** 330 g
c. No. Only 340 g solute will dissolve; 20 g remain as undissolved solid.
d. Yes, all 200 g KNO_3 will dissolve.

◆ Learning Exercise 11.3C

Predict whether the following salts are soluble (S) or insoluble (I) in water.

1.	______	NaCl	**2.**	______	$AgNO_3$	**3.**	______	$PbCl_2$
4.	______	Ag_2S	**5.**	______	$BaSO_4$	**6.**	______	Na_2CO_3
7.	______	K_2S	**8.**	______	$MgCl_2$	**9.**	______	BaS

Answers **1.** S **2.** S **3.** I **4.** I **5.** I
6. S **7.** S **8.** S **9.** I

◆ Learning Exercise 11.3D

Predict whether an insoluble salt forms in the following mixtures of soluble salts. If so, write the formula of the solid.

1. $NaCl(aq) + Pb(NO_3)_2(aq) \longrightarrow$ ______________________

2. $BaCl_2(aq) + Na_2SO_4(aq) \longrightarrow$ ______________________

3. $K_3PO_4(aq) + NaNO_{32}(aq) \longrightarrow$ ______________________

4. $Na_2S(aq) + AgNO_3(aq) \longrightarrow$ ______________________

Answers **1.** Yes; $PbCl_2$ **2.** Yes; $BaSO_4$ **3.** None **4.** Yes; Ag_2S

11.4 Percent Concentration

- The concentration of a solution is the relationship between the amount of solute (g or mL) and the amount (g or mL) of solution.
- A mass percent (mass/mass) expresses the ratio of the mass of solute to the mass of solution multiplied by 100.

$$\text{Percent (m/m)} = \frac{\text{grams of solute}}{\text{grams of solution}} \times 100$$

Study Note

Calculate mass percent concentration (% m/m) as

$$\frac{\text{grams of solute}}{\text{grams of solution}} \times 100$$

Example: What is the percent (mass/mass) when 2.4 g $NaHCO_3$ dissolves in 120 g solution?

Solution: $$\frac{2.4\text{ g }NaHCO_3}{120\text{ g solution}} \times 100 = 2.0\%\text{ (m/m)}$$

◆ Learning Exercise 11.4A

Determine the percent concentration (mass/mass or volume/volume) of each of the following solutions:

a. 18.0 g NaCl in 90.0 g solution

b. 35.2 g KCl in 425 g KCl solution

c. 1.0 g KOH in 25 g KOH solution

d. 18 mL alcohol in 350 mL mouthwash solution

Answers **a.** 20.0% **b.** 8.28% **c.** 4.0% **d.** 5.1%

Study Note

In solution problems, the percent concentration is useful as a conversion factor. The factor is obtained by rewriting the % as g solute/100 g (or mL) solution.

Example 1: How many g of KI solution are needed to prepare 225 g of a 4.0% (m/m) KI solution?

Solution: $225 \, \cancel{\text{g solution}} \times \frac{4.0 \text{ g KI}}{100 \, \cancel{\text{g solution}}} = 9.0 \text{ g KI}$

Example 2: How many grams of a 24% (m/m) NaOH solution can be prepared from 75 g NaOH?

Solution: $75 \, \cancel{\text{g NaOH}} \times \frac{100 \text{ g solution}}{24 \, \cancel{\text{g NaOH}}} = 310 \text{ g solution}$

◆ Learning Exercise 11.4B

Calculate the number of grams of solute needed to prepare each of the following solutions:

a. How many grams of glucose are needed to prepare 480 g of a 5.0% (m/m) solution?

b. How many grams of lidocaine hydrochloride are needed to prepare 50.0 g of a 2.0% (m/m) solution?

c. How many grams of KCl are needed to prepare 1250 g of a 4.00% (m/m) KCl solution?

d. How many grams of NaCl are needed to prepare 75.6 g of a 1.50% (m/m) solution?

Answers **a.** 24 g **b.** 1.0 g **c.** 50.0 g KCl **d.** 1.13 g NaCl

◆ Learning Exercise 11.4C

Use percent-concentration factors to calculate the mass of each solution that contains the amount of solute stated in each problem.

a. 8.75 g NaCl from a 3.00% (m/m) NaCl solution

b. 24 g glucose from a 5.0% (m/m) glucose solution

c. 10.5 g KCl from a 2.5% (m/m) KCl solution

d. 75.0 g NaOH from a 25.0% (m/m) NaOH solution

Answers **a.** 292 g **b.** 480 g **c.** 420 g **d.** 300 g

11.5 Molarity

- Molarity is a concentration term that describes the number of moles of solute dissolved in 1 L (1000 mL) of solution.

$$M = \frac{\text{moles of solute}}{\text{L solution}}$$

- Molarity is used to convert the moles of a solute to volume of solution and the volume of a solution to moles of the solute.
- *Dilution* is the process of mixing a solution with solvent to obtain a lower concentration.
- For dilutions, use the expression $M_1V_1 = M_2V_2$ and solve for the unknown value.

◆ Learning Exercise 11.5A

Calculate the molarity of the following solutions:

a. 1.45 mol HCl in 0.250 L HCl solution

b. 10.0 mol glucose ($C_6H_{12}O_6$) in 2.50 L glucose solution

c. 80.0 g NaOH in 1.60 L NaOH solution (Hint: Find moles of NaOH.)

d. 38.8 g NaBr in 175 mL NaBr solution

Answers **a.** 5.80 HCl **b.** 4.00 M glucose **c.** 1.25 M NaOH **d.** 1.25 M NaBr

Study Note

Molarity is used as a conversion factor to convert between the amount of solute and the volume of solution.

Example 1: How many grams of NaOH are in 0.250 L of a 5.00 M NaOH solution?

Solution: The concentration 4.00 M can be expressed as the conversion factors:

$$\frac{5.00 \text{ mol NaOH}}{1 \text{ L NaOH solution}} \quad \text{and} \quad \frac{1 \text{ L NaOH solution}}{5.00 \text{ mol NaOH}}$$

$$0.250 \text{ \sout{L solution}} \times \frac{5.00 \text{ \sout{mol NaOH}}}{1 \text{ \sout{L solution}}} \times \frac{40.0 \text{ \sout{g NaOH}}}{1 \text{ \sout{mol NaOH}}} = 50.0 \text{ g NaOH}$$

Example 2: How many mL of a 6.00 M HCl solution will provide 2.50 mol HCl?

Solution: $2.50 \text{ \sout{mol HCl}} \times \frac{1 \text{ \sout{L solution}}}{6.00 \text{ \sout{M HCl}}} \times \frac{1000 \text{ mL solution}}{1 \text{ \sout{L solution}}} = 417 \text{ mL}$

◆ Learning Exercise 11.5B

Calculate the quantity of solute in the following solutions:

a. How many moles of HCl are in 1.50 L of a 6.00 M HCl solution?

b. How many moles of KOH are in 0.750 L of a 10.0 M KOH solution?

c. How many grams of NaOH are needed to prepare 0.500 L of a 4.40 M NaOH solution? (Hint: Find moles of NaOH.)

d. How many grams of NaCl are in 285 mL of a 1.75 M NaCl solution?

Answers **a.** 9.00 mol HCl **b.** 7.50 mol KOH **c.** 88.0 g NaOH **d.** 29.2 g NaCl

◆ Learning Exercise 11.5C

Calculate the milliliters needed of each solution to obtain the given quantity of solute:

a. 1.50 mol $Mg(OH)_2$ from a 2.00 M $Mg(OH)_2$ solution

b. 0.150 mol glucose from a 2.20 M glucose solution

c. 18.5 g KI from a 3.00 M KI solution

d. 18.0 g NaOH from a 6.00 M NaOH solution

Answers **a.** 750. mL **b.** 68.2 mL **c.** 37.1 mL **d.** 75.0 mL

Study Note

Example: What is the final concentration after 250 mL water is used to dilute 150 mL of a 2.00 M NaCl solution?

Solution $M_1 = 2.00$ M $V_1 = 150$ mL $M_2 = ?$ $V_2 = 150$ mL + 250 mL = 400 mL

$$M_1V_1 = M_2V_2$$

$$M_2 = \frac{M_1V_1}{V_2} = \frac{(2.00\text{ M})(150\text{ mL})}{400\text{ mL}} = 0.75\text{ M}$$

◆ Learning Exercise 11.5D

Solve each of the following dilution problems (assume the volumes add):

a. What is the final concentration after 100 mL of a 5.0 M KCl solution is diluted with water to give a final volume of 200 mL?

b. What is the final concentration of the diluted solution if 5.0 mL of a 15% (m/v) KCl solution is diluted to 25 mL?

c. What is the final concentration after 250 mL of an 8% (m/v) NaOH is diluted with 750 mL water?

d. 160 mL water is added to 40 mL of an 1.0 M NaCl solution. What is the final concentration?

e. What volume of 6.0 M HCl is needed to prepare 300. mL of 1.0 M HCl? How much water must be added?

Answers **a.** 2.5 M **b.** 3.0% (m/v) **c.** 2% (m/m)
d. 0.20 M **e.** $V_1 = 50$ mL; add 250 mL water

Checklist for Chapter 11

You are ready to take the practice test for Chapter 11. Be sure you have accomplished the following learning goals for this chapter. If you are not sure, review the section listed at the end of the goal. Then apply your new skills and understanding to the practice test.

After studying Chapter 11, I can successfully:

_______ Identify the solute and solvent in a solution. Describe the process of dissolving an ionic solute in water (11.1).

_______ Identify the components in solutions of electrolytes and nonelectrolytes (11.2).

_______ Describe the effects of temperature and nature of the solute on its solubility in a solvent. Determine the solubility of an ionic compound (salt) in water (11.3).

_______ Calculate the percent concentration of a solute in a solution, and use percent concentration to calculate the amount of solute or solution (11.4).

_______ Calculate the molarity of a solution, and use molarity as a conversion factor to calculate between the mole (or grams) of a solute and the volume of the solution (11.5).

_______ Calculate the new concentration or new volume when a solution is diluted (11.5).

Practice Test for Chapter 11

Indicate if the following are more soluble in (A) water, a polar solvent, or (B) benzene, a nonpolar solvent.

1. _____ $I_2(g)$, nonpolar **2.** _____ $NaBr(s)$, polar
3. _____ $KI(s)$, polar **4.** _____ C_6H_{12}, nonpolar

5. When dissolved in water, $Ca(NO_3)_2(s)$ dissociates into

A. $Ca^{2+}(aq) + (NO_3)_2^{2-}(aq)$ **B.** $Ca^{+}(aq) + NO_3^{-}(aq)$ **C.** $Ca^{2+}(aq) + 2NO_3^{-}(aq)$
D. $Ca^{2+}(aq) + 2N^{5+}(aq) + 2O_3^{6-}(aq)$ **E.** $CaNO_3^{+}(aq) + NO_3^{-}(aq)$

6. CH_3CH_2OH, ethyl alcohol, is a nonelectrolyte. When placed in water it

A. dissociates completely **B.** dissociates partially **C.** does not dissociate
D. makes the solution acidic **E.** makes the solution basic

7. The solubility of NH_4Cl is 46 g in 100 g water at 40°C. How much NH_4Cl can dissolve in 500 g water at 40°C?

A. 9.2 g **B.** 46 g **C.** 100 g
D. 184 g **E.** 230 g

8. A solution containing 1.20 g sucrose in 50.0 g solution has a percent (m/m) concentration of

A. 0.600% **B.** 1.20% **C.** 2.40%
D. 30.0% **E.** 41.6%

9. The amount of lactose in 250 g of a 3.0% (m/m) lactose solution for infant formula is

A. 0.15 g **B.** 1.2 g **C.** 6.0 g
D. 7.5 g **E.** 30 g

10. The volume needed to obtain 0.40 g glucose from a 5.0% (m/m) glucose solution is

A. 1.0 mL **B.** 2.0 mL **C.** 4.0 mL
D. 5.0 mL **E.** 8.0 mL

11. The amount of NaCl needed to prepare 50.0 g of a 4.00% (m/m) NaCl solution is

A. 20.0 g **B.** 15.0 g **C.** 10.0 g
D. 4.00 g **E.** 2.00 g

12. A solution containing 6.0 g NaCl in 1500 g of solution has a mass-mass percent concentration of

A. 0.40 (m/m)% **B.** 0.25 (m/m)% **C.** 4.0 (m/m)%
D. 0.90 (m/m)% **E.** 2.5 (m/m)%

13. The moles of KOH needed to prepare 2400 mL of a 2.0 M KOH solution is

A. 1.2 mol **B.** 2.4 mol **C.** 4.8 mol
D. 12 mol **E.** 48 mol

14. The grams of NaOH needed to prepare 7.5 mL of a 5.0 M NaOH is

A. 1.5 g **B.** 3.8 g **C.** 6.7 g
D. 15 g **E.** 38 g

For questions 15 through 17, consider a 20.0-g sample of a solution that contains 2.0 g NaOH.

15. The percent (m/m) concentration of the solution is

A. 1.0% **B.** 4.0% **C.** 5%
D. 10% **E.** 20%

16. The moles of NaOH in the sample is

A. 0.050 mol **B.** 0.40 mol **C.** 1.0 mol
D. 2.5 mol **E.** 4.0 mol

17. If the solution has a volume of 0.25 L, what is the molarity of the sample?

A. 0.10 M **B.** 0.5 M **C.** 1.0 M
D. 1.5 M **E.** 2.0 M

18. Which of the following is soluble in water?

A. AgCl **B.** $BaCO_3$ **C.** K_2SO_4
D. PbS **E.** MgO

19. The insoluble salt that forms when a solution of NaCl mixes with a $Pb(NO_3)_2$ solution is

A. Na_2Pb **B.** $ClNO_3$ **C.** $NaNO_3$
D. $PbCl_2$ **E.** none

20. Which of the following salts is insoluble in water?

A. $CuCl_2$ **B.** $Pb(NO_3)_2$ **C.** K_2CO_3
D. $(NH_4)SO_4$ **E.** $CaCO_3$

21. A 20.0-mL sample of 5.0 M HCl is diluted to 100.0 mL. The final concentration of the HCl solution is

A. 10 M **B.** 5.0 M **C.** 2.0 M
D. 1.0 M **E.** 0.50 M

22. 200.0 mL water is added to 200.0 mL of a 4.00 M KNO_3 solution. The final concentration of the diluted solution is

A. 1.00 M **B.** 2.00 M **C.** 4.00 M
D. 0.500 M **E.** 0.100 M

23. 5.0 mL of a 20.0% (m/m) KOH solution is diluted to 50.0 mL. The final concentration of the KOH solution is

A. 15% (m/m) **B.** 10% (m/m) **C.** 5.0% (m/m)
D. 2.0% (m/m) **E.** 0.50% (m/m)

Answers to the Practice Test

1. B	**2.** A	**3.** A	**4.** B	**5.** C
6. C	**7.** E	**8.** C	**9.** D	**10.** E
11. E	**12.** A	**13.** C	**14.** A	**15.** D
16. A	**17.** E1	**18.** C	**19.** D	**20.** E
21. D	**22.** B	**23.** D		

Answers and Solutions to Selected Problems

11.1 The component present in the smaller amount is the solute; the larger amount is the solvent.
a. Solute, sodium chloride; solvent, water
b. Solute, water; solvent, ethanol
c. Solute, oxygen; solvent, nitrogen

11.3 **a.** Potassium chloride, an ionic solute, would be soluble in water (a polar solvent).
b. Iodine, a nonpolar solute, would be soluble in carbon tetrachloride (a nonpolar solvent).
c. Sugar, a polar solute, would be soluble in water, which is a polar solvent.
d. Gasoline, a nonpolar solute, would be soluble in carbon tetrachloride, which is a nonpolar solvent.

11.5 The positively charged hydrogen atoms in water attract the negatively charged I^- ions at the surface of the solid and pulls I^- into solution. The negatively charged oxygen atoms in water attract the positively charged K^+ ions and pull the K^+ into solution where the hydration process surrounds separate ions with water molecules.

11.7 The salt KF dissociates into ions when it dissolves in water. The weak acid HF exists as mostly molecules along with some ions when it dissolves in water.

11.9 Strong electrolytes dissociate into ions.

a. $KCl(s) \xrightarrow{H_2O} K^+(aq) + Cl^-(aq)$

b. $CaCl_2(s) \xrightarrow{H_2O} Ca^{2+}(aq) + 2Cl^-(aq)$

c. $K_3PO_4(s) \xrightarrow{H_2O} 3K^+(aq) + PO_4^{3-}(aq)$

d. $Fe(NO_3)(s) \xrightarrow{H_2O} Fe^{3+}(aq) + 3NO_3^-(aq)$

11.11 **a.** In solution, a weak electrolyte exists mostly as molecules with a few ions.
b. Sodium bromide is a strong electrolyte and forms ions in solution.
c. A nonelectrolyte does not dissociate and forms only molecules in solution.

11.13 **a.** Strong electrolyte because a K_2SO_4 solution contains only ions of K^+ and SO_4^{2-}.
b. Weak electrolyte because both ions and molecules are present in the NH_3 solution.
c. Nonelectrolyte because only molecules are present in the $C_6H_{12}O_6$ solution.

11.15 **a.** The solution must be saturated because no additional solute dissolves.
b. The solution was unsaturated because the sugar cube dissolves.

11.17 **a.** It is unsaturated because 34.0 g KCl is the maximum that dissolves in 100 g H_2O at 20°C.
b. Adding 11.0 g $NaNO_3$ in 100 g H_2O. At 20°C, 88.0 g Na_2Co_3 can dissolve so the solution is unsaturated.
c. Adding 400.0 g sugar to 125 g H_2O is 320 g in 100 g H_2O. At 20°C, only 203.9 g sugar can dissolve, which is less than 320 g. The sugar solution is saturated, and excess undissolved sugar is present.

11.19 **a.** $\frac{34.0 \text{ g KCl}}{100 \text{ g } H_2O} \times 200 \text{ g } H_2O = 68.0 \text{ g KCl}$ (This will dissolve at 20°C.)
At 20°C, 68.0 g KCl can dissolve in 200 g H_2O.
b. Because 80.0 g KCl dissolves at 50°C and 68.0 g is in solution at 20°C, the mass of solid is 80.0 g – 68.0 g = 12.0 g KCl.

11.21 **a.** In general, the solubility of solid ionic solutes increases as temperature is increased.
b. The solubility of a gaseous solute (CO_2) decreases as the temperature is increased.
c. The solubility of a gaseous solute is lowered as temperature increases. When the can of warm soda is opened, more CO_2 is released producing more spray.

11.23 **a.** Li^+ salts are soluble.
b. The Cl^- salt containing Ag^+ is insoluble.
c. Salts containing CO_3^{2-} are usually insoluble.
d. Salts containing K^+ ions are soluble.
e. Salts containing NO_3^- ions are soluble.

11.25 **a.** No solid forms; a salt containing K^+ and Na^+ is soluble.
b. Solid silver sulfide forms.

$2AgNO_3(aq) + K_2S(aq) \longrightarrow Ag_2S(s) + 2KNO_3(aq)$

$2\,Ag^+(aq) + S^{2-}(aq) \longrightarrow Ag_2S(s)$

c. Solid calcium sulfate forms.
$CaCl_2(aq) + Na_2SO_4(aq) \longrightarrow CaSO_4(s) + 2NaCl(aq)$
$Ca^{2+}(aq) + SO_4^{2-}(aq) \longrightarrow CaSO_4(s)$

11.27 The 5.0% (m/m) concentration indicates that 5.00 g glucose is in every 100 g solution. Thus, to prepare 250. g of a 5.00% (m/m) glucose solution, the total amount of grams of glucose is calculated as follows:

$$250.\ \cancel{\text{g solution}} \times \frac{5.00\text{ g glucose}}{100\ \cancel{\text{g solution}}} = 12.5\text{ g glucose}$$

factor from 5.0% (m/m)

Weigh out 12.5 glucose and add 237.5 g water to make a total of 250. g solution. Then you have a 5.00% (m/m) glucose solution.

11.29 a. $\frac{25\text{ g KCl}}{150\text{ g solution}} \times 100 = 17\%\text{ (m/m)}$

b. $\frac{8.0\text{ g CaCl}_2}{80\text{ g solution}} \times 100 = 10.\%\text{ (m/m)}$

c. $\frac{12\text{ g sugar}}{225\text{ g solution}} \times 100 = 5.3\%\text{ (m/m)}$

11.31 a. $50.0\ \cancel{\text{g solution}} \times \frac{5.0\text{ g KCl}}{100\ \cancel{\text{g solution}}} = 2.5\text{ g KCl}$

b. $1250\ \cancel{\text{g solution}} \times \frac{4.0\text{ g NH}_4\text{Cl}}{100\ \cancel{\text{g solution}}} = 50.\text{ g NH}_4\text{Cl}$

c. $250\ \cancel{\text{mL solution}} \times \frac{10.0\text{ mL acetic acid}}{100\ \cancel{\text{mL solution}}} = 25\text{ mL acetic acid}$

11.33 $355\ \cancel{\text{mL solution}} \times \frac{22.5\text{ mL alcohol}}{100\ \cancel{\text{mL solution}}} = 79.9\text{ mL alcohol}$

11.35 a. $5.0\ \cancel{\text{g LiNO}_3} \times \frac{100\text{ g solution}}{25\ \cancel{\text{g LiNO}_3}} = 20.\text{ g solution}$

b. $40.0\ \cancel{\text{g KOH}} \times \frac{100\text{ g solution}}{10.0\ \cancel{\text{g KOH}}} = 400.\text{ g solution}$

c. $2.0\ \cancel{\text{mL acetic acid}} \times \frac{100\text{ mL solution}}{10.0\ \cancel{\text{mL acetic acid}}} = 20.\text{ mL solution}$

11.37 a. $\frac{2.00\text{ mol glucose}}{4.00\text{ L solution}} = 0.500\text{ M glucose solution}$

b. $5.85\ \cancel{\text{g NaCl}} \times \frac{1\ \cancel{\text{mol NaCl}}}{58.44\ \cancel{\text{g NaCl}}} = 0.100\text{ mol NaCl}$

$$\frac{0.100\text{ mol glucose}}{40.0\ \cancel{\text{mL solution}}} \times \frac{1000\ \cancel{\text{mL}}}{1\text{ L solution}} = 2.50\text{ M NaCl solution}$$

c. $4.00\ \cancel{\text{g KOH}} \times \frac{1\ \cancel{\text{mol KOH}}}{56.11\ \cancel{\text{g KOH}}} = 0.0713\text{ mol KOH}$

$$\frac{0.0713\text{ mol KOH}}{2.00\text{ L solution}} = 0.0357\text{ M NaCl solution}$$

11.39 **a.** $\frac{1.50 \text{ mol NaOH}}{1 \text{ L solution}} \times 2.00 \text{ L} = 3.00 \text{ mol NaOH} \times \frac{40.00 \text{ g}}{1 \text{ mol}} = 120. \text{ g NaOH}$

b. $\frac{0.200 \text{ mol KCl}}{1 \text{ L solution}} \times 125 \text{ mL} \times \frac{1 \text{ L}}{1000 \text{ mL}} = 0.0250 \text{ mol KCl} \times \frac{74.55 \text{ g}}{1 \text{ mol}} = 1.86 \text{ g KCl}$

c. $\frac{3.50 \text{ mol HCl}}{1 \text{ L solution}} \times 25 \text{ mL} \times \frac{1 \text{ L}}{1000 \text{ mL}} = 0.0875 \text{ mol HCl} \times \frac{36.46 \text{ g}}{1 \text{ mol}} = 3.19 \text{ g HCl}$

11.41 **a.** $12.5 \text{ g } Na_2CO_3 \times \frac{1 \text{ mol } Na_2CO_3}{106.0 \text{ g } Na_2CO_3} = 0.118 \text{ mol } Na_2CO_3$

$0.118 \text{ mol } Na_2CO_3 \times \frac{1 \text{ L}}{0.120 \text{ mol}} \times \frac{1000 \text{ mL}}{1 \text{ L}} = 983 \text{ mL}$

b. $0.850 \text{ mol } NaNO_3 \times \frac{1 \text{ L}}{0.500 \text{ mol}} \times \frac{1000 \text{ mL}}{1 \text{ L}} = 1700 \text{ mL } (1.70 \times 10^3 \text{ mL})$

c. $30.0 \text{ g LiOH} \times \frac{1 \text{ mol LiOH}}{23.95 \text{ g LiOH}} = 1.25 \text{ mol LiOH}$

$1.25 \text{ mol LiOH} \times \frac{1 \text{ L}}{2.70 \text{ mol}} \times \frac{1000 \text{ mL}}{1 \text{ L}} = 464 \text{ mL}$

11.43 **a.** $M_1V_1 = M_2V_2 \quad M_2 = \frac{M_1V_1}{V_2} = \frac{(6.00 \text{ M})(0.150 \text{ L})}{0.500 \text{ L}} = 1.80 \text{ M}$

b. $M_1V_1 = M_2V_2 \quad 10.0 \text{ mL} \times \frac{1 \text{ L}}{1000 \text{ mL}} = 0.0100 \text{ L}$

$M_2 = \frac{M_1V_1}{V_2} = \frac{(2.50 \text{ M})(0.0100 \text{ L})}{0.250 \text{ L}} = 0.100 \text{ M}$

c. $M_1V_1 = M_2V_2 \quad M_2 = \frac{M_1V_1}{V_2} = \frac{(12.0 \text{ M})(0.250 \text{ L})}{1.00 \text{ L}} = 3.00 \text{ M}$

11.45 **a.** $M_1V_1 = M_2V_2 \quad V_2 = \frac{M_1V_1}{M_2} = \frac{(12.0 \text{ M})(50.0 \text{ mL})}{2.00 \text{ M}} = 300. \text{ mL}$

b. $M_1V_1 = M_2V_2 \quad V_2 = \frac{M_1V_1}{M_2} = \frac{(15.0 \text{ M})(18.0 \text{ mL})}{1.50 \text{ M}} = 180. \text{ mL}$

c. $M_1V_1 = M_2V_2 \quad V_2 = \frac{M_1V_1}{M_2} = \frac{(18.0 \text{ M})(4.50 \text{ mL})}{2.50 \text{ M}} = 32.4 \text{ mL}$

11.47 **a.** $M_1V_1 = M_2V_2 \quad V_2 = \frac{M_1V_1}{M_2} = \frac{(0.200 \text{ M})(255 \text{ mL})}{4.00 \text{ M}} = 12.8 \text{ mL}$

b. $M_1V_1 = M_2V_2 \quad V_2 = \frac{M_1V_1}{M_2} = \frac{(0.100 \text{ M})(715 \text{ mL})}{6.00 \text{ M}} = 11.9 \text{ mL}$

c. $M_1V_1 = M_2V_2 \quad V_2 = \frac{M_1V_1}{M_2} = \frac{(0.150 \text{ M})(100. \text{ mL})}{8.00 \text{ M}} = 1.88 \text{ mL}$

11.49 $M_1V_1 = M_2V_2$ $\quad V_2 = \frac{M_1V_1}{M_2} = \frac{(3.00\ \cancel{M})(25.0\ mL)}{0.150\ \cancel{M}} = 500.\ mL$

11.51 **a.** $50.0\ \cancel{mL} \times \frac{1\ L}{1000\ \cancel{mL}} = 0.0500\ \cancel{L} \times \frac{1.50\ mol\ KCl}{1\ \cancel{L}} = 0.0750\ mol\ KCl$

$0.0750\ \cancel{mol\ KCl} \times \frac{1\ \cancel{mol\ PbCl_2}}{2\ \cancel{mol\ KCl}} \times \frac{278.1\ g}{1\ \cancel{mol\ PbCl_2}} = 10.4\ g\ PbCl_2$

b. $50.0\ \cancel{mL} \times \frac{1\ L}{1000\ \cancel{mL}} = 0.0500\ \cancel{L} \times \frac{1.50\ mol\ KCl}{1\ \cancel{L}} = 0.0750\ mol\ KCl$

$0.0750\ \cancel{mol\ KCl} \times \frac{1\ \cancel{mol\ Pb(NO_3)_2}}{2\ \cancel{mol\ KCl}} \times \frac{1\ L\ solution}{2.00\ \cancel{mol\ Pb(NO_3)_2}} = 0.0188\ L\ solution$

$0.0188\ \cancel{L} \times \frac{1000\ mL}{1\ \cancel{L}} = 18.8\ mL\ solution$

c. $30.0\ \cancel{mL} \times \frac{1\ L}{1000\ \cancel{mL}} = 0.0300\ \cancel{L} \times \frac{0.400\ mol\ Pb(NO_3)_2}{1\ \cancel{L}} = 0.0120\ mol\ Pb(NO_3)_2$

$0.0120\ \cancel{mol\ Pb(NO_3)_2} \times \frac{2\ mol\ KCl}{1\ \cancel{mol\ Pb(NO_3)_2}} = 0.0240\ mol\ KCl$

$20.0\ \cancel{mL} \times \frac{1\ L}{1000\ \cancel{mL}} = 0.0200\ L \qquad \frac{0.0240\ mol\ KCl}{0.0200\ L} = 1.20\ M$

11.53 **a.** $15.0\ \cancel{g\ Mg} \times \frac{1\ mol\ Mg}{24.31\ \cancel{g\ Mg}} = 0.617\ mol\ Mg$

$0.617\ \cancel{mol\ Mg} \times \frac{2\ mol\ HCl}{1\ \cancel{mol\ Mg}} = 1.23\ \cancel{mol\ HCl} \times \frac{1\ L}{6.00\ \cancel{mol\ HCl}} = 0.206\ L$

$0.206\ \cancel{L} \times \frac{1000\ mL}{1\ \cancel{L}} = 206\ mL$

b. $\frac{2.00\ mol\ HCl}{1\ \cancel{L\ solution}} \times 0.500\ \cancel{L} = 1.00\ \cancel{mol\ HCl} \times \frac{1\ mol\ H_2}{2\ \cancel{mol\ HCl}} = 0.500\ mol\ H_2\ gas$

At STP, 1 mol gas has a volume of 22.4 L and $0.500\ \cancel{mol\ H_2} \times \frac{22.4\ L}{1\ \cancel{mol}} = 11.2\ L$

c. $n = \frac{PV}{RT} = \frac{(735\ \cancel{mm\ Hg})(5.20\ \cancel{L})}{\left(\frac{62.4\ \cancel{L} \cdot \cancel{mm\ Hg}}{mol \cdot \cancel{K}}\right)(298\ \cancel{K})} = 0.206\ mol\ H_2$

$0.206\ \cancel{mol\ H_2} \times \frac{2\ mol\ HCl}{1\ \cancel{mol\ H_2}} \times \frac{1}{0.0452\ L} = 9.12\ M\ HCl$

Answers to Additional Questions and Problems

11.63 Iodine is a nonpolar molecule and needs a nonpolar solvent such as hexane. Iodine does not dissolve in water because water is a polar solvent.

11.65 $80.0\ \cancel{g\ NaCl} \times \frac{100\ g\ water}{36.0\ \cancel{g\ NaCl}} = 222\ g\ water$

11.67 **a.** unsaturated solution – 200 g H_2O can dissolve up to 68 g KNO_3.
b. saturated solution – this is equal to 34 g KNO_3 in 100 g H_2O.
c. saturated solution – this is equal to 58 g KNO_3 in 100 g H_2O, exceeding the 34 g KNO_3 maximum that can dissolve in 100 g H_2O at 20°C.

11.69 When solutions of $NaNO_3$ and KCl are mixed, no insoluble product forms because all the possible combinations of salts are soluble. When KCl and $Pb(NO_3)_2$ solutions are mixed, the insoluble salt $PbCl_2$ forms.

11.71 **a.** $Ag^+(aq) + Cl^-(aq) \longrightarrow AgCl(s)$

b. none

c. $Ba^{2+}(aq) + SO_4^{2-}(aq) \longrightarrow BaSO_4(s)$

11.73 $4.5 \text{ mL propyl alcohol} \times \dfrac{100 \text{ mL solution}}{12 \text{ mL propyl alcohol}} = 38 \text{ mL of solution}$

11.75 Mass of solution: 70.0 g solute + 130.0 g solvent = 200.0 g

a. $\dfrac{70.0 \text{ g HNO}_3}{200.0 \text{ g solution}} \times 100 = 35.0\% \text{ HNO}_3$

b. $200.0 \text{ g solution} \times \dfrac{1 \text{ mL}}{1.21 \text{ g solution}} = 165 \text{ mL}$

c. $70.0 \text{ g HNO}_3 \times \dfrac{1 \text{ mol HNO}_3}{63.02 \text{ g HNO}_3} \times \dfrac{1}{0.165 \text{ L}} = 6.73 \dfrac{\text{mol}}{\text{L}} = 6.73 \text{ M}$

11.77 $60.0 \text{ g KNO}_3 \times \dfrac{1 \text{ mol KNO}_3}{101.1 \text{ g KNO}_3} \times \dfrac{1 \text{ L}}{2.50 \text{ mol KNO}_3} = 0.237 \text{ L KNO}_3 \text{ solution}$

11.79 $250 \text{ mL} \times \dfrac{1 \text{ L}}{1000 \text{ mL}} \times \dfrac{2 \text{ moles KCl}}{1 \text{ L}} \times \dfrac{74.6 \text{ g KCl}}{1 \text{ mole KCl}} = 37.3 \text{ g KCl}$

To make a 2.0 M KCl solution, weigh out 37.3 g KCl (0.500 mol) and place in a volumetric flask. Add water to dissolve the KCl and to give a final volume of 0.250 L.

11.81 **a.** $2.52 \text{ L} \times \dfrac{3 \text{ mol KNO}_3}{1 \text{ L}} \times \dfrac{101.1 \text{ g KNO}_3}{1 \text{ mol KNO}_3} = 764 \text{ g KNO}_3$

b. $0.075 \text{ L} \times \dfrac{0.506 \text{ mol Na}_2\text{SO}_4}{1 \text{ L}} \times \dfrac{142.0 \text{ g Na}_2\text{SO}_4}{1 \text{ mol Na}_2\text{SO}_4} = 5.39 \text{ g Na}_2\text{SO}_4$

c. $0.452 \text{ L} \times \dfrac{1.80 \text{ mol HCl}}{1 \text{ L}} \times \dfrac{36.45 \text{ g HCl}}{1 \text{ mol HCl}} = 2.97 \text{ g HCl}$

11.83 $60.0 \text{ mL Al(OH)}_3 \times \dfrac{1 \text{ L}}{1000 \text{ mL Al(OH)}_3} \times \dfrac{2.00 \text{ mol Al(OH)}_3}{1 \text{ L}} \times \dfrac{3 \text{ mol HCl}}{1 \text{ mol Al(OH)}_3}$

$\times \dfrac{1000 \text{ mL}}{6.00 \text{ mol}} = 60.0 \text{ mL HCl solution}$

11.85 $n = \dfrac{PV}{RT} = \dfrac{(745 \text{ mm Hg})(4.20 \text{ L})}{\left(62.4 \dfrac{\text{L} \cdot \text{mm Hg}}{\text{mol} \cdot \text{K}}\right)(308 \text{ K})} = 0.163 \text{ mol H}_2$

$0.163 \text{ mol H}_2 \times \dfrac{2 \text{ mol HCl}}{1 \text{ mol H}_2} \times \dfrac{1}{0.355 \text{ L}} = 9.17 \text{ M HCl}$

11.87 $M_1V_1 = M_2V_2$

a. $M_2 = \frac{M_1V_1}{V_2} = \frac{(0.200\ M)\ (25.0\ \cancel{mL})}{50.0\ \cancel{mL}} = 0.100\ M\ NaBr$

b. $M_2 = \frac{M_1V_1}{V_2} = \frac{(1.20\ M)\ (15.0\ \cancel{mL})}{40.0\ \cancel{mL}} = 0.450\ M\ K_2SO_4$

c. $M_2 = \frac{M_1V_1}{V_2} = \frac{(6.00\ M)\ (75.0\ \cancel{mL})}{255\ \cancel{mL}} = 1.76\ M\ NaOH$

11.89 a. $M_1V_1 = M_2V_2 \quad V_2 = \frac{M_1V_1}{M_2} = \frac{(5.00\ \cancel{M})\ (25.0\ mL)}{2.50\ \cancel{M}} = 50.0\ mL\ HCl$

b. $M_1V_1 = M_2V_2 \quad V_2 = \frac{M_1V_1}{M_2} = \frac{(5.00\ \cancel{M})\ (25.0\ mL)}{1.00\ \cancel{M}} = 125.\ mL\ HCl$

c. $M_1V_1 = M_2V_2 \quad V_2 = \frac{M_1V_1}{M_2} = \frac{(5.00\ \cancel{M})\ (25.0\ mL)}{0.500\ \cancel{M}} = 250.\ mL\ HCl$

12
Chemical Equilibrium

Study Goals

- Describe how temperature, concentration, and catalysts affect the rate of a reaction.
- Use the concept of reversible reactions to explain chemical equilibrium.
- Calculate the equilibrium constant for a reversible reaction using the concentrations of reactants and products at equilibrium.
- Use an equilibrium constant to predict the extent of reaction and to calculate equilibrium concentrations.
- Use Le Châtelier's principle to describe the shifts in equilibrium concentrations when reaction conditions change.
- Calculate the solubility product for a saturated solution; use the solubility product to calculate the molar ion concentrations.

Think About It

1. Why does a high temperature cook food faster than a low temperature?

2. Why do automobile engines now use a catalytic converter?

3. What does the size of an equilibrium constant tell you about the reactants and products?

Key Terms

Match each of the following key terms with the correct definition.

a. activation energy **b.** equilibrium **c.** catalyst
d. equilibrium constant **e.** collision theory **f.** heterogeneous equilibria

1. ____ A substance that lowers the activation energy and increases the rate of reaction.

2. ____ Equilibrium components are present in at least two different states.

3. ____ The ratio of the concentrations of products to that of the reactants raised to an exponent equal to their coefficients.

4. ____ The energy required to convert reactants to products in a chemical reaction.

5. ____ A reaction requires that reactants collide to form products.

6.____ The rate of the forward reaction is equal to the rate of the reverse reaction.

Answers **1.** c **2.** f **3.** d
4. a **5.** e **6.** b

12.1 Rates of Reaction

- The rate of a reaction is the speed at which products form.
- At higher temperatures, reaction rates increase because reactants move faster, collide more often, and produce more collisions with the required energy of activation.
- Increasing the concentration of reactants or lowering the energy of activation by adding a catalyst increases the rate of a reaction.
- The reaction rate slows when the temperature or the concentration of reactants is decreased.

◆ Learning Exercise 12.1A

Indicate the effect of each of the following on the rate of a chemical reaction:

Increase (I) Decrease (D) No effect (N)

1. ____ adding a catalyst

2. ____ running the reaction at a lower temperature

3. ____ doubling the concentrations of the reactants

4. ____ removing a catalyst

5. ____ running the experiment in a different laboratory

6. ____ increasing the temperature

7. ____ using a container with a different shape

8. ____ using lower concentrations of reactants

Answers **1.** I **2.** D **3.** I **4.** D

5. N **6.** I **7.** N **8.** D

◆ Learning Exercise 12.1B

For the following reaction, $NO_2(g) + CO(g) \rightarrow NO(g) + CO_2(g)$

indicate the effect of each as

Increase (I) Decrease (D) No effect (N)

1. _____ adding CO

2. _____ running the experiment on Wednesday

3. _____ removing NO_2

4. _____ adding a catalyst

5. _____ adding NO_2

Answers **1.** I **2.** N **3.** D **4.** I **5.** I

12.2 Chemical Equilibrium

- Chemical equilibrium is achieved when the rate of the forward reaction becomes equal to the rate of the reverse reaction.
- In a system at equilibrium, there is no change in the concentrations of reactants and products.
- At equilibrium, the concentrations of reactants and products are typically greater or less than the concentrations of products; they are not usually equal.

◆ Learning Exercise 12.2

Indicate if each of the following indicates a system at equilibrium (E) or not (NE).

a. ____The rate of the forward reaction is faster than the rate of the reverse reaction.

b. ____There is no change in the concentrations of reactants and products.

c. ____The rate of the forward reaction is equal to the rate of the reverse reaction.

d. ____ The concentrations of reactants are decreasing.

e. ____ The concentrations of products are increasing.

Answers **a.** NE **b.** E **c.** E **d.** NE **e.** NE

12.3 Equilibrium Constants

- The equilibrium constant expression for a system at equilibrium is the ratio of the concentrations of the products to the concentrations of the reactants with the concentration of each substance raised to a power equal to its coefficient in the equation.
- For the general equation, aA + bB ⇄ cC + dD, the equilibrium constant is written:

$$K_c = \frac{[C]^c[D]^d}{[A]^a[B]^b}$$

◆ Learning Exercise 12.3A

Write the expression for the equilibrium constant (K_c) for each of the following reactions.

a. $2SO_3(g) \rightleftarrows 2SO_2(g) + O_2(g)$

b. $2NO(g) + Br_2(g) \rightleftarrows 2NOBr(g)$

c. $N_2(g) + 3H_2(g) \rightleftarrows 2NH_3(g)$

d. $2NO_2(g) \rightleftarrows N_2O_4(g)$

Answers

a. $K_c = \frac{[SO_2]^2[O_2]}{[SO_3]^2}$

b. $K_c = \frac{[NOBr]^2}{[NO]^2[Br_2]}$

c. $K_c = \frac{[NH_3]^2}{[N_2][H_2]^3}$

d. $K_c = \frac{[N_2O_4]}{[NO_2]^2}$

◆ Learning Exercise 12.3B

Write the expression for the equilibrium constant (K_c) for each of the following heterogenous equilibria:

a. $H_2(g) + S(s) \rightleftarrows H_2S(g)$

b. $SiO_2(g) + 3C(s) \rightleftarrows SiC(s) + 2CO(g)$

c. $2PbS(s) + 3O_2(g) \rightleftarrows 2PbO(s) + 2SO_2(g)$

d. $SiH_4(g) + 2O_2(g) \rightleftarrows SiO(s) + 2H_2O(g)$

Answers

a. $K_c = \frac{[H_2S]}{[H_2]}$

b. $K_c = \frac{[CO]^2}{[SiO_2]}$

c. $K_c = \frac{[SO_2]^2}{[O_2]^3}$

d. $K_c = \frac{[H_2O]^2}{[SiH_4][O_2]^2}$

◆ Learning Exercise 12.3C

Calculate the K_c value for each of the following equilibrium concentrations.

a. $H_2(g) + I_2(g) \rightleftarrows 2HI(g)$
$[H_2] = 0.28$ M $[I_2] = 0.28$ M $[HI] = 2.0$ M

b. $2NO_2(g) \rightleftarrows + N_2(g) + 2O_2(g)$
$[NO_2] = 0.60$ M $[N_2] = 0.010$ M $[O_2] = 0.020$ M

c. $N_2(g) + 3H_2(g) \rightleftarrows 2NH_3(g)$
$[N_2] = 0.50$ M $[H_2] = 0.20$ M $[NH_3] = 0.80$ M

Answers

a. $K_c = \frac{[HI]^2}{[H_2][I_2]} = \frac{[2.0]^2}{[0.28][0.28]} = 51$

b. $K_c = \frac{[N_2][O_2]^2}{[NO_2]^2} = \frac{[0.010]\,[0.020]^2}{[0.60]^2} = 1.1 \times 10^{-5}$

c. $K_c = \frac{[NH_3]^2}{[N_2][H_2]^3} = \frac{[0.80]^2}{[0.50][0.20]^3} = 1.6 \times 10^{2}$

12.4 Using Equilibrium Constants

- A large K_c results when a reaction favors products; a small K_c results when a reaction favors reactants.
- The concentration of a component in an equilibrium mixture is calculated from the K_c and the concentrations of all other components.

◆ Learning Exercise 12.4A

Consider the reaction $2NOBr\,(g) \rightleftarrows 2NO(g) + Br_2(g)$

a. Write the expression for the equilibrium constant for the reaction.

b. If the equilibrium constant is 2×10^3, does the equilibrium mixture contain mostly reactants, mostly products, or do both reactants and products favor the products or the reactants? Explain.

Answers

a. $K_c = \frac{[NO]^2[Br_2]}{[NOBr]^2}$

b. A large K_c (>1) means the mixture contains mostly products.

◆ Learning Exercise 12.4B

Consider the reaction $2HI(g) \rightleftarrows H_2(g) + I_2(g)$

a. Write the expression for the equilibrium constant for the reaction.

b. If the equilibrium constant is 1.6×10^{-2}, does the equilibrium mixture contain mostly reactants, mostly products, or do both reactants and products favor the products or the reactants? Explain.

Answers

a. $K_c = \frac{[H_2][I_2]}{[2HI]^2}$

b. A small K_c (<1) means that the mixture contains mostly reactants.

◆ Learning Exercise 12.4C

Calculate the concentration of the indicated component for each of the following equilibrium systems.

a. $PCl_5(g) \rightleftarrows PCl_3(g) + Cl_2(g)$ $K_c = 1.2 \times 10^{-2}$

$[PCl_5] = 2.50$ M $[PCl_3] = 0.50$ M $[Cl_2] = ?$

b. $CO(g) + H_2O(g) \rightleftarrows CO_2(g) + H_2(g)$ $K_c = 1.6$
$[CO] = 1.0$ M $[H_2O] = 0.80$ M $[CO_2] = ?$ $[H_2] = 1.2$ M

Answers

a. $K_c = \frac{[PCl_3][Cl_2]}{[PCl_5]}$ $[Cl_2] = \frac{K_c\,[PCl_5]}{[PCl_3]} = \frac{1.2 \times 10^{-2}\,[2.5]}{[0.50]} = 0.060 \text{ M} = 6.0 \times 10^{-2} \text{ M}$

b. $K_c = \frac{[CO_2][H_2]}{[CO][H_2O]}$ $[CO_2] = \frac{K_c\,[CO][H_2O]}{[H_2]} = \frac{1.6[1.0][0.80]}{[1.2]} = 1.1 \text{ M}$

12.5 Changing Equilibrium Conditions: Le Châtelier's Principle

- A change in the concentration of a reactant or product, temperature, or volume shifts the equilibrium in the direction to relieve the stress.

◆ Learning Exercise 12.5A

Identify the effect of the each of the following on the equilibrium of the following reaction.

$$N_2(g) + O_2(g) + 180 \text{ kJ} \rightleftarrows 2NO(g)$$

A. Shift toward products **B.** Shift toward reactants **C.** No change

1.____Adding $O_2(g)$ **2.**____Removing $N_2(g)$

3.____Removing $NO(g)$ **4.**____Adding heat

5.____Reducing the volume of the container **6.**____Increasing the volume

Answers **1.** A **2.** B **3.** A **4.** A **5. A** **6.** B

◆ Learning Exercise 12.5B

Identify the effect of the each of the following on the equilibrium of the following reaction.

$$2NOBr(g) \rightleftarrows 2NO(g) + Br_2(g) + 340\ kJ$$

A. Shift toward products **B.** Shift toward reactants **C.** No change

1.____Adding $NO(g)$ **2.**____Removing $Br_2(g)$

3.____Removing $NOBr(g)$ **4.**____Adding heat

5.____Lowering the temperature **6.**____Increasing the volume

Answers **1.** B **2.** A **3.** B **4.** B **5.** A **6.** A

12.6 Equilibrium in Saturated Solutions

◆ Learning Exercise 12.6A

Write the K_{sp} expression for each of the following insoluble salts.

a. BaF_2

b. NiS

c. Ag_2CO_3

d. Ag_3PO_4

Answers

a. $BaF_2(s) \rightleftarrows Ba^{2+}(aq) + 2F^-(aq)$ $K_{sp} = [Ba^{2+}][F^-]^2$

b. $NiS(s) \rightleftarrows Ni^{2+}(aq) + S^{2-}(aq)$ $K_{sp} = [Ni^{2+}][S^{2-}]$

c. $Ag_2CO_3(s) \rightleftarrows 2Ag^+(aq) + CO_3^{2-}(aq)$ $K_{sp} = [Ag^+]^2 [CO_3^{2-}]$

d. $Ag_3PO_4(s) \rightleftarrows 3Ag^+(aq) + PO_4^{3-}(aq)$ $K_{sp} = [Ag^+]^3 [PO_4^{3-}]$

◆ Learning Exercise 12.6B

Calculate the K_{sp} value for each of the following saturated solutions.

a. CdS with $[Cd^{2+}] = [S^{2-}] = 3 \times 10^{-14}$ M

b. $AgIO_3$ with $[Ag^{+}] = [IO_3^{-}] = 1.7 \times 10^{-4}$ M

c. SrF_2 with $[Sr^{2+}] = 8.5 \times 10^{-4}$ and $[F^{-}] = 1.7 \times 10^{-3}$

d. Ag_2SO_3 with $[Ag^{+}] = 3.2 \times 10^{-5}$ and $[SO_3^{2-}] = 1.6 \times 10^{-5}$

Answers

a. $K_{sp} = 9 \times 10^{-28}$ **b.** $K_{sp} = 2.9 \times 10^{-8}$

c. $K_{sp} = 2.5 \times 10^{-9}$ **d.** $K_{sp} = 1.6 \times 10^{-14}$

◆ Learning Exercise 12.6C

Calculate the solubility (S) of each of the salts in moles per liter.

a. $CaSO_4$ $K_{sp} = 9 \times 10^{-6}$

b. $ZnCO_3$ $K_{sp} = 1.4 \times 10^{-11}$

c. $Co(OH)_2$ $K_{sp} = 1.6 \times 10^{-15}$

d. $Fe(OH)_3$ $K_{sp} = 4 \times 10^{-38}$

Answers

a. $CaSO_4$	$S = 3 \times 10^{-3}$ M	**b.** $ZnCO_3$	$S = 3.7 \times 10^{-6}$ M
c. $Co(OH)_2$	$S = 7.4 \times 10^{-6}$ M	**d.** $Fe(OH)_3$	$S = 2 \times 10^{-10}$ M

Checklist for Chapter 12

You are ready to take the self-test for Chapter 12. Be sure you have accomplished the following learning goals for this chapter. If you are not sure, review the section listed at the end of the goal. Then apply your new skills and understanding to the self-test.

After studying Chapter 12, I can successfully:

_____ Describe the factors that increase or decrease the rate of a reaction (12.1).

_____ Write the forward and reverse reactions of a reversible reaction (12.2).

_____ Explain how equilibrium occurs when the rate of a forward reaction is equal to the rate of a reverse reaction (12.2).

_____ Write the equilibrium constant expression for a reaction system at equilibrium (12.3).

_____ Calculate the equilibrium constant from the equilibrium concentrations (12.3).

_____ Use the equilibrium constant to determine whether an equilibrium favors the reactants or products (12.4).

_____ Use the equilibrium constant to determine the equilibrium concentration of a component in the reaction (12.4).

_____ Use Le Châtelier's principle to describe the shift in a system at equilibrium when stress is applied to the system (12.5).

_____ Calculate the solubility product for a saturated salt solution (12.6).

_____ Use the solubility product to calculate the molar ion concentrations of an insoluble salt (12.6).

Practice Test for Chapter 12

1. The number of molecular collisions increases when

A. more reactants are added.
B. products are removed.
C. the energy of collision is below the energy of activation.
D. the reaction temperature is lowered.
E. the reacting molecules have an incorrect orientation upon impact.

2. The energy of activation is lowered when

A. more reactants are added.
B. products are removed.
C. a catalyst is used.
D. the reaction temperature is lowered.
E. the reaction temperature is raised.

3. Food deteriorates more slowly in a refrigerator because

A. more reactants are added.
B. products are removed.
C. the energy of activation is higher.
D. fewer collisions have the energy of activation.
E. collisions have the wrong orientation upon impact.

4. A reaction reaches equilibrium when

A. the rate of the forward reaction is faster than the rate of the reverse reaction.
B. the rate of the reverse reaction is faster than the rate of the forward reaction.
C. the concentrations of reactants and products are changing.
D. fewer collisions have the energy of activation.
E. the rate of the forward reaction is equal to the rate of the reverse reaction.

5. The equilibrium constant expression for the following reaction is

$$2NOCl(g) \rightleftarrows 2NO(g) + Cl_2(g)$$

A. $\frac{[NO][Cl_2]}{[NOCl]}$ **B.** $\frac{[NOCl_2]^2}{[NO]^2[Cl_2]}$ **C.** $\frac{[NOCl_2]}{[NO][Cl_2]}$

D. $\frac{[NO][^2Cl_2]}{[NOCl]}$ **E.** $\frac{[NO]^2[Cl_2]}{[NOCl]^2}$

6. The equilibrium constant expression for the following reaction is

$$MgO(s) \rightleftarrows CO_2(g) + MgCO_3(s)$$

A. $[CO_2]$ **B.** $\frac{[CO_2][MgCO_3]}{[MgO]}$ **C.** $\frac{[MgO]}{[CO_2][MgCO_3]}$

D. $\frac{1}{[CO_2]}$ **E.** $\frac{[CO_2]}{[MgO]}$

7. The equilibrium constant expression for the following reaction is

$2PbS(s) + 3O_2(g) \rightleftarrows 2PbO(s) + 2SO_2(g)$

A. $\frac{[PbO][SO_2]}{[PbS][O_2]}$ **B.** $\frac{[PbO]^2[SO_2]^2}{[PbS]^2[O_2]^3}$ **C.** $\frac{[SO_2]^2}{[O_2]^3}$

D. $\frac{[SO_2]}{[O_2]}$ **E.** $\frac{[O_2]^3}{[SO_2]^2}$

8. The equilibrium equation that has the following equilibrium constant expression

$\frac{[H_2S]^2}{[H_2]^2[S_2]}$

A. $H_2S(g) \rightleftarrows H_2(g) + S_2(g)$
B. $2H_2S(g) \rightleftarrows H_2(g) + S_2(g)$
C. $2H_2(g) + S_2(g) \rightleftarrows 2H_2S(g)$
D. $2H_2S(g) \rightleftarrows 2H_2(g)$
E. $2H_2(g) \rightleftarrows 2H_2S(g)$

9. The value of the equilibrium constant for the following equilibrium is

$COBr_2(g) \rightleftarrows CO(g) + Br_2(g)$

$[COBr_2] = 0.93$ M $[CO] = [Br_2] = 0.42$ M

A. 0.19 **B.** 0.39 **C.** 0.42
D. 2.2 **E.** 5.3

10. The value of the equilibrium constant for the following equilibrium is

$2NO(g) + O_2(g) \rightleftarrows 2NO_2(g)$

$[NO] = 2.7$ M $[O_2] = 1.0$ $[NO_2] = 3.0$ M

A. 0.81 **B.** 1.1 **C.** 1.2
D. 8.1 **E.** 9.0

11. Calculate the $[PCl_5]$ for the decomposition of PCl_5 that has a $K_c = 0.050$.

$PCl_5(g) \rightleftarrows PCl_3(g) + Cl_2(g)$

$[PCl_3] = [Cl_2] = 0.20$ M

A. 0.01 M **B.** 0.050 M **C.** 0.20 M
D. 0.40 M **E.** 0.80 M

12. The reaction that has a much greater concentration of products at equilibrium has a K_c value of

A. 1.6×10^{-15} **B.** 2×10^{-11} **C.** 1.2×10^{-5}
D. 3×10^{-3} **E.** 1.4×10^{5}

13. The reaction that has a much greater concentration of reactants at equilibrium has a K_c value of

A. 1.1×10^{-11} **B.** 2×10^{-2} **C.** 1.2×10^{2}
D. 2×10^{4} **E.** 1.3×10^{12}

14. The reaction that has about the same concentration of reactant and products at equilibrium has a K_c value of

A. 1.4×10^{-12} **B.** 2×10^{-8} **C.** 1.2
D. 3×10^{2} **E.** 1.3×10^{7}

For questions 15–19, indicate how each of the following affects the equilibrium of the reaction shown

$$PCl_5(g) + \text{heat} \rightleftarrows PCl_3(g) + Cl_2(g)$$

A. Shifts toward products **B.** Shifts toward reactants **C.** No change

15. ____ Add more Cl_2 **16.** ____ Cool the reaction **17.** ____ Remove some PCl_3

18. ____ Add more PCl_5 **19.** ____ Remove some PCl_5

For questions 20–23, indicate whether the equilibrium will

A. Shifts toward products **B.** Shifts toward reactants **C.** No change

$$2NO(g) + O_2(g) \rightleftarrows 2NO_2(g) + \text{heat}$$

20. ____ Add more NO **21.** ____ Increase temperature

22. ____ Add a catalyst **23.** ____ Add some O_2

24. The solubility product expression for the insoluble salt $Ca_3(PO_4)_2$ is

A. $[Ca^{2+}][PO_4^{3-}]$ **B.** $[Ca^{2+}]_3[PO_4^{3-}]_2$ **C.** $[Ca^{2+}]^3[PO_4^{3-}]^2$

D. $[Ca^{2+}]^2[PO_4^{3-}]^3$ **E.** $\frac{[Ca^{2+}][PO_4^{3-}]}{[Ca_3(PO_4^{3-})_2]}$

25. The K_{sp} of CuI when a saturated solution has $[Cu^+] = 1 \times 10^{-6}$ M and $[I^-] = 1 \times 10^{-6}$ M is

A. 1×10^{-12} **B.** 1×10^{-6} **C.** 1

D. 2×10^{-6} **E.** 2×10^{-12}

Answers to the Practice Test

1. A	**2.** C	**3.** D	**4.** E	**5.** E
6. A	**7.** C	**8.** C	**9.** A	**10.** C
11. E	**12.** E	**13.** A	**14.** C	**15.** B
16. B	**17.** A	**18.** A	**19.** B	**20.** A
21. B	**22.** C	**23.** A	**24.** C	**25.** A

Answers and Solutions to Selected Text Problems

Section 12.1

12.1 **a.** The rate of a reaction relates the speed at which reactants are transformed into products.
b. Because fewer reactants will have the energy necessary to proceed to products (the activation energy) at refrigerator temperature than at room temperature, the rate of mold formation will be slower at a cooler temperature in a refrigerator.

12.3 Adding Br_2 increases the concentration of reactants, which increases the number of collisions that take place between the reactants.

12.5 **a.** Adding more reactant increases the reaction rate.
b. Increasing the temperature increases the number of collisions with the energy of activation, which increases the rate of reaction.
c. Adding a catalyst increases the reaction rate.
d. Removing a reactant decreases the reaction rate.

Section 12.2

12.7 If a reaction takes place in both a forward and reverse direction, it is called a reversible reaction.

12.9 **a.** Broken glass cannot be put back together; it is not reversible
b. In this physical process, heat melts the solid form of water, while removing heat can change liquid water back to solid. It is reversible.
c. A pan is warmed when heated and cooled when heat is removed; it is reversible.

12.11 In the expression for K_c the products are divided by the reactants with each concentration raised to a power that equals the coefficient in the equation:

a. $K_c = \frac{[CS_2][H_2]^4}{[CH_4][H_2S]^2}$ **b.** $K_c = \frac{[N_2][O_2]}{[NO]^2}$ **c.** $K_c = \frac{[CS_2][O_2]^4}{[SO_3]^2[CO_2]}$

12.13 **a.** Only one state (gases) is present; homogeneous
b. Solid and gaseous states; heterogeneous
c. Only one state (gases) is present; homogeneous
d. Gas and liquid states; heterogeneous

12.15 **a.** $K_c = \frac{[O_2]^3}{[O_3]^2}$ **b.** $K_c = [CO_2][H_2O]$

c. $K_c = \frac{[CO][H_2]^3}{[H_2O]\,[CH_4]}$ **d.** $K_c = \frac{[Cl_2]^2}{[HCl]^4[O_2]}$

12.17 $K_c = \frac{[NO_2]^2}{[N_2O_4]} = \frac{[0.21]^2}{[0.030]} = 1.5$

12.19 $K_c = \frac{[H_2O][CH_4]}{[H_2]^3[CO]} = \frac{[2.0][1.8]}{[0.30]^3[0.51]} = 260$

Section 12.4

12.21 **a.** A large K_c indicates that the equilibrium mixture contains mostly products.
b. A K_c of about 1 indicates that the equilibrium mixture contains both reactants and products.
c. A small K_c indicates that the equilibrium mixture contains mostly reactants.

12.23 $K_c = \frac{[HI]^2}{[H_2][I_2]}$

Rearrange K_c to solve for $[H_2]$, and substitute concentrations to calculate $[H_2]$.

$[H_2] = \frac{[HI]^2}{K_c\,[I_2]} = \frac{[0.030]^2}{[54]\,[0.015]} = 1.1 \times 10^{-3}$ M

12.25 $K_c = \frac{[Br_2][NO]^2}{[NOBr]^2}$

Rearranging K_c to solve for [NOBr]

$[NOBr]^2 = \frac{[Br_2][NO]^2}{K_c} = \frac{[1.0][2.0]^2}{[2.0]} = 2.0$

$[NOBr] = \sqrt{2.0} = 1.4$ M

Section 12.5

12.27 **a.** When more reactant is added to an equilibrium mixture, the product/reactant ratio is initially less than K_c.
b. According to Le Châtelier's principle, equilibrium is established when the forward reaction forms more products to make the product/reactant ratio equal the K_c again.

12.29 **a.** Adding more reactant shifts equilibrium to products.
b. Adding more product shifts equilibrium to reactants.
c. Adding heat, a reactant, shifts equilibrium to products.
d. Decreasing volume favors products with fewer moles.
e. A catalyst does not shift equilibrium.

12.31 **a.** Adding more reactant shifts equilibrium to products.
b. Adding heat, a reactant, shifts equilibrium to products.
c. Removing product shifts equilibrium to products.
d. A catalyst does not shift equilibrium.
e. Removing reactant shifts equilibrium to reactants.

Section 12.6

12.33 **a.** $MgCO_3(s) \rightleftarrows Mg^{2+}(aq) + CO_3^{2-}(aq)$ $K_{sp} = [Mg^{2+}] \times [CO_3^{2-}]$

b. $CaF_2(s) \rightleftarrows Ca^{2+}(aq) + 2F^-(aq)$ $K_{sp} = [Ca^{2+}] \times [F^-]^2$

c. $Ag_3PO_4(s) \rightleftarrows 3Ag^+(aq) + PO_4^{3-}(aq)$ $K_{sp} = [Ag^+]^3 \times [PO_4^{3-}]$

12.35 $BaSO_4(s) \rightleftarrows Ba^{2+}(aq) + SO_4^{2-}(aq)$ $K_{sp} = [Ba^{2+}] \times [SO_4^{2-}]$

$K_{sp} = [1 \times 10^{-5}][1 \times 10^{-5}] = 1 \times 10^{-10}$

12.37 $Ag_2CO_3(s) \rightleftarrows 2Ag^+(aq) + CO_3^{2-}(aq)$; $K_{sp} = [Ag^+]^2 \times [CO_3^{2-}]$

$K_{sp} = [2.6 \times 10^{-4}]^2[1.3 \times 10^{-4}] = 8.8 \times 10^{-12}$

12.39 $CuI(s) \rightleftarrows Cu^+(aq) + I^-(aq)$ $K_{sp} = [Cu^+] \times [I^-]$

$K_{sp} = [S][S] = [S]^2 = 1 \times 10^{-12}$

$[S] = \sqrt{1 \times 10^{-12}} = 1 \times 10^{-6}$ M

$[Cu^+] = 1 \times 10^{-6}$ M; $[I^-] = 1 \times 10^{-6}$ M

12.41 $AgCl(s) \rightleftarrows Ag^+(aq) + Cl^-(aq)$ $K_{sp} = [Ag^+] \times [Cl^-]$

$$[Cl] = \frac{K_{sp}}{[Ag^+]} = \frac{1.8 \times 10^{-10}}{2.0 \times 10^{-7}} = 9.0 \times 10^{-4}\text{ M}$$

Answers to Selected Questions and Problems

12.49 **a.** Adding heat, a product, shifts equilibrium toward reactants.
b. Decreasing volume favors products with fewer moles.
c. Adding a catalyst does not shift equilibrium.
d. Adding a reactant shifts equilibrium toward products.

12.51 There are mostly reactants and a few products, which gives a small equilibrium constant.

12.53 **a.** There are more products, which means that heat must be reduced; T_2 is lower than T_1.

b. Because the equilibrium mixture at T_2 has more products, the K_c for T_2 is larger than the K_c for the equilibrium mixture at T_1.

12.55 **a.** $K_c = \dfrac{[CO_2][H_2O]^2}{[CH_4][O_2]^2}$

b. $K_c = \dfrac{[N_2]^2\,[H_2O]^6}{[NH_3]^4[O_2]^3}$

c. $K_c = \dfrac{[CH_4]}{[H_2]^2}$

12.57 **a.** An equilibrium mixture with a large K_c consists of mostly products.
b. An equilibrium mixture with a K_c of about 1 consists of both products and reactants.
c. An equilibrium mixture with a small K_c consists of mostly reactants.

12.59 The numerator in the K_c expression gives the products in the equation, and the denominator gives the reactants.

a. $SO_2Cl_2(g) \rightleftarrows SO_2(g) + Cl_2(g)$

b. $Br_2(g) + Cl_2(g) \rightleftarrows 2BrCl(g)$

c. $CO(g) + 3\,H_2(g) \rightleftarrows CH_4(g) + H_2O(g)$

d. $2O_2(g) + 2NH_3(g) \rightleftarrows N_2O(g) + 3H_2O(g)$

12.61 **a.** $K_c = \dfrac{[N_2][H_2]^3}{[NH_3]^2}$

b. $K_c = \dfrac{[3.0][0.50]^3}{[0.20]^2} = 9.4$

12.63 **a.** $K_c = \frac{[N_2O_4]}{[NO_2]^2}$ Rearranging K_c for $[N_2O_4] = K_c\,[NO_2]^2$

$[N_2O_4] = 5.0[0.50]^2 = 1.3$ M

12.65 **a.** Adding a reactant shifts equilibrium to products.
b. Adding a product shifts equilibrium to reactants.
c. Adding a reactant shifts equilibrium to products.
d. Adding a product shifts equilibrium to reactants.

12.67 Decreasing the volume of an equilibrium mixture shifts the equilibrium to the side of the reaction that has the fewer number of moles. No shift occurs when there are an equal number of moles on both sides of the equation.
a. Three mol gas on the reactant side and two mol gas on the product side shifts equilibrium to products.
b. Two mol gas on the reactant side and three mol gas on the product side shifts equilibrium to reactants.
c. Six mol of gas on reactant side and one mol gas on the product side shifts equilibrium to products.
d. With an equal number of moles (2) on each side, no shift in equilibrium occurs.

12.69 **a.** $CuCO_3(s) \rightleftarrows Cu^{2+}(aq) + CO_3^{2-}(aq)$ $K_{sp} = [Cu^{2+}] \times [CO_3^{2-}]$
b. $PbF_2(s) \rightleftarrows Pb^{2+}(aq) + 2F^-(aq)$ $K_{sp} = [Pb^{2+}] \times [F^-]^2$
c. $Fe(OH)_3(s) \rightleftarrows Fe^{3+}(aq) + 3OH^-(aq)$ $K_{sp} = [Fe^{3+}] \times [OH^-]^3$

12.71 $FeS(s) \rightleftarrows Fe^{2+}(aq) + S^{2-}(aq)$
$K_{sp} = [Fe^{2+}] \times [S^{2-}] = [7.7 \times 10^{-10}] \times [7.7 \times 10^{-10}] = 5.9 \times 10^{-19}$

12.73 $Mn(OH)_2(s) \rightleftarrows Mn^{2+}(aq) + 2OH^-(aq)$
$K_{sp} = [Mn^{2+}] \times [OH^-]^2 = [3.7 \times 10^{-5}] \times [7.4 \times 10^{-5}]^2 = 2.0 \times 10^{-13}$

12.75 $CdS(s) \rightleftarrows Cd^{2+}(aq) + S^{2-}(aq)$
$K_{sp} = [Cd^{2+}] \times [S^{2-}] = 1.0 \times 10^{-24}$
$[S][S] = 1.0 \times 10^{-24}$ $[S]\ \sqrt{1.0 \times 10^{-24}} = 1.0 \times 10^{-12}$ M
$[Cd^{2+}] = 1.0 \times 10^{-12}$ and $[S^{2-}] = 1.0 \times 10^{-12}$

12.77 $BaSO_4(s) \rightleftarrows Ba^{2+}(aq) + SO_4^{2-}(aq)$ $K_{sp} = [Ba^{2+}] \times [SO_4^{2-}]$
$[SO_4^{2-}] = \frac{K_{sp}}{[Ba^{2+}]} = \frac{[1.1 \times 10^{-10}]}{[1.0 \times 10^{-3}]} = 1.1 \times 10^{-7}$ M

13
Acids and Bases

Study Goals

- Describe the characteristics of acids and bases.
- Identify conjugate acid–base pairs in Brønsted-Lowry acids and bases.
- Use the ion product of water to calculate $[H_3O^+]$, $[OH^-]$, and pH.
- Write balanced equations for reactions of an acid with metals, carbonates, and bases.
- Predict the salts that form acidic, basic, and neutral solutions.
- Describe the function of a buffer.
- Describe how titration with a base can determine the molarity of an acid.

Think About It

1. Why do a lemon, grapefruit, and vinegar taste sour?

2. What do antacids do? What are some bases listed on the labels of antacids?

3. Why are some aspirin products buffered?

Key Terms

Match each of the following key terms with the correct definition.

A. acid **B.** base **C.** pH **D.** neutralization **E.** buffer

1. _____ A substance that forms hydroxide ions (OH^-) in water and/or accepts protons (H^+)

2. _____ A reaction between an acid and a base to form a salt and water

3. _____ A substance that forms hydrogen ions (H^+) in water

4. _____ A mixture of a weak acid (or base) and its salt that maintains the pH of a solution

5. _____ A measure of the acidity (H_3O^+) of a solution

Answers **1.** B **2.** D **3.** A **4.** E **5.** C

13.1 Acids and Bases

- In water, an Arrhenius acid produces H_3O^+ and an Arrhenius base produces OH^-.
- According to the Brønsted-Lowry theory, acids are proton (H^+) donors and bases are proton acceptors.
- Protons form hydronium ions, H_3O^+, in water when they bond to polar water molecules.

◆ Learning Exercise 13.1A

Indicate if the following characteristics describe an (A) acid or (B) base.

1. ____ Turns blue litmus red

2. ____ Tastes sour

3. ____ Contains more OH^- ions than H_3O^+ ions

4. ____ Neutralizes bases

5. ____ Tastes bitter

6. ____ Turns red litmus blue

7. ____ Contains more H_3O^+ ions than OH^- ions

8. ____ Neutralizes acids

Answers **1.** A **2.** A **3.** B **4.** A **5.** B **6.** B **7.** A **8.** B

◆ Learning Exercise 13.1B

Fill in the blanks with the formula or name of an acid or base:

1. HCl ____________________

2. ________ sodium hydroxide

3. ________ sulfurous acid

4. ________ nitric acid

5. $Ca(OH)_2$ ____________________

6. H_2CO_3 ____________________

7. $Al(OH)_3$ ____________________

8. ________ potassium hydroxide

9. $HClO_4$ ____________________

10. H_3PO_3 ____________________

Answers

1. hydrochloric acid
2. NaOH
3. H_2SO_3
4. HNO_3
5. calcium hydroxide
6. carbonic acid
7. aluminum hydroxide
8. KOH
9. perchloric acid
10. phosphorous acid

13.2 Conjugate Acid–Base Pairs

- According to the Brønsted-Lowry theory, acids donate protons (H^+) to bases.
- Conjugate acid–base pairs are molecules or ions linked by the loss and gain of a proton.
- Every proton transfer reaction contains two acid–base conjugate pairs.

Study Note

Identify the conjugate acid–base pairs in the following equation:

$$HCl(aq) + H_2O(l) \longrightarrow H_3O^+(aq) + Cl^-(aq)$$

Solution: (1) HCl and Cl^- (2) H_2O and H_3O^+

◆ Learning Exercise 13.2A

Complete the following conjugate acid–base pairs:

	Conjugate Acid	Conjugate Base
1.	H_2O	________
2.	HSO_4^-	________
3.	________	F^-
4.	________	CO_3^{2-}
5.	HNO_3	________
6.	NH_4^+	________
7.	________	HS^-
8.	________	$H_2PO_4^-$

Answers
1. OH^- **2.** SO_4^{2-} **3.** HF **4.** HCO_3^-
5. NO_3^- **6.** NH_3 **7.** H_2S **8.** H_3PO_4

◆ Learning Exercise 13.2B

Identify the conjugate acid–base pairs in each of the following:

1. $HF(aq) + H_2O(l) \rightleftharpoons H_3O^+(aq) + F^-(aq)$

2. $NH_4^+(aq) + SO_4^{2-}(aq) \rightleftharpoons NH_3(aq) + HSO_4^-(aq)$

3. $NH_3(aq) + H_2O(l) \rightleftharpoons NH_4^+(aq) + OH^-(aq)$

4. $HNO_3(aq) + OH^-(aq) \rightleftharpoons H_2O(l) + NO_3^-(aq)$

Answers
1. HF/F^- and H_2O/H_3O^+ **2.** NH_4^+/NH_3 and SO_4^{2-}/HSO_4^-
3. NH_3/NH_4^+ and H_2O/OH^- **4.** HNO_3/NO_3^- and OH^-/H_2O

◆ Learning Exercise 13.2C

Write an equation with conjugate acid–base pairs starting with each of the following reactants:

1. HBr (acid) and CO_3^{2-} (base)

2. HSO_4^- (acid) and OH^- (base)

3. NH_4^+ (acid) and H_2O (base)

4. HCl (acid) and SO_4^{2-} (base)

Answers

1. $HBr(aq) + CO_3^{2-}(aq) \rightleftarrows HCO_3^-(aq) + Br^-(aq)$
2. $HSO_4^-(aq) + OH^-(aq) \rightleftarrows H_2O(l) + SO_4^{2-}(aq)$
3. $NH_4^+(aq) + H_2O(l) \rightleftarrows H_3O^+(aq) + NH_3(aq)$
4. $HCl(aq) + SO_4^{2-}(aq) \rightleftarrows Cl^-(aq) + HSO_4^-(aq)$

13.3 Strengths of Acids and Bases

- In aqueous solution, a strong acid donates nearly all its protons to water, whereas a weak acid donates only a small percentage of protons to water.
- Most hydroxides of Groups 1A (1) and 2A (2) are strong bases, which dissociate nearly completely in water.
- In an aqueous ammonia solution, NH_3, which is a weak base, accepts only a small percentage of protons to form NH_4^+.

Study Note

Only six common acids are strong acids. Other acids are considered as weak acids.

HCl	HNO_3
HBr	H_2SO_4 (first H)
HI	$HClO_4$

Example: Is H_2S a strong or weak acid?

Solution: H_2S is a weak acid because it is not one of the six strong acids.

◆ Learning Exercise 13.3A

Identify each of the following as a strong or weak acid or base:

1. HNO_3 ________ **2.** H_2CO_3 ________ **3.** $H_2PO_4^-$ ________

4. NH_3 ________ **5.** LiOH ________ **6.** H_3BO_3 ________

7. $Ca(OH)_2$ ________ **8.** H_2SO_4 ________

Answers **1.** strong acid **2.** weak acid **3.** weak acid **4.** weak base **5.** strong base **6.** weak acid **7.** strong base **8.** strong acid

◆ Learning Exercise 13.3B

Using Table 13.4, identify the stronger acid in each of the following pairs of acids:

1. HCl or H_2CO_3 ________ **2.** HNO_2 or HCN ________

3. H_2S or HBr ________ **4.** H_2SO_4 or HSO_4^- ________

5. HF or H_3PO_4 ________

Answers **1.** HCl **2.** HNO_2 **3.** HBr **4.** H_2SO_4 **5.** H_3PO_4

Study Note

In an acid–base reaction, the relative strengths of the two acids or two bases indicate whether the equilibrium position favors the reactants or products:

Example: Does the following reaction favor the reactants or products?

$$NO_3^-(aq) + H_2O(l) \rightleftarrows HNO_3(aq) + OH^-(aq)$$

Solution: The reactants contain the weaker base and acid NO_3^- and H_2O, which make the equilibrium favor the reactants. This can be represented with a long arrow to the left.

$$NO_3^-(aq) + H_2O(l) \xleftarrow[\quad\quad]{} \!\!\!\!\!\!\!\rightarrow HNO_3(aq) + OH^-(aq)$$

◆ Learning Exercise 13.3C

Indicate whether each of the following reactions favors the reactants or the products:

1. $HNO_3(aq) + H_2O(l) \rightleftarrows H_3O^+(aq) + NO_3^-(aq)$

2. $I^-(aq) + H_3O+(aq) \rightleftarrows H_2O(aq) + HI(aq)$

3. $NH_3(aq) + H_2O(l) \rightleftarrows NH_4^+(aq) + OH^-(aq)$

4. $HCl(aq) + CO_3^{2-}(aq) \rightleftarrows Cl^-(aq) + HCO_3^-(aq)$

Answers **1.** products **2.** reactants **3.** reactants **4.** products

13.4 Dissociation Constants

- An acid or base dissociation constant is the equilibrium constant when water is considered a constant.
- In the acid dissociation constant, the molar concentration of the products is divided by the molar concentration of the reactants.

$$\mathbf{HA}(aq) + H_2O(l) \rightleftharpoons \mathbf{H_3O^+}(aq) + \mathbf{A^-}(aq)$$

$$K_a = K_c\,[H_2O] = \frac{[\mathbf{H_3O^+}][A^-]}{[\mathbf{HA}]}$$

- An acid or a base with a large dissociation constant is more dissociated than an acid or base with a small dissociation constant.
- Dissociation constants greater than 1 favor the products, whereas constants smaller than 1 favor reactants.

◆ Learning Exercise 13.4A

Write the acid dissociation constant for the ionization of the following weak acids:

1. HCN

2. HNO_2

3. H_2CO_3 (first ionization only)

4. H_2S (first ionization only)

Answers

1. $K_a = \frac{[H_3O^+][CN^-]}{[HCN]}$

2. $K_a = \frac{[H_3O^+][NO_2^-]}{[HNO_2]}$

3. $K_a = \frac{[H_3O^+][HCO_3^-]}{[H_2CO_3]}$

4. $K_a = \frac{[H_3O^+][HS^-]}{[H_2S]}$

◆ Learning Exercise 13.4B

For each of the following pairs of acid dissociation constants, indicate the constant of the weaker acid.

1. 5.2×10^{-5} or 3.8×10^{-3} ____________________

2. 3.0×10^{8} or 1.6×10^{-10} ____________________

3. 4.5×10^{-2} or 7.2×1^{-6} ____________________

Answers **1.** 5.2×10^{-5} **2.** 1.6×10^{-10} **3.** 7.2×10^{-6}

◆ Learning Exercise 13.4C

Indicate whether the equilibrium favors the reactants or products for each of the following dissociation constants.

1. 5.2×10^{-5} ____________ **2.** 3.0×10^{8} ____________

3. 4.5×10^{-5} ____________ **4.** 7.2×10^{15} ____________

Answers **1.** reactants **2.** products **3.** reactants **4.** products

13.5 Dissociation of Water

- In pure water, a few water molecules transfer a proton to other water molecules producing small but equal amounts of $[H_3O^+]$ and $[OH^-] = 1 \times 10^{-7}$ mol/L.

$$H_2O(l) + H_2O(l) \rightleftarrows H_3O^+(aq) + OH^-(aq)$$

- K_w, the ion product, $[H_3O^+][OH^-] = [1 \times 10^{-7}][1 \times 10^{-7}] = 1 \times 10^{-14}$, applies to all aqueous solutions.
- In acidic solutions, the $[H_3O^+]$ is greater than the $[OH^-]$. In basic solutions, the $[OH^-]$ is greater than the $[H_3O^+]$.

Study Note

Example: What is the $[H_3O^+]$ in a solution that has $[OH^-] = 2.0 \times 10^{-9}$ M?

Solution: $K_w = [H_3O^+][OH^-] = 1.0 \times 10^{-14}$

Rearrange for $[H_3O^+]$ and substitute $[OH^-] = 2.0 \times 10^{-9}$ M

$$[H_3O^+] = \frac{1.0 \times 10^{-14}}{2.0 \times 10^{-9}} = 5.0 \times 10^{-6} \text{ M}$$

◆ Learning Exercise 13.5A

Write the $[H_3O^+]$ when the $[OH^-]$ has the following values:

a. $[OH^-] = 1.0 \times 10^{-10}$ M $[H_3O^+] =$

b. $[OH^-] = 2.0 \times 10^{-5}$ M $[H_3O^+] =$

c. $[OH^-] = 4.5 \times 10^{-7}$ M $[H_3O^+] =$

d. $[OH^-] = 8.0 \times 10^{-4}$ M $[H_3O^+] =$

e. $[OH^-] = 5.5 \times 10^{-8}$ M $[H_3O^+] =$

Answers **a.** 1.0×10^{-4} M **b.** 5.0×10^{-10} M **c.** 2.2×10^{-8} M
d. 1.3×10^{-11} M **e.** 1.8×10^{-7} M

◆ Learning Exercise 13.5B

Use the K_w to determine the $[OH^-]$ when the $[H_3O^+]$ has the following values:

a. $[H_3O^+] = 1.0 \times 10^{-3}$ M　　$[OH^-] =$

b. $[H_3O^+] = 3.0 \times 10^{-10}$ M　　$[OH^-] =$

c. $[H_3O^+] = 4.0 \times 10^{-6}$ M　　$[OH^-] =$

d. $[H_3O^+] = 2.8 \times 10^{-13}$ M　　$[OH^-] =$

e. $[H_3O^+] = 8.6 \times 10^{-7}$ M　　$[OH^-] =$

Answers　**a.** 1.0×10^{-11} M　**b.** 3.3×10^{-5} M　**c.** 2.5×10^{-9} M
d. 3.6×10^{-2} M　**e.** 1.2×10^{-8} M

13.6 The pH Scale

- The pH scale is a range of numbers from 0 to 14 related to the $[H_3O^+]$ of the solution.
- A neutral solution has a pH of 7. In acidic solutions, the pH is below 7, and in basic solutions, the pH is above 7.
- Mathematically, pH is the negative logarithm of the hydronium ion concentration:

$$pH = -\log [H_3O^+]$$

◆ Learning Exercise 13.6A

State whether the following pH values are acidic, basic or neutral:

1. ______ plasma, pH = 7.4　　**2.** ______ soft drink, pH = 2.8

3. ______ maple syrup, pH = 6.8　　**4.** ______ beans, pH = 5.0

5. ______ tomatoes, pH = 4.2　　**6.** ______ lemon juice, pH = 2.2

7. ______ saliva, pH = 7.0　　**8.** ______ eggs, pH = 7.8

9. ______ lime, pH = 12.4　　**10.** ______ strawberries, pH = 3.0

Answers　**1.** basic　**2.** acidic　**3.** acidic　**4.** acidic　**5.** acidic
6. acidic　**7.** neutral　**8.** basic　**9.** basic　**10.** acidic

◆ Learning Exercise 13.6B

Calculate the pH of each of the following solutions.

a. $[H_3O^+] = 1 \times 10^{-8}$ M ______　　**b.** $[OH^-] = 1 \times 10^{-12}$ M ______

c. $[H_3O^+] = 1 \times 10^{-3}$ M ______　　**d.** $[OH^-] = 1 \times 10^{-10}$M ______

Answers　**a.** 8.0　**b.** 12.0　**c.** 3.0　**d.** 10.0

◆ Learning Exercise 13.6C

Calculate the pH of each of the following solutions.

a. $[H_3O^+] = 5.0 \times 10^{-3}$ M

b. $[OH^-] = 4.0 \times 10^{-6}$ M

c. $[H_3O^+] = 7.5 \times 10^{-8}$ M

d. $[OH^-] = 2.5 \times 10^{-10}$ M

Answers **a.** 2.30 **b.** 8.60 **c.** 7.12 **d.** 4.40

◆ Learning Exercise 13.6D

Complete the following table:

	$[H_3O^+]$	$[OH^-]$	pH
a.	________	1×10^{-12} M	________
b.	________	________	8.0
c.	5×10^{-8} M	________	________
d.	________	________	7.0
e.	________	________	1.0

Answers

	$[H_3O^+]$	$[OH^-]$	pH
a.	1×10^{-2} M	1×10^{-12} M	2.0
b.	1×10^{-8} M	1×10^{-6} M	8.0
c.	5×10^{-8} M	2×10^{-7} M	7.3
d.	1×10^{-7} M	1×10^{-7} M	7.0
e.	1×10^{-1} M	1×10^{-13} M	1.0

13.7 Reactions of Acids and Bases

- Acids react with *active* metals to yield hydrogen gas (H_2) and the salt of the metal.
- Acids react with carbonates and bicarbonates to yield CO_2, H_2O, and the salt of the metal.
- Acids neutralize bases in a reaction that produces water and a salt.
- The net ionic equation for any neutralization is $H^+ + OH^- \longrightarrow H_2O$.
- In a balanced neutralization equation, an equal number of moles of H^+ and OH^- must react.

◆ Learning Exercise 13.7A

Complete and balance each of the following reactions of acids:

1. ____ $Zn(s)$ + ____ $HCl(aq)$ ⟶ ______ $ZnCl_2(aq)$ + ______

2. ____ $HCl(aq)$ + ______ $Li_2CO_3(aq)$ ⟶ ____________ + ____________

3. ____ $HCl(aq)$ + ______ $NaHCO_3(aq)$ ⟶ ____ $CO_2(g)$ + ______ $H_2O(l)$ + ______ $NaCl(aq)$

4. ____ $Al(s)$ + ____ $H_2SO_4(aq)$ ⟶ ______ $Al_2(SO_4)_3(aq)$ + ____________

Answers

1. $Zn(s) + 2HCl(aq) \longrightarrow ZnCl_2(aq) + H_2(g)$
2. $2HCl(aq) + Li_2CO_3(aq) \longrightarrow CO_2(g) + H_2O(l) + 2LiCl(aq)$
3. $HCl(aq) + NaHCO_3(aq) \longrightarrow CO_2(g) + H_2O(l) + NaCl(aq)$
4. $2Al(s) + 3H_2SO_4(aq) \longrightarrow Al_2(SO_4)_3(aq) + 3\,H_2(g)$

◆ Learning Exercise 13.7B

Balance each of the following neutralization reactions:

1. ____ $NaOH(aq)$ + ____ $H_2SO_4(aq)$ ⟶ ____ $Na_2SO_4(aq)$ + ____ $H_2O(l)$
2. ____ $Mg(OH)_2\,(aq)$ + ____ $HCl(aq)$ ⟶ ____ $MgCl_2(aq)$ + ____ $H_2O(l)$
3. ____ $Al(OH)_3(aq)$ + ____ $HNO_3(aq)$ ⟶ ____ $Al(NO_3)_3(aq)$ + ____ $H_2O(l)$
4. ____ $Ca(OH)_2(aq)$ + ____ $H_3PO_4(aq)$ ⟶ ____ $Ca_3(PO_4)_2(aq)$ + ____ $H_2O(l)$

Answers

1. $2NaOH(aq) + 1H_2SO_4(aq) \longrightarrow 1Na_2SO_4(aq) + 2H_2O(l)$
2. $1Mg(OH)_2(aq) + 2HCl(aq) \longrightarrow 1MgCl_2(aq) + 2H_2O(l)$
3. $1Al(OH)_3(aq) + 3HNO_3(aq) \longrightarrow 1Al(NO_3)_3(aq) + 3H_2O(l)$
4. $3Ca(OH)_2(aq) + 2H_3PO_4(aq) \longrightarrow 1Ca_3(PO_4)_2(aq) + 6H_2O(l)$

◆ Learning Exercise 13.7C

Complete each of the following neutralization reactions and then balance:

a. ____ $KOH(aq)$ + ____ $H_3PO_4(aq)$ ⟶ ____________ + ____ $H_2O(l)$

b. ____ $NaOH(aq)$ + ____________ ⟶ ____ $Na_2SO_4(aq)$ + ____________

c. ____________ + ____________ ⟶ ____ $AlCl_3(aq)$ + ____________

d. ____________ + ____________ ⟶ ____ $Fe_2(SO_4)_3(aq)$ + ____________

Answers

a. $3KOH(aq) + H_3PO_4(aq) \longrightarrow K_3PO_4(aq) + 3H_2O(l)$

b. $2NaOH(aq) + H_2SO_4(aq) \longrightarrow Na_2SO_4(aq) + 2H_2O(l)$

c. $Al(OH)_3(aq) + 3HCl(aq) \longrightarrow AlCl_3(aq) + 3H_2O(l)$

d. $2Fe(OH)_3(aq) + 3H_2SO_4(aq) \longrightarrow Fe_2(SO_4)_3(aq) + 6H_2O(l)$

13.8 Acid-Base Titration

- In a laboratory procedure called a titration, an acid sample is neutralized with a known amount of a base.
- From the volume and molarity of the base, the concentration of the acid is calculated.

◆ Learning Exercise 13.8A

Solve the following problems using the titration data given:

a. A 5.00-mL sample of HCl is placed in a flask. Titration required 15.0 mL of 0.200 M NaOH. What is the molarity of the HCl in the sample?

$$HCl(aq) + NaOH(aq) \longrightarrow NaCl(aq) + H_2O(l)$$

b. How many mL of 0.200 M NaOH are required to neutralize completely 8.50 mL of 0.500 M H_2SO_4?

$$H_2SO_4(aq) + 2\ NaOH(aq) \longrightarrow Na_2SO_4(aq) + 2H_2O(l)$$

c. A 10.0-mL sample of H_3PO_4 is placed in a flask. Titration required 42.0 mL of 0.100 M NaOH. What is the molarity of the H_3PO_4?

$$H_3PO_4(aq) + 3\ NaOH(aq) \longrightarrow Na_3PO_4(aq) + 3\ H_2O(l)$$

Answers **a.** 0.600 M **b.** 42.5 mL **c.** 0.140 M

13.9 Acid–Base Properties of Salt Solutions

- Salts of strong acids and strong bases produce neutral, aqueous solutions.
- Salts of weak acids and strong bases form basic, aqueous solutions.
- Salts of strong acids and weak bases form acidic, aqueous solutions.

Study Note

Use the cation and anion of a salt to determine the acidity of its aqueous solution.

Example: Will the salt Na_2CO_3 form an acidic, basic, or neutral aqueous solution?

Solution: A salt of a strong base (NaOH) and a weak acid (HCO_3^-) remove protons from water to produce a basic solution:

$$CO_3^{2-}(aq) + H_2O(l) \longrightarrow HCO_3^-(aq) + OH^-(aq)$$

◆ Learning Exercise 13.9A

Identify solutions of each of the following salts as acidic, basic, or neutral:

1. NaBr __________ **2.** KNO_2 __________

3. NH_4Cl __________ **4.** Li_2SO_4 __________

5. KF __________

Answers **1.** neutral **2.** basic **3.** acidic **4.** basic **5.** basic

◆ Learning Exercise 13.9B

Determine if each of the following salts dissolved in water form solutions that are acidic, basic, or neutral. If acidic or basic, write an equation for the reaction:

	Acidic, basic, or neutral	Equation
1. NaCN	__________	__________
2. LiBr	__________	__________
3. NH_4NO_3	__________	__________
4. Na_2S	__________	__________
5. $BaCl_2$	__________	__________

Answers

1. NaCN	basic	$CN^-(aq) + H_2O(l) \longrightarrow HCN(aq) + OH^-(aq)$
2. LiBr	neutral	
3. NH_4NO_3	acidic	$NH_4^+(aq) + H_2O(l) \longrightarrow H_3O^+(aq) + NH_3(aq)$
4. Na_2S	basic	$S^{2-}(aq) + H_2O(l) \longrightarrow HS^-(aq) + OH^-(aq)$
5. $BaCl_2$	neutral	

13.10 Buffers

- A buffer solution resists a change in pH when small amounts of acid or base are added.
- A buffer contains either (1) a weak acid and its salt, or (2) a weak base and its salt. The weak acid picks up excess OH^-, and the anion of the salt picks up excess H_3O^+.
- The pH of a buffer can be calculated by rearranging the K_a for $[H_3O^+]$.

◆ Learning Exercise 13.10A

State whether each of the following represents a buffer system.

a. $HCl + NaCl$ **b.** K_2SO_4

c. H_2CO_3 **d.** $H_2CO_3 + NaHCO_3$

Answers

a. No. A strong acid and its salt do not make a buffer.
b. No. A salt alone cannot act as a buffer.
c. No. A weak acid alone cannot act as a buffer.
d. Yes. A weak acid and its salt act as a buffer system.

Study Note

Rearranging the K_a for an acid HA to solve for $[H_3O^+]$ gives the following expression:

$$[H_3O^+] = K_a \times \frac{[HA]}{[A^-]}$$

Using the $[H_3O^+]$, calculate the pH of the buffer.

◆ Learning Exercise 13.10B

The K_a for acetic acid CH_3COOH is 1.8×10^{-5}.

a. What is the pH of a buffer that contains 1.0 M CH_3COOH and 1.0 M $CH_3COO^-Na^+$?

b. What is the pH of a buffer made from 0.10 M CH_3COOH and 0.10 M $CH_3COO^-Na^+$?

c. What is the pH of a buffer made from 0.10 M CH_3COOH and 1.0 M $CH_3COO^-Na^+$?

Answers

a. $[H_3O^+] = 1.8\ 10^{-5} \times \frac{[1.0\ M]}{[1.0\ M]} = 1.8 \times 10^{-5}$ $pH = [1.8 \times 10^{-5}] = 4.74$

b. $[H_3O^+] = 1.8\ 10^{-5} \times \frac{[0.1\ M]}{[0.1\ M]} = 1.8 \times 10^{-5}$ $pH = [1.8 \times 10^{-5}] = 4.74$

c. $[H_3O^+] = 1.8\ 10^{-5} \times \frac{[0.1\ M]}{[1.0\ M]} = 1.8 \times 10^{-6}$ $pH = [1.8 \times 10^{-6}] = 5.74$

Checklist for Chapter 13

You are ready to take the practice test for Chapter 13. Be sure you have accomplished the following learning goals for this chapter. If you are not sure, review the section listed at the end of the goal. Then apply your new skills and understanding to the practice test.

After studying Chapter 13, I can successfully:

_____ Describe the properties of Arrhenius acids and bases and write their names (13.1).

_____ Describe the Brønsted-Lowry concept of acids and bases; write conjugate acid–base pairs for an acid–base reaction (13.2).

_____ Write equations for the ionization of strong and weak acids and bases (13.3).

_____ Write a dissociation constant for a weak acid or base (13.4).

_____ Use the ion product of water to calculate $[H_3O^+]$ and $[OH^-]$ (13.5).

_____ Calculate pH from the $[H_3O^+]$ or $[OH^-]$ of a solution (13.6).

____ Write a balanced equation for the reactions of acids with metals, carbonates, and/or bases (13.7).

____ Calculate the molarity or volume of an acid or base from titration information (13.8).

____ Determine if a salt solution will be acidic, basic, or neutral (13.9).

____ Describe the role of buffers in maintaining the pH of a solution, and calculate the pH of a buffer solution (13.10).

Practice Test for Chapter 13

1. An acid is a compound that when placed in water yields this characteristic ion:

A. H_3O^+ **B.** OH^- **C.** Na^+
D. Cl^- **E.** CO_3^{2-}

2. $MgCl_2$ would be classified as a(n)

A. acid **B.** base **C.** salt
D. buffer **E.** nonelectrolyte

3. $Mg(OH)_2$ would be classified as a

A. weak acid **B.** strong base **C.** salt
D. buffer **E.** nonelectrolyte

4. In the K_w expression for pure H_2O, the $[H_3O^+]$ has the value

A. 1×10^{-7} M **B.** 1×10^{-1} M **C.** 1×10^{-14} M
D. 1×10^{-6} M **E.** 1×10^{-12} M

5. Of the following pH values, which is the most acidic?

A. 8.0 **B.** 5.5 **C.** 1.5
D. 3.2 **E.** 9.0

6. Of the following pH values, which is the most basic?

A. 10.0 **B.** 4.0 **C.** 2.2
D. 11.5 **E.** 9.0

For questions 7 through 9, consider a solution with $[H_3O^+] = 1 \times 10^{-11}$ M.

7. The pH of the solution is

A. 1.0 **B.** 2.0 **C.** 3.0
D. 11.0 **E.** 14.0

8. The hydroxide ion concentration is

A. 1×10^{-1} M **B.** 1×10^{-3} M **C.** 1×10^{-4} M
D. 1×10^{-7} M **E.** 1×10^{-11} M

9. The solution is

A. acidic **B.** basic **C.** neutral
D. a buffer **E.** neutralized

For questions 10 through 12, consider a solution with a $[OH^-] = 1 \times 10^{-5}$ M.

10. The hydrogen ion concentration of the solution is

A. 1×10^{-5} M **B.** 1×10^{-7} M **C.** 1×10^{-9} M
D. 1×10^{-10} M **E.** 1×10^{-14} M

11. The pH of the solution is

A. 2.0 **B.** 5.0 **C.** 9.0
D. 11 **E.** 14

12. The solution is

A. acidic **B.** basic **C.** neutral
D. a buffer **E.** neutralized

13. Acetic acid is a weak acid because

A. it forms a dilute acid solution. **B.** it is isotonic.
C. it is less than 50% ionized in water. **D.** it is a nonpolar molecule.
E. it can form a buffer.

14. A weak base when added to water

A. makes the solution slightly basic. **B.** does not affect the pH.
C. dissociates completely. **D.** does not dissociate.
E. makes the solution slightly acidic.

15. Which is an equation for neutralization?

A. $CaCO_3(s) \longrightarrow CaO(s) + CO_2(g)$
B. $Na_2SO_4(s) \longrightarrow 2Na^+(aq) + SO_4^{2-}(aq)$
C. $H_2SO_4(aq) + 2NaOH(aq) \longrightarrow Na_2SO_4(aq) + 2H_2O(l)$
D. $Na_2O(s) + SO_3(g) \longrightarrow Na_2SO_4(aq)$
E. $H_2CO_3(aq) \longrightarrow CO_2(g) + H_2O(l)$

16. What is the name given to components in the body that keep blood pH within its normal 7.35 to 7.45 range?

A. nutrients **B.** buffers **C.** metabolites
D. regufluids **E.** neutralizers

17. What is true of a typical buffer system?

A. It maintains a pH of 7.0.
B. It contains a weak base.
C. It contains a salt.
D. It contains a strong acid and its salt.
E. It maintains the pH of a solution.

18. Which of the following would act as a buffer system?

A. HCl **B.** Na_2CO_3 **C.** $NaOH + NaNO_3$
D. NH_4OH **E.** $NaHCO_3 + H_2CO_3$

19. What is the molarity of a 10.0-mL sample of HCl that is neutralized by 15.0 mL of 2.0 M NaOH?

A. 0.50 M HCl **B.** 1.0 M HCl **C.** 1.5 M HCl
D. 2.0 M HCl **E.** 3.0 M HCl

20. In a titration, 6.0 mol NaOH will completely neutralize _____ mol H_2SO_4.

A. 1.0 **B.** 2.0 **C.** 3.0
D. 6.0 **E.** 11

21. Which of the following pairs is a conjugate acid–base pair?

A. HCl/HNO_3 **B.** HNO_3/NO_3^- **C.** NaOH/KOH
D. HSO_4^-/HCO_3^- **E.** Cl^-/F^-

22. The conjugate base of HSO_4^- is

A. SO_4^{2-} **B.** H_2SO_4 **C.** HS^-
D. H_2S **E.** SO_3^{2-}

23. In which reaction does H_2O act as an acid?

A. $H_3PO_4 + H_2O \longrightarrow H_3O^+ + H_2PO_4^-$
B. $H_2SO_4 + H_2O \longrightarrow H_3O^+ + HSO_4^-$
C. $H_2O + HS^- \longrightarrow H_3O^+ + S^{2-}$
D. $NaOH + HCl \longrightarrow NaCl + H_2O$
E. $NH_3 + H_2O \longrightarrow NH_4^+ + OH^-$

24. Which of the following acids has the smallest K_a value?

A. HNO_3 **B.** H_2SO_4 **C.** HCl
D. H_2CO_3 **E.** HBr

25. Using the following K_a values, identify the strongest acid in the group.

A. 7.5×10^{-3} **B.** 1.8×10^{-5} **C.** 4.5×10^{8}
D. 4.9×10^{-10} **E.** 3.2×10^{4}

26. Which of the following salts produce an acidic aqueous solution?

A. KCl **B.** NH_4Cl **C.** Na_2SO_4
D. K_2CO_3 **E.** $NaNO_2$

27. A buffer is made with 1.0 M HF and 1.0 M NaF. If HF has a K_a of 7.2×10^{-4}, what is the pH of the buffer?

A. 3.14 **B.** 4.00 **C.** 4.14
D. 4.72 **E.** 7.20

Answers to the Practice Test

1. A	2. C	3. B	4. A	5. C
6. D	7. D	8. B	9. B	10. C
11. C	12. B	13. C	14. A	15. C
16. B	17. E	18. E	19. E	20. C
21. B	22. A	23. E	24. D	25. C
26. B	27. A			

Answers and Solutions to Selected Text Problems

Section 13.1

13.1 According to the Arrhenius theory:

a. An acid tastes sour.
b. An acid neutralizes bases.
c. An acid produces H_3O^+ ions in water.
d. Potassium hydroxide is the name of a base.
e. A base is a proton acceptor.

13.3 The names of nonoxy acids begin with *hydro-,* followed by the name of the anion. The names of oxyacids use the element root with *-ic acid.* Acids with one oxygen less than the common *-ic acid* name are named as *-ous acids.*

a. hydrochloric acid **b.** calcium hydroxide
c. carbonic acid **d.** nitric acid (common oxyacid of N)
e. sulfurous acid (one O less than common oxyacid H_2SO_4)
f. bromic acid

13.5 **a.** $Mg(OH)_2$ **b.** HF (*hydro-* indicates nonoxy acid)
c. H_3PO_4 (common oxyacid of P) **d.** LiOH
e. NH_4OH **f.** HIO_4 (one O more than common oxyacid HIO_3)

13.7 The acid donates a proton (H^+), whereas the base accepts a proton.

a. Acid (proton donor) HI; proton acceptor (base) H_2O
b. Acid (proton donor) H_2O; proton acceptor (base) F^-

Section 13.2

13.9 To form the conjugate base, remove one proton (H^+) from the acid.

a. $HF - H^+ \longrightarrow F^-$, fluoride ion is the conjugate base
b. $H_2O - H^+ \longrightarrow OH^-$, hydroxide ion is the conjugate base
c. $H_2CO_3 - H^+ \longrightarrow HCO_3^-$, bicarbonate ion is the conjugate base
d. $HSO_4^- - H^+ \longrightarrow SO_4^{2-}$, sulfate ion is the conjugate base
e. $HClO_2 - H^+ \longrightarrow ClO_2^-$, chlorite ion is the conjugate base

13.11 To form the conjugate acid, add one proton (H^+) to the base.

a. $CO_3^{2-} + H^+ \longrightarrow HCO_3^-$, bicarbonate ion is the conjugate acid
b. $H_2O + H^+ \longrightarrow H_3O^+$, hydronium ion is the conjugate acid
c. $H_2PO_4^- + H^+ \longrightarrow H_3PO_4$, phosphoric acid is the conjugate acid
d. $Br^- + H^+ \longrightarrow HBr$, hydrobromic acid is the conjugate acid
e. $ClO_4^- + H^+ \longrightarrow HClO_4$, perchloric acid is the conjugate acid

13.13 The conjugate acid is a proton donor, and the conjugate base is a proton acceptor.

a. acid H_2CO_3; conjugate base HCO_3^-; base H_2O; conjugate acid H_3O^+
b. acid NH_4^+; conjugate base NH_3; base H_2O; conjugate acid H_3O^+
c. acid HCN; conjugate base CN^-; base NO_2^-; conjugate acid HNO_2

13.15 $NH_4^+(aq) + H_2O(l) \rightleftarrows NH_3(aq) + H_3O^+(aq)$

Section 13.3

13.17 A strong acid is a good proton donor, whereas its conjugate base is a poor proton acceptor.

13.19 Use Table 13.4 to answer.

a. HBr **b.** HSO_4^- **c.** H_2CO_3

12.21 Use Table 13.4 to answer.

a. HSO_4^- **b.** HF **c.** HCO_3^-

13.23 **a.** From Table 13.4, we see that H_2O is a weaker base than HCO_3^- and that H_2CO_3 is a weaker acid than H_3O^+. Thus, the reactants are favored.

b. From Table 13.4, we see that NH_4^+ is a weaker acid than H_3O^+ and H_2O is a weaker base than NH_3. Thus, the reactants are favored.

c. From Table 13.4, we see that NH_4^+ is a weaker acid than HCl and that Cl^- is a weaker base than NH_3. Thus, the products are favored.

13.25 The reactants are favored because NH_4^+ is a weaker acid than HSO_4^-.

$$NH_4^+(aq) + SO_4^{2-}(aq) \rightleftarrows NH_3(aq) + HSO_4^-(aq)$$

Section 13.4

13.27 The smaller the K_a, the weaker the acid. The weaker acid has the stronger conjugate base.

a. H_2SO_3, which has a larger K_a than HS^-, is a stronger acid.
b. The conjugate base forms by removing a proton from the acid, HSO_3^-.
c. The stronger acid, H_2SO_3, has a weaker conjugate base.
d. The weaker acid, HS^-, has a stronger conjugate base.
e. H_2SO_3, the stronger acid, produces more ions.

13.29 $H_3PO_4(aq) + H_2O(l) \rightleftarrows H_3O^+(aq) + H_2PO_4^-(aq)$

The K_a is the ratio of the [products] divided by the [reactants] with $[H_2O]$ considered constant and part of the K_a:

$$K_a = \frac{[H_3O^+][H_2PO_4^-]}{[H_3PO_4]}$$

Section 13.5

13.31 In pure water, a small fraction of the water molecules donate a H^+ to H_2O to form H_3O^+. Every time a H_3O^+ is formed, OH^- is also formed. Therefore, the concentration of the two must be equal in pure water.

13.33 In an acidic solution, $[H_3O^+]$ is greater than $[OH^-]$, which means that the $[H_3O^+]$ is greater than 1×10^{-7} M and the $[OH^-]$ is less than 1×10^{-7} M.

13.35 A neutral solution has $[OH^-] = [H_3O^+] = 1.0 \times 10^{-7}$ M. If $[OH^-]$ is greater than 1×10^{-7}, the solution is basic; if $[H_3O^+]$ is greater than 1×10^{-7} M, the solution is acidic.

a. Acidic; $[H_3O^+]$ is greater than 1×10^{-7} M
b. Basic; $[H_3O^+]$ is less than 1×10^{-7} M
c. Basic; $[OH^-]$ is greater than 1×10^{-7} M
d. Acidic; $[OH^-]$ is less than 1×10^{-7} M

13.37 The value of the $[H_3O^+]$ multiplied by the value of the $[OH^-]$ is always equal to K_w, which is 1×10^{-14}. When $[OH^-]$ is known, the $[H_3O^+]$ can be calculated.
Rearranging the K_w gives $[H_3O^+] = \frac{K_w}{[OH^-]}$.

a. $[H_3O^+] = \frac{1.0 \times 10^{-14}}{1.0 \times 10^{-9}} = 1.0 \times 10^{-5}$ M

b. $[H_3O^+] = \dfrac{1.0 \times 10^{-14}}{1.0 \times 10^{-6}} = 1.0 \times 10^{-8}$ M

c. $[H_3O^+] = \dfrac{1.0 \times 10^{-14}}{2.0 \times 10^{-5}} = 5.0 \times 10^{-10}$ M

d. $[H_3O^+] = \dfrac{1.0 \times 10^{-14}}{4.0 \times 10^{-13}} = 2.5 \times 10^{-2}$ M

13.39 The value of the $[H_3O^+]$ multiplied by the value of the $[OH^-]$ is always equal to K_w, which is 1×10^{-14}. When $[H_3O^+]$ is known, the $[OH^-]$ can be calculated.

Rearranging the K_w gives $[OH^-] = K_w / [H_3O^+]$.

a. 1.0×10^{-11} M **b.** 2.0×10^{-9} M

c. $[OH^-] = \dfrac{1.0 \times 10^{-14}}{1.8 \times 10^{-12}} = 5.6 \times 10^{-3}$ M

d. $[OH^-] = \dfrac{1.0 \times 10^{-14}}{4.0 \times 10^{-13}} = 2.5 \times 10^{-2}$ M

Section 13.6

13.41 In neutral solutions, the $[H_3O^+]$ is equal to 1.0×10^{-7} M. The pH is the –log $[H_3O^+]$ and the –log $[1.0 \times 10^{-7}] = 7.00$. Note that the pH has two *decimal places* because the coefficient 1.0 has two significant figures.

13.43 An acidic solution has a pH less than 7. A neutral solution has a pH equal to 7. A basic solution has a pH greater than 7.

a. basic **b.** acidic **c.** basic **d.** acidic

13.45 An increase or decrease of 1 pH unit changes the $[H_3O^+]$ by a factor of 10. Thus, a pH of 3 (10^{-3} M or 0.001 M) is 10 times more acidic than a pH of 4 (10^{-4} M or 0.0001 M).

13.47 pH $= -\log[H_3O^+]$
The value of $[H_3O^+][OH^-] = K_w$, which is 1.0×10^{-14}. If $[H_3O^+]$ needs to be calculated from $[OH^-]$, then rearranging the K_w for $[H_3O^+]$ gives

$$[H_3O^+] = \frac{1.0 \times 10^{-14}}{[OH^-]}$$

a. pH $= -\log[1.0 \times 10^{-4}] = 4.00$

b. pH $= -\log[3.0 \times 10^{-9}] = 8.52$

c. $[H_3O^+] = \dfrac{1.0 \times 10^{-14}}{[1.0 \times 10^{-5}]} = 1.0 \times 10^{-9}$ pH $= -\log[1.0 \times 10^{-9}] = 9.00$

d. $[H_3O^+] = \dfrac{1.0 \times 10^{-14}}{[2.5 \times 10^{-11}]} = 4.0 \times 10^{-4}$ pH $= -\log[4.0 \times 10^{-4}] = 3.40$

13.49 On a calculator, pH is calculated by entering –log, followed by the coefficient EE (EXP) key and the power of 10 follow by the change sign (+/–) key. On some calculators the concentration is entered first (coefficient EXP – power) followed by log and +/– key.

$[H_3O^+] = \dfrac{1.0 \times 10^{-14}}{[OH^-]}$ $[OH^-] = \dfrac{1.0 \times 10^{-14}}{[H_3O^+]}$

pOH $= -\log[OH^-]$ pOH $= 14.00 -$ pH pH $= 14.00 -$ pOH

$[H_3O^+]$	$[OH^-]$	pH	pOH	Acidic, Basic, or Neutral?
1.0×10^{-8} M	**1.0×10^{-6} M**	8.00	6.00	Basic
1.0×10^{-3} M	1.0×10^{-11} M	**3.00**	11.00	Acidic
2.8×10^{-5} M	3.6×10^{-10} M	4.55	9.45	Acidic
1.0×10^{-12} M	1.0×10^{-2} M	12.00	**2.00**	Basic

Section 13.7

13.51 Acids react with active metals to form H_2 and a salt of the metal. The reaction of acids with carbonates yields CO_2, H_2O, and a salt of the metal. In a neutralization reaction, an acid and a base form a salt and H_2O.

a. $ZnCO_3(s) + 2HBr(aq) \longrightarrow ZnBr_2(aq) + CO_2(g) + H_2O(l)$
b. $Zn(s) + 2HCl(aq) \longrightarrow ZnCl_2(aq) + H_2(g)$
c. $HCl(aq) + NaHCO_3(s) \longrightarrow NaCl(aq) + H_2O(l) + CO_2(g)$
d. $H_2SO_4(aq) + Mg(OH)_2(s) \longrightarrow MgSO_4(aq) + 2\,H_2O(l)$

13.53 In balancing a neutralization equation, the number of H^+ and OH^- must be equalized by placing coefficients in front of the formulas for the acid and base.

a. $2HCl(aq) + Mg(OH)_2(s) \longrightarrow MgCl_2(aq) + 2H_2O(l)$
b. $H_3PO_4(aq) + 3LiOH(aq) \longrightarrow Li_3PO_4(aq) + 3H_2O(l)$

13.55 In balancing a neutralization equation, the number of H^+ and OH^- must be equalized by placing coefficients in front of the formulas for the acid and base.

a. $H_2SO_4(aq) + 2NaOH(aq) \longrightarrow Na_2SO_4(aq) + 2H_2O(l)$
b. $3HCl(aq) + Fe(OH)_3(aq) \longrightarrow FeCl_3(aq) + 3H_2O(l)$
c. $H_2CO_3(aq) + Mg(OH)_2(s) \longrightarrow MgCO_3(aq) + 2H_2O(l)$

Section 13.8

13.57 To a known volume of formic acid, add a few drops of indicator. Place a NaOH solution of known molarity in a buret. Add NaOH to the acid solution until one drop changes the color of the solution. Use the volume and molarity of NaOH to calculate the moles of formic acid in the sample. Then calculate the concentration from the moles and volume of formic acid.

13.59 In the equation, 1 mol HCl reacts with 1 mol NaOH.

Moles of NaOH: $28.6\ \cancel{\text{mL}} \times \frac{1\text{ L}}{1000\ \cancel{\text{mL}}} = 0.0286\ \cancel{\text{L}} \times \frac{0.145\text{ mol NaOH}}{1\ \cancel{\text{L}}} = 0.00415\text{ mol NaOH}$

$0.00415\text{ mol NaOH} \times \frac{1\text{ mol HCl}}{1\text{ mol NaOH}} = 0.00415\text{ mol HCl}$

Molarity of HCl: $5.00\ \cancel{\text{mL}} \times \frac{1\text{ L}}{1000\ \cancel{\text{mL}}} = 0.00500\text{ L} \qquad \frac{0.00415\text{ mol HCl}}{0.00500\text{ L}} = 0.829\text{ M}$

13.61 In the equation, 1 mol H_2SO_4 reacts with 2 mol KOH.

Moles of KOH: $38.2\ \cancel{\text{mL}} \times \frac{1\text{ L}}{1000\ \cancel{\text{mL}}} = 0.0382\ \cancel{\text{L}} \times \frac{0.163\text{ mol KOH}}{1\ \cancel{\text{L}}} = 0.00623\text{ mol KOH}$

Moles of H_2SO_4: $0.00623\ \cancel{\text{mol KOH}} \times \frac{1\ \cancel{\text{mol}}\ H_2SO_4}{2\ \cancel{\text{mol KOH}}} = 0.00312\text{ mol } H_2SO_4$

Molarity of H_2SO_4: $25.0\ \cancel{\text{mL}} \times \frac{1\text{ L}}{1000\ \cancel{\text{mL}}} = 0.0250\text{ L} \qquad \frac{0.00312\text{ mol } H_2SO_4}{0.0250\text{ L}} = 0.125\text{ M}$

13.63 In the equation, 1 mol H_3PO_4 reacts with 3 mol NaOH.

Moles of NaOH: $16.4\ \cancel{\text{mL}} \times \frac{1\text{ L}}{1000\ \cancel{\text{mL}}} = 0.0164\ \cancel{\text{L}} \times \frac{0.204\text{ mol NaOH}}{1\ \cancel{\text{L}}} = 0.00335\text{ mol NaOH}$

Moles of H_3PO_4: $0.00335\ \cancel{\text{mol NaOH}} \times \frac{1\ \cancel{\text{mol}}\ H_3PO_4}{3\ \cancel{\text{mol NaOH}}} = 0.00112\text{ mol } H_3PO_4$

Molarity of H_3PO_4: $50.0\ \cancel{\text{mL}} \times \frac{1\text{ L}}{1000\ \cancel{\text{mL}}} = 0.0500\text{ L} \qquad \frac{0.00112\text{ mol } H_3PO_4}{0.0500\text{ L}} = 0.0223\text{ M}$

Section 13.9

13.65 The anion of a weak acid removes a proton from H_2O to make a basic solution.

13.67 A solution of a salt with an anion from a strong acid and a cation from a weak base will form an acidic solution. A salt with an anion from a weak acid and a cation from a strong base will form a basic solution. Solutions of salts with ions of strong acids and strong bases are neutral.

a. neutral: Mg^{2+} is the cation of a strong base; Cl^- is the anion of a strong acid.
b. acidic: $NH_4^+(aq) + H_2O(l) \rightleftarrows NH_3(aq) + H_3O^+(aq)$
c. basic: $CO_3^{2-}(aq) + H_2O(l) \rightleftarrows HCO_3^-(aq) + OH^-(aq)$
d. basic: $S^{2-}(aq) + H_2O(l) \rightleftarrows HS^-(aq) + OH^-(aq)$

Section 13.9

13.69 A buffer system contains a weak acid and its salt, or a weak base and its salt.
a. This is not a buffer system because it only contains a strong base.
b. This is a buffer system; it contains the weak acid H_2CO_3 and its salt $NaHCO_3$.
c. This is a buffer system; it contains HF, a weak acid, and its salt KF.
d. This is not a buffer system because it contains the salts KCl and NaCl.

13.71 **a.** A buffer system keeps the pH of a solution constant.
b. The salt of the acid in a buffer is needed to neutralize any acid added.
c. When H^+ is added to the buffer, the F^- from NaF, the salt of the weak acid, reacts with the acid to neutralize it.

$$F^- + H_3O^+ \rightarrow HF + H_2O$$

d. When OH^- is added to the buffer solution, HF (weak acid) reacts to neutralize the OH^-.

$$HF(aq) + OH^-(aq) \rightarrow F^-(aq) + H_2O$$

13.73 Rearrange the K_a for $[H_3O^+]$ and use it to calculate the pH.

$$[H_3O^+] = 4.5 \times 10^{-4} \times \frac{[0.10\ \cancel{M}]}{[0.10\ \cancel{M}]} = 4.5 \times 10^{-4} \qquad pH = -\log[4.5 \times 10^{-4}] = 3.35$$

13.75 Rearrange the K_a for $[H_3O^+]$ and use it to calculate the pH.

$$[H_3O^+] = 7.2 \times 10^{-4} \times \frac{[0.10\ \cancel{M}]}{[0.10\ \cancel{M}]} = 7.2 \times 10^{-4} \qquad pH = -\log[7.2 \times 10^{-4}] = 3.14$$

$$[H_3O^+] = 7.2 \times 10^{-4} \times \frac{[0.060\ \cancel{M}]}{[0.120\ \cancel{M}]} = 3.6 \times 10^{-4} \qquad pH = -\log[3.6 \times 10^{-4}] = 3.44$$

The solution with 0.10 M HF is more acidic.

Answers to Additional Questions and Problems

13.83 The name of an acid from a simple nonmetallic anion is formed by adding the prefix *hydro-* to the name of the anion and changing the anion ending to *-ic acid.* If the acid has polyatomic anion, the name of the acid uses the name of the polyatomic anion and ends in *-ic acid* or *-ous acid.* There is no prefix *hydro-*. Bases are named as ionic compounds containing hydroxide anions.

a. sulfuric acid, acid **b.** potassium hydroxide, base
c. calcium hydroxide, base **d.** hydrochloric acid, acid **e.** nitrous acid, acid

13.85 Both strong and weak acids dissolve in water to give H_3O^+. They both neutralize bases, turn litmus red and phenolphthalein clear. Both taste sour and are electrolytes in solution. However, weak acids are only slightly dissociated in solution and are weak electrolytes. Strong acids, which are nearly completely dissociated in solution, are strong electrolytes.

13.87 **a.** $Mg(OH)_2$ is a strong base because all the base that dissolves is dissociated in aqueous solution.
b. $Mg(OH)_2(s) + 2HCl(aq) \rightarrow 2H_2O(l) + MgCl_2(aq)$

13.89 **a.** HF **b.** H_3O^+
c. HNO_2 **d.** HCO_3^-

13.91 The pOH = –log [OH^-], which means that pH + pOH =14.00.
a. pH 7.70, pOH = 14 – 7.70 = 6.30
b. pH 1.30, pOH = 14 – 1.30 = 12.70
c. pH 10.54, pOH 3.46
d. pH 11.73, pOH 2.27

13.93 If the pH is given, the [H_3O^+] can be found by using the relationship [H_3O^+] = 1.0×10^{-pH}. The [OH^-] can be found from [H_3O^+][OH^-] = 1×10^{-14}.

a. pH = 3.00 [H_3O^+] = 1.0×10^{-3} M [OH^-] = 1.0×10^{-11} M
b. [H_3O^+] = 3.3×10^{-7} M [OH^-] = 3.0×10^{-8} M

[H_3O^+] = 6.48 +/- 2nd *function 10^x^* (or *inv log*) = 3.3×10^{-7} M

$$[OH^-] = \frac{1.0 \times 10^{-14}}{3.3 \times 10^{-7}} = 3.0 \times 10^{-8}\ M$$

c. [H_3O^+] = 1.4×10^{-9} M [OH^-] = 7.1×10^{-6} M
d. [H_3O^+] = 1.0×10^{-11} M [OH^-] = 1.0×10^{-3} M

13.95 The concentration of OH^- can be calculated from the moles of NaOH and volume of the solution.

$$0.225\ \text{g NaOH} \times \frac{1\ \text{mol NaOH}}{40.01\ \text{g NaOH}} = 0.00563\ \text{mol NaOH}$$

$$\frac{0.00563\ \text{mol NaOH}}{0.0250\ \text{L}} = 0.225\ \text{M NaOH}$$

13.97

$$2.5\ \text{g HCl} \times \frac{1\ \text{mol HCl}}{36.46\ \text{g HCl}} = 0.069\ \text{mol HCl}$$

$$\frac{0.069\ \text{mol HCl}}{0.425\ \text{L}} = 0.16\ \text{M HCl}$$

Because HCl is a strong acid, the [H_3O^+] is also 0.16 M.
pH = –log [1.6×10^{-1} M] = 0.80 pOH = 14.00 – 0.80 = 13.20

13.99 **a.** The solution will be basic. K^+ is the cation of a strong acid; no effect on pH. The anion, F^-, reacts with water to form the weak acid, HF and OH^-.
$F^-(aq) + H_2O \rightarrow HF(aq) + OH(aq)$
b. The solution will be basic. Na^+ is the cation of a strong acid; no effect on pH. CN^-, the anion, reacts with water to form the weak acid, HCN and OH^-.
$CN^-(aq) + H_2O \rightarrow HCN(aq) + OH(aq)$
c. The solution will be acidic. NH_4^+ is the cation of a weak base, NH_4OH. The anion, NO_3^-, is from a strong acid and does not change the pH.
d. The solution will be neutral. The cation is from a strong base, and the anion is from a strong acid. None of the ions of the salt will change the pH.

13.101 In a buffer, the anion accepts H^+ and the cation provides H^+.

a. $H_2PO_4^-(aq) + H_3O^+(aq) \longrightarrow H_3PO_4(aq) + H_2O(l)$

b. $H_3PO_4(aq) + OH^-(aq) \longrightarrow H_2PO_4^-(aq) + H_2O(l)$

c. $[H_3O^+] = 7.5 \times 10^{-3} \times \frac{[0.10\ \cancel{M}]}{[0.10\ \cancel{M}]} = 7.5 \times 10^{-3}$ pH = –log (7.5 x 10^{-3}) = 2.12

13.103 **a.** One mol HCl reacts with 1 mol NaOH.

Moles of HCl: $25.0\ \cancel{mL} \times \frac{1\ L}{1000\ \cancel{mL}} = 0.0250\ \cancel{L} \times \frac{0.288\ mol\ HCl}{1\ \cancel{L}} = 0.00720\ mol\ HCl$

$0.00415\ \cancel{mol\ NaOH} \times \frac{1\ mol\ HCl}{1\ \cancel{mol\ NaOH}} = 0.00415\ mol\ HCl$

Volume of NaOH: $0.00720\ \cancel{moL} \times \frac{1\ L}{0.150\ \cancel{mol}} \times \frac{1000\ mL}{1\ \cancel{L}} = 48.0\ mL$

b. One mol H_2SO_4 reacts with 2 mol NaOH.

Moles of H_2SO_4: $10.0\ \cancel{mL} \times \frac{1\ L}{1000\ \cancel{mL}} = 0.0100\ \cancel{L} \times \frac{0.560\ mol}{1\ \cancel{L}} = 0.00560\ mol\ H_2SO_4$

$0.00560\ mol\ H_2SO_4 \times \frac{2\ \cancel{mol\ NaOH}}{1\ \cancel{mol\ H_2SO_4}} = 0.0112\ mol\ NaOH$

Volume of NaOH: $0.0112\ \cancel{moL} \times \frac{1\ L}{0.150\ \cancel{mol}} \times \frac{1000\ mL}{1\ \cancel{L}} = 74.7\ mL$

13.105 One mol H_2SO_4 reacts with 2 mol NaOH.

Moles of NaOH: $45.6\ \cancel{mL} \times \frac{1\ L}{1000\ \cancel{mL}} = 0.0456\ \cancel{L} \times \frac{0.205\ mol}{1\ \cancel{L}} = 0.00935\ mol\ NaOH$

Moles of H_2SO_4: $0.00935\ \cancel{mol\ NaOH} \times \frac{1\ \cancel{mol\ H_2SO_4}}{2\ \cancel{mol\ KOH}} = 0.00468\ mol\ H_2SO_4$

Molarity of H_2SO_4: $20.0\ \cancel{mL} \times \frac{1\ L}{1000\ \cancel{mL}} = 0.0200\ L \quad \frac{0.00468\ mol\ H_2SO_4}{0.0200\ L} = 0.234\ M$

14

Oxidation-Reduction: Transfer of Electrons

Study Goals

- Identify the atoms that are oxidized and reduced in an oxidation-reduction reaction.
- Assign an oxidation number to the atoms in a compound to determine the oxidized and reduced components.
- Use oxidation numbers to identify what is oxidized, what is reduced, the reducing agent, and the oxidizing agent.
- Balance oxidation-reduction equations using the oxidation number or the half-reaction method.
- Write the half-reactions that occur at the anode and cathode of a voltaic cell; write the shorthand cell notation.
- Describe the half-cell reactions and the overall reactions that occur in electrolytic cells.
- Use the activity series to determine if a reaction is spontaneous or requires electrical energy.

Think About It

1. What change occurs in iron metal (Fe) when it is oxidized to form rust?

2. How does the oxidation number change when an atom is reduced?

3. How does a battery provide electricity to run a flashlight or watch?

Key Terms

Match each of the following key terms with the correct definition.

a. cathode
b. oxidation
c. reduction
d. oxidizing agent
e. reducing agent
f. voltaic cell

1. _____ The reactant that is reduced

2. _____ The gain of electrons by a substance

3. _____ A cell that uses an oxidation-reduction reaction to produce electrical energy

4. _____ The loss of electrons by a substance

5. _____ The reactant that is oxidized

6. _____ The electrode in an electrochemical cell where reduction takes place

Answers **1.** d **2.** c **3.** f **4.** b **5.** e **6.** a

14.1 Oxidation and Reduction

- In an oxidation-reduction reaction, electrons are transferred from one reactant to another.
- In an oxidation, electrons are lost. In a reduction, there is a gain of electrons.
- In any oxidation-reduction reaction, the number of electrons lost must be equal to the number of electrons gained.
- A reducing agent provides the electrons (oxidized), and an oxidizing agent accepts electrons (reduced).

◆ Learning Exercise 14.1A

Study Note

Oxidation is always the loss of electrons (LEO). Reduction is always a gain of electrons (GER). A balanced reduction-oxidation equation contains an oxidation of one reactant and a reduction of the other reactant.

$$Cu(s) + 2Ag^+ \longrightarrow Cu^{2+} + 2\,Ag(s)$$

oxidation $\quad Cu^0 \longrightarrow Cu^{2+} + \mathbf{2e^-}$

reduction $\quad 2\,Ag^+ + \mathbf{2e^-} \longrightarrow 2\,Ag(s)$

In a balanced reduction-oxidation equation, the loss of electrons must be equal to the gain of electrons.

Loss of electrons = Gain of electrons

Identify each of the following as oxidation (O) or reduction (R):

1. _____ loss of two electrons

2. _____ $Zn(s) \rightarrow Zn^{2+}(aq) + 2e^-$

3. _____ $Cu^{2+}(aq) + e^- \rightarrow Cu^+(aq)$

4. _____ gain of electrons

Answers **1.** O **2.** O **3.** R **4.** R

◆ Learning Exercise 14.1B

For each of the following, indicate whether the underlined element is *oxidized* or *reduced.*

a. $4\underline{Al} + 3O_2 \longrightarrow 2Al_2O_3$ Al is ____________________

b. $\underline{Fe}^{3+} + e^- \longrightarrow Fe^{2+}$ Fe^{3+} is ____________________

c. $\underline{Cu}O + H_2 \longrightarrow Cu + H_2O$ Cu^{2+} is ____________________

d. $2\underline{Cl}^- \longrightarrow Cl_2 + 2e^-$ Cl^- is ____________________

e. $2H\underline{Br} + Cl_2 \longrightarrow 2HCl + Br_2$ Br^- is ____________________

f. $2\underline{Na} + Cl_2 \longrightarrow 2NaCl$ Na is ____________________

g. $\underline{Cu}Cl_2 + Zn \longrightarrow ZnCl_2 + Cu$ Cu^{2+} is ____________________

Answers

a. Al is oxidized to Al^{3+}; loss of electrons

b. Fe^{3+} is reduced to Fe^{2+}; gain of electrons

c. Cu^{2+} is reduced to Cu; gain of electrons

d. $2Cl^-$ is oxidized to Cl_2; loss of electrons

e. 2 Br^- is oxidized to Br_2; loss of electrons

f. Na is oxidized to Na^+; loss of electrons

g. Cu^{2+} is reduced to Cu; gain of electrons

◆ Learning Exercise 14.1C

Determine whether each of the following is an oxidation-reduction reaction. If the reaction is an oxidation-reduction, identify the element that is oxidized and the element that is reduced.

a. $2Na + Cl_2 \longrightarrow 2NaCl$

b. $Zn + 2H^+ \longrightarrow Zn^{2+} + H_2$

c. $H_2S + I_2 \longrightarrow 2HI + S$

d. $BaCl_2 + 2AgNO_3 \longrightarrow 2AgCl + Ba(NO_3)_2$

e. $2Mg + O_2 \longrightarrow 2MgO$

f. $B_2O_3 + 3Mg \longrightarrow 3MgO + 2B$

Answers

a. oxidation: $Na \longrightarrow Na^+ + 1\,e^-$ reduction: $Cl_2 + 2e^- \longrightarrow 2Cl^-$

b. oxidation: $Zn \longrightarrow Zn^{2+} + 2e^-$ reduction: $2H^+ + 2e^- \longrightarrow H_2$

c. oxidation: $S^{2-} \longrightarrow S + 2e^-$ reduction: $I_2 + 2e^- \longrightarrow 2I^-$

d. not reduction-oxidation (double replacement reaction)

e. oxidation: $Mg \longrightarrow Mg^{2+} + 2e^-$ reduction: $O_2 + 4e^- \longrightarrow 2O^{2-}$

f. oxidation: $Mg \longrightarrow Mg^{2+} + 2e$ reduction: $B^{3+} + 3e^- \longrightarrow B$

14.2 Oxidation Numbers

- An oxidation number is assigned to atoms in the reactants and products to determine the oxidation and reduction reactions.
- An increase in oxidation number indicates an oxidation; a decrease indicates a reduction.

Summary of Rules for Assigning Oxidation Numbers		
1. An element is 0.	2. A monoatomic ion is equal to its ionic charge.	
3. The sum of oxidation numbers is 0 in a compound or the charge in a polyatomic ion.		
4. Group 1A and H= +1	Group 2A = +2	
Fluorine = −1	Oxygen = −2	Group 7 = −1 except when combined with F or O

◆ Learning Exercise 14.2A

Assign oxidation numbers to the elements in each of the following:

a. PbO **b.** Fe **c.** NO_2 **d.** $CuCl_2$

e. H_2CO_3 **f.** HNO_3 **g.** $Cu(NO_3)_2$ **h.** $Cr_2O_7^{2-}$

Answers

a. PbO
+2 −2

b. Fe
0

c. NO_2
+4 −2
$N + 2(-2) = 0$
$N = +4$

d. $CuCl_2$
+2 −1

e. H_2CO_3
+1 +4 −2
$2(+1) + C + 3(-2) = 0$
$C = -2 + 6 = +4$

f. HNO_3
+1 +5 −2
$+1 + N + 3(-2) = 0$
$N = -1 + 6 = +5$

g. K_3PO_3
+1 +5 −2
$3(+1) + P + 3(-2)$
$P = -3 + 6 = +3$

h. $Cr_2O_7^{2-}$
+6 −2
$2Cr + 7(-2) = -2$
$2Cr = -2 + 14 = +12$
$Cr = +6$

◆ Learning Exercise 14.2B

Complete each of the following statements about oxidation-reduction reactions by using the term *loses* or *gains*:

a. In reduction, an element __________ electrons.

b. The oxidizing agent __________ electrons.

c. The element that ____________ electrons is oxidized.

d. The reducing agent is the element that ___________ electrons.

e The oxidation number increases when an element _____________ electrons.

f. The oxidizing agent is the substance that ___________electrons.

g. The oxidation number decreases when an element _____________ electrons.

h. In oxidation, an element __________ electrons.

Answers	**a.** gains	**b.** gains	**c.** loses	**d.** loses
	e. loses	**f.** gains	**g.** gains	**h.** loses

◆ Learning Exercise 14.2C

Study Note

The oxidizing agent gains electrons from the oxidation. The reducing agent provides electrons for reduction.

In each of the following, assign oxidation numbers to identify the element that is oxidized and the element that is reduced. For each, identify the oxidizing agent and the reducing agent.

a. $PbO(s) + CO(g) \rightarrow Pb(s) + CO_2(g)$

substance oxidized _________ substance reduced ___________

oxidizing agent _________ reducing agent ___________

b. $Fe_2O_3(s) + 3C(s) \rightarrow 2Fe(s) + 3CO(g)$

substance oxidized _________ substance reduced ___________

oxidizing agent _________ reducing agent ___________

c. $Cu(s) + 4HNO_3(aq) \rightarrow Cu(NO_3)_2(aq) + 2NO_2(g) + 2H_2O(l)$

substance oxidized _________ substance reduced ___________

oxidizing agent _________ reducing agent ___________

Answers

a. $PbO(s) + CO(g) \rightarrow Pb(s) + CO_2(g)$
+2 −2   +2 −2   0   +4 −2

substance oxidized C(+2 → +4)   substance reduced Pb(+2 → 0)
oxidizing agent Pb   reducing agent CO

b. $Fe_2O_3(s) + 3C(s) \rightarrow 2Fe(s) + 3CO(g)$
+3 −2   0   0   +2 −2

substance oxidized C(0 → +2)   substance reduced Fe(+3 → 0)
oxidizing agent Fe_2O_3 reducing agent C

c. $Cu(s) + 4HNO_3(aq) \rightarrow Cu(NO_3)_2(aq) + 2NO_2(g) + 2H_2O(l)$
0   +1 +5 −2   +2 +5 −2   +4 −2   +1 −2

substance oxidized Cu(0 → +2)   substance reduced N(+5 → +4)
oxidizing agent HNO_3 reducing agent Cu

14.3 Balancing Oxidation-Reduction Equations

- An oxidation-reduction equation is balanced by identifying the oxidized and reduced atoms from the changes in electrons.

Study Note

Balance the following equation using oxidation number method:

$$Cr(s) + HCl(aq) \longrightarrow CrCl_3(aq) + H_2$$

1. Assign oxidation numbers.

$$\underset{0}{Cr(s)} + \underset{+1\,-1}{HCl(aq)} \longrightarrow \underset{+3\,-1}{CrCl_3(aq)} + \underset{0}{H_2}$$

2. Identify the oxidized and reduced elements.

Cr is oxidized; oxidation number 0 → +3 ($3e^-$ change) × 2
2H are reduced; oxidation number 2(+1 → 0) ($2e^-$ change) × 3

oxidation: loss of $3e^- \times 2$

$$\underset{0}{Cr(s)} + \underset{+1\,-1}{2HCl(aq)} \longrightarrow \underset{+3\,-1}{CrCl_3(aq)} + \underset{0}{H_2}$$

reduction: gain of $2e^- \times 3$

3. Multiply the changes by small integers to equalize the increase and decrease in oxidation numbers. The Cr oxidation loses 3 e^- (x 2 = $6e^-$). The 2H reduction is multiplied by 3 (= $6e^-$)

$$2Cr(s) + 6HCl(aq) \longrightarrow 2CrCl_3(aq) + 3H_2$$

◆ Learning Exercise 14.3A

Use oxidation numbers to balance each of the following equations by placing appropriate coefficients in front of the formulas as needed:

a. ______$MgO(s)$ ⟶ ______$Mg(s)$ + ______$O_2(g)$

b. ______$Zn(s)$ + ______$HCl(aq)$ ⟶ ______$ZnCl_2(aq)$ + ______$H_2(g)$

c. ______$Al(s)$ + ______$CuSO_4(aq)$ ⟶ ______$Cu(s)$ + ______$Al_2(SO_4)_3(aq)$

d. ______$CO(g)$ + ______$Fe_2O_3(s)$ ⟶ ______$Fe(s)$ + ______$CO_2(g)$

e. ______$K(s)$ + ______$H_2O(l)$ ⟶ ______$K_2O(aq)$ + ______$H_2(g)$

Answers

a. $2MgO(s) \rightarrow 2Mg(s) + O_2(g)$ O loss of $2e^-$; Mg gain of $2e^-$
+2 −2 0 0

b. $Zn(s) + 2HCl(aq) \rightarrow ZnCl_2(aq) + H_2(g)$ Zn loss of $2e^-$; 2H gain of $2(1e^-)$
0 +1 −1 +2 −1 0

c. $2Al(s) + 3CuSO_4(aq) \rightarrow 3Cu(s) + Al_2(SO_4)_3(aq)$ Al loss of $3e^-$ (x 2); Cu gain of $2e^-$(x3)
0 +2 +6 −2 0 +3 +6 −2

d. $3CO(g) + Fe_2O_3(s) \rightarrow 2Fe(s) + 3CO_2(g)$ C loss of $2e^-$(x 3); Fe gain of $3e^-$(x2)
+2 −2 +3 −2 0 +4 −2

e. $2K(s) + H_2O(l) \rightarrow K_2O(aq) + H_2(g)$ K loss of $1e^-$ (x 2); 2H gain of $2(1e^-)$
0 +1 −2 +1 −2 0

Study Note

Using Half-Reaction Method to Balance Oxidation-Reduction Equations

1. Write the oxidation and reduction reactions as separate half-reactions.
2. Balance atoms other than O and H. Balance O atoms with H_2O, H with H^+, and charge with electrons.
3. Use small numbers as coefficients to equalize the electron lost and gain.
4. Combine half-reactions, combine like species, and cancel electrons.

Consider the following unbalanced oxidation-reduction equation:

$$I^-(aq) + SO_4^{2-}(aq) \rightarrow H_2S(g) + I_2(g)$$

1. Write two half-reactions and balance atoms other than O and H.

$\mathbf{2}I^-(aq) \rightarrow I_2(g)$ $\quad\quad$ $SO_4^{2-}(aq) \rightarrow H_2S(g)$

2. Balance O with H_2O and H with H^+:

$SO_4^{2-}(aq) \rightarrow H_2S(g) + \mathbf{4H_2O}(l)$ $\quad\quad$ $SO_4^{2-}(aq) + \mathbf{10H^+}(aq) \rightarrow H_2S(g) + 4H_2O(l)$

Balance charge using electrons:

$2I^-(aq) \rightarrow I_2(g) + \mathbf{2e^-}$ $\quad\quad$ $SO_4^{2-}(aq) + 10H^+(aq) + \mathbf{8e^-} \rightarrow H_2S(g) + 4H_2O(l)$

3 Multiply by small numbers to equalize electron loss and gain:

$[2I^-(aq) \rightarrow I_2(g) + 2e^-] \times 4$ $\quad$ $(= 8e^-$ loss)

$8I^-(aq) \rightarrow 4I_2(g) + \mathbf{8e^-}$ $\quad\quad$ $SO_4^{2-}(aq) + 10H^+(aq) + \mathbf{8e^-} \rightarrow H_2S(g) + \mathbf{4}H_2O(l)$

4 Add half-reactions, cancel electrons, and combine like species.

$8I^-(aq) + SO_4^{2-}(aq) + 10H^+(aq) \cancel{+ 8e^-} \rightarrow 4I_2(g) + H_2S(g) + 4H_2O(l) \cancel{+8e^-}$

$8I^-(aq) + SO_4^{2-}(aq) + 10H^+(aq) \rightarrow 4I_2(g) + H_2S(g) + 4H_2O(l)$ $\quad$ balanced

◆ Learning Exercise 14.3C

Use half-reactions to balance the following oxidation-reduction equations:

a. $NO_3^- + S \rightarrow NO_2 + H_2SO_4$

b. $MnO_4^- + Cl^- \rightarrow Mn^{2+} + Cl_2$

c. $Cr_2O_7^{2-}$ + Fe^{2+} → Cr^{3+} + Fe^{3+}

d. $NO_2 + ClO^-$ → $NO_3^- + Cl^-$

e. $BrO_3^- + MnO_2$ → $Br^- + MnO_4^-$

Answers

a. $6NO_3^- + S + 6H^+$ → $6NO_2 + H_2SO_4 + 2H_2O$

b. $2MnO_4^-$ + $10Cl^-$ + $16H^+$ → $2Mn^{2+}$ + $5Cl_2 + 8H_2O$

c. $Cr_2O_7^{2-}$ + $6Fe^{2+} + 14H^+$ → $2Cr^{3+}$ + $6Fe^{3+} + 7H_2O$

d. $2NO_2 + ClO^-$ + H_2O → $2NO_3^- + Cl^-\ 2H^+$

e. $BrO_3^- + 2MnO_2$ + H_2O → $Br^- + 2MnO_4^-$ + $2H^+$

14.4 Electrical Energy from Oxidation-Reduction Reactions

- In an electrochemical cell, the half-reactions of an oxidation-reduction reaction are physically separated so the electrons flow through an external circuit.
- In a voltaic cell, the flow of electron through an external circuit generates electrical energy.
- Oxidation takes place at the anode; reduction takes place at the cathode.
- Batteries are examples of electrochemical cells that provide electrical energy.

◆ Learning Exercise 14.4A

For each of the following voltaic cells, write the cell notation, diagram the cell, write the half-reactions at the anode and cathode, the balanced equation, and indicate the direction of electron flow.

a. Mg anode in a Mg^{2+} solution $Mg(NO_3)_2$ and a Ag cathode in a Ag^+ solution $AgNO_3$.

b. Cr anode in a Cr^{3+} solution $Cr(NO_3)_3$ and an Al cathode in a Al^{3+} solution $Al(NO_3)_3$.

c. Fe anode in a Fe^{2+} solution $Fe(NO_3)_2$ and a Ni cathode in a Ni^+ solution $Ni(NO_3)_2$.

Answers

a. $Mg(s)\,|\,Mg^{2+}(aq)\,\|\,Ag^{+}(aq)\,|\,Ag(s)$

Anode: $Mg(s) \rightarrow Mg^{2+}(aq) + 2e^{-}$

Cathode: $Ag^{+}(aq) \rightarrow Ag(s) + e^{-}$

$Mg(s) + 2Ag^{+}(aq) \rightarrow Mg^{2+}(aq) + 2Ag(s)$

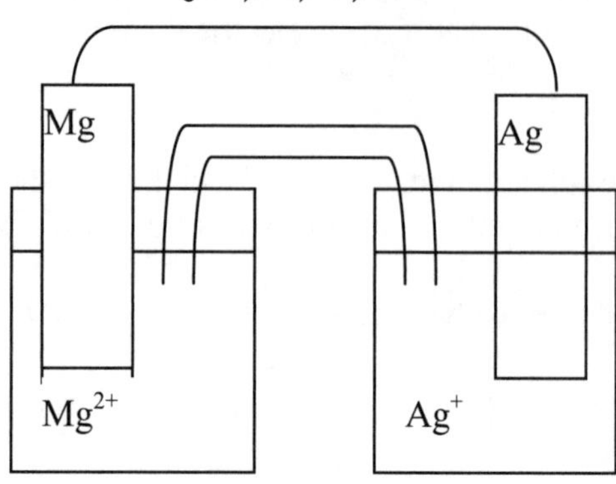

b. $Al(s)\,|\,Al^{3+}(aq)\,\|\,Cr^{3+}(aq)\,|\,Cr(s)$

Anode: $Al(s) \rightarrow Al^{3+}(aq) + 3e^{-}$

Cathode: $Cr^{3+}(aq) + 3e \rightarrow Cr(s)$

$Cr^{3+}(aq) + Al(s) \rightarrow Cr(s) + Al^{3+}(aq)$

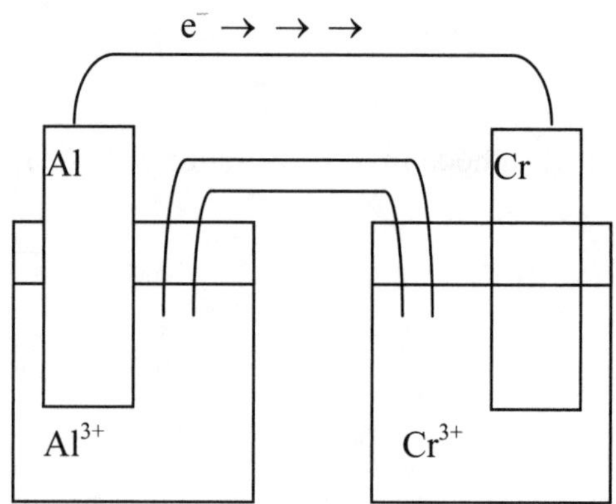

c. $Fe(s)\,|\,Fe^{2+}(aq)\,\|\,Ni^{2+}(aq)\,|\,Ni(s)$

Anode: $Fe(s) \rightarrow Fe^{2+}(aq) + 2e^{-}$

Cathode: $Ni^{2+}(aq) \rightarrow Ni(s) + 2e^{-}$

$Fe(s) + Ni^{2+}(aq) \rightarrow Fe^{2+}(aq) + Ni(s)$

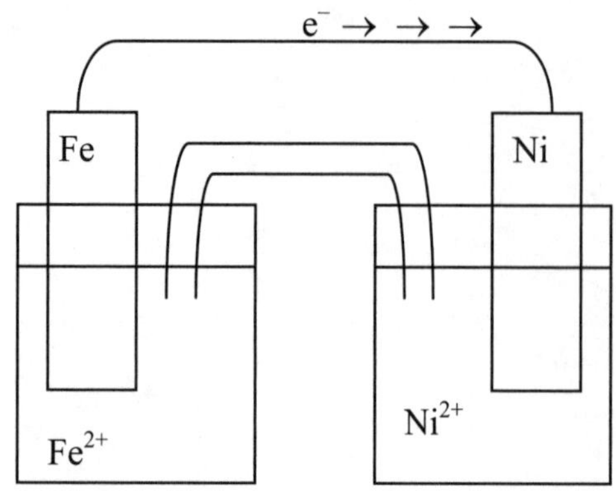

◆ Learning Exercise 14.4B

Write the half-reactions for the anode and cathode and the overall cell reaction for the following cell notations:

a. $Sr(s) \mid Sr^{2+}(aq) \parallel Sn^{4+}(aq), Sn^{2+}(aq) \mid Pt$

b. $Cr(s) \mid Cr^{3+}(aq) \parallel Ni^{2+}(aq) \mid Ni(s)$

c. $Ag(s) \mid Ag^{+}(aq) \parallel Au^{3+}(aq) \mid Au(s)$

Answers

a. Anode: $Sr(s) \rightarrow Sr^{2+}(aq) + 2e^-$
Cathode: $Sn^{4+}(aq) + 2e^- \rightarrow Sn^{2+}(aq)$
$Sr(s) + Sn^{4+}(aq) \rightarrow Sr^{2+}(aq) + Sn^{2+}(aq)$

b. Anode: $Cr(s) \rightarrow Cr^{3+}(aq) + 3e^- \quad \times 2$
Cathode: $Ni^{2+}(aq) + 2e^- \rightarrow Ni(s) \times 3$
$2Cr(s) + 3Ni^{2+}(aq) \rightarrow 2Cr^{2+}(aq) + 3Ni(s)$

c. Anode: $Ag(s) \rightarrow Ag^{+}(aq) + e^- \quad \times 3$
Cathode: $Au^{3+}(aq) + 3e^- \rightarrow Au(s) \quad \times 1$
$3Ag(s) + Au^{3+}(aq) \rightarrow 3Ag^{+}(aq) + Au(s)$

14.5 Oxidation-Reduction Reactions That Require Electrical Energy

- The activity series arranges element in order of their ability to oxidize spontaneously when combined with the ions of any metal lower on the list.
- An oxidation-reduction reaction is not spontaneous when a less active metal is combined with the ions of a more active metal.
- In electrolysis, an electrolytic cell requires external electric current to drive a nonspontaneous reaction.

◆ Learning Exercise 14.5A

Use the activity series to determine the most active metal in each of the following pairs:

a. Fe(*s*) or Pb(*s*)

b. Ag(*s*) or Na(*s*)

c. Zn(*s*) or Ca(*s*)

d. Al(*s*) or Pb(*s*)

e. Fe(*s*) or Ni(*s*)

Answers

a.	Fe(*s*)	**b.**	Na(*s*)	**c.**	Ca(*s*)
d.	Al(*s*)	**e.**	Fe(*s*)		

◆ Learning Exercise 14.5B

Using the activity series, predict whether each of the following reactions occur spontaneously:

a. $Cu(s) + Sn^{2+}(aq) \rightarrow Cu^{2+}(aq) + Sn(s)$ ____________________

b. $Pb^{2+}(aq) + Mg(s) + \rightarrow Mg^{2+}(aq) + Pb(s)$ ____________________

c. $2Ag(s) + Ni^{2+}(aq) \rightarrow Ni^{2+}(aq) + 2Ag(s)$ ____________________

d. $Zn(s) + 2H^{+}(aq) \rightarrow Zn^{2+}(aq) + H_2(g)$ ____________________

e. $2Cr(s) + 3Ca^{2+}(aq) \rightarrow 2Cr^{3+}(aq) + 3Ca(s)$ ____________________

Answers

a. Not spontaneous: Cu(*s*) is less active than Sn(*s*).

b. Spontaneous: Mg(*s*) is more active than Pb(*s*).

c. Not spontaneous: Ag(*s*) is less active than Ni(*s*).

d. Spontaneous: Zn(*s*) is more active than $H_2(g)$.

e. Not spontaneous: Cr(*s*) is less active than Ca(*s*).

◆ Learning Exercise 14.5C

1. Oxalic acid $H_2C_2O_4$ present in plants such as spinach reacts with permanganate.

$$H_2C_2O_4^{2-}(aq) + MnO_4^{-}(aq) \rightarrow Mn^{2+}(aq) + CO_2(g)$$

a. Balance the equation in acidic solution.

b. If 25.0 mL of 0.0200 M MnO_4^- ($KMnO_4$) is required to react 5.00 mL of $H_2C_2O_4$, what is the molarity of the $C_2O_4^{2-}$ solution?

2. Iodine reacts with thiosulfate, $S_2O_3^{2-}$ solution:

$$I_2(s) + S_2O_3^{2-}(aq) \rightarrow I^-(aq) + S_4O_6^{2-}(g)$$

a. Balance the equation in acidic solution.

b. If 37.6 mL of 0.250 M $S_2O_3^{2-}$ solution is required to complete react I_2, how many grams of I_2 are present in the sample?

Answers

1. a. $5H_2C_2O_4(aq) + 6H^+ + 2MnO_4^-(aq) \rightarrow 2Mn^{2+}(aq) + 10CO_2(g) + 8H_2O$

b. $0.0250\ \text{L} \times \dfrac{0.0200\ \text{mol}\ MnO_4^-}{1\ \text{L}} \times \dfrac{5\ \text{mol}\ H_2C_2O_4}{2\ \text{mol}\ MnO_4^-} \times \dfrac{1}{0.00500\ \text{L}} = 0.250\ \text{M}$

2. a. $I_2(s) + 2S_2O_3^{2-}(aq) \rightarrow 2I^-(aq) + + S_4O_6^{2-}(g)$

b. $0.0376\ \text{L} \times \dfrac{0.250\ \text{mol}\ S_2O_4^{2-}}{1\ \text{L}} \times \dfrac{1\ \text{mol}\ I_2}{2\ \text{mol}\ S_2O_4^{2-}} \times \dfrac{253.8\ \text{g}\ I_2}{1\ \text{mol}\ I_2} = 1.19\ \text{g}\ I_2$

Checklist for Chapter 14

You are ready to take the practice test for Chapter 14. Be sure you have accomplished the following learning goals for this chapter. If you are not sure, review the section listed at the end of the goal. Then apply your new skills and understanding to the practice test.

After studying Chapter 14, I can successfully:

____ Identify what is oxidized and reduced in an oxidation-reduction reaction (14.1).

____ Assign oxidation numbers to the atoms in an equation (14.2).

____ Use oxidation numbers to determine the oxidized element, reduced element, oxidizing agent, and reducing agent (14.2).

____ Balance an oxidation-reduction equation using oxidation numbers (14.3).

____ Balance an oxidation-reduction equation using half-reactions (14.3).

____ Write the half-reactions for the anode and the cathode of a voltaic cell (14.4).

____ Write the shorthand cell notation for the half-reactions for the anode and the cathode of a voltaic cell (14.4).

____ Write the half-cell reactions for an electrolytic cell (14.5).

____ Use the activity series for metals to determine whether an oxidation-reduction reaction is spontaneous (14.5).

____ Calculate the mass of a substance used or produced using an oxidation-reduction equation (14.5).

Practice Test for Chapter 14

Identify whether the element in each of the following is oxidized (O) or reduced (R).

1. ____ Gains electrons

2. ____ An oxidizing agent

3. ____ Loses electrons

4. ____ A reducing agent

5. ____ Oxidation number increases

For questions 6 to 10, indicate the oxidation number of the indicated element as
A. +1 **B.** +2 **C.** +3 **D.** +4 **E.** +5

6. ____ N in HNO_2

7. ____ P in P_2O_5

8. ____ C in HCO_3^-

9. ____ Mn in MnO_2

10. ____ Ca in $CaSO_4$

For questions 11 to 15, indicate the oxidation number of the indicated element as
A. 0 **B.** –1 **C.** –2 **D.** –3 **E.** –4

11. ____ P in Na_3P

12. ____ N in N_2H_4

13. ____ C in CH_4

14. ____ Br in Br_2

15. ____ F in OF_2

For questions 16 to 18, consider the following half-reaction in acidic solution:

$ClO_2^- \rightarrow Cl^-$

16. What is the number of H_2O in the balanced half-reaction?
A. 1 **B.** 2 **C.** 3 **D.** 4 **E.** 5

17. What is the number of H^+ in the balanced half-reaction?
A. 1 **B.** 2 **C.** 3 **D.** 4 **E.** 5

18. How many electrons are in the balanced half-reaction?
A. 1 **B.** 2 **C.** 3 **D.** 4 **E.** 5

For questions 19 to 21, consider the following half-reaction in acidic solution:

$Cr_2O_7^{2-} \rightarrow Cr^{3+}$

19. What is the number of H_2O in the balanced half-reaction?
A. 2 **B.** 4 **C.** 5 **D.** 7 **E.** 14

20. What is the number of H^+ in the balanced half-reaction?
A. 2 **B.** 6 **C.** 7 **D.** 12 **E.** 14

21. How many electrons are in the balanced half-reaction?
A. 2 **B.** 4 **C.** 6 **D.** 10 **E.** 14

22. The equation that has the cell notation is

$Al(s) \mid Al^{3+}(aq) \parallel Fe^{2+}(aq) \mid Fe(s)$

A. $Al(s) + Fe^{2+}(aq) \rightarrow Al^{3+}(aq) + Fe(s)$

B. $Al^{3+}(aq) + Fe(s) \rightarrow Al(s) + Fe^{2+}(aq)$

C. $Al^{3+}(aq) + Fe(s) \rightarrow Al(s) + Fe^{2+}(aq)$

D. $Al^{3+}(aq) + Fe^{2+}(aq) \rightarrow Fe(s) + Al(s)$

E. $Al(s) + Fe(s) \rightarrow Fe^{2+}(aq) + Al^{3+}(aq)$

Consider the following metals and ions in order from most to least active:

$Mg(s) \rightarrow Mg^{2+}(aq) + 2e^-$

$Cr(s) \rightarrow Cr^{3+}(aq) + 3e^-$

$Pb(s) \rightarrow Pb^{2+}(aq) + 2e^-$

$Ag(s) \rightarrow Ag^{+}(aq) + e^-$

23. Which of the following reactions is spontaneous?

A. $3Pb(s) + 2Cr^{3+}(aq) \rightarrow 3Pb^{2+}(aq) + 2Cr(s)$

B. $Mg(s) + 2Ag^{+}(aq) \rightarrow Mg^{2+}(aq) + 2Ag(s)$

C. $2Cr^{3+}(aq) + 3Pb(s) \rightarrow 3Pb^{2+}(aq) + 2Cr(s)$

D. $2Ag(s) + Pb^{2+}(aq) \rightarrow Pb(s) + 2Ag^{+}(s)$

E. $3Ag(s) + Cr^{3+}(aq) \rightarrow 3Ag^{+}(aq) + Cr^{3+}(s)$

24. Which of the following reactions requires external source of energy?

A. $2Mg(s) + 2Cr^{3+}(aq) \rightarrow 2Cr(s) + 3Mg^{2+}(aq)$

B. $Pb(s) + 2Ag^{+}(aq) \rightarrow Pb^{2+}(aq) + Pb^{2+}(aq)$

C. $Mg(s) + Pb^{2+}(aq) \rightarrow Mg^{2+}(aq) + Pb(s)$

D. $Mg(s) + 2Ag^{+}(aq) \rightarrow Mg^{2+}(aq) + Ag(s)$

E. $3Pb(s) + 2Cr^{3+}(aq) + \rightarrow 3Pb^{2+}(aq) + 2Cr(s)$

25. In the electroplating of an aluminum bowl, an aluminum anode is placed in a Al^{3+} solution $Al(NO_3)_3$. The bowl to be aluminum plated is the cathode. The anode and cathode are wired to a battery. The reaction at the anode is

A. $Al^{3+}(aq) + 3e^- \rightarrow Al(s)$

B. $Al^{3+}(aq) \rightarrow Al(s) + 3e^-$

C. $Al(s) + 3e^- \rightarrow Al^{3+}(aq)$

D. $Al(s) \rightarrow Al^{3+}(aq) + 3e^-$

E. $Al(s) + Al^{3+}(aq) \rightarrow 2\ Al(s)$

Answers to the Practice Test

1. R	**2.** R	**3.** O	**4.** O	**5.** O
6. C	**7.** E	**8.** D	**9.** D	**10.** B
11. D	**12.** C	**13.** E	**14.** A	**15.** B
16. B	**17.** D	**18.** D	**19.** D	**20.** E
21. C	**22.** A	**23.** B	**24.** E	**25.** D

Answers and Solutions to Selected Text Problems

Section 14.1

Answers to Selected Problems and Questions

14.1 Oxidation is the loss of electrons; reduction is the gain of electrons.
a. When Na^+ gains electrons, the reaction is a reduction.
b. When Ni loses electrons, the reaction is an oxidation.
c. When Cr^{3+} gains electrons, the reaction is a reduction.
d. When H^+ gains electrons, the reaction is a reduction.

14.3 An oxidized substance has lost electrons; a reduced substance has gain electrons.
a. Zn loses electrons and is oxidized. Cl_2 gains electrons and is reduced.
b. Br^- (in NaBr) loses electrons and is oxidized. Cl_2 gains electrons and is reduced.
c. Pb loses electrons and is oxidized. O_2 gains electrons and is reduced.
d. Sn^{2+} loses electrons and is oxidized. Fe^{3+} gains electrons and is reduced.

14.5 **a.** A reducing agent provides electrons for reduction; it is the substance that is oxidized.
b. An oxidizing agent accepts electrons for oxidation; it is the substance that gains electrons.

14.7 **a.** Zn is the reducing agent. Cl_2 is the oxidizing agent
b. Br^-(in NaBr) is the reducing agent. Cl_2 is the oxidizing agent
c. Pb is the reducing agent. O_2 is the oxidizing agent.
d. Sn^{2+} is the reducing agent. Fe^{3+} is the oxidizing agent

14.9 **a.** An element has an oxidation number of zero; Cu = 0.
b. An element has an oxidation number of zero; F in F_2 = 0.
c. The oxidation number of a monoatomic ion is equal to its charge; Fe^{2+} = +2.
d. An element has an oxidation number of zero; O in O_2 = 0.

14.11 **a.** The monoatomic ions in KCl are K^+ and Cl^-. Oxidation numbers: K = +1, Cl = –1
b. The monoatomic ions in MnO_2 are Mn^{4+} and O^{2-}. Oxidation numbers: Mn is +4, O is –2
c. In CO (covalent polar), the O is assigned an oxidation number –2. The calculation gives an oxidation number C = +2.

$CO = C + -2 = 0 \quad$ Thus, $C = 0 + 2 = +2$

d. The monoatomic ions in Mn_2O_3 are Mn^{3+} and O^{2-}. Oxidation numbers: Mn = +3, O = –2.

14.13 **a.** In $AlPO_4$ (ionic, polyatomic ion), the Al^{3+} is assigned an oxidation number +3. In PO_4^{3-}, the O is assigned an oxidation number = –2. The calculation makes P = +5.

$PO_4^{3-} = P + 4(-2) = -3 \quad$ Thus, $P = -3 + 8 = +5$

b. In SO_3^{2-} (polyatomic ion), the O is assigned an oxidation number = –2. The calculation makes S = +4.

$SO_3^{2-} = S + 3(-2) = -2 \quad$ Thus, $S = -2 + 6 = +4$

c. In Cr_2O_3, the O is assigned an oxidation number –2. The calculation makes Cr = +3.

$Cr_2O_3 = 2Cr + 3(-2) = 0 \quad$ Thus, $2Cr = 0 + 6 = +6 \quad Cr = +6/2 = +3$

d. In NO_3^- (polyatomic ion), the O is assigned an oxidation number = –2. The calculation makes N = +5.

$NO_3^- = N + 3(-2) = -1 \quad$ Thus, $N = -1 + 6 = +5$

14.15 **a.** In HSO_4^-, the H is assigned an oxidation number +1 and O = -2.

$HSO_4^- = +1 + S + 4(-2) = -1$ Thus, $S = -1 + 8 - 1 = +6$

b. In H_3PO_3, the H is assigned an oxidation number +1 and the O is assigned an oxidation number = –2. The calculation makes P = +3.

$H_3PO_3 = 3(+1) + P + 3(-2) = 0$ Thus, $P = -3 + 6 = +3$

c. In $Cr_2O_7^{2-}$, the O is assigned an oxidation number = –2. The calculation makes Cr = +6.

$Cr_2O_7^{2-} = 2Cr + 7(-2) = -2$ Thus, $2Cr = -2 + 14 = +12$ and $Cr = +12/2 = +6$

d. In Na_2CO_3, the Na^+ is assigned an oxidation number +1 and O is assigned an oxidation number = –2. The calculation makes C = +4.

$Na_2CO_3 = 2(+1) + C + 3(-2) = 0$ Thus, $C = -2 + 6 = 4$

14.17 **a.** HNO_3 H = +1, O = –2

$HNO_3 = +1 + N + 3(-2) = 0$ $N = -1 + 6 = +5$

b. C_3H_6 H = +1

$C_3H_6 = 3C + 6(+1) = 0$ $3C = -6$ and $C = -6/3 = -2$

c. K_3PO_4 K = +1, O = –2

$K_3PO_4 = 3(+1) + P + 4(-2)$ $P = -3 + 8 = +5$

d. CrO_4^{2-} O = –2

$CrO_4^{2-} = Cr + 4(-2) = -2$ $Cr = +8 - 2 = +6$

14.19 Assign oxidation numbers and determine which one increases and which one decreases. The substance with an increase in oxidation number is oxidized and is also the reducing agent. The substance with a decrease in oxidation number is reduced and is also the oxidizing agent.

a. $2NiS + 3O_2 \rightarrow 2NiO + 2SO_2$

+2 –2   0   +2 –2   +4 –2

Ni: +2 → +2 no change

S^2: -2 → +4 in SO_2 Oxidation number increases.

O: 0 → 2– Oxidation number decreases.

S^{2-} (in NiS) is oxidized; O_2 is reduced. NiS is the reducing agent, and O_2 is the oxidizing agent.

b. $Sn^{2+} + 2Fe^{3+} \rightarrow Sn^{4+} + 2Fe^{2+}$

+2   3+   +4   +2

Sn +2 → +4 Oxidation number increases.

Fe: +3 → +2 Oxidation number decreases.

Sn^{2+} is oxidized; Fe^{3+} is reduced. Sn^{2+} is the reducing agent, and Fe^{3+} is the oxidizing agent.

c. $CH_4 + 2O_2 \rightarrow CO_2 + 2H_2O$

–4 +1   0   +4 –2   +1 –2

C: -4 → +4 Oxidation number increases.

O: 0 → –2 Oxidation number decreases.

C (in CH_4) is oxidized; O_2 is reduced. CH_4 is the reducing agent, and O_2 is the oxidizing agent.

d. $2Cr_2O_3 + 3Si \rightarrow 4Cr + 3SiO_2$

+3 –2   0   0   +4 –2

Cr: +3 → 0 Oxidation number decreases.

Si: 0 → +4 Oxidation number increases.

Si is oxidized; Cr^{3+} (in Cr_2O_3) is reduced. Si is the reducing agent, and Cr_2O_3 is the oxidizing agent.

14.21 **a.** $PbS(s) + O_2(g) \rightarrow PbO(s) + SO_2(g)$
+2 −2 0 +2 −2 +4 −2
S: −2 → +4 6e⁻ lost (oxidation)
O: 0 → −2 2e⁻ gain (reduction) x 3 = 6e⁻
$2PbS(s) + 3O_2(g) \rightarrow 2PbO(s) + 2SO_2(g)$

b. $Fe(s) + Cl_2(g) \rightarrow FeCl_3(s)$
0 0 +3 −1
Fe: 0 → +3 = 3e⁻ lost x 2 = 6e⁻
Cl: 0 → 2(1) e⁻ gain x 3 = 6e⁻
$2Fe(s) + 3Cl_2(g) \rightarrow 2FeCl_3(s)$

c. $Al(s) + H_2SO_4(aq) \rightarrow Al_2(SO_4)_3(aq) + H_2(g)$
0 +1 +6 −2 +3 +6 −2 0
Al: (0) → +3 = 3e⁻ lost x 2 = 6e⁻
H: 2(+1) → 0 = 2e⁻ gain x 3 = 6e⁻
$2Al(s) + 3H_2SO_4(aq) \rightarrow Al_2(SO_4)_3(aq) + 3H_2(g)$

14.23 **a.** Balance charge with e^-: $Sn^{2+}(aq) \rightarrow Sn^{4+}(aq) + 2e^-$

b. $Mn^{2+}(aq) \rightarrow MnO_4^-(aq)$
Balance O with H_2O: $Mn^{2+}(aq) + 4H_2O(l) \rightarrow MnO_4^-(aq)$
Balance H with H^+: $Mn^{2+}(aq) + 4H_2O(l) \rightarrow MnO_4^-(aq) + 8H^+(aq)$
Balance charge with e^-: $Mn^{2+}(aq) + 4H_2O(l) \rightarrow MnO_4^-(aq) + 8H^+(aq) + 5e^-$

c. $Cr_2O_7^{2-}(aq) \rightarrow Cr^{3+}(aq)$
Balance Cr: $Cr_2O_7^{2-}(aq) \rightarrow 2Cr^{3+}(aq)$
Balance O with H_2O: $Cr_2O_7^{2-}(aq) \rightarrow 2Cr^{3+}(aq) + 7H_2O(l)$
Balance H with H^+: $14H^+(aq) + Cr_2O_7^{2-}(aq) \rightarrow 2Cr^{3+}(aq) + 7H_2O(l)$
Balance charge with e^-: $14H^+(aq) + Cr_2O_7^{2-}(aq) + 6e^- \rightarrow 2Cr^{3+}(aq) + 7H_2O(l)$

d. $ClO_3^-(aq) \rightarrow ClO_2(aq)$
Balance O with H_2O: $ClO_3^-(aq) \rightarrow ClO_2(aq) + H_2O(l)$
Balance H with H^+: $ClO_3^-(aq) + 2H^+(aq) \rightarrow ClO_2(aq) + H_2O(l)$
Balance charge with e^-: $ClO_3^-(aq) + 2H^+(aq) + e^- \rightarrow ClO_2(aq) + H_2O(l)$

14.25 **a.** $Ag(s) \rightarrow Ag^+(aq) + e^-$
$2H^+(aq) + NO_3^-(aq) + e^- \rightarrow NO_2(g) + H_2O(l)$
Overall: $2H^+(aq) + Ag(s) + NO_3^-(aq) \rightarrow NO_2(g) + Ag^+(aq) + H_2O(l)$

b. $[Fe^{2+}(aq) \longrightarrow Fe^{3+}(aq) + e^-]$ x 6
$6H^+(aq) + ClO_3^-(aq) + 6e^- \longrightarrow Cl^-(aq) + 3H_2O(l)$
Overall: $6H^+(aq) + 6Fe^{2+}(aq) + ClO_3^-(aq) \longrightarrow 6Fe^{3+}(aq) + Cl^-(aq) + 3H_2O(l)$

c. $[4H^+(aq) + NO_3^-(aq) + 3e^- \rightarrow NO(g) + 2H_2O(l)]$ x 4
$[2H_2O(l) + S(s) \rightarrow SO_2(g) + 4H^+(aq) + 4e^-]$ x 3
Overall: $4H^+(aq) + 4NO_3^-(aq) + 3S(s) \rightarrow 4NO(g) + 2H_2O(l) + 3SO_2(g)$

d. $2S_2O_3^{2-}(aq) \rightarrow S_4O_6^{2-}(aq) + 2e^-$
$Cu^{2+}(aq) + 2e^- \rightarrow Cu(s)$
Overall: $2S_2O_3^{2-}(aq) + Cu^{2+}(aq) \rightarrow S_4O_6^{2-}(aq) + Cu(s)$

e. $[PbO_2(s) + 4H^+ + 2e^- \rightarrow Pb^{2+}(aq) + 2H_2O(l)]$ x 5
$[Mn^{2+}(aq) + 4H_2O(l) \rightarrow MnO_4^-(aq) + 8H^+(aq) + 5e^-]$ x 2
Overall: $4H^+(aq) + 5PbO_2(s) + 2Mn^{2+}(aq) \rightarrow 5Pb^{2+}(aq) + 2MnO_4^-(aq) + 2H_2O(l)$

14.27 Oxidation occurs at the anode; reduction occurs at the cathode. In the cell diagram, the oxidation half-cell is written on the left side of the double vertical line, and the reduction half-cell is written on the right side.

a. Anode reaction: $Pb(s) \mid Pb^{2-}(aq)$ = $Pb(s) \rightarrow Pb^{2+}(aq) + 2e^-$
Cathode reaction: $Cu^{2+}(aq) \mid Cu(s)$ = $Cu^{2+}(aq) + 2e^- \rightarrow Cu(s)$
Overall reaction: $Cu^{2+}(aq) + Pb(s) \rightarrow Cu(s) + Pb^{2+}(aq)$

b. Anode reaction: $Cr(s) \mid Cr^{2+}(aq)$ = $Cr(s) \rightarrow Cr^{2+}(aq) + 2e^-$
Cathode reaction: $Ag^+(aq) \mid Ag(s)$ = $Ag^+(aq) + e^- \rightarrow Ag(s)$
Overall reaction: $2Ag^+(aq) + Cr(s) \rightarrow 2Ag(s) + Cr^{2+}(aq)$

14.29 **a.** The anode is a Cd metal electrode in a Cd^{2+} solution. The anode reaction is:
$Cd(s) \rightarrow Cd^{2+}(aq) + 2e^-$
The cathode is a Sn metal electrode in a Sn^{2+} solution. The cathode reaction is:
$Sn^{2+}(aq) + 2e^- \rightarrow Sn(s)$
The shorthand notation (oxidation//reduction) for this cell is:
$Cd(s)|Cd^{2+}(aq)||\ Sn^{2+}(aq)|Sn(s)$

b. The anode is a Zn metal electrode in a Zn^{2+} solution. The anode reaction is:
$Zn(s) \rightarrow Zn^{2+}(aq) + 2e^-$
The cathode is a C(graphite) electrode, where Cl_2 gas is reduced to Cl^-. The cathode reaction is:
$Cl_2(g) + 2e^- \rightarrow 2Cl^-(aq)$
The shorthand cell notation (oxidation//reduction) is:
$Zn(s)|Zn^{2+}(aq)||\ Cl^-(aq), Cl_2(g)|C(\text{graphite})$

14.31 **a.** The Cd(*s*) has lost electrons, which makes the half-reaction an oxidation.
b. Cd metal is oxidized.
c. Because this is oxidation, it takes place at the anode.

14.33 **a.** The Zn(*s*) has lost electrons, which makes the half-reaction an oxidation.
b. Zn metal is oxidized.
c. Because this is oxidation, it takes place at the anode.

14.35 **a.** The half-reaction to plate tin is $Sn^{2+}(aq) + 2e^- \rightarrow Sn(s)$.
b. The iron is the cathode.
c. Because Fe is above Sn in the activity series, the plating of Sn^{2+} onto Fe is not spontaneous. Energy from electrolysis is needed to make the reaction proceed.

14.37 Because Fe is above Sn in the activity series, Fe is more active and will oxidize when exposed to air and water forming rust.

Answers to Selected Additional Questions and Problems

14.45 Reactions b, c, and d all involve loss and gain of electrons; b, c, and d are oxidation-reduction reactions.
a. No change in oxidation numbers: Ag = +1, N = +5, Na = +1, Cl = –1
b. Yes. $Li = 0 \rightarrow Li^+ = +1, N = 0 \rightarrow N^{3-} = -3$
c. Yes. $Ni = 0 \rightarrow Ni^{2+} = +2 \quad Pb^{2+} = +2 \rightarrow Pb = 0$
d. Yes. $K = 0 \rightarrow K^+ = +1, H^+ \rightarrow H = 0$

14.47 **a.** Fe^{3+} is gaining electrons; this is a reduction.
b. Fe^{2+} is losing electrons; this is an oxidation.

14.49

a. Co_2O_3	$O = -2$	Calculate: $2Co + 3(-2) = 0$	$Co = 6/2 = +3$
b. $KMnO_4$	$K = +1, O = -2$	Calculate: $+1 + Mn + 4(-2) = 0$	$Mn = -1 + 8 = +7$
c. SF_6	$F = -1$	Calculate: $S + 6(-1) = 0$	$S = +6$
d. ClO_3^-	$O = -2$	Calculate: $Cl + 3(-2) = -1$	$Cl = -1 + 6 = +5$
e. PO_4^{3-}	$O = -2$	Calculate: $P + 4(-2) = -3$	$P = -3 + 8 = +5$

14.51 **a.** $FeCl_2(aq) + Cl_2(g) \rightarrow FeCl_3(aq)$
+2 −1 0 +3 −1
Fe^{2+} is oxidized, and Cl_2 is reduced.
$2FeCl_2(aq) + Cl_2(g) \rightarrow 2FeCl_3(aq)$

b. $Si(s) + Cr_2O_3(s) \rightarrow Cr(s) + SiO_2(s)$
0 +3 −2 0 +4 −2
Si is oxidized, and Cr^{3+} is reduced.
$3Si(s) + 2Cr_2O_3(s) \rightarrow 4Cr(s) + 3SiO_2(s)$

c. $Cr_2O_3(s) + Al(s) \rightarrow Cr(s) + Al_2O_3(s)$
+3 −2 0 0 +3 −2
Al is oxidized, and Cr^{3+} is reduced.
$Cr_2O_3(s) + 2Al(s) \rightarrow 2Cr(s) + Al_2O_3(s)$

d. $P_2O_5(g) + C(s) \rightarrow P(g) + CO(g)$
+5 −2 0 0 +2 −2
C is oxidized, and P^{5+} is reduced.
$P_2O_5(g) + 5C(s) \rightarrow 2P(g) + 5CO(g)$

14.53 **a.** Balance charge with electrons: $Zn(s) \rightarrow Zn^{2+}(aq) + 2e^-$

b. Balance O with H_2O: $SnO_2^{2-}(aq) + H_2O(l) \rightarrow SnO_3^{2-}(aq)$
Balance H with H^+: $SnO_2^{2-}(aq) + H_2O(l) \rightarrow SnO_3^{2-}(aq) + 2H^+(aq)$
Balance charge with electrons: $SnO_2^{2-}(aq) + H_2O(l) \rightarrow SnO_3^{2-}(aq) + 2H^+(aq) + 2e^-$

c. Balance Cr atoms: $Cr_2O_7^{2-}(aq) \rightarrow 2Cr^{3+}(aq)$
Balance O with H_2O: $Cr_2O_7^{2-}(aq) \rightarrow 2Cr^{3+}(aq) + 7\,H_2O(l)$
Balance H with H^+: $Cr_2O_7^{2-}(aq) + 14H^+(aq) \rightarrow 2Cr^{3+}(aq) + 7\,H_2O(l)$
Balance charge with electrons: $Cr_2O_7^{2-}(aq) + 14H^+(aq) + 6e^- \rightarrow 2Cr^{3+}(aq) + 7\,H_2O(l)$

d. Balance O with H_2O: $NO_3^-(aq) \rightarrow NO(g) + 2\,H_2O(l)$
Balance H with H^+: $NO_3^-(aq) + 4H^+(aq) \rightarrow NO(g) + 2\,H_2O(l)$
Balance charge with electrons: $NO_3^-(aq) + 4H^+(aq) + 3e^- \rightarrow NO(g) + 2\,H_2O(l)$

14.55 Write half-reactions, multiply by small numbers to equalized electrons lost and gained, add together and combine common species.

a. $Zn(s) \rightarrow Zn^{2+}(aq) + 2e^-$
$[NO_3^-(aq) + 2H^+(aq) + e^- \rightarrow NO_2(g) + H_2O(l)] \times 2$
Overall: $Zn(s) + 2NO_3^-(aq) + 4\,H^+(aq) \rightarrow Zn^{2+}(aq) + 2NO_2(g) + 2H_2O(l)$

b. $[MnO_4^-(aq) + 8\,H^+(aq) + 5e^- \rightarrow Mn^{2+}(aq) + 4H_2O(l)] \times 2$
$[SO_3^{2-}(aq) + H_2O(l) \rightarrow SO_4^{2-}(aq) + 2H^+(aq) + 2e^-] \times 5$
Overall: $2MnO_4^-(aq) + 5SO_3^{2-}(aq) + 6H^+(aq) \rightarrow 2Mn^{2+}(aq) + 5SO_4^{2-}(aq) + 3H_2O(l)$

c. $[2I^-(aq) \rightarrow I_2(g) + 2e^-] \times 3$
$ClO_3^-(aq) + 6H^+(aq) + 6e^- \rightarrow Cl^-(aq) + 3H_2O(l)$
Overall: $ClO_3^-(aq) + 6I^-(aq) + 6H^+(aq) \rightarrow Cl^-(aq) + 3I_2(g) + 3H_2O(l)$

d. $[C_2O_4^{2-}(aq) \rightarrow 2CO_2(g) + 2e^-] \times 3$
$Cr_2O_7^{2-}(aq) + 14H^+(aq) + 6e^- \rightarrow 2Cr^{3+}(aq) + 7H_2O(l)$
Overall: $Cr_2O_7^{2-}(aq) + 3C_2O_4^{2-}(aq) + 14H^+(aq) \rightarrow 2Cr^{3+}(aq) + 6CO_2(g) + 7H_2O(l)$

14.57 In the activity series, a metal oxidizes spontaneously when combined with the ions in solutions of any metal below it

a. Because Cu is below H_2 in the activity series, the reaction will not be spontaneous.
b. Because Fe is above Ni in the activity series, the reaction will be spontaneous.
c. Because Ag is below Cu in the activity series, the reaction will not be spontaneous.
d. Because Cr is above Ni in the activity series, the reaction will be spontaneous.
e. Because Zn is above Cu in the activity series, the reaction will be spontaneous.
f. Because Zn is above Pb in the activity series, the reaction will be spontaneous.

14.59 **a.** The anode is Fe.
b. The cathode is Ni.
c. The half-reaction at the anode is $Fe(s) \rightarrow Fe^{2+}(aq) + 2e^-$.
d. The half-reaction at the cathode is $Ni^{2+}(aq) + 2e^- \rightarrow Ni(s)$.
e. The overall reaction is $Fe(s) + Ni^{2+}(aq) \rightarrow Fe^{2+}(aq) + Ni(s)$.
f. The cell notation is $Fe(s)| Fe^{2+}(aq)|| Ni^{2+}(aq)|Ni(s)$.

14.61 In the activity series, Fe is above Ni, Pb, and Ag, which means it is oxidized. However, it is below Ca and Al, which means it cannot be oxidized and therefore will not reduce Ca^{2+} or Al^{3+}.

a. $Ca^{2+}(aq)$ will not be reduced by an iron strip.
b. $Ag^+(aq)$ will be reduced by an iron strip.
c. $Ni^{2+}(aq)$ will be reduced by an iron strip.
d. $Al^{3+}(aq)$ will not be reduced by an iron strip.
e. $Pb^{2+}(aq)$ will be reduced by an iron strip.

14.63

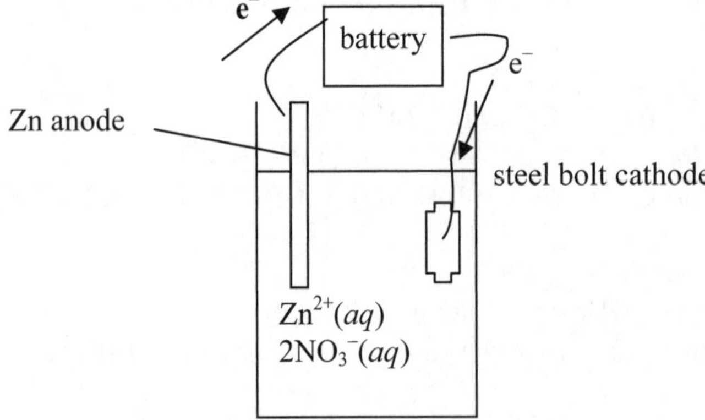

a. The anode is a bar of zinc.
b. The cathode is the steel bolt.
c. $Zn(s) \rightarrow Zn^{2+}(aq) + 2e^-$
d. $Zn^{2+}(aq) + 2e^- \rightarrow Zn(s)$
e. The purpose of the zinc coating is to prevent rusting of the bolt by H_2O and O_2.

14.65 **a.** $Pb(s) + SO_4^{2-}(aq) \rightarrow PbSO_4(s) + 2e^-$
b. Pb(*s*) loses electrons; it is oxidized.
c. The oxidation half-reaction takes place at the anode.

14.67 **a.** $3[Ag(s) \rightarrow Ag^+(aq) + e^-] \times 3$

$$\underline{NO_3^-(aq) + 4H^+(aq) + 3e^- \rightarrow NO(g) + 2H_2O(l)}$$

$$3Ag(s) + NO_3^-(aq) + 4H^+(aq) \rightarrow 3Ag^+(aq) + NO(g) + 2H_2O(l)$$

b. $15.0\ \cancel{\text{g Ag}} \times \frac{1\ \cancel{\text{mol Ag}}}{107.9\ \cancel{\text{g Ag}}} \times \frac{1\ \cancel{\text{mol NO}}}{3\ \cancel{\text{mol Ag}}} \times \frac{22.4\ \text{L gas}}{1\ \cancel{\text{mol NO}}} = 1.04\ \text{L NO}(g)\ \text{at STP}$

14.69 **a.** $[CuS(s) + 4H_2O(l)\ (aq) \rightarrow CuSO_4(aq) + 8H^+ + 8e^-] \times 3$

$$\underline{[HNO_3(aq) + 3H^+ + 3e^- \rightarrow NO(g) + 2H_2O(l)] \times 8}$$

$$3CuS(s) + 8HNO_3(aq) \rightarrow 3CuSO_4(aq) + 8NO(g) + 4H_2O(l)$$

b. $24.8\ \cancel{\text{g CuS}} \times \frac{1\ \cancel{\text{mol CuS}}}{95.62\ \cancel{\text{g CuS}}} \times \frac{8\ \cancel{\text{mol HNO}_3}}{3\ \cancel{\text{mol CuS}}} \times \frac{1000\ \text{mL HNO}_3}{16.0\ \cancel{\text{mol HNO}_3}} = 43.2\ \text{mL HNO}_3$

15
Nuclear Radiation

Study Goals

- Identify the types of radiation as alpha particles, beta particles, or gamma radiation.
- Describe the methods required for proper shielding for each type of radiation.
- Write an equation for an atom that undergoes radioactive decay.
- Identify some radioisotopes used in nuclear medicine.
- Calculate the amount of radioisotope that remains after a given number of half-lives.
- Describe nuclear fission and fusion.

Think About It

1. What is nuclear radiation?

2. Why do you receive more radiation if you live in the mountains or travel on an airplane?

3. In nuclear medicine, iodine-125 is used for detecting a tumor in the thyroid. What does the number 125 used in the name indicate?

4. How does nuclear fission differ from nuclear fusion?

5. Why is there a concern about radon in our homes?

Key Terms

Match each of the following key terms with the correct definition.

a. radioactive nucleus **b.** half-life **c.** curie
d. nuclear fission **e.** alpha particle

1.____ A particle identical to a helium nucleus produced in a radioactive nucleus

2.____ The time required for one-half of a radioactive sample to undergo radioactive decay

3.____ A unit of radiation measurement equal to 3.7×10^{10} disintegrations per second

4.____ A process in which large nuclei split into smaller nuclei with the release of energy

5.____ A nucleus that spontaneously emits radiation

Answers **1.** e **2.** b **3.** c **4.** d **5.** a

15.1 Natural Radioactivity

- Radioactive isotopes have unstable nuclei that break down (decay), spontaneously emitting alpha (α), beta (β^-), positron (β^+), and gamma (γ) radiation.
- An alpha particle is the same as a helium nucleus; it contains two protons and two neutrons. A beta particle is a high-energy electron and a positron is a high-energy positive electron. A gamma ray is high-energy radiation.
- Because radiation can damage the cells in the body, proper protection must be used: shielding, time limitation, and distance.

◆ Learning Check 15.1A

Study Note

It is important to learn the symbols for the radiation particles in order to describe the different types of radiation:

$^{1}_{1}H$ or $^{1}_{1}p$	$^{1}_{0}n$	$^{0}_{-1}\beta$ or $^{0}_{-1}e$	$^{4}_{2}He$ or $^{4}_{2}\alpha$	$^{0}_{+1}\beta$ or $^{0}_{+1}e$
proton	*neutron*	*electron*	*alpha particle*	*positron*

Match the description in column B with the terms in column A:

A	B
1. ____ $^{18}_{8}O$	**a.** Symbol for a beta particle
2. ____ γ	**b.** Symbol for an alpha particle
3. ____ β^+	**c.** An atom that emits radiation
4. ____ radioactive isotope	**d.** Symbol for positron
5. ____ $^{4}_{2}He$	**e.** Symbol for an atom of oxygen
6. ____ β	**f.** Symbol for gamma radiation

Answers **1.** e **2.** f **3.** d **4.** c **5.** b **6.** a

◆ Learning Check 15.1B

Discuss some things you can do to minimize the amount of radiation received if you work with a radioactive substance. Describe how each method helps to limit the amount of radiation you would receive.

Answer

Shielding such as clothing and gloves stops alpha and beta particles from reaching your skin, whereas lead or concrete will absorb gamma rays. Limiting the time spent near radioactive samples reduces exposure time. Increasing the distance from a radioactive source reduces the intensity of radiation.

◆ Learning Check 15.1C

What type(s) of radiation (alpha, beta, and/or gamma) would each of the following shielding materials protect you from?

a. clothing ________________________ **b.** skin ________________________

c. paper ________________________ **d.** concrete ________________________

e. lead wall________________________

Answers **a.** alpha, beta **b.** alpha **c.** alpha, beta
d. alpha, beta, gamma **e.** alpha, beta, gamma

15.2 Nuclear Equations

- A balanced nuclear equation represents the changes in the nuclei of radioisotopes.
- The new isotopes and the type of radiation emitted can be determined from the symbols that show the mass numbers and atomic numbers of the isotopes in the nuclear reaction.

  Radioactive nucleus ⟶ new nucleus + radiation

  Total of the mass numbers are equal

$$^{11}_{6}\text{C} \longrightarrow {}^{7}_{4}\text{Be} + {}^{4}_{2}\text{He}$$

  Total of the atomic numbers are equal

- A new radioactive isotope is produced when a nonradioactive isotope is bombarded by a small particle such as a proton, an alpha, or a beta particle.

$$^{10}_{5}\text{B} + {}^{4}_{2}\text{He} \longrightarrow {}^{13}_{7}\text{N} + {}^{1}_{0}\text{n}$$

stable nucleus	*bombarding particle (α)*	*new nucleus*	*neutron emitted*

◆ Learning Check 15.2A

> **Study Note**
> When balancing nuclear equations for radioactive decay,
> 1. The mass number of the reactant must equal the sum of the mass numbers of the products.
> 2. The atomic number of the reactant must equal the sum of the atomic numbers of the products.

Write a nuclear symbol that completes each of the following nuclear equations:

a. $^{66}_{29}\text{Cu} \longrightarrow {}^{66}_{30}\text{Zn} + ?$ **a.** __________

b. $^{127}_{53}\text{I} \longrightarrow {}^{1}_{0}\text{n} + ?$ **b.** __________

c. $^{238}_{92}\text{U} \longrightarrow {}^{4}_{2}\text{He} + ?$ **c.** __________

d. $^{24}_{11}\text{Na} \longrightarrow {}^{0}_{-1}\text{e} + ?$ **d.** __________

e. $? \longrightarrow {}^{30}_{14}\text{Si} + {}^{0}_{-1}\text{e}$ **e.** __________

Answers **a.** $^{0}_{-1}\text{e}$ **b.** $^{126}_{53}\text{I}$ **c.** $^{234}_{90}\text{Th}$ **d.** $^{24}_{12}\text{Mg}$ **e.** $^{30}_{13}\text{Al}$

◆ Learning Check 15.2B

Study Note

In balancing nuclear transmutation equations (bombardment by small particles),

1. The sum of the mass numbers of the reactants must equal the sum of the mass numbers of the products.
2. The sum of the atomic numbers of the reactants must equal the sum of the atomic numbers of the products.

Complete the following equations for bombardment reactions:

a. $^{40}_{20}\text{Ca} + ? \longrightarrow {}^{40}_{19}\text{K} + {}^{1}_{1}\text{H}$ **a.** ____________

b. $^{27}_{13}\text{Al} + {}^{1}_{0}\text{n} \longrightarrow {}^{24}_{11}\text{Na} + ?$ **b.** ____________

c. $^{10}_{5}\text{B} + {}^{1}_{0}\text{n} \longrightarrow {}^{4}_{2}\text{He} + ?$ **c.** ____________

d. $^{23}_{11}\text{Na} + ? \longrightarrow {}^{23}_{12}\text{Mg} + {}^{1}_{0}\text{n}$ **d.** ____________

e. $^{197}_{79}\text{Au} + {}^{1}_{1}\text{H} \longrightarrow ? + {}^{1}_{0}\text{n}$ **e.** ____________

Answers **a.** $^{1}_{0}\text{n}$ **b.** $^{4}_{2}\text{He}$ **c.** $^{7}_{3}\text{Li}$ **d.** $^{1}_{1}\text{H}$ **e.** $^{197}_{80}\text{Hg}$

15.3 Radiation Measurement

- A Geiger counter is used to detect radiation. When radiation passes through the gas in the counter tube, some atoms of gas are ionized producing an electrical current.
- The activity of a radioactive sample measures the number of nuclear transformations per second. The curie (Ci) is equal to 3.7×10^{10} disintegrations in 1 second. The becquerel (Bq) is equal to 1 disintegration per second. The radiation dose absorbed by a gram of material such as body tissue is measured in units of rad and gray.
- The biological damage of different types of radiation on the body is measured in units of rem and sievert.

◆ Learning Check 15.3

Match each type of measurement unit with the radiation process measured.

a. curie **b.** becquerel **c.** rad **d.** gray **e.** rem

1.____An activity of one disintegration per second

2.____The amount of radiation absorbed by 1 g material

3.____An activity of 3.7×10^{10} disintegrations per second

4.____The biological damage caused by different kinds of radiation

5.____A unit of absorbed dose equal to 100 rads

Answers **1.** b **2.** c **3.** a **4.** e **5.** d

15.4 Half-Life of a Radioisotope

- The half-life of a radioactive sample is the time required for one-half of the sample to decay (emit radiation).
- Most radioisotopes used in medicine, such as Tc-99m and I-131, have short half-lives. By comparison, many naturally occurring radioisotopes, such as C-14, Ra-226, and U-238, have long half-lives. For example, potassium-42 has a half-life of 12 hr, whereas potassium-40 takes 1.3×10^9 years for one-half of the radioactive sample to decay.

◆ Learning Check 15.4

a. Suppose you have an 80-mg sample of iodine-125. If iodine-125 has a half-life of 60 days, how many mg are radioactive

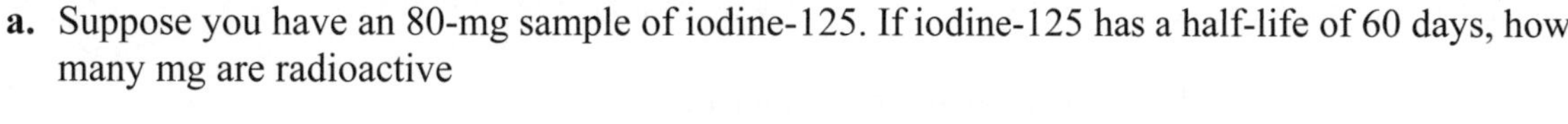

(1) after one half-life?

(2) after two half-lives?

(3) after 240 days?

b. ^{99m}Tc has a half-life of 6 hr. If a technician picked up a 16-mg sample at 8 AM, how much of the radioactive sample remained at 8 PM that same day?

c. Phosphorus-32 has a half-life of 14 days. How much of a 240-μg sample will be radioactive after 56 days?

d. Iodine-131 has a half-life of 8 days. How many days will it take for 80 mg of I-131 to decay to 5 mg?

e. Suppose a group of archaeologists digs up some pieces of a wooden boat at an ancient site. When a sample of the wood is analyzed for C-14, scientists determine that 12.5% or 1/8 of the original amount of C-14 remain. If the half-life of carbon-14 is 5730 years, how long ago was the boat made?

Answers **a.** (1) 40 mg (2) 20 mg (3) 5 mg **b.** 4.0 mg
c. 15 μg **d.** 32 days **e.** 17 200 years ago

15.5 Medical Applications Using Radioactivity

- In nuclear medicine, radioactive isotopes are given that go to specific sites in the body.
- For diagnostic work, radioisotopes are used that emit gamma rays and produce nonradioactive products.
- By detecting the radiation emitted by medical radioisotopes, evaluations can be made about the location and extent of an injury, disease, or tumor, blood flow, or the level of function of a particular organ.

◆ Learning Check 15.5

Write the nuclear symbol for each of the following radioactive isotopes:

a. _______Iodine-131 used to study thyroid gland activity

b. _______Phosphorus-32 used to locate brain tumors

c. _______Sodium-24 used to determine blood flow and to locate a blood clot or embolism

d. _______Nitrogen-13 is used in positron emission tomography

Answers **a.** ${}^{131}_{53}I$ **b.** ${}^{32}_{15}P$ **c.** ${}^{24}_{11}Na$ **d.** ${}^{13}_{7}N$

15.6 Nuclear Fission and Fusion

- In fission, a large nucleus breaks apart into smaller pieces releasing one or more types of radiation, and a great amount of energy.
- In fusion, small nuclei combine to form a larger nucleus, which releases great amounts of energy.

◆ Learning Check 15.6

Discuss the nuclear processes of fission and fusion for the production of energy.

Answer *Nuclear fission* is a splitting of the atom into two or more nuclei accompanied by the release of large amounts of energy and radiation. In the process of *nuclear fusion*, two or more nuclei combine to form a heavier nucleus and release a large amount of energy. However, fusion requires a considerable amount of energy to initiate the process.

Checklist for Chapter 15

You are ready to take the practice test for Chapter 15. Be sure you have accomplished the following learning goals for this chapter. If you are not sure, review the section listed at the end of the goal. Then apply your new skills and understanding to the practice test.

After studying Chapter 15, I can successfully:

____ Describe alpha, beta, and gamma radiation (15.1).

____ Write a nuclear equation showing mass numbers and atomic number for radioactive decay (15.2).

____ Write a nuclear equation for the formation of a radioactive isotope (15.2).

____ Describe the detection and measurement of radiation (15.3).

____ Calculate the amount of radioisotope remaining after one or more half-lives (15.4).

____ Describe the use of radioisotopes in medicine (15.5).

____ Describe the processes of nuclear fission and fusion (15.6).

Practice Test for Chapter 15

1. The correctly written symbol for an atom of sulfur would be
A. ${}^{30}_{16}Su$ **B.** ${}^{14}_{30}Si$ **C.** ${}^{30}_{16}S$ **D.** ${}^{30}_{16}Si$ **E.** ${}^{16}_{30}S$

2. Alpha particles are composed of
A. protons **B.** neutrons **C.** electrons
D. protons and electrons **E.** protons and neutrons

3. Gamma radiation is a type of radiation that
A. originates in the electron shells
B. is most dangerous
C. is least dangerous
D. is the heaviest
E. goes the shortest distance

4. The charge on an alpha particle is
A. −1 **B.** +1 **C.** −2 **D.** +2 **E.** +4

5. Beta particles formed in a radioactive nucleus are
A. protons **B.** neutrons **C.** electrons
D. protons and electrons **E.** protons and neutrons

For questions 6–10, select from the following:
A. ${}^{0}_{-1}X$ **B.** ${}^{4}_{2}X$ **C.** ${}^{1}_{1}X$ **D.** ${}^{1}_{0}X$ **E.** ${}^{0}_{0}X$

6. An alpha particle

7. A beta particle

8. A gamma ray

9. A proton

10. A neutron

---

11. Shielding from gamma rays is provided by
A. skin **B.** paper **C.** clothing **D.** lead **E.** air

12. The skin will provide shielding from
A. alpha particles **B.** beta particles **C.** gamma rays
D. ultraviolet rays **E.** X rays

13. The radioisotope iodine-131 is used as a radioactive tracer for studying thyroid gland activity. The symbol for iodine-131 is
A. I **B.** $_{131}I$ **C.** $^{131}_{53}I$ **D.** $^{53}_{131}I$ **E.** $^{78}_{53}I$

14. When an atom emits an alpha particle, its mass number will
A. increase by 1. **B.** increase by 2. **C.** increase by 4.
D. decrease by 4. **E.** not change

15. When a nucleus emits a beta particle, the atomic number of the new nucleus
A. increases by 1 **B.** increase by 2 **C.** decreases by 1
D. decreases by 2 **E.** will not change

16. When a nucleus emits a gamma ray, the atomic number of the new nucleus
A. increases by 1 **B.** increase by 2 **C.** decreases by 1
D. decreases by 2 **E.** will not change

For questions 17 to 20, select the particle that completes each of the equations.
A. neutron **B.** alpha particle **C.** beta particle **D.** gamma ray

17. $^{126}_{50}Sn \longrightarrow ^{126}_{51}Sb + ?$ **18.** $^{69}_{30}Zn \longrightarrow ^{69}_{31}Ga + ?$

19. $^{99m}_{43}Tc \longrightarrow ^{99}_{43}Tc + ?$ **20.** $^{149}_{62}Sm \longrightarrow ^{145}_{60}Nd + ?$

21. What symbol completes the following reaction?

$$^{14}_{7}N + ^{1}_{0}n \longrightarrow ? + ^{1}_{1}H$$

A. $^{15}_{8}O$ **B.** $^{15}_{6}C$ **C.** $^{14}_{8}O$ **D.** $^{14}_{6}C$ **E.** $^{15}_{7}N$

22. To complete this nuclear equation, you need to write

$$^{54}_{26}Fe + ? \longrightarrow ^{57}_{28}Ni + ^{1}_{0}n$$

A. an alpha particle **B.** a beta particle **C.** gamma **D.** neutron **E.** proton

23. The name of the unit used to measure the number of disintegrations per second is
A. curie **B.** rad **C.** rem **D.** gray **E.** sievert

24. The rem and the sievert are units used to measure
A. activity of a radioactive sample
B. biological damage of different types of radiation
C. radiation absorbed
D. background radiation
E. half-life of a radioactive sample

25. Radiation can cause

A. nausea **B.** a lower white cell count **C.** fatigue **D.** hair loss **E.** all of these

26. Radioisotopes used in medical diagnosis

A. have short half-lives
B. emit only gamma rays
C. locate in specific organs
D. produce nonradioactive nuclei
E. all of these

27. The time required for a radioisotope to decay is measured by its

A. half-life **B.** protons **C.** activity **D.** fusion **E.** radioisotope

28. Oxygen-15 used in imaging has a half-life of 2 min. How many half-lives have occurred in the 10 minutes it takes to prepare the sample?

A. 2 **B.** 3 **C.** 4 **D.** 5 **E.** 6

29. Iodine-131 has a half-life of 8 days. How long will it take for a 160-mg sample to decay to 10 mg?

A. 8 days **B.** 16 days **C.** 32 days **D.** 40 days **E.** 48 days

30. Phosphorus-32 has a half-life of 14 days. After 28 days, how many milligrams of a 100-mg sample will still be radioactive?

A. 75 mg **B.** 50 mg **C.** 40 mg **D.** 25 mg **E.** 12.5 mg

31. The "splitting" of a large nucleus to form smaller particles accompanied by a release of energy is called

A. radioisotope **B.** fission **C.** fusion **D.** rem **E.** half-life

32. The process of combining small nuclei to form larger nuclei is

A. radioisotope **B.** fission **C.** fusion **D.** rem **E.** half-life

33. The fusion reaction

A. occurs in the sun
B. forms larger nuclei from smaller nuclei
C. requires extremely high temperatures
D. releases a large amount of energy
E. all of the these

Answers to the Practice Test

1. C	**2.** E	**3.** B	**4.** D	**5.** C
6. B	**7.** A	**8.** E	**9.** C	**10.** D
11. D	**12.** A	**13.** C	**14.** D	**15.** A
16. E.	**17.** C	**18.** C	**19.** D	**20.** B
21. D	**22.** A	**23.** A	**24.** B	**25.** E
26. E	**27.** A	**28.** D	**29.** C	**30.** D
31. B	**32.** C	**33.** E		

Answers and Solutions to Selected Problems

Section 15.1

15.1 **a.** An α-particle and a helium nucleus both contain 2 protons and 2 neutrons. However, an α-particle has no electrons and carries a 2+ charge. Alpha-particles are emitted from unstable nuclei during radioactive decay.

b. α, ${}^{4}_{2}He$

15.3 **a.** ${}^{39}_{19}K$, ${}^{40}_{19}K$, ${}^{41}_{19}K$

b. Each isotope has 19 protons and 19 electrons, but they differ in the number of neutrons present. Potassium-39 has 20 neutrons, potassium-40 has 21 neutrons, and potassium-41 has 22 neutrons.

15.5

Medical Use	Nuclear Symbol	Mass Number	Number of Protons	Number of Neutrons
Heart imaging	${}^{201}_{81}Tl$	201	81	120
Radiation therapy	${}^{60}_{27}Co$	60	27	33
Abdominal scan	${}^{67}_{31}Ga$	67	31	36
Hyperthyroidism	${}^{131}_{53}I$	131	53	78
Leukemia treatment	${}^{32}_{15}P$	32	15	17

15.7 **a.** α, ${}^{4}_{2}He$ **b.** ${}^{1}_{0}n$ **c.** β, ${}^{0}_{-1}e$ **d.** ${}^{15}_{7}N$ **e.** ${}^{125}_{53}I$

15.9 **a.** β (or e) **b.** α (or He) **c.** n **d.** Na **e.** C

15.11 **a.** Because β-particles move faster than α-particles, they can penetrate further into tissue.

b. Ionizing radiation breaks bonds and forms reactive species that cause undesirable reactions in the cells.

c. X-ray technicians leave the room to increase their distance from the radiation source. They are also shielded by a thick wall or one that contains a lead lining.

d. Wearing gloves shields the skin from α and β radiation.

Section 15.2

15.13 The mass number of the radioactive atom is reduced by four when an alpha particle is emitted. The unknown product will have an atomic number that is two less than the atomic number of the radioactive atom.

a. ${}^{208}_{84}Po \rightarrow {}^{204}_{82}Pb + {}^{4}_{2}He$ **b.** ${}^{232}_{90}Th \rightarrow {}^{228}_{88}Ra + {}^{4}_{2}He$

c. ${}^{251}_{102}No \rightarrow {}^{247}_{100}Fm + {}^{4}_{2}He$ **d.** ${}^{220}_{86}Rn \rightarrow {}^{216}_{84}Po + {}^{4}_{2}He$

15.15 **a.** ${}^{25}_{11}Na \rightarrow {}^{25}_{12}Mg + {}^{0}_{-1}e$ **b.** ${}^{20}_{8}O \rightarrow {}^{20}_{9}F + {}^{0}_{-1}e$

c. ${}^{92}_{38}Sr \rightarrow {}^{92}_{39}Y + {}^{0}_{-1}e$ **d.** ${}^{42}_{19}K \rightarrow {}^{42}_{20}Ca + {}^{0}_{-1}e$

15.17 a. ${}^{26}_{14}\text{Si} \rightarrow {}^{26}_{13}\text{Al} + {}^{0}_{+1}\text{e}$ **b.** ${}^{54}_{27}\text{Co} \rightarrow {}^{54}_{26}\text{Fe} + {}^{0}_{+1}\text{e}$

c. ${}^{77}_{37}\text{Rb} \rightarrow {}^{77}_{36}\text{Kr} + {}^{0}_{+1}\text{e}$ **d.** ${}^{93}_{45}\text{Rh} \rightarrow {}^{93}_{44}\text{Ru} + {}^{0}_{+1}\text{e}$

15.19 a. ${}^{28}_{13}\text{Al} \rightarrow ? + {}^{0}_{-1}\text{e}$ $? = {}^{28}_{14}\text{Si}$

b. $? \rightarrow {}^{86}_{36}\text{Kr} + {}^{1}_{0}\text{n}$ $? = {}^{87}_{36}\text{Kr}$

c. ${}^{66}_{29}\text{Cu} \rightarrow {}^{66}_{30}\text{Zn} + ?$ $? = {}^{0}_{-1}\text{e}$

d. $? \rightarrow {}^{4}_{2}\text{He} + {}^{234}_{90}\text{Th}$ $? = {}^{238}_{92}\text{U}$

e. ${}^{188}_{80}\text{Hg} \rightarrow ? + {}^{0}_{+1}\text{e}$ $? = {}^{188}_{79}\text{Au}$

15.21 a. ${}^{9}_{4}\text{Be} + {}^{1}_{0}\text{n} \rightarrow ?$ $? = {}^{10}_{4}\text{Be}$

b. ${}^{32}_{16}\text{S} + ? \rightarrow {}^{32}_{15}\text{P}$ $? = {}^{0}_{-1}\text{e}$

c. $? + {}^{1}_{0}\text{n} \rightarrow {}^{24}_{11}\text{Na} + {}^{4}_{2}\text{He}$ $? = {}^{27}_{13}\text{Al}$

d. To balance the mass numbers, the unknown product must have a mass of 1. Balancing the number of protons gives an atomic number of 1. The unknown product is a proton.
${}^{27}_{13}\text{Al} + {}^{4}_{2}\text{He} \rightarrow {}^{30}_{14}\text{Si} + ?$ $? = {}^{1}_{1}\text{H}$

Section 15.3

15.23 a. When radiation enters the Geiger counter, it ionizes a gas in the detection tube. The ions created in the tube move toward an electrode of opposite charge (recall that opposite electrical charges attract one another). This flow of charge produces an electric current, which is detected by the instrument.

b. The becquerel (Bq) is the SI unit for activity. The curie (Ci) is the original unit for activity of radioactive samples.

c. The SI unit for absorbed dose is the gray (Gy). The rad (radiation absorbed dose) is a unit of radiation absorbed per gram of sample. It is the older unit.

d. A kilogray is 1000 gray (Gy), which is equivalent to 100 000 rads.

15.25 a. $3.0\ \cancel{\text{Ci}} \times \dfrac{3.7 \times 10^{10}\ \text{dis}/\cancel{\text{s}}}{1\ \cancel{\text{Ci}}} \times 20.\ \cancel{\text{s}} = 2.2 \times 10^{12}$ disintegrations

b. $70.0\ \cancel{\text{kg}} \times \dfrac{4.20\ \mu\text{Ci}}{1\ \cancel{\text{kg}}} = 294\ \mu\text{Ci}$

15.27 While flying a plane, a pilot is exposed to higher levels of background radiation because there is less atmosphere to act as a shield against cosmic radiation.

Section 15.4

15.29 Half-life is the time required for one-half of a radioactive sample to decay.

15.31 **a.** After one half-life, one-half of the sample would be radioactive: 80.0 mg x 1/2 = 40.0 mg.

b. After two half-lives, one-fourth of the sample would still be radioactive

$$80.0\text{ mg} \xrightarrow{(1)} 40.0\text{ mg} \xrightarrow{(2)} 20.0\text{ mg}$$

c. $18\ \cancel{\text{hr}} \times \dfrac{1\text{ half-life}}{6.0\ \cancel{\text{hr}}} = 3.0$ half-lives

$$80.0\text{ mg} \xrightarrow{(1)} 40.0\text{ mg} \xrightarrow{(2)} 20.0\text{ mg} \xrightarrow{(3)} 10.0\text{ mg}$$

d. $24\ \cancel{\text{hr}} \times \dfrac{1\text{ half-life}}{6.0\ \cancel{\text{hr}}} = 4.0$ half-lives

$$80.0\text{ mg} \xrightarrow{(1)} 40.0\text{ mg} \xrightarrow{(2)} 20.0\text{ mg} \xrightarrow{(3)} 10.0\text{ mg} \xrightarrow{(4)} 5.00\text{ mg}$$

15.33 The radiation level in a radioactive sample is cut in half with each passing half-life. To answer the question, we must first determine the number of half-lives. ¼ = ½ x ½ = 2 half-lives

Because each half-life is 64 days, it will take 128 days for the radiation level of strontium-85 to fall to one-fourth of its original value. 2 half-lives x 64 days/half-life = 128 days

To determine the amount of time for the strontium-85 to drop to one-eighth its original activity, we calculate the number of half-lives. 1/8 = ½ x ½ x ½ = 3 half-lives

Because each half-life is 64 days, it will take 192 days for the radiation level of strontium-85 to fall to one-eighth of its original value. 3 half-lives x 64 days/half-life = 192 days

Section15.5

15.35 **a.** Because the elements calcium and phosphorus are part of bone, any calcium and/or phosphorus atom, regardless of isotope, will be carried to and become part of the bony structures in the body. Once there, the radiation emitted by the radioisotope can be used for diagnosis or treatment of bone diseases.

b. Strontium is chemically similar to calcium, so it too will be carried to the bones. Once in the bone, the radiation emitted can destroy healthy bone and bony structures.

15.37 $4.0\ \cancel{\text{mL}} \times \dfrac{45\ \mu\text{Ci}}{1\ \cancel{\text{mL}}} = 180\ \mu\text{Ci}$

Section 15.6

15.39 Nuclear fission is the splitting of a large atom into smaller fragments with a simultaneous release of large amounts of energy.

15.41 ${}^{235}_{92}\text{U} + {}^{1}_{0}\text{n} \rightarrow {}^{131}_{50}\text{Sn} + ? + 2\,{}^{1}_{0}\text{n}$? = ${}^{103}_{42}\text{Mo}$

15.43 **a.** fission **b.** fusion **c.** fission **d.** fusion

Answers to Additional Problems

15.49 Both carbon-12 and carbon-14 contain six protons and six electrons, but there are only six neutrons in a carbon-12 nucleus while a carbon-14 nucleus has eight. Carbon-12 is a stable isotope, but carbon-14 is radioactive and will emit radiation.

15.51 **a.** Alpha (α) and beta (β) radiation consist of particles emitted from an unstable nucleus, whereas gamma (γ) rays are radiation emitted as pure energy.

b. Alpha radiation is abbreviated as α, ${}^{4}_{2}\alpha$, and ${}^{4}_{2}\text{He}$. Beta radiation is abbreviated as β, β^-, ${}^{0}_{-1}\beta$, and ${}^{0}_{-1}\text{e}$. Gamma radiation is abbreviated as γ and ${}^{0}_{0}\gamma$.

c. Alpha particles cannot penetrate skin, beta particles penetrate 4 to 5 mm into body tissue, and gamma radiation easily passes through body tissues.

d. Lightweight clothing or a piece of paper will shield against alpha particles, heavy clothing and gloves shield against beat particles, thick concrete and lead will shield against gamma rays.

15.53 **a.** ${}^{225}_{90}\text{Th} \rightarrow {}^{221}_{88}\text{Ra} + {}^{4}_{2}\text{He}$ **b.** ${}^{210}_{83}\text{Bi} \rightarrow {}^{206}_{81}\text{Tl} + {}^{4}_{2}\text{He}$

c. ${}^{137}_{55}\text{Cs} \rightarrow {}^{137}_{56}\text{Ba} + {}^{0}_{-1}\text{e}$ **d.** ${}^{126}_{50}\text{Sn} \rightarrow {}^{126}_{51}\text{Sb} + {}^{0}_{-1}\text{e}$

15.55 **a.** ${}^{180}_{80}\text{Hg} \rightarrow {}^{176}_{78}\text{Pt} + {}^{4}_{2}\text{He}$

b. ${}^{126}_{50}\text{Sn} \rightarrow {}^{126}_{51}\text{Sb} + {}^{0}_{-1}\text{e}$

c. ${}^{49}_{25}\text{Mn} \rightarrow {}^{49}_{24}\text{Cr} + {}^{0}_{+1}\text{e}$

15.57 **a.** ${}^{11}_{6}\text{C}$

b.

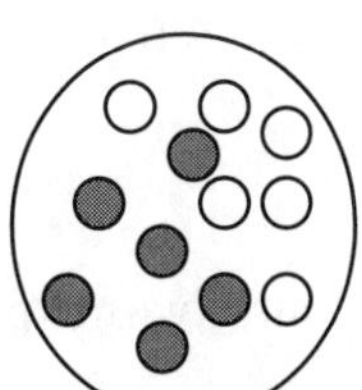

15.59

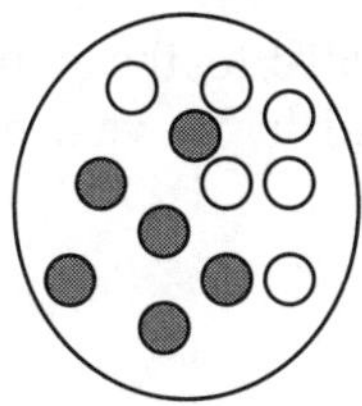

15.61 **a.** ${}^{14}_{7}\text{N} + {}^{4}_{2}\text{He} \rightarrow ? + {}^{1}_{1}\text{H}$ $? = {}^{17}_{8}\text{O}$

b. ${}^{27}_{13}\text{Al} + {}^{4}_{2}\text{He} \rightarrow {}^{30}_{14}\text{Si} + ?$ $? = {}^{1}_{1}\text{H}$

c. ${}^{235}_{92}\text{U} + {}^{1}_{0}\text{n} \rightarrow {}^{90}_{38}\text{Sr} + 3\,{}^{1}_{0}\text{n} + ?$ $? = {}^{143}_{54}\text{Xe}$

d. $? \rightarrow {}^{127}_{54}\text{Xe} + {}^{0}_{+1}\text{e}$ $? = {}^{127}_{55}\text{Cs}$

15.63 a. $^{16}_{8}O + ^{16}_{8}O \rightarrow ^{4}_{2}He + ?$ $\quad ? = ^{28}_{14}Si$

b. $^{249}_{98}Cf + ^{18}_{8}O \rightarrow ? + 4\,^{1}_{0}n$ $\quad ? = ^{263}_{106}Sg$

c. $^{222}_{86}Rn \rightarrow ^{4}_{2}He + ?$ $\quad ? = ^{218}_{84}Po$

Then the polonium-218 decays as follows:

$^{218}_{84}Po \rightarrow ^{4}_{2}He + ?$ $\quad ? = ^{214}_{82}Pb$

d. $^{106}_{47}Ag \rightarrow ^{106}_{46}Pd + ?$ $\quad ? = ^{0}_{+1}e$

15.65 Half of a radioactive sample decays with each half-life:

½ lives (1) (2)

1.2 g ⟶ 0.60 g ⟶ 0.30 g

Therefore, the amount of phosphorus-32 will drop to 0.30 g in two half-lives, which is 28 days. One half-life is 14 days. 28 days/2 half-lives = 14 days/half-life

15.67 a. $^{131}_{53}I \longrightarrow ^{0}_{-1}e + ^{131}_{54}Xe$

b. First, we must determine the number of half-lives.

$40\ \text{days} \times \dfrac{1\ \text{half-life}}{8.0\ \text{days}} = 5.0\ \text{half-lives}$

Now we can calculate the number of grams of iodine-131 remaining:

(1) (2) (3) (4) (5)

12.0 g → 6.00 g → 3.00 g → 1.50 g → 0.750 g → 0.375 g

c. One-half of a radioactive sample decays with each half-life:

½ lives (1) (2) (3) (4)

48 g ⟶ 24 g ⟶ 12 g ⟶ 6.0 g ⟶ 3.0 g

When 3.0 g remain, four half-lives must have passed. Because each half-life is 8.0 days, we can calculate the number of days that the sample required to decay to 3.0 g.

$4\ \text{half-lives} \times \dfrac{8.0\ \text{days}}{1\ \text{half-life}} = 32\ \text{days}$

15.69 First, calculate the number of half-lives that have passed since the nurse was exposed:

$36\ \text{hr} \times \dfrac{1\ \text{half-life}}{12\ \text{hr}} = 3.0\ \text{half-lives}$

Because the activity of a radioactive sample is cut in half with each half-life, the activity must have been double its present value prior to each half-life. For three half-lives, we need to double the value 3 times. $2.0\ \mu Ci \times (2 \times 2 \times 2) = 16\ \mu Ci$

Check: (1) (2) (3)

16 μCi → 8.0 μCi → 4.0 μCi → 2.0 μCi

15.71 First, calculate the number of half-lives:

$24\ \text{hr} \times \dfrac{1\ \text{half-life}}{6.0\ \text{hr}} = 4.0\ \text{half-lives}$

Now calculate the amount of technetium-99^{m} that remains after four half-lives have passed:

(1) (2) (3) (4)

120 mg → 60 mg → 30 mg → 15 mg → 7.5 mg

15.73 Irradiating foods kills bacteria that are responsible for food-borne illnesses and food spoilage. As a result, shelf-life of the food is extended.

15.75 Nuclear fission is the splitting of a large atom into smaller fragments with a simultaneous release of large amounts of energy. Nuclear fusion occurs when two (or more) nuclei combine (fuse) to form a larger species, with a simultaneous release of large amounts of energy.

15.77 Fusion reactions naturally occur in the stars, such as our sun.

16
Organic Chemistry

Study Goals

- From its properties, classify a compound as organic or inorganic.
- Describe some properties of alkanes.
- Draw the complete and condensed structural formulas for alkanes.
- Identify the functional groups in organic compounds.
- Use the IUPAC system to name alkanes, alkenes, and alkynes.
- Write equations for hydrogenation of alkenes and alkynes.
- Describe the formation of a polymer from alkene monomers.
- Describe and name aromatic compounds.
- Name and write formulas for alcohols and ethers.
- Classify alcohols as primary, secondary, or tertiary.
- Write the structure of products from the oxidation of alcohols.
- Name and write formulas for aldehydes, ketones, carboxylic acids, esters, amines, and amides.
- Write the products for the esterification of carboxylic acids and alcohols.
- Write the products for the amidation of amines.

Think About It

1. In a salad dressing, why is the layer of vegetable oil separate from the water layer?

2. What two elements are found in all organic compounds?

3. What are functional groups?

4. A margarine is partially hydrogenated. What does that mean?

16.1 Organic Compounds

- Organic compounds are compounds of carbon that typically have covalent bonds, low melting and boiling points, burn vigorously, are nonelectrolytes, and are soluble in nonpolar solvents.
- Alkanes are hydrocarbons that have only single bonds, C—C and C—H.
- Each carbon in an alkane has four bonds arranged so that the bonded atoms are in the corners of a tetrahedron.

◆ Learning Exercise 16.1

Identify the following as typical of organic (O) or inorganic (I) compounds:

1.____ have covalent bonds	**2.** ____ have low boiling points
3.____ burn in air	**4.** ____ are soluble in water
5.____ have high melting points	**6.** ____ are soluble in nonpolar solvents
7.____ have ionic bonds	**8.** ____ form long chains
9.____ contain carbon	**10.** ____ do not burn in air

Answers					
	1. O	**2.** O	**3.** O	**4.** I	**5.** I
	6. O	**7.** I	**8.** O	**9.** O	**10.** I

16.2 Alkanes

- An expanded structural formula shows a separate line from a carbon atom to each bonded atom; a condensed structural formula depicts each carbon atom and its attached hydrogen atoms as a group.

  Example:

Expanded Structural Formula	Condensed Structural Formula	Molecular Formula
H H H | | | H—C—C—C—H | | | H H H	$CH_3—CH_2—CH_3$	C_3H_8

- In the IUPAC system used to name organic compounds, the stem indicates the number of carbon atoms, and the suffix *-ane* indicates single bonds (alkane). The names of the first five alkanes are shown:

Name	Number of Carbon Atoms	Condensed Structural Formula
Methane	1	CH_4
Ethane	2	$CH_3—CH_3$
Propane	3	$CH_3—CH_2—CH_3$
Butane	4	$CH_3—CH_2—CH_2—CH_3$
Pentane	5	$CH_3—CH_2—CH_2—CH_2—CH_3$

- A branched chain alkane contains at least one alkyl branch or substituent. Replacing the *-ane* of the alkane name with *-yl* gives the alkyl names of carbon side groups.
- The longest continuous chain is named as the parent alkane, and the substituents attached to the chain are numbered and listed alphabetically in front of the name of the parent chain.

```
       CH3
        |
CH3—CH—CH2—CH3    2-methylbutane
```

- The alkanes are nonpolar, less dense than water, and mostly unreactive, except they burn vigorously.
- An alkane undergoes combustion with oxygen to produce carbon dioxide, water, and heat.

$$CH_4(g) + 2O_2(g) \longrightarrow CO_2(g) + 2H_2O(g) + \text{Heat}$$

◆ Learning Exercise 16.2A

Match the statements shown with the correct term:

A. alkane | **B.** condensed structural formula | **C.** alkyl group
D. combustion | **E.** hydrocarbons

1.____ A hydrocarbon that contains only carbon–carbon single bonds.

2.____ The chemical reaction of an alkane and oxygen to produce CO_2, H_2O, and heat.

3.____ The type of formula that shows the arrangement of the carbon atoms grouped with their attached H atoms.

4.____ A substituent of one or more carbon atoms attached to a longer carbon chain.

5.____ Organic compounds that consist of only carbon and hydrogen atoms.

Answers: **1.** A **2.** D **3.** B **4.** C **5.** E

◆ Learning Exercise 16.2B

Write the name for each of the following alkanes:

1. $CH_3{-}CH_2{-}CH_3$ ____________________

2. $CH_3{-}CH_3$ ____________________

3. $CH_3{-}CH_2{-}CH_2{-}CH_3$ ____________________

4. $CH_3{-}CH_2{-}CH_2{-}CH_2{-}CH_2{-}CH_3$ ____________________

Answers: **1.** propane **2.** ethane **3.** butane **4.** hexane

◆ Learning Exercise 16.2C

Provide a correct IUPAC name for the following compounds:

CH_3 (on C-2)
1. $CH_3{-}CH{-}CH_3$ ____________________

CH_3 (on C-3), CH_3 (on C-5)
2. $CH_3{-}CH_2{-}CH{-}CH_2{-}CH{-}CH_3$ ____________________

CH_3 (on C-2), CH_3 (on C-5)
3. $CH_3{-}CH{-}CH_2{-}CH_2{-}CH{-}CH_2{-}CH_3$ ____________________

CH_3 (above C-2), CH_3 (below C-2)
4. $CH_3{-}C{-}CH_2{-}CH_3$ ____________________

Answers: **1.** 2-methylpropane **2.** 2,4-dimethylhexane
3. 2,5-dimethylheptane **4.** 2,2-dimethylbutane

◆ Learning Exercise 16.2D

Write the correct condensed formula for the following compounds:

1. hexane ____________________

2. methane ____________________

3. 2, 3-dimethylbutane ____________________

4. 2, 3, 4-trimethylpentane ____________________

Answers:

1. CH_3—CH_2—CH_2—CH_2—CII_2—CII_3 **2.** CH_4

3.
```
        CH3 CH3
         |   |
  CH3—CH—CH—CH3
```

4.
```
       CH3      CH3
        |        |
  CH3—CH——CH——CH——CH3
             |
            CH3
```

◆ Learning Exercise 16.2E

Write a balanced equation for the complete combustion of the following:

1. propane ____________________

2. hexane ____________________

3. pentane ____________________

Answers: **1.** $C_3H_8(g) + 5O_2(g) \longrightarrow 3CO_2(g) + 4H_2O(g)$ + Heat
2. $2C_6H_{14}(g) + 19O_2(g) \longrightarrow 12CO_2(g) + 14H_2O(g)$ + Heat
3. $C_5H_{12}(g) + 8O_2(g) \longrightarrow 5CO_2(g) + 6H_2O(g)$ + Heat

16.3 Functional Groups

- The *functional group* in an organic molecule is an atom or group of atoms where specific chemical reactions occur.
- Alkenes are hydrocarbons that contain one or more double bonds (C=C); alkynes contain a triple bond (C≡C).
- Alcohols contain a hydroxyl (OH) group; ethers have an oxygen atom (—O—) between alkyl groups.
- Aldehydes contain a carbonyl group (C=O) bonded to at least one H atom; ketones contain the carbonyl group bonded to two alkyl groups.
- Carboxylic acids have a carboxyl group attached to hydrogen (—COOH); esters contain the carboxyl groups attached to an alkyl group.
- In amines, alkyl groups replace one or more of the H atoms in ammonia, NH_3; amides contain a carboxyl group attached to nitrogen.

◆ Learning Check 16.3A

Classify the organic compounds shown according to the following functional groups:

a. alkane **b.** alkene **c.** alcohol **d.** ether **e.** aldehyde

1._____ $CH_3{-}CH_2{-}CH{=}CH_2$ **2.**_____ $CH_3{-}CH_2{-}CH_3$

3._____ $CH_3{-}CH_2{-}\overset{\displaystyle O}{\overset{\|}{C}}{-}H$ **4.**_____ $CH_3{-}CH_2{-}CH_2{-}OH$

5._____ $CH_3{-}CH_2{-}O{-}CH_2{-}CH_3$ **6.**_____ $CH_3{-}CH_2{-}CH_2{-}CH_3$

Answers **1.** b **2.** a **3.** e **4.** c **5.** d **6.** a

◆ Learning Exercise 16.3B

Classify the following compounds by their functional groups:

a. alcohol **b.** aldehyde **c.** ketone **d.** ether **e.** amine

1. ____ $CH_3{-}CH_2{-}CH_2{-}\overset{\displaystyle O}{\overset{\|}{C}}{-}H$ **2.** ____ $CH_3{-}CH_2{-}CH_2{-}NH_2$

3. ____ $CH_3{-}CH_2{-}\overset{\displaystyle O}{\overset{\|}{C}}{-}CH_2{-}CH_3$ **4.** ____ $CH_3{-}CH_2{-}O{-}CH_3$

5. ____ $CH_3{-}\overset{\displaystyle O}{\overset{\|}{C}}{-}CH_2{-}CH_3$ **6.** ____ $CH_3{-}\overset{\displaystyle O}{\overset{\|}{C}}{-}H$

7. ____ $CH_3{-}CH_2{-}\overset{\displaystyle NH_2}{\overset{|}{C}H}{-}CH_3$ **8.** ____ $CH_3{-}CH_2{-}\overset{\displaystyle OH}{\overset{|}{C}H}{-}CH_3$

Answers				
	1. b	**2.** e	**3.** c	**4.** d
	5. c	**6.** b	**7.** e	**8.** a

16.4 Alkenes and Alkynes

- The IUPAC names of alkenes are derived by changing the *-ane* ending of the parent alkane to *-ene*.
- In alkenes, the longest carbon chain containing the double bond is numbered from the end nearest the double bond.

$CH_3{-}CH{=}CH_2$ propene (propylene)

$CH_2{=}CH{-}CH_2{-}CH_3$ 1-butene

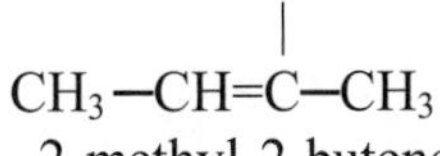

2-methyl-2-butene

- The alkynes are a family of unsaturated hydrocarbons that contain a triple bond. They use naming rules similar to the alkenes, but the parent chain ends with *-yne.*

$HC{\equiv}CH$ ethyne

$CH_3{-}C{\equiv}CH$ propyne

- Hydrogenation adds hydrogen atoms to the double bond of an alkene or the triple bond of an alkyne to yield an alkane.

$$CH_2{=}CH_2 + H_2 \xrightarrow{Pt} CH_3{-}CH_3$$

$$HC{\equiv}CH + 2H_2 \rightarrow CH_3{-}CH_3$$

◆ Learning Exercise 16.4A

Write the IUPAC (and common name, if one) for each of the following alkenes:

1. $CH_3{-}CH{=}CH_2$

2. $CH_3{-}CH{=}CH{-}CH_3$

3. $CH_3{-}CH{=}\overset{\overset{\large CH_3}{|}}{C}{-}CH_2{-}CH_3$

4. $CH_2{=}CH{-}\overset{\overset{\large Cl}{|}}{CH}{-}CH_2{-}\overset{\overset{\large CH_3}{|}}{CH}{-}CH_3$

Answers

1. propene (propylene)
2. 2-butene
3. 3-methyl-2-pentene
4. 3-chloro-5-methyl-1-hexene

◆ Learning Exercise 16.4B

Write the IUPAC and common name (if any) of each of the following alkynes.

1. $HC{\equiv}CH$

2. $CH_3{-}C{\equiv}CH$

3. $CH_3{-}CH_2{-}C{\equiv}CH$

4. $CH_3{-}\overset{\overset{\large CH_3}{|}}{CH}{-}C{\equiv}C{-}CH_3$

Answers

1. ethyne (acetylene)
2. propyne
3. 1-butyne
4. 4-methyl-2-pentyne

◆ Learning Exercise 16.4C

Draw the condensed structural formula for each of the following:

1. 2-pentyne **2.** 2-chloro-2-butene

3. 2-bromo-3-methyl-2-pentene **4.** 2-methyl-3- hexyne

Answers

1. $CH_3{-}C{\equiv}C{-}CH_2{-}CH_3$

2. $CH_3{-}CH{=}C(Cl){-}CH_3$

```
               Cl
               |
CH3—CH=C—CH3
```

3. $CH_3{-}C(Br){=}C(CH_3){-}CH_2{-}CH_3$

```
      Br
      |
CH3—C=C—CH2—CH3
        |
        CH3
```

4. $CH_3{-}CH_2{-}C{\equiv}C{-}CH(CH_3){-}CH_3$

```
                        CH3
                        |
CH3—CH2—C≡C—CH—CH3
```

◆ Learning Exercise 16.4D

Write the products of the following addition reactions:

1. $CH_3{-}CH{=}CH_2 + H_2 \xrightarrow{Pt}$

2. $CH_3{-}CH{=}CH{-}CH_2{-}CH_3 + H_2 \xrightarrow{Pt}$

3. $CH_3{-}CH{\equiv}CH{-}CH_3 + 2H_2 \xrightarrow{Pt}$

Answers

1. $CH_3{-}CH_2{-}CH_3$
2. $CH_3{-}CH_2{-}CH_2{-}CH_2{-}CH_3$
3. $CH_3{-}CH_2{-}CH_2{-}CH_3$

16.5 Polymers

- *Polymers* are large molecules prepared from the bonding of many small units called *monomers*.
- Many synthetic polymers are made from small alkene monomers.

◆ Learning Check 16.5A

Write the formula of the alkene monomer that would be used for each of the following polymers:

```
    H   H   H   H   H   H
    |   |   |   |   |   |
1. —C———C———C———C———C———C—
    |   |   |   |   |   |
    H   H   H   H   H   H
```

2. 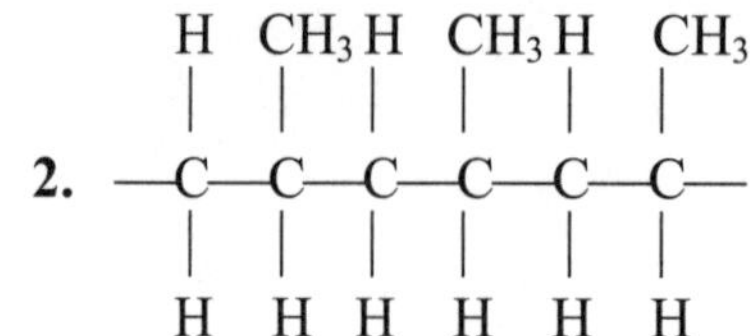

3. 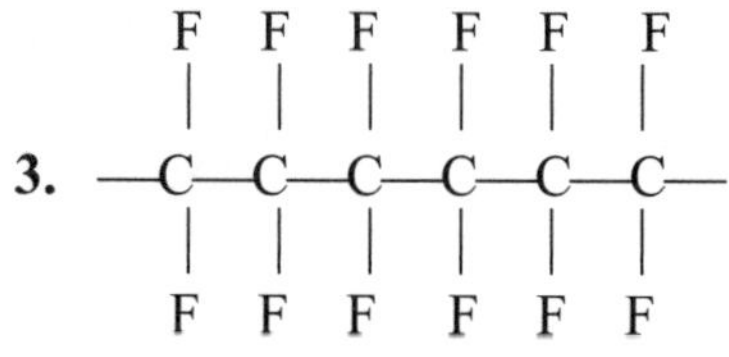

```
                         CH3
                          |
Answers   1. H2C=CH2   2. H2C=CH        3. F2C=CF2
```

Answers **1.** $H_2C{=}CH_2$ **2.** $H_2C{=}C(CH_3)H$ **3.** $F_2C{=}CF_2$

◆ Learning Check 16.5B

Write three sections of the polymer that would result when 1,1-difluoroethene is the monomer unit.

Answer

```
 F   H   F   H   F   H
 |   |   |   |   |   |
—C———C———C———C———C———C—
 |   |   |   |   |   |
 F   H   F   H   F   H
```

16.6 Aromatic Compounds

- Most aromatic compounds contain benzene, a cyclic structure containing six CH units. The structure of benzene is represented as a hexagon with a circle in the center.
- The names of many aromatic compounds use the parent name benzene, although many common names were retained as IUPAC names, such as toluene.

◆ Learning Exercise 16.6

Write the IUPAC (or common name) for each of the following.

a.

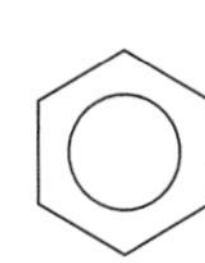

b.

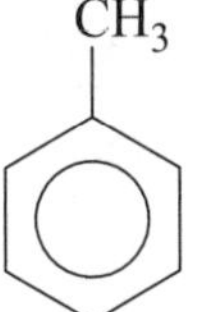

c.

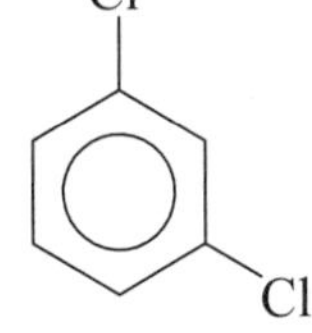

d.

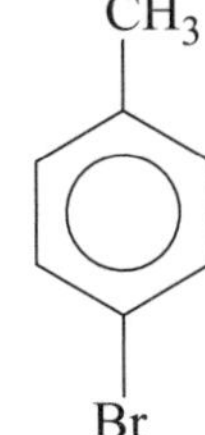

Answers **1.** benzene **2.** methylbenzene; toluene
3. 1, 3-dichlorobenzene **4.** 4-bromotoluene

16.7 Alcohols and Ethers

- An alcohol contains the hydroxyl group —OH attached to a carbon chain.
- In the IUPAC system, alcohols are named by replacing the *-ane* of the alkane name with *-ol*. The location of the –OH group is given by numbering the carbon chain. Simple alcohols are generally named by their common names, with the alkyl name preceding the term alcohol. For example, CH_3—OH is methyl alcohol, and CH_3—CH_2—OH is ethyl alcohol.
- When a hydroxyl group is attached to a benzene ring, the compound is a phenol.
- In a primary alcohol, there is one alkyl group attached to the carbon atom bonded to the –OH. In a secondary alcohol, there are two alkyl groups, and in a tertiary alcohol there are three alkyl groups.
- An ether contains an oxygen atom attached by single bonds to two carbon atoms —O—.
- Simple ethers are named using the names of the alkyl groups attached to the oxygen atom.
- Primary alcohols oxidize to aldehydes and secondary alcohols are oxidized to ketones, but tertiary alcohols do not oxidize.

◆ Learning Exercise 16.7A

Match the following terms with the statements shown:

a. primary alcohol **b.** secondary alcohol **c.** tertiary alcohol
d. phenol **e.** ether

1. ___An organic compound with one alkyl group bonded to the carbon with the —OH group.

2. ___An alcohol that oxidizes to a ketone.

3. ___An organic compound that contains an oxygen atom —O— attached to two alkyl groups.

4. ___ An organic compound with three alkyl groups bonded to the carbon with the —OH group.

5. ___ An organic compound that contains a benzene ring bonded to a hydroxyl group.

Answers **1.** a **2.** b **3.** e **4.** c **5.** d

◆ Learning Exercise 16.7B

Give the correct IUPAC and common name (if any) for each of the following compounds:

1. $CH_3{-}CH_2{-}OH$ **2.** $CH_3{-}CH_2{-}CH_2{-}OH$

3. 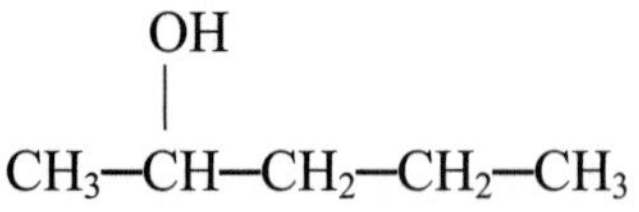
$$\begin{array}{l} \quad\;\; OH \\ \quad\;\; | \\ CH_3{-}CH{-}CH_2{-}CH_2{-}CH_3 \end{array}$$

4. 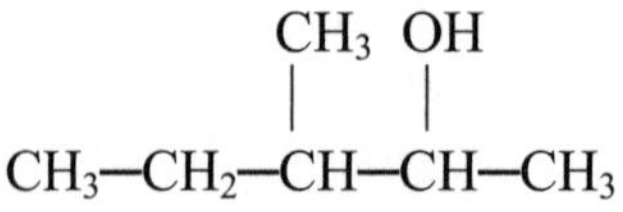
$$\begin{array}{l} \qquad\qquad\quad CH_3\;\; OH \\ \qquad\qquad\quad\;\; | \qquad | \\ CH_3{-}CH_2{-}CH{-}CH{-}CH_3 \end{array}$$

5. 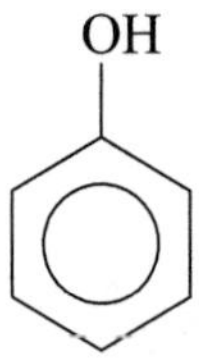 (benzene ring with OH)

Answers **1.** ethanol (ethyl alcohol) **2.** 1-propanol (propyl alcohol)
3. 2-pentanol **4.** 3-methyl-2-pentanol
5. phenol

◆ Learning Exercise 16.7C

Write the structural formula for each of the following compounds:

1. 2-butanol **2.** 2-chloro-1-propanol

3. 2,4-dimethyl-3-pentanol **4.** 3-methylphenol

Answers

1. 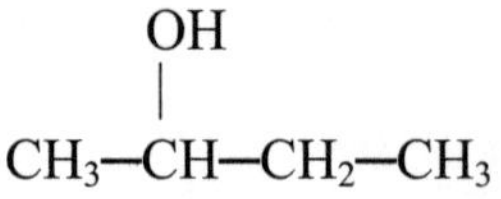
$$\begin{array}{l} \quad\;\; OH \\ \quad\;\; | \\ CH_3{-}CH{-}CH_2{-}CH_3 \end{array}$$

2.
$$\begin{array}{l} \quad\;\; Cl \\ \quad\;\; | \\ CH_3{-}CH{-}CH_2{-}OH \end{array}$$

3.
$$\begin{array}{l} \quad\;\; CH_3\; OH\;\; CH_3 \\ \quad\;\; | \qquad | \qquad | \\ CH_3{-}CH{-}CH{-}CH{-}CH_3 \end{array}$$

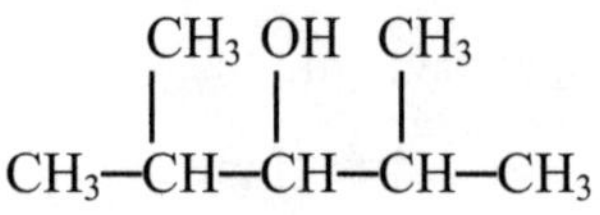

4. 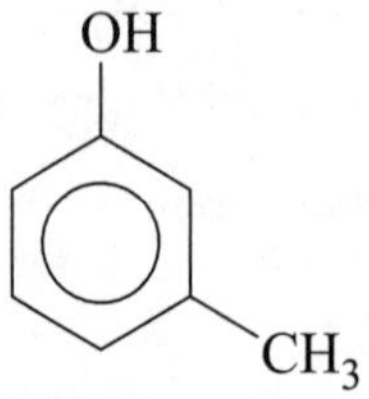 (benzene ring with OH and CH_3 in meta position)

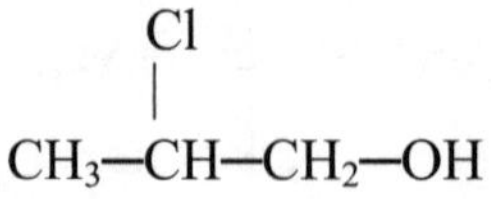

Study Note

Alcohols are classified as primary, secondary, or tertiary.
Example: Identify the following as primary, secondary, or tertiary alcohols.
Solution: Determine the number of alkyl group attached to the hydroxyl carbon atom.

$$CH_3{-}CH_2{-}OH \qquad CH_3{-}\underset{}{\overset{\displaystyle CH_3}{\overset{|}{C}H}}{-}OH \qquad CH_3{-}\underset{\underset{\displaystyle CH_3}{|}}{\overset{\displaystyle CH_3}{\overset{|}{C}}}{-}OH$$

Primary (1°) Secondary (2°) Tertiary (3°)

◆ Learning Exercise 16.7D

Classify each of the following alcohols as primary (1°), secondary (2°), or tertiary (3°):

1. $CH_3{-}CH_2{-}OH$ ________

2. $CH_3{-}CH_2{-}\overset{\displaystyle OH}{\overset{|}{C}H}{-}CH_3$ ________

3. $CH_3{-}\underset{\underset{\displaystyle CH_3}{|}}{\overset{\displaystyle OH}{\overset{|}{C}}}{-}CH_2{-}CH_3$ ________

4. $CH_3{-}\underset{\underset{\displaystyle CH_3}{|}}{\overset{\displaystyle CH_3}{\overset{|}{C}}}{-}CH_2{-}CH_2{-}OH$ ________

Answers **1.** primary (1°) **2.** secondary (3°) **3.** tertiary (3°) **4.** primary (1°)

◆ Learning Exercise 16.7E

Write the condensed structural formulas of the products expected in the oxidation reaction of each of the following reactants:

1. $CH_3{-}CH_2{-}CH_2{-}CH_2{-}OH \xrightarrow{[O]}$

2. $CH_3{-}\overset{\displaystyle OH}{\overset{|}{C}H}{-}CH_3 \xrightarrow{[O]}$

3. $CH_3{-}CH_2{-}\overset{\displaystyle CH_3}{\overset{|}{C}H}{-}CH_2{-}OH \xrightarrow{[O]}$

Answers

1. $CH_3{-}CH_2{-}CH_2{-}\overset{\displaystyle O}{\overset{\|}{C}}{-}H$

2. $CH_3{-}\overset{\displaystyle O}{\overset{\|}{C}}{-}CH_3$

3. $CH_3{-}CH_2{-}\overset{\displaystyle CH_3}{\overset{|}{C}H}{-}\overset{\displaystyle O}{\overset{\|}{C}}{-}H$

16.8 Aldehydes and Ketones

- In an aldehyde, the carbonyl group appears at the end of a carbon chain attached to at least one hydrogen atom.
- In a ketone, the carbonyl group occurs between carbon groups and has no hydrogens attached to it.
- In the IUPAC system, aldehydes and ketones are named by replacing the *-e* in the longest chain containing the carbonyl group with *-al* for aldehydes and *-one* for ketones. The location of the carbonyl group in a ketone is given if there are more than four carbon atoms in the chain.

$$CH_3{-}\overset{\overset{\large O}{\|}}{C}{-}H \qquad CH_3{-}\overset{\overset{\large O}{\|}}{C}{-}CH_3$$

ethanal (acetaldehyde) — propanone (dimethyl ketone)

◆ Learning Exercise 16.8A

Write the correct IUPAC (or common name) for the following aldehydes and ketones:

1. $CH_3{-}\overset{\overset{\large O}{\|}}{C}{-}H$

2. $CH_3{-}CH_2{-}CH_2{-}CH_2{-}\overset{\overset{\large O}{\|}}{C}{-}H$

3. $CH_3{-}\overset{\overset{\large O}{\|}}{C}{-}CH_3$

4. $CH_3{-}\overset{\overset{\large O}{\|}}{C}{-}CH_2{-}CH_2{-}CH_3$

5. $CH_3{-}CH_2{-}\overset{\overset{\large CH_3}{|}}{CH}{-}CH_2{-}CH_2{-}\overset{\overset{\large O}{\|}}{C}{-}H$

6. $CH_3{-}CH_2{-}\overset{\overset{\large O}{\|}}{C}{-}CH_2{-}CH_3$

Answers

1. ethanal; acetaldehyde
2. pentanal
3. propanone; dimethyl ketone, acetone
4. 2-pentanone; methyl propyl ketone
5. 4-methylhexanal
6. 3-pentanone; diethyl ketone

◆ Learning Exercise 16.8B

Write the correct condensed formulas for the following aldehydes and ketones:

1. ethanal

2. 2-methylbutanal

3. 2-chloropropanal

4. ethylmethylketone

5. 3-hexanone

6. benzaldehyde

Answers

1. $CH_3-\overset{\overset{O}{\|}}{C}-H$

2. $CH_3-CH_2-\overset{\overset{CH_3}{|}}{CH}-\overset{\overset{O}{\|}}{C}-H$

3. $CH_3-\overset{\overset{Cl}{|}}{CH}-\overset{\overset{O}{\|}}{C}-H$

4. $CH_3-CH_2-\overset{\overset{O}{\|}}{C}-CH_3$

5. $CH_3-CH_2-\overset{\overset{O}{\|}}{C}-CH_2-CH_2-CH_3$

6. $C_6H_5-\overset{\overset{O}{\|}}{C}H$

16.9 Carboxylic Acids and Esters

- In the IUPAC system, a carboxylic acid is named by replacing the *-ane* ending with *-oic acid.* Simple acids usually are named by the common naming system using the prefixes: **form-** (1C), **acet-** (2C), **propion-** (4C), **butyr-** (4C), followed by ***-ic acid.***

$H-\overset{\overset{O}{\|}}{C}-OH$	$CH_3-\overset{\overset{O}{\|}}{C}-OH$	$CH_3-CH_2-CH_2-\overset{\overset{O}{\|}}{C}-OH$
methanoic acid (formic acid)	ethanoic acid (acetic acid)	butanoic acid (butyric acid)

- In the presence of a strong acid, carboxylic acids react with alcohols to produce esters and water.

◆ Learning Exercise 16.9A

Give the IUPAC and common names for each of the following carboxylic acids:

1. $CH_3-\overset{\overset{O}{\|}}{C}-OH$

2. $CH_3-CH_2-\overset{\overset{O}{\|}}{C}-OH$

3. $CH_3-\overset{\overset{CH_3}{|}}{CH}-CH_2-\overset{\overset{O}{\|}}{C}-OH$

4.

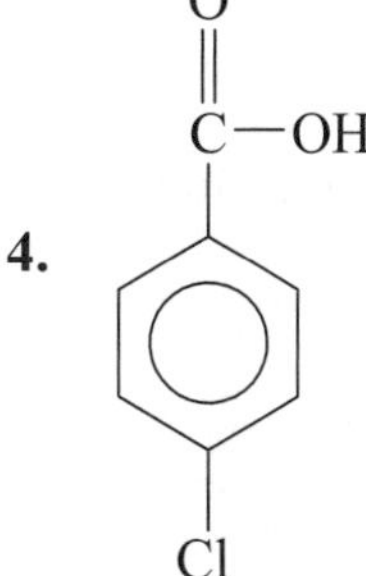

Answers
1. ethanoic acid (acetic acid) **2.** propanoic acid (propionic acid)
3. 3-methylbutanoic acid **4.** 4-chlorobenzoic acid

◆ Learning Exercise 16.9B

A. Write the formulas for the following carboxylic acids:

1. acetic acid

2. 2-methylbutanoic acid

3. benzoic acid

4. 3-chloropropionic acid

5. formic acid

6. 3-chloropentanoic acid

Answers **1.** $CH_3-\overset{\overset{\displaystyle O}{\|}}{C}-OH$

2. $CH_3-\overset{\overset{\displaystyle CH_3}{|}}{CH}-CH_2-\overset{\overset{\displaystyle O}{\|}}{C}-OH$

3. 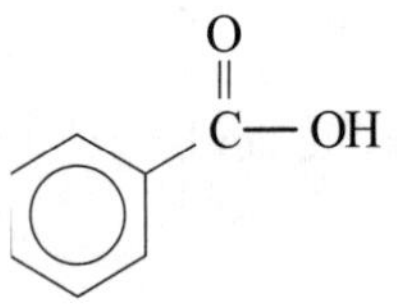 $C_6H_5-\overset{\overset{\displaystyle O}{\|}}{C}-OH$ (benzene ring bonded to the carbonyl carbon)

4. $Cl-CH_2-CH_2-\overset{\overset{\displaystyle O}{\|}}{C}-OH$

5. $H-\overset{\overset{\displaystyle O}{\|}}{C}-OH$

6. $CH_3-CH_2-\overset{\overset{\displaystyle Cl}{|}}{CH}-CH_2-\overset{\overset{\displaystyle O}{\|}}{C}-OH$

◆ Learning Exercise 16.9C

Write the products of the following reactions.

1. $CH_3-\overset{\overset{\displaystyle O}{\|}}{C}-OH + CH_3-OH \xrightarrow{H^+}$

2. $H-\overset{\overset{\displaystyle O}{\|}}{C}-OH + CH_3-CH_2-OH \xrightarrow{H^+}$

3. $CH_3-CH_2-\overset{\overset{\displaystyle O}{\|}}{C}-OH + CH_3-CH_2-OH \xrightarrow{H^+}$

Answers

1. $CH_3-\overset{\overset{\large O}{\|}}{C}-O-CH_3 + H_2O$
2. $H-\overset{\overset{\large O}{\|}}{C}-O-CH_2-CH_3 + H_2O$
3. $CH_3-CH_2-\overset{\overset{\large O}{\|}}{C}-O-CH_2-CH_3 + H_2O$

16.10 Amines and Amides

- Amines are derivative of ammonia (NH_3), in which alkyl or aromatic groups replace one or hydrogen atoms.
- Simple amines are named with common names in which the names of the alkyl group are listed alphabetically preceding the suffix *-amine.*

CH_3-NH_2	$CH_3-NH-CH_3$	$CH_3-\overset{\overset{\large CH_3}{\vert}}{N}-CH_3$
methylamine	dimethylamine	trimethylamine

- Amides are derivatives of carboxylic acids in which an amine group replaces the —OH group in the acid.
- Amides are named by replacing the *-ic acid* or *-oic acid* ending by *-amide.*

$CH_3-\overset{\overset{\large O}{\|}}{C}-NH_2$ ethanamide (acetamide)

◆ Learning Exercise 16.10A

Name each of the amines.

1. $CH_3-\overset{\overset{\large H}{\vert}}{N}-CH_2CH_3$

2. $CH_3-CH_2-\overset{\overset{\large CH_3}{\vert}}{N}-CH_3$

3. $CH_3-CH_2-CH_2-CH_2-\overset{\overset{\large H}{\vert}}{N}-CH_2-CH_3$

4. (benzene ring with NH_2 and CH_3 substituents in meta positions)

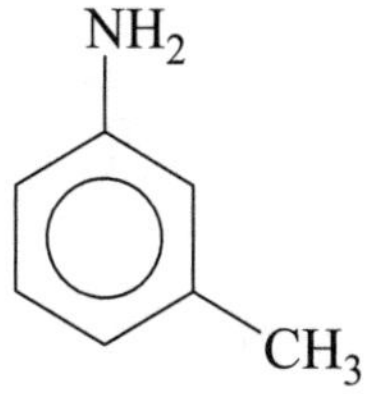

Answers
1. ethylmethylamine
2. ethyldimethylamine
3. butylethylamine
4. 3-methylaniline

◆ Learning Exercise 16.10B

Write the structural formulas of the following amines:

1. propylamine

2. ethylmethylamine

3. dimethylamine

4. aniline

Answers

1. $CH_3{-}CH{-}CH_2{-}NH_2$

2. $CH_3{-}NH{-}CH_2{-}CH_3$

3. $CH_3{-}NH{-}CH_3$

4. 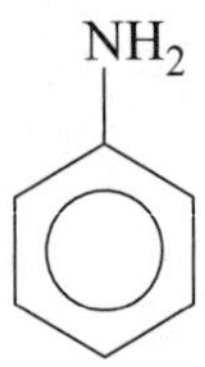 NH_2 (on a benzene ring)

Learning Exercise 16.10C

Name the following amides:

1. $CH_3{-}CH_2{-}\overset{O}{\overset{\|}{C}}{-}NH_2$ ______________________

2. 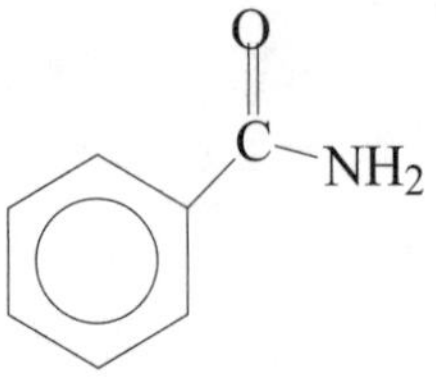 $\overset{O}{\overset{\|}{C}}{-}NH_2$ (on a benzene ring) ______________________

3. $CH_3{-}CH_2{-}CH_2{-}CH_2{-}\overset{O}{\overset{\|}{C}}{-}NH_2$ ______________________

4. $CH_3{-}\overset{O}{\overset{\|}{C}}{-}NH_2$ ______________________

Answers

1. propanamide (propionamide)

2. benzamide

3. pentanamide

4. ethanamide (acetamide)

◆ Learning Exercise 16.10D

Write the structural formulas for each of the following amides:

1. propanamide

2. 2-methylbutanamide

3. 3-chloropentanamide

4. benzamide

Answers

1. $CH_3-CH_2-\overset{\overset{\Large O}{\|}}{C}-NH_2$

2. $CH_3-CH_2-\overset{\overset{\Large CH_3}{|}}{CH}-\overset{\overset{\Large O}{\|}}{C}-NH_2$

3. $CH_3-CH_2-\overset{\overset{\Large Cl}{|}}{CH}-CH_2-\overset{\overset{\Large O}{\|}}{C}-NH_2$

4. $C_6H_5-\overset{\overset{\Large O}{\|}}{C}-NH_2$ (benzene ring)

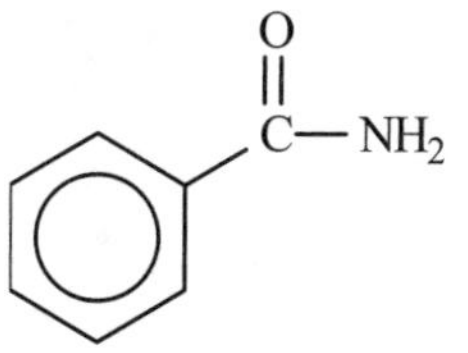

◆ Learning Exercise 16.10E

Write the structural formulas(s) of the amides formed in each of the following reactions:

1. $CH_3-CH_2-\overset{\overset{\Large O}{\|}}{C}-OH + NH_3 \xrightarrow{\text{Heat}}$

2. $CH_3-\overset{\overset{\Large O}{\|}}{C}-OH + NH_3 \xrightarrow{\text{Heat}}$

Answers

1. $CH_3-CH_2-\overset{\overset{\Large O}{\|}}{C}-NH_2$

2. $CH_3-\overset{\overset{\Large O}{\|}}{C}-NH_2$

Checklist for Chapter 16

You are ready to take the self-test for Chapter 16. Be sure you have accomplished the following learning goals for this chapter. If you are not sure, review the section listed at the end of the goal. Then apply your new skills and understanding to the self-test.

After studying Chapter 16, I can successfully:

____ Identify properties as characteristic of organic or inorganic compounds (16.1).

____ Use the IUPAC system to name alkanes (16.2).

____ Identify the functional groups in organic compounds (16.3).

____ Identify the structural features of alkenes and alkynes (16.4).

____ Name alkenes and alkynes using IUPAC rules and write their structural formulas (16.4).

____ Describe the process of forming polymers from alkene monomers (16.5).

____ Write the names and structures for compounds that contain a benzene ring (16.6).

____ Classify an alcohol as primary, secondary, or tertiary (16.7).

____ Give the IUPAC or common name of an alcohol; draw the structural formula from the name (16.7).

____ Write the IUPAC and common names and draw structural formulas of aldehydes and ketones (16.8).

____ Write the IUPAC and common names and draw structural formula of carboxylic acids (16.9).

____ Write the IUPAC or common names and structural formulas of esters (16.9).

____ Write the common names of amines and amides draw their structural formulas (16.10).

Practice Test for Chapter 16

Indicate whether each of the following structural formulas are correct (C) or not correct (N):

1. ____

```
H—C—C—H
```

2. ____

```
  H  H  H
  |  |  |
H—C—C—C—H
  |  |  |
  H  H  H
```

3. ____

```
  H  H  H
  |  |  |
H—C—C—N—H
     |  |
     H  H
```

4. ____

```
  H  H  O
  |  |  ||
H—C=C—C—O—H
```

Indicate whether the following characteristics are typical of organic (O) compounds or inorganic (I) compounds.

5.___ higher melting points

6.___ covalent bonds

7.___ soluble in water

8.___ ionic bonds

9. ___ burn easily in air

10. ___ soluble in nonpolar solvents

Match the name of the hydrocarbon with each structure:

A. propane **B.** 3-methylbutane **C.** 2-methylbutane
D. hexane **E.** 2,4-dimethylhexane

11. $CH_3—CH_2—CH_3$

12. $CH_3—CH_2—CH_2—CH_2—CH_2—CH_3$

13.
```
              CH3
               |
CH3—CH2—CH—CH3
```

14.
```
      CH3          CH3
       |            |
CH3—CH—CH2—CH— CH2—CH3
```

15. The correctly balanced equation for the complete combustion of ethane is

A. $C_2H_6 + O_2 \rightarrow 2CO + 3H_2O$
B. $C_2H_6 + O_2 \rightarrow CO_2 + H_2O$
C. $C_2H_6 + 2O_2 \rightarrow 2CO_2 + 3H_2O$
D. $2C_2H_6 + 7O_2 \rightarrow 4CO_2 + 6H_2O$
E. $2C_2H_6 + 4O_2 \rightarrow 4CO_2 + 6H_2O$

Classify the family for each of the compounds in problems 16 to 21:

A. alkane **B.** alkene **C.** alcohol **D.** aldehyde
E. ketone **F.** ether **G.** amine

16. ____
```
            O
            ||
CH3—CH2—C—CH3
```

17. ____ $CH_3—CH_2—CH_2—OH$

18. ____
```
            CH3
             |
CH3—CH=C—CH3
```

19. ____ $CH_3—CH_2—O—CH_3$

20. ____ $CH_3—CH_2—NH—CH_3$

21. ____
```
      O
      ||
CH3—C—H
```

In questions 22 to 24, match the name of the alkene or alkyne with the structural formula:

A. 1-butene **B.** 2-butene **C.** 3-butene
D. 2-butyne **E.** 1-butyne

22. ___ $CH_3—CH_2—C\equiv CH$

23. ___ $CH_3—CH_2—CH=CH_2$

24. ___ $CH_3—CH=CH—CH_3$

25. Hydrogenation of $CH_3—CH=CH_2$ gives

A. $3CO_2 + 6H_2$ **B.** $CH_3—CH_2—CH_3$ **C.** $CH_2=CH—CH_3$
D. no reaction **E.** $CH_3—CH_2—CH_2—CH_3$

In questions 26 to 29, match the names of the aromatic compounds with their structural formulas:

A. 

B. 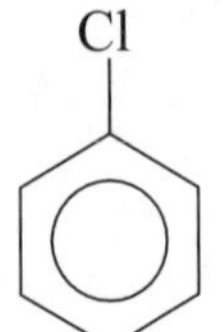

C. 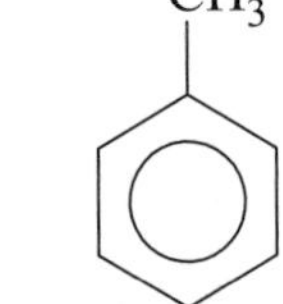

D. 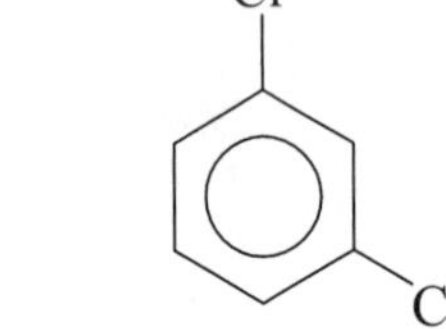

26. ___ chlorobenzene

27. ___ benzene

28. ___ toluene

29. ___ 1, 3-chlorobenzene

Match the names of the following compounds with their structures:

A. 1-propanol **B.** 3-propanol **C.** 2-propanol
D. ethyl methyl ether **E.** diethyl ether

30. $CH_3—\underset{}{\overset{\text{OH}}{\overset{|}{\text{CH}}}}—CH_3$

31. $CH_3—CH_2—CH_2—OH$

32. $CH_3—O—CH_2—CH_3$

33. $CH_3—CH_2—O—CH_2—CH_3$

34. The compound $CH_3—\overset{\text{O}}{\overset{\|}{\text{C}}}—CH_3$ is formed by the oxidation of

A. 2-propanol **B.** propane **C.** 1-propanol
D. dimethyl ether **E.** methyl ethyl ketone

In questions 35 to 38, match each structure with its functional group:
A. alcohol **B.** aldehyde **C.** carboxylic acid **D.** ester **E.** ketone

35.___ $CH_3—CH_2—\overset{\text{O}}{\overset{\|}{\text{C}}}—O—CH_3$

36. ___ $CH_3—CH_2—\overset{\text{O}}{\overset{\|}{\text{C}}}—H$

37.___ $CH_3—\overset{\text{O}}{\overset{\|}{\text{C}}}—CH_2—CH_3$

38. ___ $CH_3—CH_2—\overset{\text{O}}{\overset{\|}{\text{C}}}—OH$

For questions 39 to 42, match the structure that goes with each of the following names:

A. 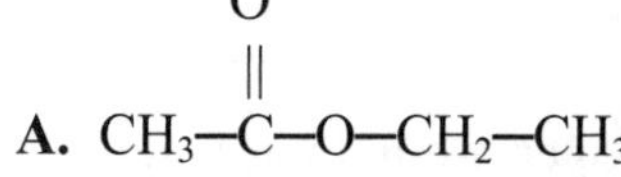

B. $CH_3-O-\overset{\overset{\large O}{||}}{C}-CH_2-CH_3$

C. $CH_3-\overset{\overset{\large O}{||}}{C}-O-H$

D. $CH_3-CH_2-CH_2-\overset{\overset{\large O}{||}}{C}-OH$

E. $CH_3-CH_2-CH_2-\overset{\overset{\large O}{||}}{C}-O-CH_3$

39._____ butyric acid

40._____ methyl propanoate

41._____ ethyl acetate

42._____ acetic acid

43. Identify the carboxylic acid and alcohol needed to produce

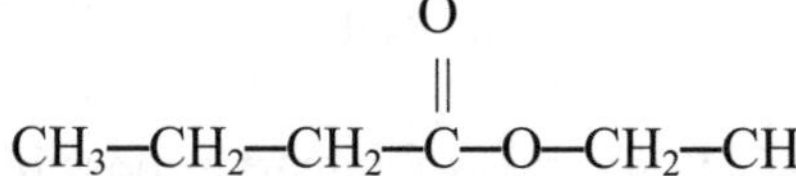

A. propanoic acid and ethanol
B. acetic acid and 1-pentanol
C. acetic acid and 1-butanol
D. butanoic acid and ethanol
E. hexanoic acid and methanol

Match the amines and amides in questions 44 to 47 with the following names:

A. ethyl dimethyl amine
B. ethanamide
C. propanamide
D. diethyl amine
E. butanamide

44. ____ $CH_3-CH_2-\overset{\overset{\large CH_3}{|}}{N}-CH_3$

45. ____ $CH_3-CH_2-CH_2-\overset{\overset{\large O}{||}}{C}-NH_2$

46. ____ $CH_3-CH_2-NH-CH_2-CH_3$

47. ____ $CH_3-CH_2-\overset{\overset{\large O}{||}}{C}-NH_2$

Answers to Practice Test

1. N	**2.** C	**3.** N	**4.** C	**5.** I
6. O	**7.** I	**8.** I	**9.** O	**10.** O
11. A	**12.** D	**13.** C	**14.** E	**15.** D
16. E	**17.** C	**18.** B	**19.** F	**20.** G
21. D	**22.** E	**23.** A	**24.** B	**25.** B
26. B	**27.** A	**28.** C	**29.** D	**30.** C
31. A	**32.** D	**33.** E	**34.** A	**35.** D
36. B	**37.** E	**38.** C	**39.** D	**40.** B
41. A	**42.** C	**43.** D	**44.** A	**45.** E
46. D	**47.** C			

Answers and Solutions to Selected Text Problems

16.1 Organic compounds contain C and H and sometimes O, N, or a halogen atom. Inorganic compounds usually contain elements other than C and H.

a. inorganic **b.** organic **c.** organic
d. inorganic **e.** inorganic **f.** organic

16.3 **a.** Inorganic compounds are usually soluble in water.
b. Organic compounds have lower boiling points than most inorganic compounds.
c. Organic compounds often burn in air.
d. Inorganic compounds are more likely to be solids at room temperature.

16.5 **a.** ethane **b.** ethane **c.** NaBr **d.** NaBr

16.7 VSEPR theory predicts that the four bonds attached to CH_4 will be as far apart as possible, which means that the hydrogen atoms in the bonds are at the corners of a tetrahedron.

16.9 **a.** Pentane is the alkane with a carbon chain of five carbon atoms.
b. Ethane is the alkane with a carbon chain of two carbon atoms.
c. Hexane is the alkane with a carbon chain of six carbon atoms.

16.11 **a.** CH_4 **b.** $CH_3—CH_3$ **c.** $CH_3—CH_2—CH_2—CH_2—CH_3$

16.13 **a.** same molecule **b.** isomers of C_5H_{12} **c.** isomers of C_6H_{14}

16.15 **a.** 2-fluorobutane **b.** 2,2-dimethylpropane
c. 2-chloro-3-dimethylpentane

16.17 Draw the main chain with the number of carbon atoms in the ending. For example, butane has a main chain of four carbon atoms, and hexane has a main chain of six carbon atoms. Attach substituents on the carbon atoms indicated. For example, in 3-methylpentane, a $CH_3—$ group is bonded to carbon 3 of a five-carbon chain.

```
         CH3                                  Cl
          |                                   |
a. CH3—CH—CH2—CH3              b. CH3—CH2—C—CH2—CH3
                                              |
                                              Cl

         CH3  CH3        CH3
          |    |          |
c.  CH3—CH—CH—CH2—CH—CH3
```

16.19 **a.** $CH_3—CH_2—CH_2—CH_2—CH_2—CH_2—CH_3$
b. An alkane with seven carbon atoms would be liquid at room temperature.
c. Alkanes are insoluble in water.
d. Alkanes are less dense than water and float on water.

16.21 In combustion, a hydrocarbon reacts with oxygen to yield CO_2 and H_2O.

a. $2C_2H_6 + 7O_2 \longrightarrow 4CO_2 + 6H_2O$ **b.** $C_3H_8 + 5O_2 \longrightarrow 3CO_2 + 4H_2O$

c. $2C_8H_{18} + 25O_2 \longrightarrow 16CO_2 + 18H_2O$

16.23 **a.** Alcohols contain a hydroxyl group (—OH).
b. Alkenes have carbon-carbon double bonds.
c. Aldehydes contain a C=O bonded to at least one H atom.
d. Esters contain a carboxyl group attached to an alkyl group.

16.25 **a.** Ethers have an —O— group.
b. Alcohols have a —OH group.
c. Ketones have a C=O group between alkyl groups.
d. Carboxylic acids have a —COOH group.
e. Amines contain a N atom.

16.27 **a.** An alkene has a double bond. **b.** An alkyne has a triple bond.

16.29 **a.** Ethene contains two carbon atoms with a carbon–carbon double bond.
b. 2-Methyl-1-propene contains three carbon atoms with a carbon–carbon double bond and a methyl group on carbon 2.
c. 2-Pentyne contains five carbon atoms with a carbon–carbon triple bond between carbon 2 and carbon 3.

16.31 **a.** Propene is the three-carbon alkene. $H_2C{=}CH{-}CH_3$
b. 1-Pentene is the five-carbon compound with a double bond between carbon 1 and carbon 2.
$H_2C{=}CH{-}CH_2{-}CH_2{-}CH_3$
c. 2-Methyl-1-butene has a four-carbon chain with a double bond between carbon 1 and carbon 2 and a methyl attached to carbon 2.

```
      CH3
      |
H2C=C—CH2—CH3
```

16.33 **a.** When H_2 is added to 1-pentene, the product is pentane $CH_3{-}CH_2{-}CH_2{-}CH_2{-}CH_3$
b. When H_2 is added to 2-butene, the product is butane $CH_3{-}CH_2{-}CH_2{-}CH_3$
c. When H_2 is added to an 2-hexene, the product is hexane
$CH_3{-}CH_2{-}CH_2{-}CH_2{-}CH_2{-}CH_3$

16.35 A polymer is a long-chain molecule consisting of many repeating smaller units. These smaller units are called monomers.

16.37 Teflon is a polymer of the monomer tetrafluoroethene.

```
     F  F               F  F  F  F  F  F
     |  |               |  |  |  |  |  |
3  F—C=C—F   ——→      —C—C—C—C—C—C—
                        |  |  |  |  |  |
                        F  F  F  F  F  F
```

16.39 The six-carbon ring with alternating single and double bonds is benzene. Benzene with a methyl group is commonly called toluene.

a. 2-chlorotoluene **b.** ethylbenzene **c.** 1,3,5-trichlorobenzene

16.41 **a.**

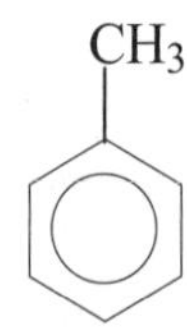

b.

c.

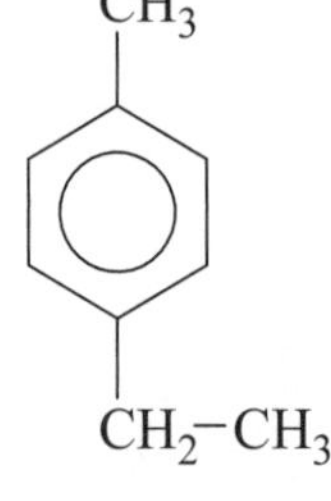

16.43 **a.** This compound has a two-carbon chain (ethane). The final *–e* is dropped and *–ol* added to indicate an alcohol. The IUPAC name is ethanol.

b. This compound has a four-carbon chain with a hydroxyl attached to carbon 2. The IUPAC name is 2-butanol.

c. This compound, which has a five -carbon chain with a hydroxyl attached to carbon 2, is named 2-pentanol.

d. When a benzene ring contains an —OH group, it is called phenol.

16.45 **a.** 1-Propanol has a three-carbon chain with a hydroxyl attached to carbon 1.

CH_3—CH_2—CH_2—OH

b. Methyl alcohol has a hydroxyl attached to a one-carbon alkane CH_3—OH.

c. 3-Pentanol has a five-carbon chain with a hydroxyl attached to carbon 3.

```
                OH
                |
CH3—CH2—CH—CH2—CH3
```

d. 2-Methyl-2-butanol has a four-carbon chain with a methyl and -OH attached to carbon 2.

```
         OH
         |
CH3—C—CH2—CH3
         |
        CH3
```

16.47 In a primary (1°) alcohol, the carbon bonded to the hydroxyl group (—OH) is attached to one alkyl group except for methanol; to two alkyl groups in a secondary alcohol (2°); and to three alkyl groups in a tertiary alcohol (3°).

a. 1° **b.** 1° **c.** 3°

16.49 **a.** With an ethyl on one side of —O— and methyl on the other, the common name of this compound is ethyl methyl ether.

b. Three-carbon propyl groups on each side of —O— makes this compound dipropyl ether.

c. Methyl propyl ether has a one-carbon group and a three-carbon group attached to oxygen by single bonds.

16.51

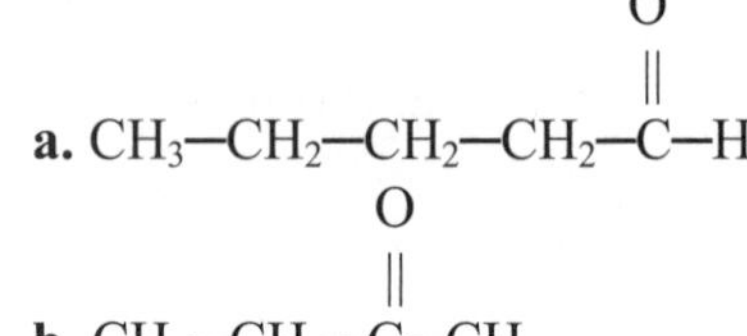


```
              O
              ||
b. CH3—CH2—C—CH3
```

c. $CH_3-\overset{\overset{O}{\|}}{C}-CH_2-\overset{\overset{CH_3}{|}}{CH}-CH_3$

16.53 **a.** acetaldehyde **b.** methyl propyl ketone **c.** formaldehyde

16.55 **a.** propanal **b.** 2-methyl-3-pentanone **c.** benzaldehyde

16.57

a. $CH_3-\overset{\overset{O}{\|}}{C}-H$ Acetaldehyde is an aldehyde with two carbons.

b. $CH_3-\overset{\overset{O}{\|}}{C}-CH_2-CH_2-CH_3$ 2-Pentanone has a ketone group on carbon 2 of a five-carbon chain.

c. $CH_3-\overset{\overset{O}{\|}}{C}-CH_2-CH_2-CH_2-CH_3$

16.59 **a.** ethanoic acid; acetic acid
b. propanoic acid; propionic acid
c. 4-hydroxybenzoic acid (IUPAC)

16.61 **a.** $CH_3-CH_2-\overset{\overset{O}{\|}}{C}-OH$

b. $C_6H_5-\overset{\overset{O}{\|}}{C}-OH$ (benzene ring bonded to the carbonyl carbon)

c. $Cl-CH_2-\overset{\overset{O}{\|}}{C}-OH$

d. $HO-CH_2-CH_2-\overset{\overset{O}{\|}}{C}-OH$

16.63 **a.** aldehyde **b.** ester **c.** ketone **d.** carboxylic acid

16.65 **a.** $CH_3-\overset{\overset{O}{\|}}{C}-O-CH_3$ The carbonyl portion of the ester has two carbons bonded to a methyl group.

b. $CH_3-CH_2-CH_2-\overset{\overset{O}{\|}}{C}-OCH_3$ The carbonyl portion of the ester is a four-carbon chain bonded to a one-carbon methyl group.

16.67 A carboxylic acid and an alcohol react to give an ester with the elimination of water.

a. $CH_3-CH_2-\overset{\overset{O}{\|}}{C}-O-CH_2-CH_2-CH_3$

b. $$CH_3-CH_2-CH_2-CH_2-\overset{\overset{\displaystyle O}{\|}}{C}-O-\overset{\overset{\displaystyle CH_3}{|}}{CH}-CH_3$$

16.69 **a.** The name of this ester is methyl methanoate (methyl formate). The carbonyl portion of the ester contains one carbon; the name is derived from methanoic (formic) acid. The alkyl portion is methyl.

b. The name of this ester is methyl ethanoate (methyl acetate). The carbonyl portion of the ester contains two carbons. The name is derived from ethanoic (acetic) acid. The alkyl portion is methyl.

c. The name of this ester is methyl butanoate (methyl butyrate). The carbonyl portion of the ester contains four carbons; the name is derived from butanoic (butyric) acid. The alkyl portion is methyl.

16.71

a. $CH_3-\overset{\overset{\displaystyle O}{\|}}{C}-O-CH_3$ Acetic acid is the two carbon carboxylic acid. Methanol gives a one-carbon alkyl group.

b. $H-\overset{\overset{\displaystyle O}{\|}}{C}-O-CH_2-CH_2-CH_2-CH_3$ Formic acid is the carboxylic acid bonded to the four-carbon butanol.

c. $CH_3-CH_2-CH_2-CH_2-\overset{\overset{\displaystyle O}{\|}}{C}-O-CH_2-CH_3$ Pentanoic acid is the carboxylic acid bonded to ethanol.

d. $CH_3-CH_2-\overset{\overset{\displaystyle O}{\|}}{C}-O-CH_2-CH_2-CH_3$ Propanoic acid is the carboxylic acid bonded to propanol.

16.73 The common name of an amine consists of naming the alkyl groups bonding to the nitrogen atom in alphabetical order.

a. An ethyl group attached to $-NH_2$ is ethylamine.

b. Two alkyl groups attach to nitrogen as methyl and propyl for methylpropylamine.

c. Diethylmethylamine

16.75 **a.** Ethanamide (acetamide) tells us that the carbonyl portion has two carbon atoms.

b. Butanamide (butyramide) is a chain of four carbon atoms bonded to an amino group.

c. Methanamide (formamide)

16.77 **a.** This is an amide of propionic acid, which has three carbon atoms.

$$CH_3-CH_2-\overset{\overset{\displaystyle O}{\|}}{C}-NH_2$$

b. 2-Methyl indicates that a methyl is bonded to carbon 2 in an amide chain of five carbon atoms.

$$CH_3-CH_2-CH_2-\overset{\overset{\displaystyle CH_3}{|}}{CH}-\overset{\overset{\displaystyle O}{\|}}{C}-NH_2$$

c. $\mathrm{H{-}\overset{\overset{\displaystyle O}{\|}}{C}{-}NH_2}$

Answers to Additional Questions and Problems

16.85 **a.** butane; organic compounds have low melting points
b. butane; organic compounds burn vigorously in air
c. potassium chloride; inorganic compounds have high melting points
d. potassium chloride; inorganic compounds (ionic) produce ions in water
e. butane; organic compounds are more likely to be gases at room temperature

16.87 **a.** carboxylic acid **b.** alkene **c.** ester
d. amine **e.** aldehyde

16.89

a. $\mathrm{CH_3{-}CH_2{-}\overset{\overset{\displaystyle CH_2{-}CH_3}{|}}{C}H{-}CH_2{-}CH_2{-}CH_3}$

b. $\mathrm{CH_3{-}\overset{\overset{\displaystyle CH_3}{|}}{C}H{-}\overset{\overset{\displaystyle CH_3}{|}}{C}H{-}CH_2{-}CH_3}$

c. $\mathrm{Cl{-}CH_2{-}CH_2{-}\underset{\underset{\displaystyle Cl}{|}}{\overset{\overset{\displaystyle CH_3}{|}}{C}}{-}CH_2{-}CH_2{-}CH_2{-}CH_3}$

16.91 **a.** alcohol **b.** alkene **c.** aldehyde
d. alkane **e.** carboxylic acid **f.** amine

16.93 **a.** This compound contains a five-carbon chain with a double bond between carbon 1 and carbon 2 and a methyl group attached to carbon 2. The IUPAC name is 2-methyl-1-pentene.
b. This compound contains a five-carbon chain with a triple bond between carbon 1 and carbon 2. The IUPAC name is 1-butyne.
c. This compound contains a five-carbon chain with a double bond between carbon 2 and carbon 3. The IUPAC name is 2-pentene.

16.95 **a.** toluene **b.** 2-chlorotoluene **c.** 4-ethyltoluene

16.97 **a.** 1° **b.** 2° **c.** 1°

16.99 **a.**

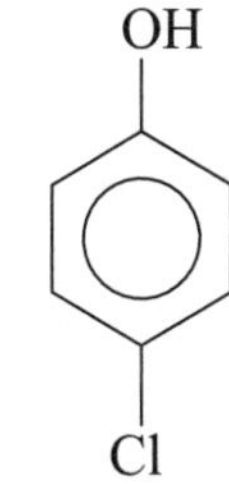

b. $\mathrm{CH_3{-}\overset{\overset{\displaystyle CH_3}{|}}{C}H{-}\overset{\overset{\displaystyle OH}{|}}{C}H{-}CH_2{-}CH_3}$

c. $\mathrm{CH_3{-}CH_2{-}\overset{\overset{\displaystyle O}{\|}}{C}{-}CH_2{-}CH_3}$

16.101

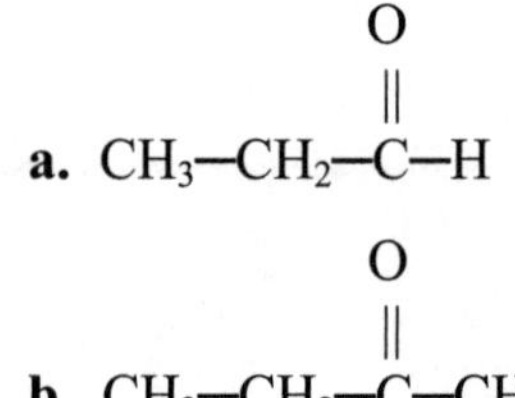

16.103 **a.** 4-chloro-3-hydroxybenzaldehyde **b.** 3-chloropropanal
c. 2-chloro-3-pentanone

16.105 **a.** 4-Chlorobenzaldehyde is benzene with an aldehyde group and a chlorine atom on carbon 4.

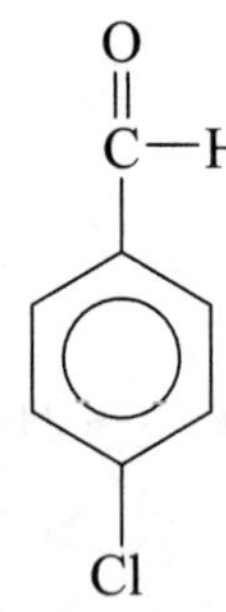

b. 3-Chloropropionaldehyde is a three-carbon aldehyde with a chlorine located two carbons from the carbonyl group.

$Cl{-}CH_2{-}CH_2{-}\overset{\overset{\displaystyle O}{\|}}{C}{-}H$

c. In ethyl methyl ketone, the ketone carbon is attached to a methyl and an ethyl group.

$CH_3{-}\overset{\overset{\displaystyle O}{\|}}{C}{-}CH_2{-}CH_3$

16.107 Primary alcohols oxidize to aldehydes. Secondary alcohols oxidize to ketones.

a. $CH_3{-}CH_2{-}\overset{\overset{\displaystyle O}{\|}}{C}{-}H$

b. $CH_3{-}\overset{\overset{\displaystyle O}{\|}}{C}{-}CH_2{-}CH_2{-}CH_3$

c. $CH_3{-}CH_2{-}CH_2{-}\overset{\overset{\displaystyle O}{\|}}{C}{-}H$

16.109 **a**. 3-methylbutanoic acid
b. ethyl benzoate
c. ethyl propanoate; ethyl propionate

16.111 **a.** $CH_3{-}CH_2{-}NH_2$

b. $CH_3{-}NH{-}CH_3$

c. $CH_3{-}CH_2{-}\overset{\overset{\displaystyle CH_2{-}CH_3}{|}}{N}{-}CH_2{-}CH_3$

17
Biochemistry

Study Goals

- Distinguish between monosaccharides, disaccharides, and polysaccharides.
- Write cyclic structures for monosaccharides.
- Describe the structural units and bonds in disaccharides and polysaccharides.
- Distinguish between saturated and unsaturated fatty acids.
- Write the structure of a triacylglycerol obtained from glycerol and fatty acids.
- Draw the structures of the products from hydrogenation and saponification of triacylglycerols.
- Describe steroids and their role in hormones.
- Classify proteins by their functions in the cells.
- Draw the structures of amino acids.
- Write the structural formulas of dipeptides.
- Identify the structural levels of proteins as primary, secondary, tertiary, and quaternary.
- Describe the lock and key and induced fit models of enzyme action.
- Identify the nitrogen bases, sugars, and nucleotides in DNA and RNA.
- Describe the double helix of DNA.
- Explain the process of DNA replication.
- Describe the transcription process during the synthesis of mRNA.
- Use the codons in the genetic code to describe protein synthesis.

Think About It

1. What carbohydrates are present in table sugar, milk, and wood?

2. How fats used to make soaps?

3. What are some uses of protein in the body?

4. What are some functions of enzymes in the cells of the body?

5. How does DNA determine your height, or the color of your hair or eyes?

17.1 Carbohydrates

- Carbohydrates are classified as monosaccharides (simple sugars), disaccharides (two monosaccharide units), and polysaccharides (many monosaccharide units).
- Monosaccharides are aldehydes (aldoses) or ketones (ketoses) with hydroxyl groups on all other carbon atoms.
- Important monosaccharides are the aldohexoses glucose and galactose and the ketohexose fructose.
- The predominant form of monosaccharides is the cyclic form of five or six atoms. The cyclic structure forms by a reaction between an OH on carbon 5 in hexoses with the carbonyl group of the same molecule.
- The formation of a new hydroxyl group on carbon 1 (or 2 in fructose) gives α and β forms of the cyclic structure of a monosaccharide.

◆ Learning Exercise 17.1A

Match the following key terms with the descriptions shown:

A. carbohydrate **B.** glucose **C.** disaccharide **D.** cellulose **E.** polysaccharide

1.____ A simple or complex sugar composed of a carbon chain with an aldehyde or ketone group and several hydroxyl groups

2.____ A carbohydrate that contains many monosaccharides linked by glycosidic bonds

3.____ An unbranched polysaccharide that cannot be digested by humans

4.____ A hexoaldose that is the most prevalent monosaccharide in the diet

5.____ A carbohydrate that contains two monosaccharides linked by a glycosidic bond

Answers **1.** A **2.** E **3.** D **4.** B **5.** C

◆ Learning Exercise 17.1B

Indicate the number of monosaccharide units (one, two, or many) in each of the following carbohydrates:

1. Sucrose, a disaccharide _______ **2.** Cellulose, a polysaccharide _______

3. Glucose, a monosaccharide _______ **4.** Amylose, a polysaccharide _______

5. Maltose, a disaccharide _______

Answers: **1.** two **2.** many **3.** one **4.** many **5.** two

◆ Learning Exercise 17.1C

Identify the following monosaccharides as aldo- or ketotrioses, tetroses, pentoses, or hexoses:

```
1. CH2OH       2.   H   O           3.  CH2OH        4.   H   O        5.  H   O
   |                 \ //               |                  \ //             \ //
   C=O                C                 C=O                 C                C
   |                  |                 |                   |                |
   CH2OH          H—C—OH           HO—C—H              H—C—OH          H—C—OH
                      |                 |                   |                |
                  H—C—OH           HO—C—H             HO—C—H           H—C—OH
                      |                 |                   |                |
                 HO—C—H             H—C—OH              H—C—OH           CH2OH
                      |                 |                   |
                      CH2OH             CH2OH           H—C—OH
                                                            |
                                                            CH2OH
```

1. ______________________ **2.** ______________________

3. ______________________ **4.** ______________________

5. ______________________

Answers **1.** ketotriose **2.** aldopentose **3.** ketohexose
4. aldohexose **5.** aldotetrose

◆ Learning Exercise 17.1D

Draw the structure for the following monosaccharides:

glucose galactose fructose

Answers:

```
        O                 O
        ||                ||
        C—H               C—H              CH2OH
        |                 |                |
   H—C—OH             H—C—OH               C=O
        |                 |                |
  HO—C—H             HO—C—H           HO—C—H
        |                 |                |
   H—C—OH            HO—C—H            H—C—OH
        |                 |                |
   H—C—OH             H—C—OH           H—C—OH
        |                 |                |
        CH3OH             CH3OH            CH3OH
     glucose           galactose         fructose
```

◆ Learning Exercise 17.1E

Write the cyclic structures (α-forms) for the following:

1. glucose **2.** galactose **3.** fructose

***Answers*:**

α-Glucose

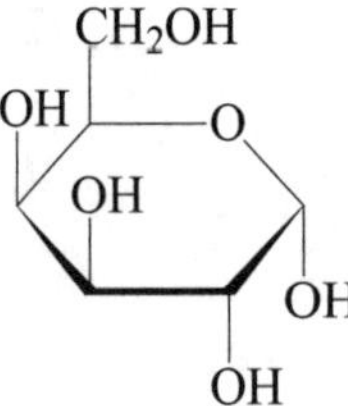

α-Galactose

α-Fructose

17.2 Disaccharides and Polysaccharides

- Disaccharides are glycosides, two monosaccharides units joined together by a glycosidic bond: monosaccharide(1) + monosaccharide (2) ⟶ disaccharide + H_2O
- In maltose, two glucose units are linked by an α-1,4-glycosidic bond. The α-1,4 indicates that the —OH of the alpha form at carbon 1 is bonded to the —OH on carbon 4 of the other glucose molecule.
- When a disaccharide is hydrolyzed by water, the products are a glucose unit and one other monosaccharide.

  Maltose + H_2O ⟶ Glucose + Glucose
  Lactose + H_2O ⟶ Glucose + Galactose
  Sucrose + H_2O ⟶ Glucose + Fructose
- Polysaccharides are polymers of monosaccharide units.
- Starches consist of amylose, an unbranched chain of glucose, whereas amylopectin is a branched polymer of glucose. Glycogen, the storage form of glucose in animals, is similar to amylopectin, but has more branching.
- Cellulose is also a polymer of glucose, but in cellulose the glycosidic bonds are β bonds rather than α bonds as in the starches. Humans can digest starches to obtain energy, but not cellulose. However, cellulose is important as a source of fiber in our diets.

◆ Learning Exercise 17.2A

For the following disaccharides, state (a) the monosaccharide units, (b) the type of glycosidic bond, and (c) the name of the disaccharide.

1. CH_2OH O OH HO OH CH_2OH O OH OH OH OH

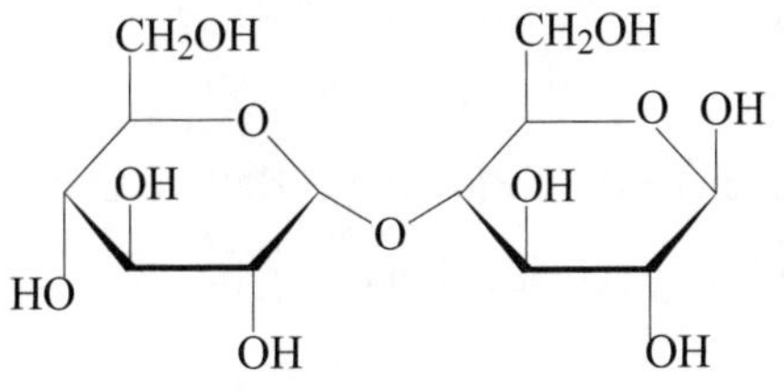

2. CH_2OH HO O OH OH O CH_2OH O OH OH OH

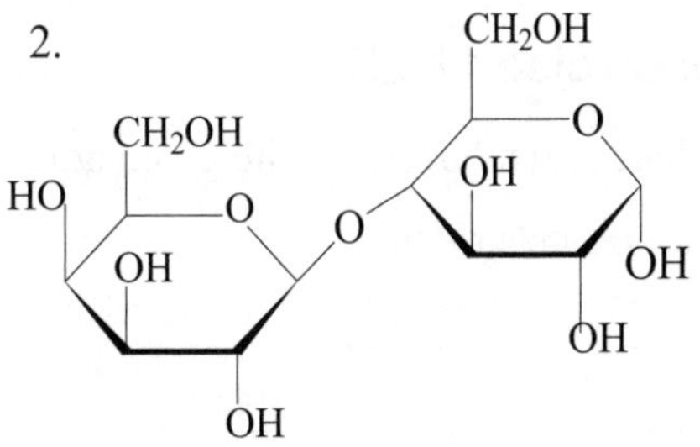

3. CH_2OH O OH HO OH O CH_2OH O HO CH_2OH OH

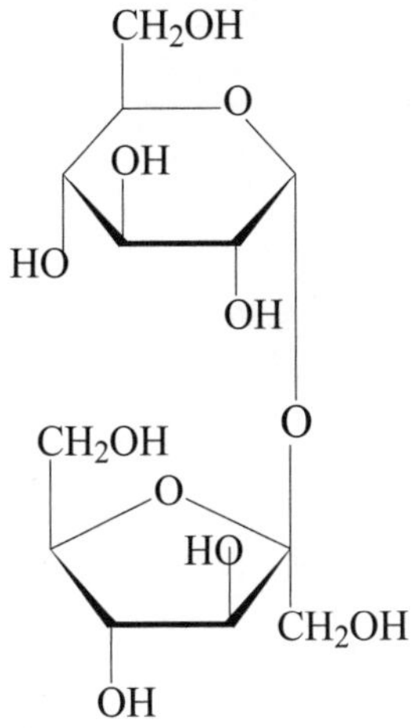

4. CH_2OH O OH HO OH O CH_2OH O OH OH OH

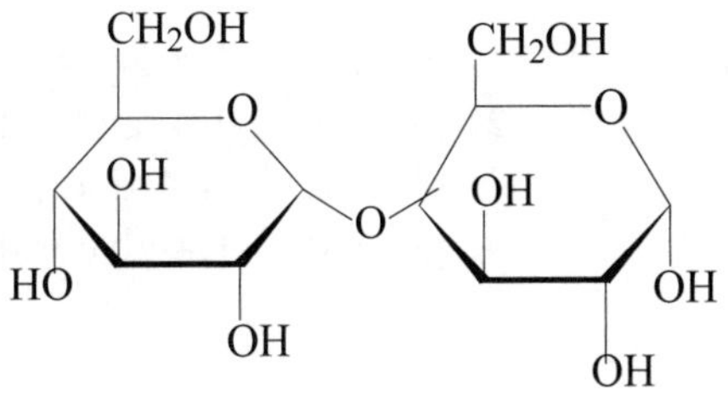

	a. Monosaccharide(s)	**b.** Type of glycosidic bond	**c.** Name of disaccharide
1.			
2.			
3.			
4.			

Answers:	**1.** **(a)** two glucose units	**(b)** α-1,4-glycosidic bond	**(c)** β-maltose
	2. **(a)** galactose + glucose	**(b)** β-1,4-glycosidic bond	**(c)** α-lactose
	3. **(a)** fructose + glucose	**(b)** α-1, β-2 glycosidic bond	**(c)** sucrose
	4. **(a)** two glucose units	**(b)** α-1,4-glycosidic bond	**(c)** α-maltose

◆ Learning Exercise 17.2B

List the monosaccharides and describe the glycosidic bonds in each of the following carbohydrates:

	Monosaccharides	Type(s) of glycosidic bonds
1. amylose	______	______
2. amylopectin	______	______
3. glycogen	______	______
4. cellulose	______	______

Answers:
1. glucose; α-1,4-glycosidic bonds
2. glucose; α-1,4- and α-1,6-glycosidic bonds
3. glucose; α-1,4- and α-1,6-glycosidic bonds
4. glucose; β-1,4-glycosidic bonds

17.3 Lipids

- Lipids are nonpolar compounds that are not soluble in water.
- Fatty acids are carboxylic acids that may be saturated, monounsaturated, or polyunsaturated.
- The triacylglycerols in fats and oils are esters of glycerol and three fatty acids.
- Fats from animal sources contain more saturated fatty acids and have higher melting points than fats found in most vegetable oils.
- Steroids are lipids containing the steroid nucleus, which is a fused structure of four rings.
- The hydrogenation of unsaturated fatty acids converts double bonds to single bonds.
- In saponification, a fat heated with a strong base produces glycerol and the salts of the fatty acids or soaps.

◆ Learning Exercise 17.3A

Match each of the following terms with the correct statement:

a. lipid **b.** fatty acid **c.** triacylglycerol
d. saponification **e.** steroid

1._____A type of compound that is not soluble in water, but in nonpolar solvents

2._____The reaction of a triacylglycerol with a strong base producing salts called soaps and glycerol

3._____A lipid consisting of glycerol bonded to three fatty acids

4._____A lipid composed of a multicyclic ring system

5._____Long-chain carboxylic acid found in triacylglycerols

Answers **1.** a **2.** d **3.** c **4.** e **5.** b

◆ Learning Exercise 17.3B

Draw the structural formulas of linoleic acid, stearic acid, and oleic acid.

1. linoleic acid

2. stearic acid

3. oleic acid

Which of these three fatty acids

a.___ is the most saturated

b.___ is the most unsaturated

c.___ has the lowest melting point

d.___ has the highest melting point

e.___ is found in vegetables

e.___ is from animal sources

Answers:

1. linoleic acid $CH_3{-}(CH_2)_4{-}CH{=}CH{-}CH_2{-}CH{=}CH{-}(CH_2)_7{-}\overset{\overset{\displaystyle O}{\|}}{C}{-}OH$

2. stearic acid $CH_3{-}(CH_2)_{16}{-}\overset{\overset{\displaystyle O}{\|}}{C}{-}OH$

3. oleic acid $CH_3{-}\ (CH_2)_7{-}CH{=}CH{-}(CH_2)_7{-}\overset{\overset{\displaystyle O}{\|}}{C}{-}OH$

a. 2 **b.** 1 **c.** 1 **d.** 2 **e.** 1 and 3 **f.** 2

◆ Learning Exercise 17.3C

Consider the following fatty acid called oleic acid

$$CH_3{-}(CH_2)_7{-}CH{=}CH{-}(CH_2)_7{-}\overset{\overset{\displaystyle O}{\|}}{C}{-}OH$$

1. Why is the compound considered an acid?

2. Is it a saturated or unsaturated compound? Why?

3. Is it likely to be a solid or a liquid at room temperature?

4. Why is it not soluble in water?

Answers
1. contains a carboxylic acid group
2. unsaturated; double bond
3. liquid
4. it has a long hydrocarbon chain

◆ Learning Exercise 17.3D

Write the structure and name of the triacylglycerol formed from the following:

1. Glycerol and three palmitic acids, $CH_3{-}(CH_2)_{14}{-}\overset{\overset{\large O}{\|}}{C}{-}OH$

2. Glycerol and three myristic acids, $CH_3{-}(CH_2)_{12}{-}\overset{\overset{\large O}{\|}}{C}{-}OH$

Answers:

1. 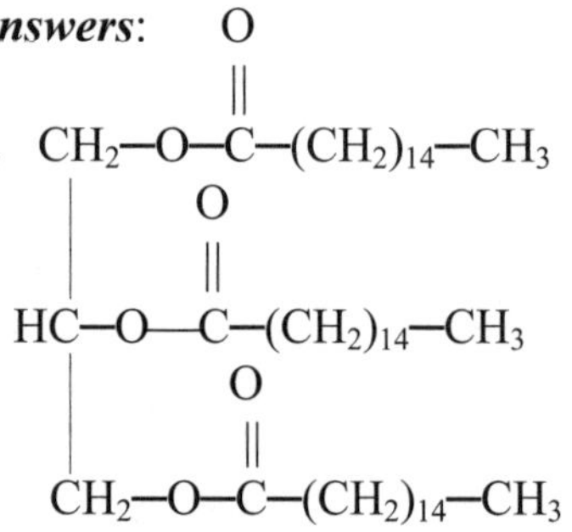
$$\begin{array}{l} CH_2{-}O{-}\overset{\overset{O}{\|}}{C}{-}(CH_2)_{14}{-}CH_3 \\ | \\ HC{-}O{-}\overset{\overset{O}{\|}}{C}{-}(CH_2)_{14}{-}CH_3 \\ | \\ CH_2{-}O{-}\overset{\overset{O}{\|}}{C}{-}(CH_2)_{14}{-}CH_3 \end{array}$$

2.
$$\begin{array}{l} CH_2{-}O{-}\overset{\overset{O}{\|}}{C}{-}(CH_2)_{12}{-}CH_3 \\ | \\ HC{-}O{-}\overset{\overset{O}{\|}}{C}{-}(CH_2)_{12}{-}CH_3 \\ | \\ CH_2{-}O{-}\overset{\overset{O}{\|}}{C}{-}(CH_2)_{12}{-}CH_3 \end{array}$$

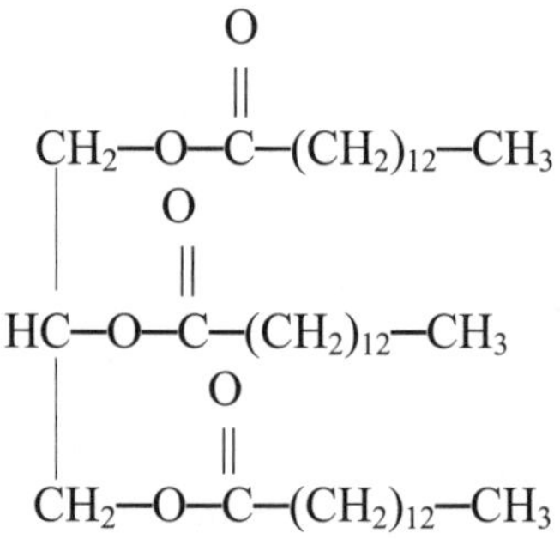

◆ Learning Exercise 17.3E

Write the structural formulas of the following triacylglycerols:

1. Glyceryl tristearate (Tristearin)

2. Glyceryl trioleate (Triolein)

Answers

1. 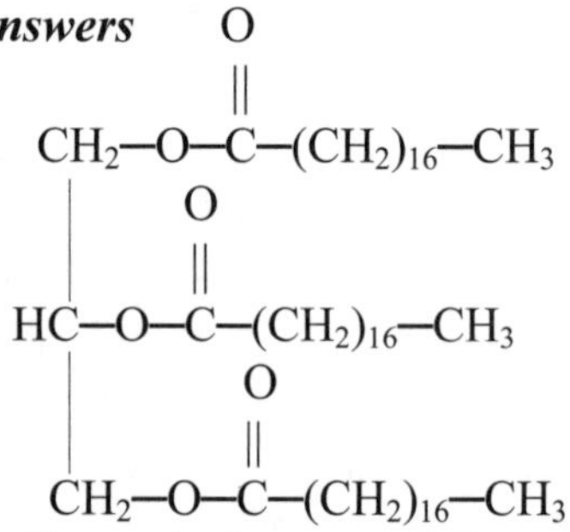
$$\begin{array}{l} CH_2{-}O{-}\overset{\overset{O}{\|}}{C}{-}(CH_2)_{16}{-}CH_3 \\ | \\ HC{-}O{-}\overset{\overset{O}{\|}}{C}{-}(CH_2)_{16}{-}CH_3 \\ | \\ CH_2{-}O{-}\overset{\overset{O}{\|}}{C}{-}(CH_2)_{16}{-}CH_3 \end{array}$$

Glyceryl tristearate (Tristearin)

2. 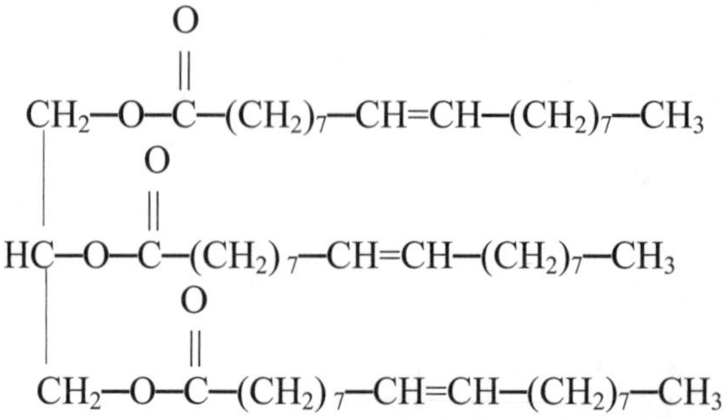
$$\begin{array}{l} CH_2{-}O{-}\overset{\overset{O}{\|}}{C}{-}(CH_2)_7{-}CH{=}CH{-}(CH_2)_7{-}CH_3 \\ | \\ HC{-}O{-}\overset{\overset{O}{\|}}{C}{-}(CH_2)_7{-}CH{=}CH{-}(CH_2)_7{-}CH_3 \\ | \\ CH_2{-}O{-}\overset{\overset{O}{\|}}{C}{-}(CH_2)_7{-}CH{=}CH{-}(CH_2)_7{-}CH_3 \end{array}$$

Glyceryl trioleate (Triolein)

◆ Learning Exercise 17.3F

Write the equations for the following reactions of glyceryl trioleate (triolein):

1. hydrogenation with a nickel catalyst

2. saponification with NaOH

Answers:

1.

$$\begin{array}{l} CH_2-O-\overset{\overset{\displaystyle O}{\|}}{C}-(CH_2)_7-CH=CH-(CH_2)_7-CH_3 \\ | \\ HC-O-\overset{\overset{\displaystyle O}{\|}}{C}-(CH_2)_7-CH=CH-(CH_2)_7-CH_3 \\ | \\ CH_2-O-\overset{\overset{\displaystyle O}{\|}}{C}-(CH_2)_7-CH=CH-(CH_2)_7-CH_3 \end{array} + 3H_2 \xrightarrow{Ni} \begin{array}{l} CH_2-O-\overset{\overset{\displaystyle O}{\|}}{C}-(CH_2)_{16}-CH_3 \\ | \\ HC-O-\overset{\overset{\displaystyle O}{\|}}{C}-(CH_2)_{16}CH_3 \\ | \\ CH_2-O-\overset{\overset{\displaystyle O}{\|}}{C}-(CH_2)_{16}-CH_3 \end{array}$$

2.

$$\begin{array}{l} CH_2-O-\overset{\overset{\displaystyle O}{\|}}{C}-(CH_2)_7-CH=CH-(CH_2)_7-CH_3 \\ | \\ HC-O-\overset{\overset{\displaystyle O}{\|}}{C}-(CH_2)_7-CH=CH-(CH_2)_7-CH_3 \\ | \\ CH_2-O-\overset{\overset{\displaystyle O}{\|}}{C}-(CH_2)_7-CH=CH-(CH_2)_7-CH_3 \end{array} + 3NaOH \rightarrow \begin{array}{l} CH_2-OH \\ | \\ HC-OH \\ | \\ CH_2-OH \end{array}$$

$$+ 3\ Na^+\ {}^-O-\overset{\overset{\displaystyle O}{\|}}{C}-(CH_2)_7-CH=CH-(CH_2)_7-CH_3$$

◆ Learning Exercise 17.3G

1. Write the structure of the steroid nucleus.

2. Write the structure of cholesterol.

Answers

1.

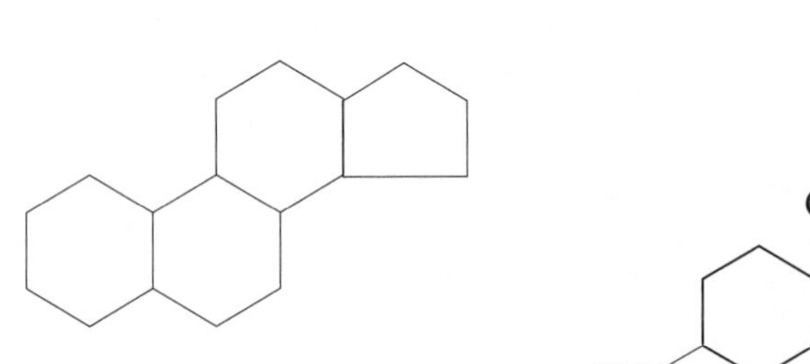

2.

CH_3 CH_3 CH_3 CH_3 CH_3 HO

17.4 Proteins

- Some proteins are enzymes or hormones, whereas others are important in structure, transport, protection, storage, and contraction of muscles.
- The molecular building blocks of proteins are a group of 20 amino acids.
- In an amino acid, a central (alpha) carbon is attached to an amino group, a carboxyl group, and a side chain, which is a characteristic group for each amino acid.
- The particular side chain makes each amino acid polar, nonpolar, acidic, or basic. Nonpolar amino acids contain hydrocarbon side chains, whereas polar amino acids contain electronegative atoms such as oxygen (–OH) or sulfur (–SH). Acidic side chains contain a carboxylic acid group and basic side chains contain an amino group ($-NH_2$).
- A peptide bond is an amide bond between the carboxyl group of one amino acid and the amino group of the second.

```
         CH3  O  H  CH2—OH
 +        |   ||  |   |
H3N—CH—C—N—CH—COO-
              peptide bond
```

- Short chains of amino acids are called peptides. Long chains of amino acids are called proteins.

◆ Learning Exercise 17.4A

Match one of the following functions of a protein with the examples:

a. structural	**b.** contractile	**c.** storage	**d.** transport
e. hormonal	**f.** enzyme	**g.** protection	

1.______hemoglobin carries oxygen in blood **2.**______amylase hydrolyzes starch

3.______egg albumin, a protein in egg white **4.**______hormone that controls growth

5.______collagen in connective tissue **6.**______immunoglobulin

7.______keratin, a major protein of hair **8.**______lipoprotein carries lipids in blood

Answers: **1.** d **2.** f **3.** c **4.** e
5. a **6.** g **7.** a **8.** d

◆ Learning Exercise 17.4B

Using the appropriate side chain, complete the structural formula of each of the following amino acids. Indicate whether the amino acid would be polar, nonpolar, acidic, or basic.

glycine

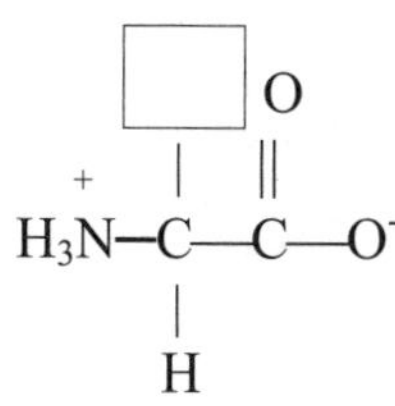

alanine

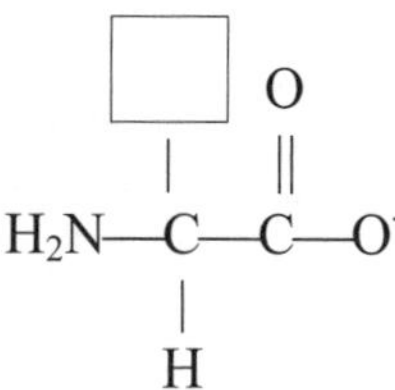

serine

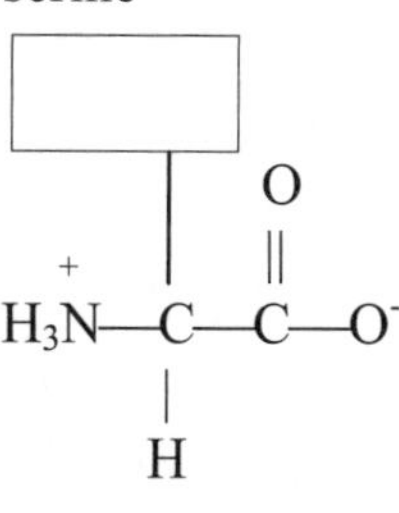

aspartic acid

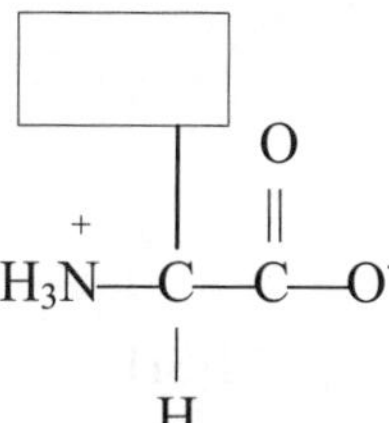

Answers:

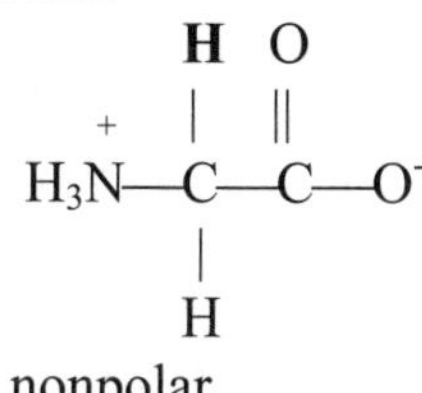

nonpolar

CH_3 O

$H_3\overset{+}{N}$—C—C—O^-

H

nonpolar

CH_2—OH O

$H_3\overset{+}{N}$—C—C—O^-

H

polar

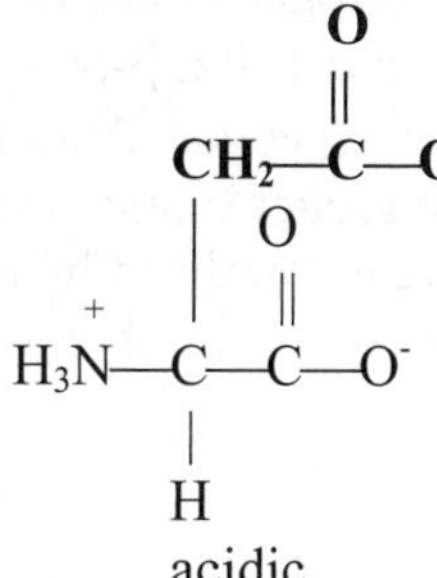

acidic

◆ Learning Exercise 17.4C

Draw the structural formulas of the following di- and tripeptides.

1. Ser-Gly

2. Cys-Val

3. Gly-Ser-Cys

Answers:

$$1.\quad \begin{array}{cccccc} & \text{HOCH}_2 & \text{O} & \text{H} & & \\ & | & \| & | & & \\ \overset{+}{\text{H}_3\text{N}}— & \text{CH}— & \text{C}— & \text{N}— & \text{CH}_2— & \text{COO}^- \end{array}$$

$$2.\quad \begin{array}{cccccc} & & & & \text{CH}_3 & \\ & & & & | & \\ & \text{HSCH}_2 & \text{O} & \text{H} & \text{CH—CH}_3 & \\ & | & \| & | & | & \\ \overset{+}{\text{H}_3\text{N}}— & \text{CH}— & \text{C}— & \text{N}— & \text{CH}— & \text{COO}^- \end{array}$$

$$3.\quad \begin{array}{ccccccccc} & & \text{O} & & \text{HOCH}_2 & \text{O} & & \text{CH}_2\text{SH} & \\ & & \| & & | & \| & & | & \\ \overset{+}{\text{H}_3\text{N}}— & \text{CH}_2— & \text{C}— & \text{N}— & \text{CH}— & \text{C}— & \text{N}— & \text{CH}— & \text{COO}^- \\ & & & | & & & | & & \\ & & & \text{H} & & & \text{H} & & \end{array}$$

17.5 Protein Structure

- The primary structure of a protein is the sequence of amino acids.
- In the secondary structure, hydrogen bonds between different sections of the peptide produce a characteristic shape such as an α-helix, β-pleated sheet, or a triple helix.
- In the tertiary structure, the polypeptide chain folds upon itself to form a three-dimensional shape with hydrophobic side groups on the inside and hydrophilic side groups on the outside surface. The tertiary structure is stabilized by interactions between side groups.
- In a quaternary structure, two or more subunits must combine for biological activity.

◆ Learning Exercise 17.5A

Identify the following descriptions of protein structure as primary or secondary structure:

1. _________ Hydrogen bonding forms an alpha (α)-helix.
2. _________ Hydrogen bonding occurs between C=O and N—H within a peptide chain.
3. _________ The sequence of amino acids linked by peptide bonds.
4. _________ Hydrogen bonds between protein chains form a pleated-sheet structure.

Answers: **1.** secondary **2.** secondary **3.** primary **4.** secondary

◆ Learning Exercise 17.5B

Identify the following descriptions of protein structure as tertiary or quaternary:

1. ________ A disulfide bond joining distant parts of a peptide
2. ________ The combination of four protein subunits
3. ________ Hydrophilic side groups attracted to water
4. ________ A salt bridge forms between two oppositely charged side chains

Answers: **1.** tertiary **2.** quaternary **3.** tertiary **4.** tertiary

17.6 Proteins as Enzymes

- Enzymes are proteins that accelerate the rate of biological reactions by lowering the activation energy of a reaction.
- Within the structure of the enzyme, a small pocket called the active site has a specific shape that fits a specific substrate.
- In the lock-and-key model or the induced-fit model, an enzyme and substrate form an enzyme-substrate complex so the reaction of the substrate can be catalyzed at the active site.

◆ Learning Exercise 17.6A

Indicate whether each of the following characteristics of an enzyme is *true or false.*

An enzyme

1. _____ is a biological catalyst.
2. _____ is much larger than a substrate.
3. _____ does not change the equilibrium of a reaction.
4. _____ must be obtained from the diet.
5. _____ greatly increases the rate of a cellular reaction.
6. _____ is needed for every reaction that takes place in the cell.
7. _____ recognizes only a small group of substrates.
8. _____ lowers the activation energy of a biological reaction.

Answers **1.** T **2.** F **3.** T **4.** F
5. T **6.** T **7.** F **8.** T

◆ Learning Exercise 17.6B

Match the following terms with the following descriptions:

a. active site　　**b.** substrate　　**c.** enzyme-substrate complex
d. lock and key　　**e.** induced fit

1._____the combination of an enzyme with a substrate

2._____a model of enzyme action in which the rigid shape of the active site exactly fits the shape of the substrate

3._____has a tertiary structure that fits the structure of the active site

4._____a model of enzyme action in which the shape of the active site adjusts to fit the shape of a substrate

5._____the portion of an enzyme that binds to the substrate and catalyzes the reaction

Answers **1.** c　　**2.** d　　**3.** b　　**4.** e　　**5.** a

17.7 Nucleic Acids

- Nucleic acids are composed of four nitrogenous bases, five-carbon sugars, and a phosphate groups.
- Deoxyribonucleic acid (DNA) and ribonucleic acid (RNA) are polymers of nucleotides. Each nucleotide consists of a nitrogen base, a sugar, and a phosphate group.
- In DNA, the nitrogen bases are adenine, thymine, guanine, or cytosine. In RNA, uracil replaces thymine. In DNA, the sugar is deoxyribose; in RNA, the sugar is ribose.
- The two strands of DNA are held together in a double helix by hydrogen bonds between complementary base pairs, A with T, and G with C.
- During DNA replication, new DNA strands form along each original DNA strand.
- Complementary base pairing ensures the correct pairing of bases to give identical copies of the original DNA.

◆ Learning Exercise 17.7A

Complete the following statements:

a. DNA　　**b.** RNA　　**c.** double helix　　**d.** adenine
e. hydrogen bonds　　**f.** complementary base pair　　**g.** daughter DNA　　**h.** cytosine

1. _____ The shape of DNA with a sugar-phosphate backbone and base pairs linked in the center

2. _____ The genetic material containing nucleotides with adenine, cytosine, guanine, and thymine

3. _____ The nucleic acid that is a single strand of nucleotides of adenine, cytosine, guanine, and uracil

4. _____ The attractions between base pairs that connect the two DNA strands

5. _____ The bases guanine and cytosine in the double helix

6. _____ The new DNA strand that forms during DNA replication

7. _____ The nitrogen base that bonds to thymine

Answers　**1.** c　　**2.** a　　**3.** b　　**4.** e
　　　　　5. f　　**6.** g　　**7.** d

◆ Learning Exercise 17.7B

1. Write the names and abbreviations for the nitrogen bases in each of the following:

   DNA____

   RNA____

2. Write the name of the sugar in each of the following nucleotides:

   DNA____

   RNA____

Answers

1. DNA: adenine (A), thymine (T), guanine (G), cytosine (C)
   RNA: adenine (A), uracil (U), guanine (G), cytosine (C)
2. DNA: deoxyribose RNA: ribose

◆ Learning Exercise 17.7C

Name each of the following nitrogen bases:

a.

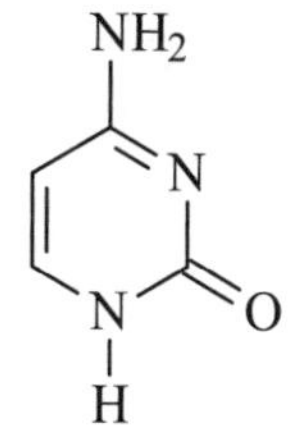

b.

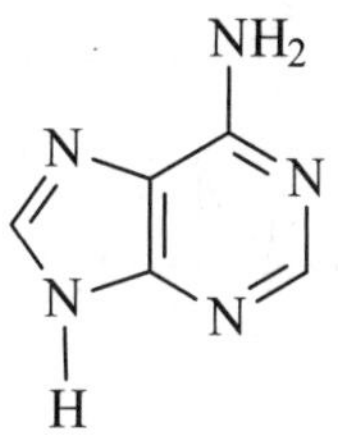

c.

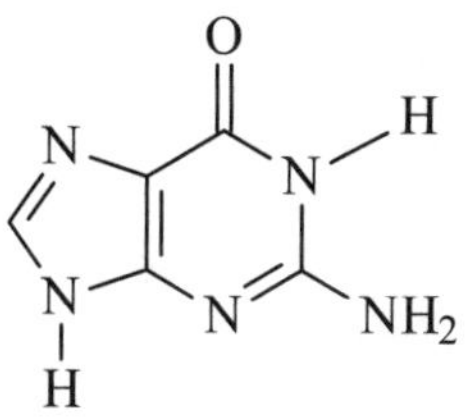

d.

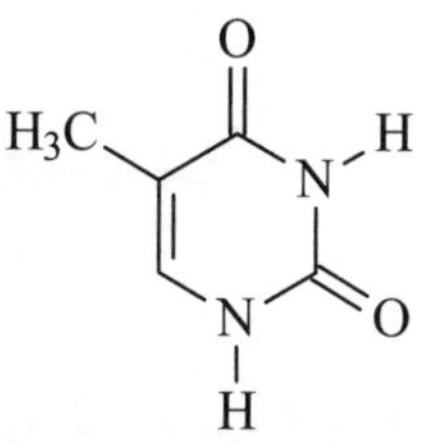

Answers **1.** cytosine **2.** adenine **3.** guanine **4.** thymine

◆ Learning Exercise 17.7D

Write the structural formula for deoxycytidine 5'-monophosphate (dCMP).

Answer

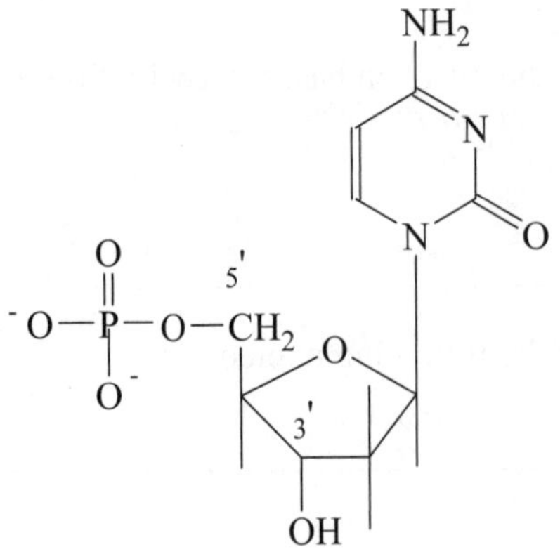

◆ Learning Exercise 17.7E

Identify the nucleotides in the following dinucleotide:

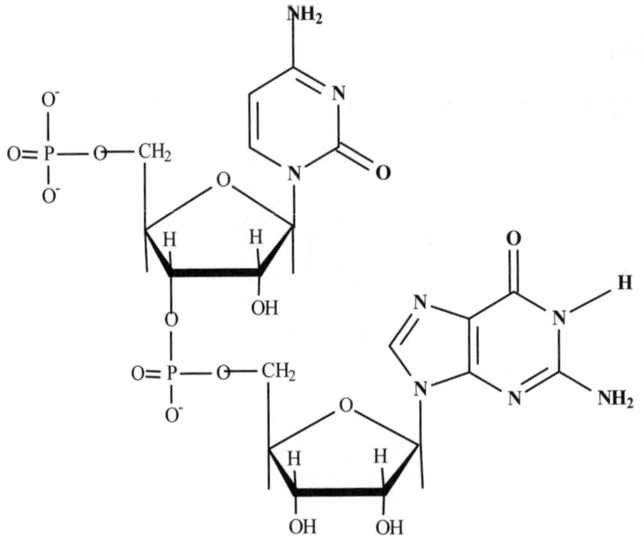

Answer
Cytidine 5'-monophosophate and guanosine 5'-monophosphate.

◆ Learning Exercise 17.7 F

Complete each DNA section by writing the complementary strand:

1. ATGCTTGGCTCC

2. AAATTTCCCGGG

3. GCGCTCAAATGC

Answers:

1. TACGAACCGAGG

2. TTTAAAGGGCCC

3. CGCGAGTTTACG

◆ Learning Exercise 17.7G

How does the replication of DNA produce identical copies of the DNA?

Answer In the replication process, the bases on each strand of the separated parent DNA are paired with their complementary bases. Because each complementary base is specific for a base in DNA, the new DNA daughter strands exactly duplicate the original strands of DNA.

17.8 Protein Synthesis

- The three types of RNA differ by function in the cell: Ribosomal RNA makes up most of the structure of the ribosomes, messenger RNA carries genetic information from the DNA to the ribosomes, and transfer RNA places the correct amino acids in the protein.
- Transcription is the process by which RNA polymerase produces mRNA from one strand of DNA.
- The bases in the mRNA are complementary to the DNA, except U is paired with A in DNA.
- The production of mRNA occurs when certain proteins are needed in the cell.
- The genetic code consists of a sequence of three bases (triplet) that specifies the order for the amino acids in a protein.
- The codon AUG signals the start of transcription, and codons UAG, UGA, and UAA signal stop.
- Proteins are synthesized in a translation process in which tRNA molecules bring the appropriate amino acids to the ribosome where each amino acid is bonded by a peptide bond to a growing peptide chain.
- When the polypeptide is released, it takes on its secondary and tertiary structures to become a functional protein in the cell.

◆ Learning Exercise 17.8A

Match each of the following characteristics with a specific type of RNA: mRNA, tRNA, or rRNA.

1. ______ most abundant type in a cell

2. ______ has the shortest chain of nucleotides

3. ______ carries information from DNA to the ribosomes for protein synthesis

4. ______ major component of ribosomes

5. ______ carries specific amino acids to the ribosome for protein synthesis

Answers **1.** rRNA **2.** tRNA **3.** mRNA **4.** rRNA **5.** tRNA

◆ Learning Exercise 17.8B

Write the corresponding section of an mRNA produced from each of the following.

1. C—A—T—T—C—G—G—T—A

2. G—T—A—C—C—T—A—A—C—G—T—C—C—G

Answers:

1. G—U—A—A—G—C—C—A—U
2. C—A—U—G—G—A—U—U—G—C—A—G—G—C

◆ Learning Exercise 17.8C

Indicate the amino acid coded for by the following mRNA codons:

1. UUU ______________ **2.** GCG ________________

3. AGC ______________ **4.** CCA ________________

5. GGA ______________ **6.** ACA ________________

7. AUG ______________ **8.** CUC ________________

9. CAU ______________ **10.** GUU ________________

Answers:

1. Phe	**2.** Ala	**3.** Ser	**4.** Pro	**5.** Gly
6. Thr	**7.** Start/Met	**8.** Leu	**9.** His	**10.** Val

◆ Learning Exercise 17.8D

Write the mRNA that would form for the following section of DNA. For each codon in the mRNA, write the amino acid that would be placed in the protein by a tRNA.

1. DNA strand: CCC—TCA—GGG—CGC

mRNA: ______—______—______—______

amino acid order: __________—_______—________—________

2. DNA: ATA—GCC—TTT—GGC—AAC

mRNA: ______—______—______—______—______

amino acid order: __________—_______—________—________—________

Answers

1. mRNA: GGG—AGU—CCC—GCG
Gly—Ser—Pro—Ala
2. mRNA: UAU—CGG—AAA—CCG—UUG
Tyr—Arg—Lys—Pro—Leu

Check List for Chapter 17

You are ready to take the practice test for Chapter 17. Be sure you have accomplished the following learning goals for this chapter. If you are not sure, review the section listed at the end of the goal. Then apply your new skills and understanding to the practice test.

After studying Chapter 17, I can successfully:

____ Classify carbohydrates as monosaccharides, disaccharides, and polysaccharides (17.1).
____ Classify a monosaccharide (aldose or ketose), and indicate the number of carbon atoms (17.1).
____ Draw the open-chain structures for glucose, galactose, and fructose (17.1).
____ Draw or identify the cyclic structures of monosaccharides (17.1).
____ Describe the monosaccharide units and linkages in disaccharides (17.2).
____ Describe the structural features of amylose, amylopectin, glycogen, and cellulose (17.2).
____ Identify a fatty acid as saturated or unsaturated (17.3).
____ Write the triacylglycerol produced by the reaction of glycerol and fatty acids (17.3).
____ Draw the product from the hydrogenation or saponification of a triacylglycerol (17.3).
____ Describe the structure of a steroid and cholesterol (17.3).
____ Classify proteins by their functions in the cells (17.4).
____ Draw the structure for an amino acid (17.4).
____ Describe a peptide bond; draw the structure for a peptide (17.4).
____ Distinguish between the primary and secondary structures of a protein (17.5).
____ Distinguish between the tertiary and quaternary structures of a protein (17.5).
____ Describe the lock-and-key and induced-fit models of enzyme action (17.6).
____ Identify the components of nucleic acids RNA and DNA (17.7).
____ Describe the nucleotides contained in DNA and RNA (17.7).
____ Describe the primary structure of nucleic acids (17.7).
____ Describe the structures of RNA and DNA (17.7).
____ Explain the process of DNA replication (17.7)
____ Describe the structures and characteristics of the three types of RNA (17.8).
____ Describe the synthesis of mRNA (transcription) (17.8).
____ Describe the function of the codons in the genetic code (17.8).
____ Describe the role of translation in protein synthesis (17.8).

Practice Test for Chapter 17

1. The name "carbohydrate" came from the fact that

A. carbohydrates are hydrates of water.
B. carbohydrates contain hydrogen and oxygen in a 2:1 ratio.
C. carbohydrates contain a great quantity of water.
D. all plants produce carbohydrates.
E. carbon and hydrogen atoms are abundant in carbohydrates.

2. What functional group(s) is (are) in the open chains of monosaccharides?

A. hydroxyl groups
B. aldehyde groups
C. ketone groups
D. hydroxyl and carbonyl groups
E. carbonyl group

3. What is the classification of the following sugar?

CH_2OH
|
C=O
|
CH_2OH

A. aldotriose **B.** ketotriose **C.** aldotetrose
D. ketotetrose **E.** ketopentose

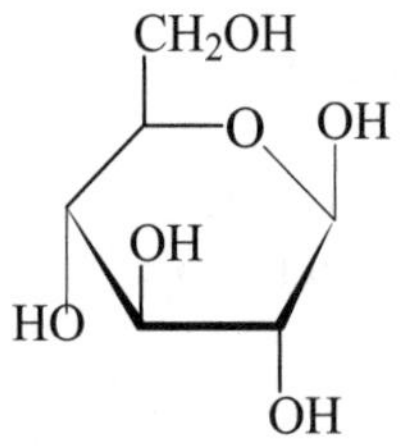

CH_2OH O OH OH HO OH

4. The structure is the cyclic structure of an

A. fructose **B.** glucose **C.** ribose
D. glyceraldehyde **E.** galactose

For questions 5 to 10, select the carbohydrate that is

A. amylose **B.** cellulose **C.** glycogen **D.** lactose **E.** sucrose

5.____ composed of many glucose units linked by α-1,4-glycosidic bonds

6.____ contains glucose and galactose

7.____ composed of glucose units joined by both α-1,4- and α-1,6-glycosidic bonds

8.____ composed of glucose units joined by β-1,4-glycosidic bonds

9.____ produced as a storage form of energy in plants

10.____ used for structural purposes by plants

11. A triacylglycerol is a

A. carbohydrate **B.** lipid **C.** protein **D.** oxyacid **E.** soap

12. A fatty acid that is unsaturated is usually

A. from animal sources and liquid at room temperature
B. from animal sources and solid at room temperature
C. from vegetable sources and liquid at room temperature
D. from vegetable sources and solid at room temperature
E. from both vegetable and animal sources and solid at room temperature

For questions 13 to 15, consider the following compound:

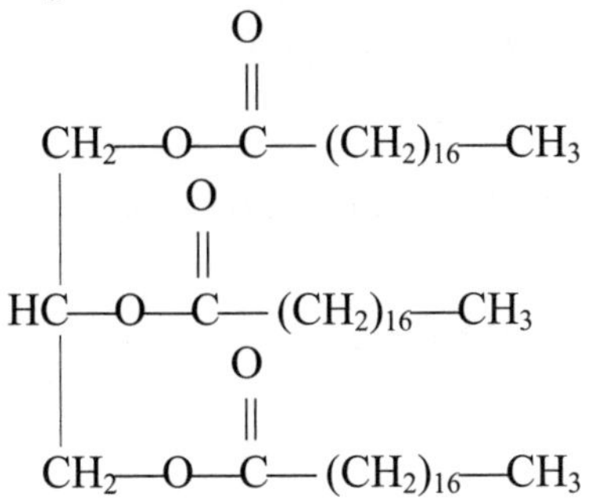

$$\begin{array}{l} CH_2-O-\overset{O}{\overset{\|}{C}}-(CH_2)_{16}-CH_3 \\ | \\ HC-O-\overset{O}{\overset{\|}{C}}-(CH_2)_{16}-CH_3 \\ | \\ CH_2-O-\overset{O}{\overset{\|}{C}}-(CH_2)_{16}-CH_3 \end{array}$$

13. The molecule shown above was formed by

A. esterification **B.** combustion **C.** saponification
D. emulsification **E.** oxidation

14. If this molecule were reacted with strong base such as NaOH, the products would be

A. glycerol and fatty acids **B.** glycerol and water
C. glycerol and soap **D.** an ester and salts of fatty acids
E. an ester and fatty acids

15. The compound would be

A. saturated, and a solid at room temperature
B. saturated, and a liquid at room temperature
C. unsaturated, and a solid at room temperature
D. unsaturated, and a liquid at room temperature
E. supersaturated, and a liquid at room temperature

16. Which amino acid is nonpolar?

A. serine **B.** aspartic acid **C.** valine **D.** cysteine **E.** glutamine

17. Which amino acid will form disulfide cross-links in a tertiary structure?

A. serine **B.** aspartic acid **C.** valine **D.** cysteine **E.** glutamine

18. Which amino acid has a basic side chain?

A. serine **B.** aspartic acid **C.** valine **D.** cysteine **E.** glutamine

19. The sequence Tyr-Ala-Gly

A. is a tripeptide **B.** has two peptide bonds **C.** has tyrosine with free $-NH_2$ end
D. has glycine with the free–COOH end **E.** All of these

20. The type of bonding expected between lysine and aspartic acid is a

A. ionic bond **B.** hydrogen bond **C.** disulfide bond
D. hydrophobic attraction **E.** hydrophilic attraction

21. What type of bond is used to form the α-helix structure of a protein?

A. peptide bond **B.** hydrogen bond **C.** ionic bond
D. disulfide bond **E.** hydrophobic attraction

22. What type of bonding places portions of the protein chain in the center of a tertiary structure?

A. peptide bonds **B.** ionic bonds **C.** disulfide bonds
D. hydrophobic attraction **E.** hydrophilic attraction

In questions 23 to 27, identify the protein structural levels that each of the following statements describe:

A. primary **B.** secondary **C.**tertiary
D. quaternary **E.** pentenary

23.____ peptide bonds **24**____ a pleated sheet

25.____ two or more protein subunits **26.**____ an α-helix

27.____ disulfide bonds

28. Enzymes are

A. biological catalysts **B.** polysaccharides **C.** insoluble in water
D. lipids **E.** named with an "ose" ending

For problems 29 to 33, select answers from the following: (**E** = enzyme; **S** = substrate; **P** = product)

A. S $\longrightarrow$ P **B.** EP $\longrightarrow$ E + P **C.** E + S $\longrightarrow$ ES
D. ES $\longrightarrow$ EP **E.** EP $\longrightarrow$ ES

29.____ The enzymatic reaction occurring at the active site

30.____ The release of product from the enzyme

31.____ The first step in the lock-and-key theory of enzyme action

32.____ The formation of the enzyme-substrate complex

33.____ The final step in the lock-and-key theory of enzyme action

34. A nucleotide contains

A. a nitrogen base **B.** a nitrogen base and a sugar
C. a phosphate and a sugar **D.** a nitrogen base and a deoxyribose
E. a nitrogen base, a sugar, and a phosphate

35. The double helix in DNA is held together by

A. hydrogen bonds **B.** ester linkages **C.** peptide bonds
D. salt bridges **E.** disulfide bonds

36. The process of producing DNA in the nucleus is called

A. complementation **B.** replication **C.** translation
D. transcription **E.** mutation

37. Which occurs in RNA but **NOT** in DNA?

A. thymine **B.** cytosine **C.** adenine
D. phosphate **E.** uracil

For questions 38 to 45, select answers from the following nucleic acids:

A. DNA **B.** mRNA **C.** tRNA **D.** rRNA

38._____ A double helix consisting of two chains of nucleotides held together by hydrogen bonds between nitrogen bases

39._____ A nucleic acid that uses deoxyribose as the sugar

40._____ A nucleic acid produced in the nucleus, which migrates to the ribosomes to direct the formation of a protein

41._____ It brings the proper amino acid to the ribosome to build the peptide chain

42._____ It has nitrogen bases of adenine, cytosine, guanine, and thymine

For questions 43 to 46, select answers from the following:

A. A—G—C—C—T—A
| | | | | |
T—C—G—G—A—T

B. A—U—U—G—C—U—C

C. A—G—T—U—G—U—
| | | | | |
T—C—A—A—C—A—

D. U—U—U **E.** A—T—G—T—A—T

43._____ A section of mRNA

44._____ An impossible section of DNA

45._____ A codon for phenylalanine

46._____ A section from a DNA molecule

For questions 47 to 50, arrange the following statements:
A. DNA forms a complementary copy of itself called mRNA.
B. Protein is formed and breaks away.
C. tRNA picks up specific amino acids.
D. mRNA goes to the ribosomes.

Of the previous statements, select the order in which they occur during protein synthesis.

47.____ First step **48.**____ Second step **49.**____ Third step

50.____ Fourth step

Answers to the Practice Test

1. B	**2.** D	**3.** B	**4.** B	**5.** A
6. D	**7.** C	**8.** B	**9.** A	**10.** B
11. B	**12.** C	**13.** A	**14.** C	**15.** A
16. C	**17.** D	**18.** E	**19.** E	**20.** A
21. B	**22.** D	**23.** A	**24.** B	**25.** D
26. B	**27.** C	**28.** A	**29.** D	**30.** B
31. C	**32.** C	**33.** B	**34.** E	**35.** A
36. B	**37.** E	**38.** A	**39.** A	**40.** B
41. C	**42.** A	**43.** B	**44.** C	**45.** D
46. A	**47.** A	**48.** D	**49.** C	**50.** B

Answers and Solutions to Selected Text Problems

Section 17.1

17.1 Hydroxyl (—OH) groups and a carbonyl (C=O) are found in all monosaccharides.

17.3 A ketopentose has five carbon atoms with a ketone functional group and hydroxyl groups on the other carbon atoms.

17.5 **a.** This monosaccharide is a ketose; it has a carbonyl between two carbon atoms.
b. This monosaccharide is an aldose; it has a CHO, an aldeyde group.
c. This monosaccharide is a ketose; it has a carbonyl between two carbon atoms.
d. This monosaccharide is an aldose; it has a CHO, an aldeyde group.
e. This monosaccharide is an aldose; it has a CHO, an aldeyde group.

17.7 In galactose, the hydroxyl on carbon four extends to the left, whereas in glucose it goes to the right.

17.9 In the cyclic structure of glucose, there are five carbon atoms and an oxygen atom in the ring.

17.11 **a.** This is the α-form because the —OH on carbon 1 is down.
b. This is the α-form because the —OH on carbon 1 is down.

Section 17.2

17.13 **a.** When lactose is hydrolyzed, galactose and glucose are produced. The glycosidic bond is a β-1,4 bond because the ether bond is up from carbon 1 of the galactose, which is on the left in the drawing to carbon 4 of the glucose on the right. β-lactose is the name of this disaccharide because the free hydroxyl is up.

b. When this disaccharide is hydrolyzed, two molecules of glucose are produced. The glycosidic bond is an α-1,4 bond because the ether bond is down from the one carbon of the glucose on the left to the four carbon of the glucose on the right. α-Maltose is the name of this disaccharide because the free hydroxyl is down.

17.15 **a.** Another name for table sugar is sucrose.
b. Lactose is the disaccharide found in milk and milk products.
c. Maltose is also called malt sugar.
d. When lactose is hydrolyzed, the products are the monosaccharides galactose and glucose.

17.17 **a.** Cellulose is not digestible by humans because we do not have the enzymes necessary to break the β-1,4-glycosidic bonds in cellulose.
b. Amylose and amylopectin are the storage forms of carbohydrates in plants.
c. Amylose is the polysaccharide that contains only α-1,4 glycosidic bonds.
d. Glycogen contains many α-1,4 and α-1,6 bonds, and is the most highly branched polysaccharide.

Section 17.3

17.19 **a.** Lauric acid has only carbon–carbon single bonds; it is saturated.
b. Linolenic has three carbon–carbon double bonds; it is unsaturated.
c. Palmitoleic has one carbon–carbon double bond: it is unsaturated.
d. Stearic acid has only carbon–carbon single bonds; it is saturated.

17.21 Tripalmitin has three palmitic acids (16 carbon saturated fatty acid) forming ester bonds with glycerol.

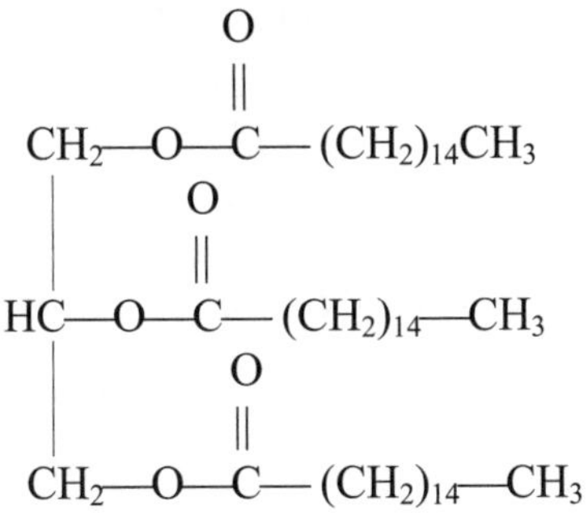

$$
\begin{array}{l}
CH_2-O-\overset{\overset{\large O}{\|}}{C}-(CH_2)_{14}CH_3 \\
| \\
HC-O-\overset{\overset{\large O}{\|}}{C}-(CH_2)_{14}-CH_3 \\
| \\
CH_2-O-\overset{\overset{\large O}{\|}}{C}-(CH_2)_{14}-CH_3
\end{array}
$$

17.23 Safflower oil contains fatty acids with two or three double bonds; olive oil contains a large amount of oleic acid, which has a single (monounsaturated) double bond.

17.25 **a.** Partial hydrogenation means that some of the double bonds in the unsaturated fatty acids have been converted to single bonds.
b. Because the margarine now has mostly saturated fatty acids that can interact more strongly, it will be a solid.

17.27

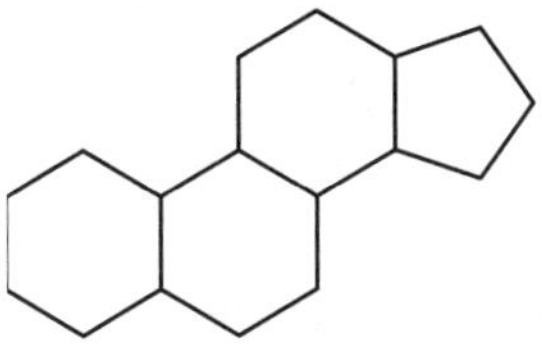

Section 17.4

17.29 All amino acids contain a carboxylic acid group and an amino group on the alpha carbon.

17.31 **a.** 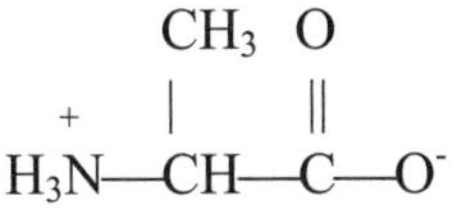 $\overset{+}{H_3N}-\underset{}{\overset{\overset{\large CH_3}{|}}{CH}}-\overset{\overset{\large O}{\|}}{C}-O^-$ **b.** $\overset{+}{H_3N}-\overset{\overset{\overset{\overset{\large CH_3}{|}}{HO-CH}}{|}}{CH}-\overset{\overset{\large O}{\|}}{C}-O^-$

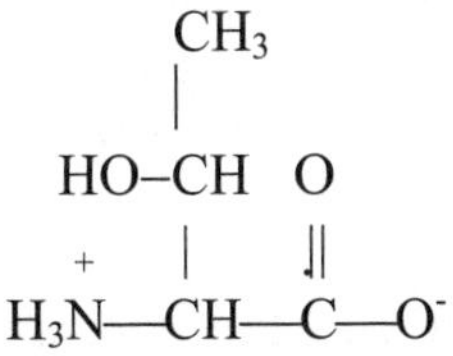

c. $\overset{+}{H_3N}-\overset{\overset{\overset{\overset{\large C_6H_5}{|}}{CH_2}}{|}}{CH}-\overset{\overset{\large O}{\|}}{C}-O^-$

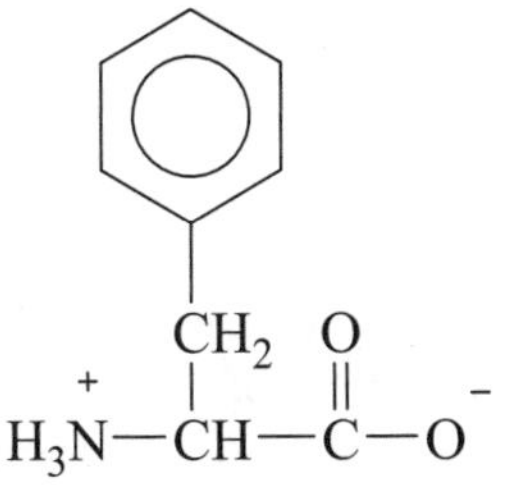

17.33 **a.** Alanine is hydrophobic (nonpolar) because it has a methyl (hydrocarbon) side group.
b. Threonine is hydrophilic (polar) because it has a polar —OH side group.
c. Phenylalanine is hydrophobic (nonpolar) with a nonpolar benzene ring in its side group.

17.35 The abbreviations of most amino acids are derived from the first three letters in the name.
a. alanine **b.** valine **c.** lysine **d.** cysteine

17.37 In a peptide, the amino acids are joined by peptide bonds (amide bonds). The first amino acid has a free amine group, and the last one has a free carboxyl group.

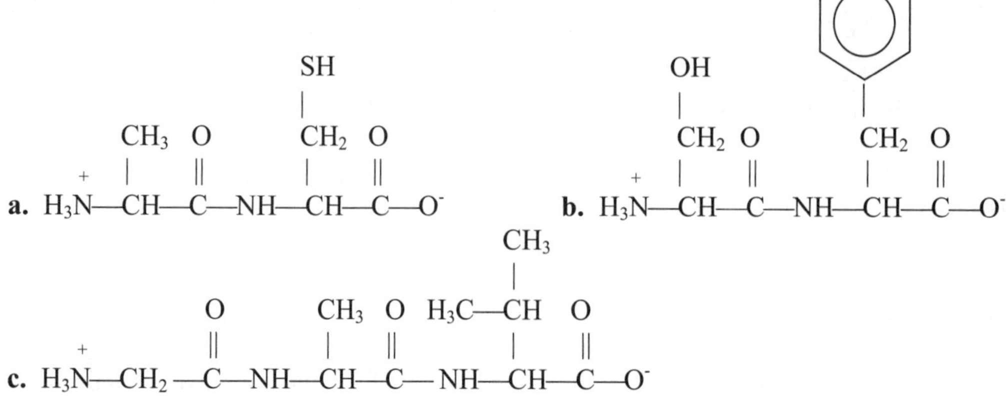

17.39 The possible primary structure of a tripeptide of one valine and two serines are Val-Ser-Ser, Ser-Val-Ser and Ser-Ser-Val.

17.41 In an alpha helix, there are hydrogen bonds formed between the carbonyl oxygen atoms and the hydrogen atom in the amine groups in different turns of the helix. In a beta-pleated sheet, the hydrogen bonds occur between two adjacent protein chains or between different parts of a long protein.

17.43 **a.** The two cysteine residues have -SH groups, which react to form a disulfide bond.
b. Serine has a polar -OH group that can form a hydrogen bond with the carboxyl group of aspartic acid.
c. Two leucine residues that are nonpolar would have a hydrophobic interaction.

17.45 **a.** The —SH side group of cysteine can form disulfide cross-links.
b. Leucine and valine will be found on the inside of the protein because they have nonpolar side groups and are hydrophobic.
c. The polar cysteine and aspartic acid would be on the outside of the protein to react with water.
d. The order of the amino acid (the primary structure) provides the side chains that determine the tertiary structure of the protein.

17.47 **a.** An enzyme has a tertiary structure that recognized the substrate.
b. The combination of the enzyme and substrate is the enzyme-substrate complex.
c. The substrate has a structure that complements the structure of the enzyme.

17.49 **a.** The equation for an enzyme-catalyzed reaction is
$E + S \rightleftharpoons ES \longrightarrow E + P$
E = enzyme, S = substrate, ES = enzyme-substrate complex, P = products
b. The active site is a region or pocket within the tertiary structure of an enzyme that accepts the substrate, aligns the substrate for reaction, and catalyzes the reaction.

Section 17.7

17.51 DNA contains two purines, adenine (A) and guanine (G), and two pyrimidines, cytosine (C) and thymine (T). RNA contains the same bases, except thymine (T) is replaced by the pyrimidine uracil (U).
a. DNA **b.** Both DNA and RNA

17.53 The two DNA strands are held together by hydrogen bonds between the nitrogen bases in each strand.

17.55 **a.** Because T pairs with A, if one strand of DNA has the sequence AAAAAA, the second strand would be TTTTTT.
b. Because C pairs with G, if one strand of DNA has the sequence GGGGGG, the second strand would be CCCCCC.
c. Because T pairs with A and C pairs with G, if one strand of DNA has the sequence AGTCCAGGT, the second strand would be TCAGGTCCA.
d. Because T pairs with A and C pairs with G, if one strand of DNA has the sequence CTGTATACGTTA, the second strand would be GACATATGCAAT.

17.57 Once the two DNA strands separate, DNA polymerase begins to pair each base along each strand with its complementary base. A is paired with T, and C is paired with G. Then each base is joined to the new, growing DNA strand.

17.59 The three types of RNA are the messenger RNA (mRNA), ribosomal RNA (rRNA), and transfer RNA (tRNA).

17.61 In transcription, the sequence of nucleotides on a DNA template (one strand) is used to produce the base sequences of a messenger RNA. The DNA unwinds, and one strand is copied as complementary bases are placed in the mRNA molecule. In RNA, U (uracil) is paired with A in DNA.

17.63 In mRNA, C, G, and A pair with G, C, and T in DNA. However, in mRNA, U will pair with A in DNA. The strand of mRNA would have the following sequence: GGC—UUC—CAA—GUG.

17.65 A codon is a sequence of three bases (triplet) in mRNA that code for a specific amino acid in a protein.

Answers to Additional Questions and Problems

17.73 They differ only at carbon 4. The –OH in glucose is on the right side, and in galactose it is on the left side.

17.75

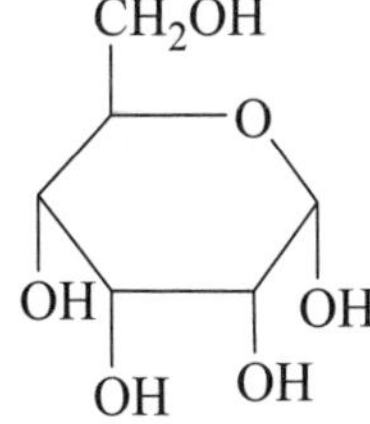

α-gulose

CH_2OH
O OH
OH
OH OH

β-gulose

17.77

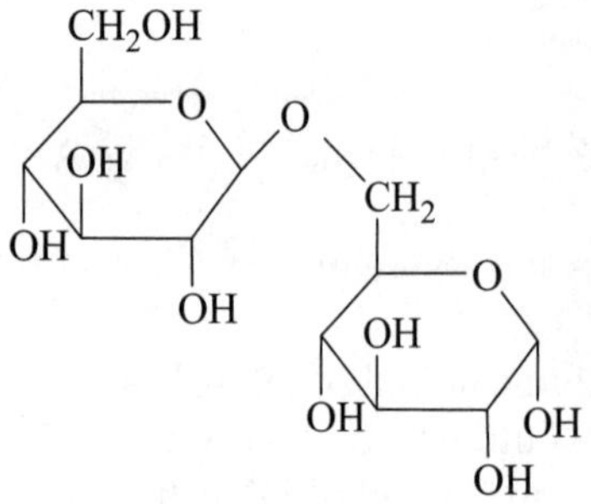

CH_2OH
O O
OH
CH_2
OH
OH O
OH
OH OH
OH

17.79

```
           O  H        O  H         O
  +        ||  |       ||  |        ||
H3N—CH—C—N—CH—C—N—CH—C—O⁻
     |            |              |
   CH2OH      (CH2)4           CH2
                  | +            |
                 NH3            C—O⁻
                                 ||
                                 O
```

$$H_3\overset{+}{N}-\underset{\substack{|\\CH_2OH}}{CH}-\overset{O}{\overset{\|}{C}}-\overset{H}{\overset{|}{N}}-\underset{\substack{|\\(CH_2)_4\\|\\\overset{+}{N}H_3}}{CH}-\overset{O}{\overset{\|}{C}}-\overset{H}{\overset{|}{N}}-\underset{\substack{|\\CH_2\\|\\C-O^-\\\|\\O}}{CH}-\overset{O}{\overset{\|}{C}}-O^-$$

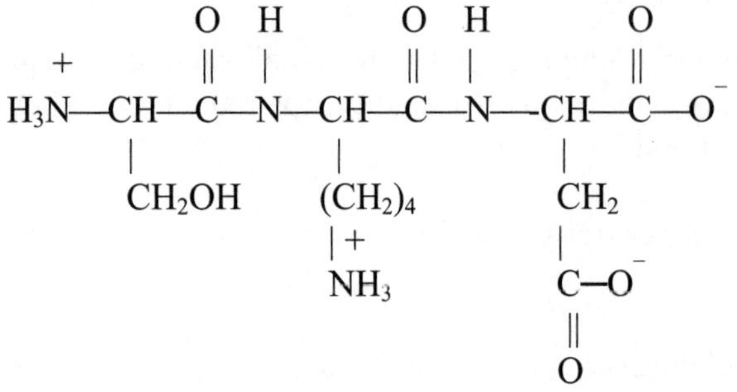

17.81 **a.** thymine and deoxyribose **b.** adenine and ribose
c. cytosine and ribose **d.** guanine and deoxyribose

17.83 **a.** CTGAATCCG
b. ACGTTTGATCGT
c. TAGCTAGCTAGC

17.85 **a.** mRNA **b**. mRNA